Talking with Texas Writers

Talking with Texas Writers
Twelve Interviews

By PATRICK BENNETT

 Texas A&M University Press   COLLEGE STATION

Copyright © 1980 by Patrick Bennett
All rights reserved

Library of Congress Cataloging in Publication Data

Bennett, Patrick, 1931-
  Talking with Texas writers.

  CONTENTS: Larry McMurty.—A. C. Greene.—John Graves. [etc.]
  1. Authors, American—Texas—Interviews. 2. Authors, American—20th century—Interviews. 3. Authorship. 4. American literature—Texas—History and criticism. 5. American literature—20th century—History and criticism. 6. Texas in literature. I. Title.
  PS266.T4B4   810'.9'9764   80-5516
  ISBN 0-89096-099-2 (cloth)
  ISBN 0-89096-105-0 (pbk.)

Manufactured in the United States of America
FIRST PAPERBACK EDITION

For Shay
My favorite conversationalist

Contents

Preface ix

Introduction 3

Larry McMurty: *Thalia, Houston, and Hollywood* 15

A. C. Greene: *Molding Past into Art* 37

John Graves: *A Hard Scrabble World* 63

Max Apple: *Voices in Fiction* 89

Shelby Hearon: *Time, Sex, and God* 111

Leon Hale: *Optimist as Novelist* 135

Preston Jones: *In the Jaws of Time* 157

Elmer Kelton: *Racial Friction Out West* 179

Frances Mossiker: *The Method of Madame Mossiker* 205

William Goyen: *A Poet Telling Stories* 227

Larry L. King: *Turning On the Memory Machine* 249

Tom Lea: *The Book as Art* 269

Works of the Writers 291

Index 297

Preface

The grand designs of aesthetic architecture persist over thousands of years, but the details change with the invention of new technology. Movable type freed Tolstoy from the necessity of mnemonic verse devices, but *War and Peace* became an epic with Homeric overtones. Colored inks ultimately gave us Krazy Kat and Peanuts. The writing down of probing, thoughtful conversations goes back beyond the Platonic dialogues and the Book of Job. However, the invention of the tape recorder makes this collection possible. Had I taken notes on a typewriter or in longhand, methods I used for years in writing for newspapers and magazines, the following chapters would have been cast in a form nearer to that of a *New Yorker* profile. I would not have had such an abundance of exact quotations. How accurately, really, did James Boswell recall the exact words of Samuel Johnson? Were those the reasonings of Socrates or of Plato? Without debating whether such a thing would have been desirable, I will venture that the world would be more certain of the answers to these questions if Boswell and Plato had possessed tape recorders.

A dab of my material is originally from pencil notes. This material was first used in my earlier articles on Shelby Hearon and A. C. Greene which appeared in the *Abilene Reporter-News* and Sam Pendergrast's *Oeste* magazine. However, that part of my conversation with Tom Lea which first appeared in the *Southwest Review* was from taped talk.

My heaviest debts in this collection are obviously owed to the twelve writers who generously lent me their knowledge and opinions during many happy days of good talk. A. C. Greene and Shelby Hearon also helped in other ways. Shay, my wife, accompanied me on most of my wanderings, explored the books with me, and suggested some of the better lines of questioning. Our son David was patient while I kept his tape recorder a full year, and our son Patrick was just patient. Joe Specht was a tremendous help with the list of the authors' works. Joe Stamey, Gene Rister, and Marilyn Hart read parts of the manuscript. Others who helped are Jacky English, Judith Sample, Anna Donaldson, June Jennings, Katy Rister, Alice Specht, Mary Harper, Jack Holden, Gary Stephenson, Gene Patty, and Tony Kinsey.

PATRICK BENNETT

McMurry College
Abilene, Texas
June, 1980

Talking with Texas Writers

Introduction

One warm May afternoon a group of us from McMurry hunted out the hardscrabble farm near Glen Rose that John Graves is trying to bring back to life between sessions with his typewriter. The roads were rough and not easy to follow, but we got there. Hup, Graves's English sheep dog, came bounding out to meet us like an eighty-five-pound welcome wagon on four feet. You knew at a glance that Hup was not the Passenger who fit so snugly into the canoe of Graves's classic *Goodbye to a River*. "I never had anything this good-natured around before," said Graves. "He's just what you see. He's absolutely benevolent. He likes the cat; he likes chickens. He doesn't like snakes very much."

Graves came along behind Hup, at a more sedate pace, dressed in khakis, shyly friendly himself. He is perhaps the writer most admired and respected by his fellow Texas writers. We accompanied him to the screened-in porch of the farmhouse, where he made coffee for the group—there were five of us. Hup ran around the outside periphery, frantic to get inside with all those friendly petters.

"Oh, you can let him in. I don't want to leave him in very long because he's got ticks. He's a clumsy mutt, a Mr. Magoo; he doesn't see too well because of all that hair."

It wasn't long before we had to put Hup back out because he kept getting tangled up with the tape-recorder wires. Graves said, "More people in Glen Rose know Hup than me."

In his doggish way Hup overstated our welcome, but while wandering around Texas collecting opinions for this book, I haven't been confronted with any biting dogs. Texas writers have been open and hospitable. They also seem to be hardworking and unassuming.

A few months after the Glen Rose visit, I phoned Graves one morning to check on Hup's name, the proper spelling of a dog's name being a subject that seldom works through into normal conversation. I was in a hurry and framed my question with stumbling ineptness.

"How does Hup spell his name?" For a man as sensitive to the language as John Graves, such a mismating of thought and idiom must ordinarily sound as cacophonous as a squeaking door opened during a Beethoven quartet. This time he didn't laugh or appear to notice. "One *p.*" He hurried on to a possibility that had been troubling him since our visit: he cautioned me against praising Texas writers too highly. In a subsequent letter, he also said: "I hope you'll keep in mind and sight the fact that Texas literature . . . is just a segment of a whole and has to stand ultimately on how well it stacks up against writing from N.Y.C. and Minnesota or whatever."

Graves is right of course. Texas writing must also be judged against the best British writing, and against the best French, German, Russian, Italian—all the great worldwide Republic of Letters. Texas writers must be ranked among themselves, and they must also be ranked ultimately against the standards of the world at large.

Barbed-wire fences were often the topic of writers Roy Bedichek, Walter Prescott Webb, and other Texans because fences have been an important instrument of civilization on the American plains. Conceptual fences are also needed for rational thought. If this book builds a fence around Texas literature, however, let's hold it to about four strands of wire, a fence through which you can see a long way in any direction, one through which intellectual winds can circulate with freedom.

It seems a couple of light years from John Graves's hilly farm to the Houston street where I found the home of Max Apple, a writer whose finely crafted short stories sell in an era when there is no market for short stories. A Texan is usually pictured as a tall cowboy who gets from one place to another on horseback. Apple is short, urban, Michigan-born, and Jewish, and he runs for exercise. But the Texan of legend is open and friendly, and Apple is both. His wife was ill, but Apple talked to me anyhow because he knew I had come a long way. He got me a cup of coffee, and while we were talking, the Apple children, six-year-old Jessica and three-year-old Sam escaped from the babysitter to join us. Sam wanted to play with his tool set, but his father asked him to quit using the hammer because its bangs interfered with my tape recorder. Apple obviously gets along well with his children, and both ended by sitting in his lap.

Several persons I've talked to were dubious about whether Apple is a Texas writer. What is a Texas writer anyway? In the little West

Texas cow and cotton town where I grew up, most people thought a Texas writer should be someone who wrote like Zane Grey. The cowboys who ambled around the courthouse square on Saturday nights saw nothing inconsistent in Grey's rootin'-tootin' picture of the West, and neither did my father, who had once, on the hurricane deck of a U.S. Cavalry pony, pursued Pancho Villa along the Mexican border. We got little help from the public schools, where Texas history was a distinct course mandated by law but where Texas literature was ignored.

Intellectuals of that era probably considered a Texas writer somebody who wrote like J. Frank Dobie. A great deal of the fuzzy thinking about the nature and markings of a Texas writer probably originated with Dobie, who served as the Dr. Johnson of Texas letters in the first half of this century. Dobie talked a lot about "southwestern literature." In 1929, "Pancho" Dobie launched his pioneering University of Texas course in regional literature. According to legend, Dobie went to the budget council in 1928 with a proposed course in "The Literature of the Southwest." The council told him there was no such animal. The following year he returned with a proposed course retitled "Life and Literature of the Southwest" with the observation that, while they might deny the existence of literature in the Southwest, they could hardly deny that life existed there. A moral sometimes missed in this yarn is that precious little literature or life either existed in this vast area before the twentieth century. Of the few brave souls who risked their scalps in the wilds of Texas, a surprising number were literate and managed to scribble books, but it would have been a miracle if they had produced much writing that could command our attention as literature. Dobie, a hard man to shake loose from reality, recognized this. He broke the boundaries of Texas and scraped over the writing production of the entire region, even adopting the work of mere tourists such as Willa Cather.

The residue of confusion left by Dobie's solution is illustrated by a well-known essay from *In a Narrow Grave*, by Larry McMurtry, a Texas writer with a beautiful style and barbed wit. The essay is entitled "Southwestern Literature?" which presumably means that he will question the merits of New Mexicans Paul Horgan and Mary Austin, Oklahomans Lynn Riggs and Stanley Vestal, and others. However, McMurtry speedily informs the reader that he is beginning "a critique of Texas letters." He rules out Katherine Anne Porter as a Texas writer, although she was born near Brownwood, apparently on the ground that she is too good. In the end it comes down to McMurtry wanting to lay the ghosts of Dobie, Webb, and Bedichek to clear the way for the present wave of Texas writers.

This is a book about Texas writers and their opinions. "Southwestern" has nothing to do with it. For our purposes a Texas writer is one who has spent his formative years in Texas, regardless of where he lives now, or one who has moved to Texas and become a resident. Easy enough. This definition might also include those writers who moved to Texas, lingered a significant amount of time, and moved on. This is a gray area that includes such authors as Amelia Barr. The last cases may provide wonderful debate topics for graduate students and junior professors on long, idle afternoons at Scholz's Beer Garden in Austin. None of the authors included in this book, fortunately, fall into the third category.

By the definition above, Texas writers include Larry L. King of Putnam and Midland, who now lives in Washington, D.C., and Bill Goyen of Trinity and Houston, who now lives in Los Angeles and New York. Max Apple grew up in Michigan, but he moved to Houston and is now a Texas writer. Someone writing a book about Michigan writers may wish to include Apple; that too is okay, because the two classifications need not be mutually exclusive.

Finally, my definition of a Texas writer has nothing to do with subject matter. The Tom Lea who wrote *The Brave Bulls* is still a Texas writer; the Edna Ferber who wrote *Giant* is not.

Now that our four-strand fence is up, the reader will want to know why I cut these particular writers out of the large herd of contemporary Texas authors. I wanted writers producing now, with work still in their typewriters. Each of the dozen here has particularly interested me, but the reasons for that interest have varied.

Apple, for instance, has written short stories of such wit that they sold in the current shrunken market and made his reputation. *Zip* is a warm, funny novel, but it was the short stories that fascinated me. Apple is a man of the city—you read a long way before you find a tree or a flower in his work. *Zeitgeist* pervades his fiction, and using contemporary names is only part of it.

William Goyen has an international reputation. What interested me was the variety of forms in which Goyen has written well. He is best known for his novels and short stories, but he has also written criticism, poetry, nonfiction, as many plays as Preston Jones has, and even songs. His fiction mood ranges from the guilt-haunted *House of Breath* to the broadly funny *Fair Sister*. Goyen has consistently experimented, rather than simply repeating successes. Of the dozen writers, he has probably attracted the most critical interest over the years.

Goyen fascinated me, but I finally gave up hope that he would visit Texas in time to be interviewed for this book. I telephoned editor Margaret Hartley, an old friend of Goyen, at the *Southwest Review*. She advised me to get in touch with Professor John Igo in San Antonio, because Igo had talked with Goyen recently. Igo said that Goyen now lives in Los Angeles, where his wife, actress Doris Roberts, has been portraying the mother in the television series *Angie*. On the phone Mrs. Goyen told me that Bill had gone back to New York to consult his publishers and to write. I finally found the novelist himself at the Goyens' old New York apartment.

John Graves is the writer's writer in Texas, and there was no question about whether I wanted to include him in this book. His *Goodbye to a River* and *Hard Scrabble* are works of art fashioned from pure Texas clay. Graves was interested in man's truce with nature before ecology became fashionable. He thinks clearly and then writes in wonderful style, one of the more distinctive styles of our era. I hope that someday somebody collects his short stories, in spite of his protests, and I would like to read those novels in his trunk.

I've known A. C. Greene longer than most of the others in the dozen. Many Texas authors have manned typewriters at the *Abilene Reporter-News*—Edward Anderson, Duvan Polk, Jane Gilmore Rushing, Carlton Stowers, and Kathryn Duff, to name a few. When I arrived there, I heard more stories about Greene than about all the rest: about how he drove a Rolls Royce as a cub, how he collected bricks from Abilene streets and built a wall on his desk, about the explosive scene in the publisher's office when Greene quit—or was fired, depending on whether you take the labor or the management viewpoint.

The reason I chose Greene, however, is because of the high quality of his work. He is best described as a "man of letters." Like Thomas Carlyle, he uses history as material, but neither of them can properly be described as a historian. Their personalities, like chili peppers, pervade their best work to an extent that can't be missed. Greene has a sharp critical mind also, and somebody ought to collect his Texas book criticism from the *Dallas Times-Herald*.

Leon Hale laughs at his fellow human beings, but he also understands and sympathizes, and I felt that he would be a good choice for the dozen. Like Don Marquis and Franklin P. Adams before him, Hale writes a humor column in a metropolitan daily, the *Houston Post* in this case. Between newspaper chores he has managed to write some books pervaded by his gentle South Texas humor, books filled with strong, likable characters. *Bonney's Place* has to be one of the best beer-joint novels ever written.

I first met Shelby Hearon at a Fort Worth conference for librarians, where there was a panel of writers that included Gary Cartwright, Al Dewlen, Preston Jones, Greene, and Hearon. My wife, Shay, who is a librarian, smuggled me inside by pinning on me the name tag of an absent friend. At intermission I introduced myself to Hearon. The novelist, who misses little, glanced curiously at my name tag.

"I'm *not* Joe Specht," I said.

"Oh, I've always wanted to do that," she said, and laughed.

Hearon is a good laugher and talker, as well as a first-rate novelist. After lunch she talked with us a while, and I eventually wrote a newspaper article about the conversation, which started me on the line of thought that finally led to this book.

I chose to go back to talk to Hearon because she seems to me the Texas writer who is thoroughly and completely at home in the novel form. Witty and intellectual, probing deeply into the female psyche, Hearon speaks through the medium of the novel as though it were tailored for her. *The Second Dune, Hannah's House,* or *A Prince of a Fellow* might well make a good play or movie, but there would be certain valuable aspects missing, aspects belonging only to the novel.

Preston Jones seemed a natural choice for my Texas dramatist. The New Mexico–born Dallas actor had written the three marvelous plays of *A Texas Trilogy* and two plays since. At the time we talked, he was working on another fine play, *Remember,* which was to be his last because of his unforeseen and tragically early death.

Elmer Kelton would be acknowledged as a Texas writer even by those readers in the first half of this century in my hometown. Kelton knows the cowboy life and writes convincingly about it. His last three novels in particular have a quality that recommended him to me. *The Time It Never Rained* captures the West Texas experience in a way no other novel has done, but my personal favorite is *The Good Old Boys,* with its comic hero, Hewey Calloway.

Kelton reminded me of a lesson I have to relearn every once in a while: never jump to conclusions. His record collection mixes country and western music with grand opera. His wife, Ann, is from Ebensee, near Salzburg, in Austria, where opera grows like mesquite trees in West Texas. I jumped to the conclusion that Kelton liked western music because he grew up in cow country and that Ann taught him the beauties of Mozart and Puccini. Kelton corrected me; he acquired his taste for opera "from a band teacher I had in high school, a tough-minded old European professional musician who hadn't seen a note of decent music written in the twentieth century."

Larry L. King has fashioned literature out of a sharecropper viewpoint and pore-boy vocabulary. He has blended these skillfully with his own wide reading and years of experience at our political vortex in Washington. Texas politics and broad humor run from *The One-eyed Man* through his theatrical success *The Best Little Whorehouse in Texas*. His magazine essays, infused with so much life that they make strong hardback collections, cover a broader range.

Tom Lea is in a category alone. He is a master painter and illustrator who in middle life also began to write masterly fiction and nonfiction. Lea is a link with Dobie and the elder gods of Texas letters, but it was because of his writing that I felt he must be included.

Lea didn't much want to use the tape recorder, finally agreeing with reluctance. "I know what you're up against," he said. "I once tried to take some tape in the outback of Australia. I've also tried to tape a polo player in Argentina, and the stuff turned out to be crap. I didn't know what they were saying on half of it. I'm skeptical about it, but at the same time my heart bleeds for you because you want to get the information." In spite of his doubts and my bumbling, the recording was better than average. The words are plain. Behind them you can hear a bird singing his heart out. A distant airplane passes. I hear myself introduced to Sarah Lea when she came to his studio to tell her husband that she was leaving on some errands.

Larry McMurtry has produced a group of strong novels since he burst into Texas letters with *Horseman Pass By* in 1961, when he was twenty-five. McMurtry's Texas is recognizably that of Dobie, Kelton, and Lea, but the time is fifty to one hundred years later. McMurtry writes sensitive and exciting prose, with a lot of funny action that is always vaguely tinged with sadness. I like his books, and it would have been unthinkable to leave him out.

Frances Mossiker has written some superb books, and I chose her because she represents a cosmopolitan strain in Texas letters. She shows that a Texan is quite capable of fathoming the French mind. Mossiker has taken the reader by the hand and guided him through the maze of French court politics, and for good measure she has re-created the English Jacobean colonial enterprise.

In person Mossiker has all the charm and good talk you associate with her favorite eras in French history. "May I get you some sherry?" she asked, as soon as we were seated. "Sunday morning just seems to mean sherry."

I wanted to include representatives of other literary forms, but a wider selection didn't seem practical. I looked into poetry. Some interesting poets were suggested, such as Vassar Miller of Houston, William Burford of Dallas, and my old mentor Everett Gillis of Lubbock. I finally decided to stick with prose; poets are suspended in an area between meaning and melody. Historians also seem a clan apart. I have long admired C. L. Sonnichsen's *Tularosa*, and Frank Vandiver can bring a dead general back to life. Rupert Richardson, my old professor, lives right around the corner. Historians, however, are generally judged on other than literary grounds. Goyen and Lea have written poetry, and Mossiker and Greene have written history, but I chose all of them for other reasons.

Finally, the distance between two covers of a normal book had most to do with limiting the number of my authors. Texas has a lot of writers, and they range high and wide in form, style, and subject matter. Donald Barthelme of Houston writes like a surrealistic S. J. Perelman for the *New Yorker;* John Rechy of El Paso tells about the homosexual underworld in *City of Night;* D. L. Coburn of Dallas won a Pulitzer Prize with his Broadway hit about an old man and an old woman, *The Gin Game*. There are many others.

The dozen writers included here have produced good, solid work, and they have written several shelves of books. The novel has been a favorite form, with 48 published or due at this writing and many others in progress or with agents. They have also written 48 nonfiction books, although this is a catchall category that takes in everything from critical essays to history, while ranging in length from Greene's slender, nostalgic *A Christmas Tree* to Lea's two-volume history, *The King Ranch*. Goyen and Apple have 4 volumes of short stories between them. Jones, King, and Goyen have together a total of 15 produced plays, and McMurtry has a filmed screenplay. Finally, Goyen and Lea have slim volumes of poetry. When you add in some miscellaneous works that don't fit neatly, that's 123 in all. These books have won nineteen awards from the Texas Institute of Letters.

The group is not particularly young, at this time ranging in age from the late thirties to the early seventies. Their average age is fifty-four, and the middle of their age range is fifty-five. That may be because it takes a while to build any kind of literary reputation, to be noticed. Or it may say something about the conditions that have produced the current bumper crop of Texas writers. Is it significant that, counting Lea, who saw the conflict up close as a *Life* magazine artist, six of the writers are World War II veterans?

William James advises landladies to ask potential roomers about their metaphysics. Writers seldom are equipped with a formal and consistent philosophy, but a Texas writer does generally have a religious creed, or at least a church background, even if faith dropped away with his milk teeth. It colors his work. A Baptist backslider is shaped differently from a fallen-away Roman Catholic. By somewhat arbitrarily assigning my writers a creed on the basis of upbringing or present status, I find there are five Methodists, two Jews, two Presbyterians, an Episcopalian, a Roman Catholic, and a Baptist.

Getting around to see everybody has involved a good deal of travel, some of it memorable. One snowy February day, as Shay and I returned from talking to Preston Jones, Shay drove out on an ice-covered bridge a tad too quickly, and the car spun around to head back toward Dallas. I drove the rest of the way, squinting through the snowflakes to follow a highway that became just two ruts in the snow.

One August night, after we talked until dark with McMurtry, the novelist and James, his son, drove back to Archer City with us to eat at the Dairy Queen. Rain clouds were closing in. A tornado had ripped a gash through nearby Wichita Falls the previous year, and the waitresses in the glass-enclosed fast-food place were torn between their duty to serve us our burritos and their desire to shut down and seek more substantial shelter. After we ate, the first volley of raindrops came down. The McMurtrys had their own problem of driving twenty miles over twisting rural roads to the ranch. Shay and I drove home three hours through the rainstorm.

In collecting my material, I discovered a good many things. A surface observation, for example, is that Lea writes letters in a beautifully hand-lettered ink script unlike the pencil scrawl of his manuscripts. Another is that McMurtry dashes off typewritten notes on canary second sheets for correspondence. Goyen has a roadrunner, brother to Dobie's paisano, on his letterhead, and Hearon sends friends picture postcards with interesting art reproductions and the like on the reverse side.

At a deeper level, I learned that a writer is not always capable of discussing the implications of his own work. Even the most literal-minded student in a college English class can grasp that some symbol, theme, motif, or overriding concern is important to a writer. It jumps out of every chapter. Yet the writer himself may not think so, and in fact, may deny that this is so.

Overall, however, writers are much more introspective than plumbers, printers, and college professors. Writers think about what they do, and they can express themselves accurately.

I discovered that the dividing line between fact and fiction is nowhere near as firmly drawn as I supposed. The reader should find interesting the remarks of Hale, Greene, Graves, King, McMurtry, and others on this topic. Fiction often seems to be a sort of emotional autobiography with the facts transformed in a surrealistic, Freudian way. Nonfiction seems to introduce material that is true only to the spirit of the literal facts that surround it.

It appears to me that Texas writers, as a group, don't have a very high "self-image," to borrow a useful term from pop psychology. They like one another, and they aren't noticeably worse than any other group about slipping knives into the backs of their friends, but there doesn't seem to be much *esprit de corps* or much optimism about the quality of native writing. That is certainly inconsistent with Texas character as perceived in Boston, Chicago, and New York. The national publishers are in the East, and the Texas writers—the ones in this book, at any rate—tend to evaluate themselves and their colleagues through the eyes of eastern editors. In one sense this may be right; those easterners are among the world's best, and anyway some of them are born Texans. But in another sense it is like having chefs flown down from Boston to judge the annual chili cookoff at Terlingua.

The colleges and universities of Texas, however, are deeply interested in the writers among us. They have squirreled away as many original manuscripts as the writers will give up, and Texas writers in general are flattered to be asked. Candidates for Ph.D.s can smelter and mold this material into dissertations, and, if there should be a Shakespeare among us, future generations should know far more about him than we do about Shakespeare himself from the joyful, careless Elizabethans.

My group of writers is too small to be statistically significant among the many Texas authors today, but I will note that four of them have Rice University connections. Graves and Goyen have bachelor's degrees from Rice and were influenced by teacher George Williams there. McMurtry earned his master's at Rice and taught there, and Apple now teaches there, both in some courses once taught by Williams.

I have learned again that writing down conversation is a curious process. To collect the living tones of human dialogue and reflect their quality somehow in mere words on a page is much like the craft of the still-life painter who translates a spherical tomato and a conical carrot onto the flat plane of a stretched canvas. A Rembrandt might go at it one way, a Matisse another, and a Juan Gris differently still.

I have made some effort to retain the individual flavor of each writer's speech in these conversations. Writing teachers frequently urge students to write the way they speak. Good advice up to a point. Most of us, however, fill all the speaking gaps with "ands" and "you knows," lean on volume for emphasis, start a sentence in one direction only to abandon it for another tack when in midphrase we hatch a more promising thought. That wonderful unscrambler inside the listener's brain reassembles a fair likeness of the idea of the speaker with marvelous art and quickness. The tape recorder, on the other hand, like the camera, captures it all—the verbal warts, hiccups, sighs, and overworked pet phrases of the speaker. A literal transcription does not reflect what the listener heard. The writer must put down the reality of the conversation rather than the literal, jumbled record. Yet, make no mistake, in these conversations I have remained as literal as the written word would gracefully allow, and when in doubt I have opted for the exact word on the tape.

I cut to the bone my own contributions to the dialogue, although at the times of the talks I traded my share of stories and theories. Since a good story bears repeating, several of the writers heard the same yarns from me. To include the latter would make the book read like the ancient chronicles in which a battle is described and then a messenger runs to the king to deliver a complete verbal replay of the original battle narrative.

The issues we explored in a particular conversation are those any serious reader might be curious about after reading the work of the particular author. Certain themes—ecology, religion, race, and sex are examples—may recur often in a writer's work; we talked about those. We also discussed the way in which writers write. They were more at ease with that question, and a writer's method to some extent explains the form or even the content of his work. Or perhaps it's the other way around. The working habits of writers will be of interest to readers who are themselves interested in doing a bit of writing.

We naturally talked of things that had influenced their writing — teachers, events, fellow Texas writers, and other authors a long way off in miles and years. Every author, whether he is writing his autobiography or preparing a historical work about an emperor of China, must draw on his own life and experience. With a woman's experience, Mossiker is most effective in examining the lives of women, whether they wore silks in a French court or buckskins in primitive America. We poked into the relationship between the work and the writer's experience of life.

The writers often discussed work they planned or actually had in progress at the time we talked. Some of these projects will no doubt be in print by now. The reader might enjoy comparing what was planned with the accomplished fact.

Finally, we discussed Texas writers at large, the writers they see on friendly terms, those they respect, and those they enjoy reading. A picture of the Texas literary community emerges.

Larry McMurtry: *Thalia, Houston, and Hollywood*

LARRY MCMURTRY was born June 3, 1936, in Wichita Falls, the largest town near the Archer County home of the McMurtrys. He earned his B.A. at North Texas State in 1958 and his M.A. at Rice in 1960 and studied further at Stanford. McMurtry's first novel, *Horseman Pass By* (1961), and the later *The Last Picture Show* (1966) were made into highly successful motion pictures (with the title of the first changed to *Hud*). After ten books and thirty-two years, McMurtry left Texas. He settled near Washington, D.C., and now operates a rare-book store in Georgetown.

McMurtry had intended to return to Archer City for a visit in early July, 1979, but research in Montana for a movie screenplay interfered. Then he and his teenage son, James, took their time driving down the eastern side of the Rockies, looking at whatever colleges lay on their way, arriving in Texas in mid-August, when I talked with him.

Out from Archer City, twenty miles along country roads through flat farm and grazing land, is the McMurtry house, an old-fashioned wooden one-story affair painted white, with a wide front porch. The family has lived in Archer City for years, with others occupying this house on the ranch until recently.

For our talk we went into the living room. There wasn't much furniture in the house; McMurtry and James were just snatching a few days of late-summer baching there. Double doors opened into the dining room, where a typewriter sat on a substantial wooden table. Behind was the kitchen.

The novelist is a slender man, just under six feet tall and weighing about 160 pounds. He has dark-brown hair and brown eyes, and his tortoise-shell glasses give him a scholarly look. He talks with a soft voice in a flat, unemotional way.

BENNETT: What writers had influenced you most when you began writing?

MCMURTRY: That's hard to answer, because that's casting back in memory quite a distance now. I was more influenced by nineteenth-century writers than by twentieth-century writers. I've read pretty widely in nineteenth-century fiction, and I think the greatest novelists belong to that era. Oddly enough, I think my main influences were not American writers. I think they were probably George Eliot, Thomas Hardy, Tolstoy, and the Russians and French. I read a lot of Balzac, Stendhal. I read Dickens. Of American writers, I suppose Faulkner probably hit me the hardest; I didn't much like the nineteenth-century Americans. I still don't somehow. One sort of historical influence on me was Kerouac. I think it was because, at the time *On the Road* was published, American writing had been stodgy for quite a while. The English departments had been dominated by the New Critics for twenty years, and everything was very symbolical and academic and heavily written. Kerouac came along and opened it up. It was a breath of air. A lot of writers of my generation were stimulated by Kerouac. Many of them went on past him, as they should have. Still, he was very important at the time when we were developing. I still have a fondness for Kerouac and Ginsberg. But for permanent influences, I think the nineteenth-century novelists.

BENNETT: Do you read many Texas writers?

MCMURTRY: Not a whole lot. I did most of my reading of Texas writing when I was working on the chapter on southwestern literature for *In a Narrow Grave*. Basically, I read Dobie and Webb and Bedichek, and I read them thoroughly. I had, of course, read George Sessions Perry and several others, but there wasn't much fiction that was interesting. It was mostly marginal at the time I began writing.

BENNETT: What do you think of Perry's two books?

MCMURTRY: Actually he wrote five or six, but only *Walls Rise Up* and *Hold Autumn in Your Hand* are any good. Most of them are either extremely Southern folksy or are straight *Saturday Evening Post*, formula fiction. There was practically nothing that I think of as an influence. Of course, I later read my own contemporaries among Texas writers as they developed. And I remember reading William Goyen, and the first book or two by William Humphrey when they first came out.

BENNETT: What about humorists? Did you read them?

MCMURTRY: No, not really. I undoubtedly read Mark Twain but without particularly thinking of him as a humorist. I did not read Thurber, White, Perelman, and people like that until quite late. I read them now, but I didn't read them then. I'm sure I was in my mid-thirties before I started reading those writers.

BENNETT: There is a strong humorous streak in your earliest work.

McMURTRY: That's true. If I had any comic influences, I suspect they were the nineteenth-century English—Dickens, George Eliot. I think it was mainly an extraliterary influence. I think my humor is from growing up in a country where stories were still told and where a comic sense was still important. I have heard a lot of funny stories, and many of them must have trickled into my books. At least that style of comedy, basically an oral style, found its way into the books. I don't think it came from literature.

BENNETT: Let's go back a little. When did you graduate from Archer City High School?

McMURTRY: 1954. I started out at Rice, left Rice as a sophomore, because Rice was a scientific institute then, and the math was just miles beyond me. I went to North Texas State, took a B.A., went back to Rice, took an M.A., left Rice, went to Stanford on a Stegner Fellowship for 1960–61, and taught at TCU the next year. That was the year *Horseman Pass By* was made into *Hud*. A little movie money, goofed around a year, went back to Rice in '63, and stayed there officially until '71, although effectively only until '69. I commuted and taught for one semester in '71, and that was it.

BENNETT: Where have you taught since then?

McMURTRY: The first year I moved to Washington, which was 1969–70, I taught a semester at George Mason just to be doing something, and then I taught a year at American University, and then I quit for good. Since then I've been located basically in Washington, D.C., although I live in rural Virginia, in a little town called Waterford, about forty-five miles from Washington. In '71, the year I finally quit teaching, I opened a rare-book shop in Georgetown with a partner, and it's been going ever since.

BENNETT: Did you start out with magazine writing?

McMURTRY: No. When I went back to Rice as a graduate student in 1958, I started writing *Horseman Pass By* and basically wrote it in the fall of '58. I didn't get it published until 1961. I revised it and fiddled around with it. I wrote another novel, one that eventually became *Leaving Cheyenne*. I had two novels in manuscript when I went to Stanford. *Horseman Pass By* finally got picked up a couple of years after I originally started it, and it was published in the spring of '61. At that time one or two excerpts from it were published in magazines. One was published in the *Southwest Review*. That was all. I had published nothing in magazines, and to this day I haven't published a lot—I mean, compared to how much I write. Actually I now do a good deal of incidental journalism of one kind or another. I was appalled last year to discover that I had written nearly thirty different pieces of one kind or another about film. Twenty-two of them are a column that I did for *American Film* for two years. I'm collecting those in a book [*Film Flam*] this fall, which will be published by the Encino Press. But I have never been comfortable with magazine writing. Having started out publishing books, where you have considerable freedom from editorial tinkering and harassment, I've never adjusted very well to the kinds of things you have to put up with when you write a lot for magazines. I have accumulated a fair amount of magazine work, but I didn't start it for several years after I began publishing. Then I wrote two little pieces for the *Texas Quarterly* and a couple of pieces for *Holiday*, and nothing much else for a long time.

BENNETT: Those were included in *In a Narrow Grave?*

McMURTRY: Some were in that book. But of the nine essays in there, only five or six had been published in magazines. They represented about ten years of incidental journalism. The rest I wrote specifically for that book. In the late sixties I began to publish more in magazines just because I was around Washington where people would ask me. Quick money, and I'd do it. I've never gone out of my way to write for magazines, and I've never been fully pleased with anything I've written for them.

BENNETT: When I saw you at Hardin-Simmons University last fall, you said you had "spent the summer in Archer City, mostly brooding at the Dairy Queen," and that you were writing an essay on Dairy Queens.

McMURTRY: I'm still writing on that. It's right up there on the mantle. It's a long essay; it'll probably turn out to be a short book. I know I'm after something, but I'm not quite sure yet what. I suppose it's really an essay about storytelling and the way it has changed in the last hundred years. It takes off on a brilliant essay by Walter Benjamin and kind of applies the things he says to my own local experience here in Archer County. I'm not quite sure where that essay is going to end up. I don't think it will be magazine length, though. This is already a hundred pages and hasn't really found its channel yet.

BENNETT: Joe Specht picked up some North Texas State literary magazines with some short stories by you in them.

MCMURTRY: No, they were mostly fragments from *Horseman Pass By*, before I started *Horseman Pass By*, and at the time I thought of them as short stories. Later I realized they were parts of a novel, and two out of three of them eventually found their way into it. I feel the short story is a dying medium, dying because there is no place to publish them, certainly not pay for them. Two hundred were published in the United States last year, and two hundred thousand were written. Talent follows money. It is a difficult art. I can't write them at all. Of my generation, Max Apple possibly. I don't miss the short story much. I don't like to read them. I like to read Flannery O'Connor, who was a kind of genius of the form.

BENNETT: Didn't you write for the *Texas Observer*?

MCMURTRY: No, that's a total myth. I was never associated with that group. I lived in Austin pretty much after the old, original gang had broken up. I lived there for maybe seven months in 1963, and I wrote only one piece for them, on the Astrodome. I didn't even write that for them; I wrote it for the *New York Times*. For various reasons the *Times* didn't use it, and I gave it to the *Observer*.

BENNETT: When did you get interested in writing?

MCMURTRY: Fairly late. Well, I suppose it wasn't late, since Conrad didn't get interested until he was forty, and I published my first book when I was twenty-four. But I didn't start writing until I was a junior in college, and even then it was half-serious. I got serious about it when I was a senior and started writing this novel to see if I could. I read an immense amount, I was literary, but I really didn't think much about writing until I was twenty-one.

BENNETT: What started you?

MCMURTRY: It happened so long ago I really don't remember. I was in college, and kids around me were writing, and I was an English major. I suppose out of curiosity to see if I could do it. I was a great reader, so it was natural at some point, an act of imitation.

BENNETT: Did you have anybody to encourage you?

MCMURTRY: I had a couple of good teachers, yes. They were very stimulating to me. One of them was a philosopher named Bill Linden; he wasn't a writing teacher. The other was an English professor who taught writing, James Brown. I don't know how much that really motivated me. Once I really got to doing it, and found that I liked it, I didn't really need a lot of pushing. It was useful to be in the university atmosphere. And I enjoyed my year at Stanford, mainly because I got to know an interesting bunch of writers, and we talked about books.

But I don't know exactly what the direct relation would be between that and writing.

BENNETT: Did you take some sort of degree at Stanford?

MCMURTRY: No, it's a good, one-year fellowship called the Stegner Fiction Fellowship. The Stegner class was maybe ten people, most of whom were fairly far along on writing and about ready to publish a book. Stegner was gone a lot. They brought in interesting outside lecturers, Frank O'Connor and Malcolm Cowley while I was there. I think we had an exceptional class, which has since produced at least twenty-five books. Ken Kesey was in the class, and Peter Beagle, and a good Australian writer, and an interesting Canadian. It was quite stimulating. The best part was meeting one another and hanging out together. The main value of a creative-writing class, it seems to me, is to keep the writer going. There are so many stages in a writer's development when he may decide that this is all just futile and that he doesn't have much talent and that many other people can do exactly what he's doing just as well. He may have long stretches when he's so isolated from the world of letters that the impetus dies, the appetite dies.

BENNETT: When you taught creative writing at Rice, did you attempt to give the same sort of experience to your students?

MCMURTRY: I basically just attempted to stimulate them. I suppose I started out with some idea of encouraging them to write, but in the end I actively tried to discourage them from writing. Over the long term I began to be really suspicious of the emotional effect of overencouraging young writers. I have seen too many people who really had no business trying to be writers encouraged to the point where they invested a great deal of psychic energy in it, and emotional energy, and felt like failures for years because they couldn't bring it off somehow. I became very dubious of pushing kids. I came to teach a sort of literary appreciation course in which I tried to get them to read things they otherwise might not encounter, and if that stimulated them to write, fine. Most of the kids that are really going to write will go ahead and do it anyway. I became rather pessimistic and dark in my last years as a teacher.

BENNETT: John Graves said much the same thing.

MCMURTRY: He was teaching at TCU the year I was there. I have seen a lot of good writers use teaching as an excuse to escape from writing, and I never wanted to do that. I wouldn't be a writer if I didn't want to write, and I don't think I would feel guilty about it if I decided

I wasn't a writer anymore and stopped. But I have known several writers who lost themselves in teaching, always with a great deal of guilt about not writing. I know one fine writer who would write two- or three-thousand-word critiques of his students' stories.

BENNETT: Tell me about your writing habits.

MCMURTRY: I've always had a strong belief in regularity as the guiding principle for prose writers. You have to be as regular as you can be. I'm a fast writer, basically. I always write first thing in the morning, and I write a fixed number of pages a day, five pages double-spaced if I'm writing the first draft of a novel. I don't do that much on an essay, but on the first draft of a novel—which I think is what I'm meant to do—I write five pages, and then I stop. Usually it doesn't take me more than an hour or an hour and a half if I'm regular about it, and I'm almost obsessively regular once I start a novel. I seldom miss a day from page one to the end of the book. I'm much more flexible in revision, which I do at a faster pace, twice that pace usually. Revision is not gut work; it's head work. But I do believe in being regular, doing it every day, and just so much a day, no more, and then doing something else. Of course, there are fairly rare times, at the end of a book when I want to get it finished, or when I need to get off one project and onto another, I'll work longer hours. But not often.

BENNETT: I gather that you use a typewriter to write.

MCMURTRY: Oh, yes, indeed. I can't sign a check in longhand. I've always written on the typewriter, and I can't really imagine not having a typewriter.

BENNETT: Do you choose your own titles?

MCMURTRY: I'm very superstitious about titles. Until I get the title, I don't know what kind of book I'm going to write. Every single one of my books except *Moving On* has been written for the title. *Moving On* was the only title I didn't choose; that book kept squirming out from under my titles. I wanted to call it *Patsy Carpenter*, and there was ample precedent for naming it after the central character. But the publisher didn't like it, and they moved publication up to spring, and somebody suggested *Moving On*.

BENNETT: Do you use an outline when you write a novel?

MCMURTRY: No, I don't. I consider it a process of discovery, writing a novel. But I always start with an ending. My novels begin with a scene that forms itself in my consciousness, which I recognize as a culminating scene. I can tell that the scene ends something, like the closing of the picture show in a small town, which is a kind of natural symbol. Often this scene will refine itself in fairly high definition before I write a word. It's been to the point where I see the people, and I hear the conversation, and I know what the last words are going to be, and I know that something's ended. I don't know exactly what's ended, and the writing of the novel is a process in which I discover how these people got themselves to this scene. I usually simply go back arbitrarily a year or two years in time, or whatever, with the characters that I have, and the scene, and sort of work toward it. I get tremendous surprises. People pop in that I had not expected, who aren't in the final scene perhaps, totally surprising characters. Sometimes novels zig to the left or zig to the right as I go through them, but I've always ended up at the final scene. I've never missed. So far I've always ended up with exactly what I thought I would end up with, although not always with exactly the kind of book I thought I'd have. I don't prejudge that. The final scene contains, sort of, the thematic resolutions of whatever story you're telling. Then I go back to find the story; I'm perfectly comfortable with that. Of course, I have written several hundred pages with the final scene in sight, and I can see that certain things are going to have to happen. I probably could outline the last quarter or third of the book if I really wanted to. But I very seldom do.

BENNETT: Do you actually write the terminal scene early?

MCMURTRY: I hardly ever actually write it down. Once in a while, if there's a particularly vivid, distinct conversation or something like that, I might jot it down. But I never take notes. I've never relied on notebooks. I just figure I'll remember it.

BENNETT: Would you give me an example or two of these climaxing scenes?

MCMURTRY: I envision not necessarily a climaxing but a culminating or terminal scene—the closing of the picture show, the funeral of an old cowman, a young writer drowning his book in a river, et cetera.

BENNETT: But you do occasionally make some jottings in advance?

MCMURTRY: I might make a few jottings, particularly names. If I spend any time on anything, it's naming my characters and naming the places where they live, things like that. I think personal names are very important, and you want to have the right names. If I jot anything down, it will be a list of names. Maybe I won't use half of them, and maybe they won't get attached to the characters that I think they will get attached to, but I'll always do that. I've been thinking about a novel for a couple of years now that I would really like to write, a novel about nineteenth-century Texas, particularly a trail-driving novel, since it seems to me that the trail drives were an extremely crucial experience, odd in that the whole period of the trail drives was so extremely brief, and yet out of it grew such an extraordinarily potent myth. That fascinates me a bit, and I've been vaguely working toward a trail-driving novel. But all I've done in the way of actual work is that every time I think of a good name, or see one, or chance upon one anywhere, in my reading perhaps, I jot it down. Place names, things like that.

BENNETT: Your names seem quite fitting.

MCMURTRY: I was driving through Little Rock on my way here, and I saw a delivery truck on the other lane of the freeway. It just zipped past. it was from a place called Pickles Gap. I don't know where that is; I never heard of it, but I thought, That's a really good name, Pickles Gap, I'll have to remember that. I don't know when I'll use it. Maybe I'll use it in the trail-driving novel, maybe I won't, but it certainly caught my eye. I knew right away that it was something that I wanted.

BENNETT: So you just pick up names where you find them.

MCMURTRY: I don't have any kind of system. I have a lot of books in my study, and when I'm really in a tight for a name, I run my eyes down the shelves. I take one name off one book and another name off another book. I've done that a lot.

BENNETT: Authors and publishers?

MCMURTRY: Yes. Particularly if I'm writing a contemporary novel and don't need a colorful name particularly, just an appropriate name, I'll just put two names together off the spines of my books. But I do feel good about them. I think that names have got to seem to fit the characters.

BENNETT: In the West Texas novels the names seem rooted in the area. Very typical.

MCMURTRY: Those are easy, the easiest ones.

BENNETT: How much revision do you do?

MCMURTRY: I normally do three drafts, never more and seldom less. The first draft is long and kind of an exploratory draft, with a lot of guesswork involved in it, some of it unsuccessful guesswork. Frequently in the first draft of a book there will be an element of redundancy, and you will write the same scene several times, an important scene in the novel, and you won't recognize perhaps you're doing that. The second draft is basically a cutting draft, in which you eliminate the bad guesses, pure mistakes, redundancies, and overwriting of all kinds. In the first draft, when you're trying to develop a character, you let conversations run on for pages if you want to. In the second draft you tighten that. The third draft is stylistic basically. I don't pay much attention to style in the first two drafts; I write fairly rapidly, and I'm trying to visualize the scenes I'm describing as intensely as possible. The third draft is the stylistic draft. I may get down to two eventually. I never want to go above three, because in a sense you participate in the emotions of the book every time you do a draft, and I think three times is about as many times as you can participate in those emotions and keep them alive. It goes cold. I revised *Horseman Pass By* too much. I was really dead on it long before I published it.

BENNETT: How many drafts did you put *Horseman Pass By* through?

MCMURTRY: I think five. Not all of it was my own idea. I did have a certain amount of editorial conflict over that book, and I did make some changes in it ultimately that were suggested by my editor, changes I personally wouldn't have made probably. I think that I would have done three, or at most four, by myself. I would not have done the fifth.

BENNETT: Have you profited by editorial suggestions?

MCMURTRY: I haven't had all that many. The first book was really the only one in which I had a lot of editorial trouble. It was perfectly well meant. My editor was a man who now runs the fiction workshop at a university in the Middle West. He's a novelist himself, and a good novelist. We did not exactly work from the same principles as fiction writers. Yet he was convinced enough of his principles, and he was somewhat older than I, and he was a very persuasive editor. In the original version of the book I had the cattle killed right away, and the book was about the disintegration of the ranching family as a result of the loss of their herd or their work. The editor felt that to kill the herd right away destroyed a certain element of suspense in the narrative which he wanted to keep. After a certain amount of argument, a young writer is particularly vulnerable to an intelligent editor. You tend to think, Well, he knows better than I know. Eventually I gave in. Also, I really wanted to get the book published. Also, by that time I had revised it so many times that I had kind of stopped caring about it one way or the other. So I did as he suggested. I still think it was a mistake. Not that it matters much; the book would not have been a great book if I had kept it my way, and it's not altogether the worse for having done it his way. However, I did think it made the end unrealistic: the collapse of the old man is too abrupt. The movie unfortunately kept the same structure, and again the collapse is too abrupt. That's the only problem I had with the way it was finally structured: just overnight the old man, who was a terrifically strong, vigorous old man, is dying. There was not time, doing it that way, to develop a natural pattern of deterioration. After that book I've never had any problem, never had any substantial editorial difficulty with anyone. None at all with most books. So little that one hardly knows if the editors are even reading.

BENNETT: Do you have any advice for young writers?

MCMURTRY: My advice is simple. At certain stages I think it is just as important to read as to write. It is extremely important for young writers to read an awful lot, onmivorously, and particularly to read very thoroughly in whatever form they expect to write in, whether it's poetry, fiction, short stories, or whatever. The only other advice I have is to be regular. I think it's very important to write a certain amount every day if you're any kind of a writer. If you're working on a project, I don't think you'll get it done if you're hit-or-miss and intermittent. The only secret I've ever discovered is that you have to do it continuously, just as musicians have to practice. You don't practice well every day; some days you write better than others. That's no problem, because you're doing several drafts, and you'll catch it. If you're flat one time, you'll be sharp the next go-round.

BENNETT: I find some novelists advising aspiring fiction writers not to read fiction.

MCMURTRY: I don't think that's good advice at all. But again, you have to consider that any writing career or life is a matter of stages. In the early stages, when you're developing, I think it's very important that you read heavily in the form that you're trying to write in, because you go through a series of natural imitative phases. You're hot on Flaubert one week, and you're hot on Kerouac the next. That's perfectly natural. It's also natural that, after you have been writing ten or fifteen years, you gradually stop reading in the form that you're working in. If only as a means of relaxation, you don't want to write novels half a day and read them the other half. That's why at a certain point the fiction reading of most fiction writers trails off a bit and tends to be spasmodic. I will not read much fiction most of the year; then I may read eight or ten novels at a whack. But basically I'll read outside that area. I'll read a pile of autobiographies, or memoirs, or a lot of travel literature, or whatever—history. After you've been writing a number of years, you develop your style if you're going to, and you cease to be affectable in the way that young writers are. You cease to be, you know, turned on by reading a fiction writer. It's practically impossible after fifteen or twenty years for a writer to hit you hard enough, for a new writer to make any serious impact on the way you write. But it's perfectly possible when you're much younger, and it's one thing that gets you from stage to stage.

BENNETT: Have you ever kept a journal?

MCMURTRY: I never have. I've always felt silly doing that, and I'm not a good keeper of journals. I've made a stab or two at it, and never got past one page. I don't have a two-page journal anywhere. If I'm going to write, I'd rather be writing fiction rather than something I'm going to reprocess and turn into fiction. I don't lead that interesting a life anyway; I don't have much to write down.

BENNETT: I've just finished reading Arnold Bennet's journals.

MCMURTRY: That's good, yes. I like Arnold Bennet very much. He's a good writer, somewhat unappreciated right now, although he's coming back a bit. *Clayhanger*'s wonderful.

BENNETT: I certainly enjoyed his journals.

MCMURTRY: I like to read journals too. I read them all the time, but I just don't like to keep them.

BENNETT: In your novels do you have a major theme or aim that runs through all of them?

MCMURTRY: I don't think it runs through all of them. Obviously in the first three there's the large social action that I observed as I grew up, which was the move off the land toward the cities and the gradual disintegration of the rural way of life in this part of Texas, and the small-town way of life too. The first three books attacked that theme from a country and small-town perspective, and the next three attacked it from the perspective of people who have left the country and found themselves in the city, a sort of transitional generation. I think that *Horseman, Leaving Cheyenne,* and *The Last Picture Show* have a common concern. The next three do too—*Moving On, All My Friends,* and *Terms of Endearment.* The last book, *Somebody's Darling,* is apart from that. I finished that movement so far as I'm concerned. I don't think I'm going to write about that anymore, at least not for a while. I'm not quite sure what I will have my say about next.

BENNETT: Few youngsters go to college intending to major in English. Did you intend to, by the way?

MCMURTRY: Yes, I started out and finished up an English major.

BENNETT: I read a scholarly English publication in which a writer said the theme of *The Last Picture Show* is the progressive isolation of the little West Texas town.

MCMURTRY: I don't think I saw that. I don't keep up with criticism well. But that's basically and broadly unarguable. That's obviously one thing at work in it, showing the vitality seeping out of small-town life.

BENNETT: Women are often the central figures in your later novels. Arnold Bennet thought he understood women. Do you think you understand women?

MCMURTRY: My interest in women characters has always been strong. One of my problems is finding men worth having in the same book with my women. Women are always the most admirable characters in my novels. I think it's really hard to say whether I understand women or not. I feel I write about them well, but that's not necessarily to say that I understand them. My writing frequently convinces women that I understand them, but I don't know whether that means I really do, or whether it means they are easily persuaded, or that my writing is especially persuasive when it comes to descriptions of women. I can't rule. I enjoy writing about them, and I've had a lot of interesting responses. I'm interested in old men and kids too, but men of my age don't interest me for some reason, and men capable of happy marriage don't interest me.

BENNETT: What do you think of the women's movement?

MCMURTRY: I don't think about it a whole lot, to tell you the truth. My approach to women in terms of writing, and in terms of everything else for that matter, is sheerly intuitive. I don't rationalize about it very much. Catch it as catch can.

BENNETT: You often use country-western music in your novels.

MCMURTRY: It has been the background music of my life. I even lived in an apartment once owned by Lightning Hopkins's manager.

BENNETT: Although I don't recall much in *Somebody's Darling*.

MCMURTRY: Not so much. There's one or two uses, that's all. I have been very sparing with it. You can't overwork it. And I'm a little dated. I haven't kept up particularly. Most of that appears back in the '50s and '60s, and I don't know if I could use it so skillfully if I had to be contemporary.

BENNETT: Do you like country-western music?

MCMURTRY: Sure I like it. I've never had any problem with it. Mainly I used it as a sort of source of stories. Quite a bit of it has narrative words.

BENNETT: But you don't rush out to buy the latest records.

MCMURTRY: No. I guess long ago I had to choose between buying all the books I wanted to read or all the records I wanted to listen to, and I chose books.

BENNETT: I keep hearing that the residents of Archer City are annoyed with your books, particularly *The Last Picture Show*.

MCMURTRY: The people at Archer City are not mad at me. They may not exploit the publicity coming from my books because they can't or don't know how. But there was little criticism of me for the movie; it brought a lot of money into town. There is now a move to save the old movie house at Archer City, and I don't know just what I think of that.

BENNETT: I gather that you're quite intuitive about your writing.

MCMURTRY: Pretty much. I'm not totally. I have some preconceptions when I go into a book, but not many. Not so many that I'm inhibited from suddenly writing a different kind of book from that I had expected to write. If it happens, it happens. I tend to go with the flow. Fiction writing is not a particularly cerebral process with me. It's a semiconscious process that becomes intellective in the last stage, or at least I'm only conscious of it as being intellective in the last stage. I write essays far more painfully than I write fiction. I never suffer much writing fiction. I may not visualize the story I am constructing successfully, or conceive it successfully. I often make bad guesses, or wait too long to write until I'm really just not interested anymore—that's a common problem with fiction writers. They have the book they think they always wanted to write; things intervene, other books pop up, and by the time they get around to writing it, they're not that interested. My last novel was a sort of case in point. I had always wanted to write a Hollywood novel, and another book about Jill Peel, and yet somehow by the time I got around to it, some of the original energy had gone. I don't know what happened to *Somebody's Darling*. I wasn't really stirred by it, even as I went along. Then, too, the idiom of California is easy, and that deceived me. Because you happen to know how people talk, you feel you know more about Californians than you really do. But that's just part of the game; you do the best you can.

BENNETT: *Somebody's Darling* didn't please all the critics, but I enjoyed it.

MCMURTRY: It's an enjoyable read. It was probably more of a disappointment to me than it was to most people who read it. One, because it never came up to the vision I had of it long before I tried to write it. Two, because I discovered that I didn't have much business writing about Los Angeles, that my grasp was superficial. I had been there a lot, but I hadn't lived there like I've lived in Texas. I was on very thin ground, and I ultimately wrote rather a thin book as a result. Another reason it was unsatisfactory to me was that most of my books have a certain amount of satisfying emotion in them; something works out so that, somewhere along the way, a feeling is satisfactorily expressed—this is less so in *Somebody's Darling* than in any other book. Consequently, it was an unpleasant writing experience, the only one I've ever had. It was the only time I've not felt really engaged; it was forced.

BENNETT: Jill Peel was a likable, strong character.

MCMURTRY: Pretty well, yes.

BENNETT: Joe Percy is marvelous.

MCMURTRY: Joe Percy I liked a lot. I've often wished that I had done only the first section and used it as a short novel or something. The first section has life. I struggled with several technical problems in that novel that I don't think I overcame. Perhaps my approach was a bit conservative. That first section should have been the last section somehow, and it should have been the only section in the first person. I should have written the whole novel in the third person, probably, but I kept feeling that if I took Joe Percy's section out of first person it would lose a kind of immediacy that it really needed. I always felt there was something misfitting about the conception of that book. Oh, well, water under the bridge. I'm not one to brood.

BENNETT: The Owen section——

MCMURTRY: It was unpleasant to me. Amazingly, many liked it.

BENNETT: It was very fitting.

MCMURTRY: Fitting yes. But I'm surprised how many people liked that section.

BENNETT: And the two screenwriters.

MCMURTRY: Oh, I liked them. If there was anything that redeemed the book for me, it was the screenwriters.

BENNETT: A principal interest with you seems to be the development of characters through time.

MCMURTRY: That becomes a very interesting thing to a novelist, one of the most interesting. In the nineteenth century, writers got to do that because the form was expansive and allowed for huge novels, three-volume novels. Nowadays to satisfy that desire, which is a crucial desire, is important for a novelist. One of the prime abilities for a novelist is the ability to convey the passage of time, moving people from generation to generation, or at least decade to decade. Consequently it is very appealing to be able to take a character and carry him through more than one book, or to pick up a character who is a minor character in one book and give him a book of his own. Joe Percy is a minor character in *Moving On*, barely mentioned in *All My Friends*, a major character in *Somebody's Darling*. Jill's a minor character in *All My Friends*, a major character in *Somebody's Darling*. Aurora Greenway is the same way: barely mentioned in *Moving On*, and really I gave her a book in *Terms of Endearment*. That's very attractive to me.

BENNETT: That's the way you overcome the limitation of the short novel.

McMURTRY: Yes. The pressure to keep a book's size down so it can sell for a certain price is constant as production costs rise. It's really bad. I hate to publish novels that cost more than ten dollars, but you have to cut way down to produce a ten-dollar book. *Moving On* is the only novel in which I've indulged myself.

BENNETT: You've tried ellipses in other books.

McMURTRY: Yes, of material. Gaps in time. Youth and middle age and old age.

BENNETT: Have you got much criticism for your use of sex?

McMURTRY: Not really, no, hardly ever. It's been a long time since anybody lifted an eyebrow.

BENNETT: Why did you select the name Thalia for your little town?

McMURTRY: That's really lost in the mists of time. There was a little town named Thalia, which was immediately pointed out to me after *Horseman Pass By* was published. I probably had a subliminal memory of it, because I've gone through it on various family trips. It was just a grocery store–post office, and I remembered it without really remembering what it was. I liked the name.

BENNETT: Isn't Thalia the muse of comic poetry?

McMURTRY: I knew that, and I knew what it meant at one time. I don't even know what it means any more in Greek. But I imagine that little town just caught my eye at some point as I was driving past it.

BENNETT: Is there much autobiographical material in *Horseman* and the small-town novels?

McMURTRY: No, there really isn't. It's almost all invented.

BENNETT: I assume some very minor characters might be based on real persons.

McMURTRY: Very minor. A character that's going to appear once, a bit of local color. The only one I can remember is the night watchman in *Horseman Pass By,* and I can't remember him, but I remember there is one. That is the way you can use a real person, and the only way as far as I'm concerned. Very little of it is overtly autobiographical. Only the place is autobiographical.

BENNETT: You pick up some characters from *Horseman* in *Picture Show.* Lem the Lion, for instance, you pick up as Sam the Lion, but he changes from black to white.

McMURTRY: You know, I don't even remember that. I don't think I thought of those two as the same character, although to tell the truth I have practically no memory of *Horseman Pass By.* I think I blotted it out because I worked on it too much or something. I don't remember that book, and I don't want to reread it, so I don't think I'll ever know the answer to any of that.

BENNETT: Are any of the fathers in your books related to your own father?

McMURTRY: I don't think so, except as an embodiment of certain principles maybe. Not in terms of personality at all.

BENNETT: Did you know any boys like Sonny and Duane of *The Last Picture Show?*

McMURTRY: I've always known kids like that. There's always kids like that around these oil towns. They may have one parent, and they may not exactly be living with that one parent. And the other parent is dead or divorced. I know two or three people like that.

BENNETT: Do you intend to return to the small-town material?

McMURTRY: Who can say? Not me. That's what normally happens to novelists in their middle years: they start subconsciously recycling material that they used earlier, generally with more technical fluency but less depth and less emotional force. I don't want to do that. There might be a time when I'll want to revisit it and see. It doesn't have to be bad; you can do it well sometimes. It is important to be conscious that you're doing it if you do it well.

BENNETT: I think of your last four books as the Houston-Hollywood novels. Do you have an overall plan? Are they going somewhere?

McMURTRY: No, not really. I don't think of them as grouped. *All My Friends, Moving On,* and *Terms of Endearment* I can see as a trilogy. I always wanted to write a trilogy. I see sequence in that set of characters and books, not that I had them in mind fully, but I did know that I was going to write a sequence of books. Now, the Hollywood novel is a pickup, a sort of accidental character that hung over that I could pick up. I don't know exactly what I intended the whole trilogy to consider, thematically. If it's about anything, it's about couples.

BENNETT: What couples do you mean?

MCMURTRY: If you look at them, the novels are just filled with couples, all kinds, all three of them. There are all the marriages in *Terms of Endearment* and in *Moving On*, three or four—offset, of course, by people who weren't coupled for one reason or another. There are all the unachieved couples in *All My Friends*, with just Emma and Flap at the center. Then there are the hopeful whoopee couples in *Terms of Endearment*.

BENNETT: Another character you pick up in your Hollywood novel, it occurs to me, is Godwin.

MCMURTRY: Yes, that's an easy thing to do. It's nice to have a character like Godwin you can pop in once in a while. He stands outside of it, of course. I think that's what I was interested in during those three books: a set of perspectives on marriage and couples.

BENNETT: You have picked up the structure of *Leaving Cheyenne* in *Somebody's Darling*. Did you intend that?

MCMURTRY: Pretty much, but I wasn't comfortable with it. A better way would have been to write it in the third person. I made a deliberate choice not to do that, although I actually started translating it into third person and went about a third of the way. I just didn't want to lose Joe Percy in the first person. I didn't like the fact that it echoes *Leaving Cheyenne* and uses that device.

BENNETT: Of course the time gaps are not as long. Did you pick up that device somewhere?

MCMURTRY: It's really the *As I Lay Dying* device.

BENNETT: Have you ever decided what happened to Danny Deck?

MCMURTRY: No, I've never given it a moment's thought.

BENNETT: Do you think you might pick him up sometime?

MCMURTRY: No, he's totally gone.

BENNETT: What are you working on now?

MCMURTRY: I'm working on a screenplay about coal development in Montana. This is a fiction film, but it doesn't exactly have a story yet. I've got a sort of fragmentary story, about some people who want to make a film about the fight that is being made against the coal development there by ranchers and the Cheyenne Indians. My task is to take that sociological phenomenon and find a story to embody it.

BENNETT: How many screenplays have you written?

MCMURTRY: Ten, I guess. Just one has become a film, *The Last Picture Show*.

BENNETT: I gather screenwriting has always been that way.

MCMURTRY: It's always that way. If you have a realistic attitude toward it, there's nothing wrong with it. One out of every hundred and fifty projects gets made. Just do the best you can and hope that sooner or later your number will come up. I'm perfectly comfortable with it. It's not something I would lose any sleep over.

BENNETT: Do you find it rewarding?

MCMURTRY: No, it's not satisfying at all in literary terms, but one would be a fool to expect it to be. You're just providing a blueprint for a possible movie. It's the first stage in the development of a movie. It's dependent on the efforts of other people for it to be fleshed out into a film. It's not like a novel, in which you control the whole thing and are responsible for every sentence. It's a different form entirely. Consequently I'm not very troubled if something doesn't happen. If it does, why, fine! Not long after *The Last Picture Show*, I did a script called *Streets of Laredo* for John Wayne, James Stewart, and Henry Fonda. It was an end-of-West western. Three old men stumble into a last adventure, and they're old, and the West is over. Everybody loved it except the three actors, so we didn't make it. I've sometimes thought I might see what would happen if I did it as a novel.

BENNETT: Do you feel there is any tradition of the West now?

MCMURTRY: The Old West has been gone for some time, and in the approaching time it will not only be gone but forgotten. That's what interests me. People, I think, will get to a place where it will be painful to be reminded of it. It is presented as better, and they don't like to be reminded of something that was better. I feel a sense of loss, but I never particularly wanted it while it was still partly available.

BENNETT: Are you at present thinking about a novel?

MCMURTRY: I'll write a novel, probably this fall, but I haven't worried much about it yet.

BENNETT: How long does a novel take?

MCMURTRY: X times five. Five pages times however many days, however long the novel is. Sundays and all.

BENNETT: Do you have any favorites among your own novels?

MCMURTRY: I suppose that my two favorites are *All My Friends Are Going to Be Strangers* and *Terms of Endearment*. Those are the only two that I can stand to think about at all. I think *Terms of Endearment* is a better book, a more mature book. *All My Friends* is a lucky book, in that I wrote it after *Moving On*, and I was quite tired, but I had a sort of momentum going, and I thought: I might just do a quick book. I wrote it rapidly, and I think it has an unself-conscious tone that I probably could not have got if I had tried. I'm really happy with it. Every time I pick it up, I'm amazed at how easy it is to read.

BENNETT: This afternoon I glanced again at *The Last Picture Show*, and it's very readable.

MCMURTRY: That's readable, but in a more simplistic way.

BENNETT: Do you have any particular system for generating ideas?

MCMURTRY: None at all. They just happen. I'm seldom at a loss, but it's not systematic.

BENNETT: You don't keep ideas on notebooks or index cards?

MCMURTRY: I don't keep anything. I just sit down and write.

BENNETT: Does it bother you to kill off characters?

MCMURTRY: You live with a character a long time. If it's a character you like, you acquire a certain level of affection for him, and it's sad to stop writing about him. I always hate to finish any book, because I've become comfortable with these people and could keep writing about them ad infinitum. But, you know, I don't anguish very much about the death of any character.

BENNETT: Have you written any novels or other things that haven't surfaced?

MCMURTRY: No. Just movie scripts.

BENNETT: There is a good deal of iconoclasm in your *In a Narrow Grave*. Have you ever regretted any of it?

MCMURTRY: Nope, not a bit.

BENNETT: Religion seems to have chiefly a comic significance in your novels. It doesn't come up when a character dies, for instance.

MCMURTRY: That's right.

BENNETT: Do you have any comment on that?

MCMURTRY: I think that's exactly right, that it is regarded as a source of comedy, and I don't have any more profound uses for it. I've always felt Texas isn't as religious as it thinks it is anyway. Underneath there is a strong undercurrent of heresy and paganism.

BENNETT: You don't have much violence in your novels.

MCMURTRY: I try to keep violence on a comic level too. I find it hard to use. I try to avoid it in writing. I try to avoid it in reality. I can't believe Texas is getting more violent than it has been. I read *Murder in Space City*, and I'm amazed at the weakness of sanctions in Texas. People kill family or friends often without even getting a ticket.

BENNETT: John Graves said you stopped by to see him while you were in Texas last spring.

McMURTRY: I see John Graves once in a while, yes. He's probably the only Texas writer I see with any regularity apart from Max Crawford, whom I see frequently.

BENNETT: Was he in that Stanford class?

McMURTRY: Yes, years later, not when I was.

BENNETT: Could we talk about your contemporaries?

McMURTRY: I don't think it's a good idea to talk about one's contemporaries. It can only lead to trouble. I know most of my contemporaries, and I'll end up getting acquainted with most of the ones I don't know, and to pop off about them wouldn't be wise.

August, 1979

A. C. Greene: *Molding Past into Art*

A. C. GREENE was born November 4, 1923, in Abilene, Texas. He earned his B.A. at Abilene Christian University in 1948 and later studied at Hardin-Simmons University and at the University of Texas in Austin. He was in the U.S. Navy and the Marines in World War II. He has operated a bookstore and worked on newspapers in Abilene and Dallas.

I first met Greene in the mid-1960s when he came to Abilene to settle the estate of his parents, who had been killed in an automobile accident. My companions and I happened onto Greene on the corner of North Second and Cypress outside the stairs leading up to the old *Reporter-News* city room. The conversation of Greene and my companions ran mostly to "Whatever happened to Old Charley?" but I was introduced. When he heard that I was the *Reporter-News* arts man, Greene said, "You're following in a great tradition." It was a typical Greene remark, generous to me and also recognizing his place in the "great tradition."

At Greene's North Dallas home, we went upstairs to a large book-lined room, which is library and workroom. There were the inevitable desk and typewriter, but Greene said that he habitually works in an apartment that he rents to get clear of the phone and other distractions. He doesn't throw things away. In our talk, he mentioned that he still has his Coca-Cola uniform from the years he was a deliveryman. When an early magazine article was mentioned, he poked around on shelves and in a closet until he found it. Various photographs, documents, and artifacts hung on the walls. All the time he was talking, good intelligent talk. He remarked that he now makes part of his living talking on radio.

Greene is five feet ten inches tall and weighs 195 pounds. He has a good crop of graying brown hair, and his hazel eyes are bordered by dark-framed spectacles.

Since Greene is former book critic for the *Dallas Times Herald*, I asked his opinion about which writers I should include in this volume.

GREENE: Angus Cameron was in Dallas one Sunday morning, and I had written a column about the new generation of Texas writers. I had made the remark in it that Frank Dobie was the worst thing that ever happened to Texas writing. The reasoning was that everybody tried to write like Frank Dobie. They all got this folkloric .... Dobie was a good writer, and I wasn't knocking Dobie. Anyway, Angus read this column, and he came up to see me. He said, "I was Frank Dobie's editor at Little, Brown for several of his books, and I was interested in your reasoning." He had just been down to see Dobie at Paisano.

BENNETT: There are lots of Texans writing these days.

GREENE: So many people in Texas letters have gotten right up to the point of—I wouldn't call it great; that's not the qualification I'm trying to make—right up to the point of *being writers,* and stopped. They remain professors or historians or newspapermen, whatever it is. There's always some qualification.

BENNETT: Who are your favorites among living Texas writers?

GREENE: Oh, John Graves is far and away my favorite. I like McMurtry too, when he's writing McMurtry and not for a peer-group audience. Although she doesn't like to be called a Texas writer, Katherine Anne Porter. She was born down around Indian Creek in Brown County, wherever that is. I went out and spent half a day looking for it one time; never did find it. I like Tom Lea; I loved *The Wonderful Country* and *The Hands of Cantu*—they evoke a period so well. Of course, they'd have to evoke it for me, because I wasn't alive by three hundred years in one case.

BENNETT: What about Shelby Hearon?

GREENE: *Armadillo in the Grass* is an excellent book, and I like *Hannah's House.* I wish she hadn't written that book on Barbara Jordan. It's not that there is anything wrong with it; it's just that it took her away from the kind of writing she ought to be doing.

BENNETT: What about Bev Lowry?

GREENE: She hasn't done that much writing yet. Now John Graves has only done two books, but, my God, if he had only done one or two pieces in *Texas Monthly,* the quality of his writing would be evident.

BENNETT: Leon Hale?

GREENE: Leon is one of those Texas writers who hasn't quite broken over the edge yet. He's still a newspaperman who writes. I think *Bonney's Place* shows a great deal. Just because a man's a newspaperman doesn't mean he's not a good writer, but as long as he considers himself a newspaperman first, he'll always be a newspaperman.

BENNETT: Then there's Max Apple.

GREENE: Max Apple may eventually be, or may be right now, the most important writer in Texas. It's just that I'm not ready to consider him a Texas writer. He hasn't written about Texas; he doesn't write from a Texas viewpoint. Texas background has had no evident influence on him. He writes as a university professor.

BENNETT: Ben Capps?

GREENE: The critics need to take a serious look at Ben. In a sense he has been overlooked, and he deserves better.

BENNETT: D. L. Coburn?

GREENE: Don, I think, will succeed as a playwright, because Don is a born pro. I'd like to see how his next couple of plays do, even though *Gin Game* proves how good he is. He impresses me as the kind of guy who *does* it, who sits down and writes without talking about it.

BENNETT: Preston Jones?

GREENE: Preston may have more heart than Don, and I think Preston's current play, *Remember,* is exceptional. But I don't know if Preston will be able to transcend the Theater Center.

BENNETT: Mary Lasswell?

GREENE: She represented a stage in Texas writing. She was writing in the sixties the way they were writing in the thirties. But it quit being Texas writing.

BENNETT: Dr. Rupert Richardson?

GREENE: As a Texas historian, I think Rupert Richardson may be the best. Eugene Barker stumbled into the Spanish archives, but Rupe stumbled into Texas history. It's a shame he didn't come east and do a history on this side of the state so he could establish himself with these people. There's never been a good East Texas history done, never.

BENNETT: Larry King?

GREENE: Larry King represents the kind of Texas writer who flees Texas but can't escape. Even though his writing style is totally different from, say, William Humphrey's or Larry McMurtry's, it still resists Texas and embraces it at the same time. He is an important writer, and when Larry wants to express himself, he does so beautifully.

BENNETT: Winston Estes?

GREENE: I'm glad to see somebody writing about contemporary Texas, or the Texas of my generation at least.

BENNETT: There's Gary Cartwright.

GREENE: He and Bud Shrake are the closest of friends. They came out of Fort Worth, they've come out of a sports background. Bud has tried to express himself in fiction, and Gary has just made a living. But I think his *Hundred Yard War* is one of the best football fiction books I've ever read, and I think Gary is a good writer. *Blood Will Tell* is very strong. Gary is approaching the point at which sheer professionalism is making him a good writer.

BENNETT: Which of the other sports novelists do you like the best?

GREENE: Dan Jenkins naturally is the most famous. *Semi-Tough* made him a million dollars, literally, but it is a weak book. But Dan is a guy who has really never written up to his talents. If he's not careful, he'll be too successful to be serious. I know Dan well. He and I worked at the *Times Herald* together for a couple of years, and we used to share a lot of things, because he was raised by a grandfather and grandmother who were both stout Campbellites. Dan and I shared certain beginnings, you might say.

BENNETT: You think of Bud Shrake apart from them.

GREENE: Bud has shown signs of really breaking out. He wrote a book called *Blessed McGill*, which was supposed to be the life of a saint in New Mexico. It was a tongue-in-cheek kind of thing. It was handled well, but not great. His *But Not for Love* was too full of the rich-man bravado kind of thing, and the in-crowd thing, but there's never been another book quite like it written in Texas. Bud got deeply into all that Austin business. Austin is the deathbed of writers. You go to Austin and you die; I've never seen it fail. As far as Texas writers go, I think he's important. I think somebody needs to inspect him without illusions. Bud is very open about himself once he understands you're not trying to put him on, or put him down, or put him off. And he wants to be a good writer. I think he'd just love to flee from everything and write two or three books. Maybe he will some of these days. He's written good work.

BENNETT: Do you know William Humphrey?

GREENE: No. He is a very difficult man even to get in touch with. Humphrey wrote a little book called *The Spawning Run* which is one of the funniest things I ever read. It's about salmon fishing in England and sex and the difference between Americans and the British. Humphrey is a good writer, but he gets off into his legendary stance, as I call it, too quickly. *The Ordways* is flawed by that, and so was *Proud Flesh*. *Proud Flesh* was so Faulkneresque and so Deep South that I couldn't get into it, much less finish it.

BENNETT: Who else?

GREENE: Well, of course, Frances Mossiker hasn't written about

Texas, even though she is a native of Dallas and has written several critically successful books. She wrote *The Queen's Necklace, Napoleon and Josephine, The Affair of the Poisons, Pocahontas*. I told her that she's gradually coming closer and closer to Texas. Leon Harris is another good Texas writer who has written mainly about non-Texas topics.

BENNETT: Elizabeth Forsythe?

GREENE: Her first book is pretty good. I read it in manuscript.

BENNETT: Are there any Texas poets with national reputations?

GREENE: Two or three. There was a young guy out at Southern Methodist University who was in the Yale Younger Poets series. There's R. G. Vliet; he's a good poet. He's up in Iowa now, but he was in Texas for years. But once again he's not primarily a poet; he's an academician. I can't blame them; they have to make a living. Oh, the poets will tell you there's some great poetry being done.

BENNETT: If they paid them a dollar a line, they couldn't get by.

GREENE: Not if they paid them a dollar a word.

BENNETT: Does it take anything out of your writing to have a radio show?

GREENE: Sure it does. Once again, I'm like the people I've been hollering about; I've got to make a living. I wish I didn't. I wish I could be just a writer.

What about Donald Barthelme? He considers himself a Texas writer. Then there's Bill Goetzmann, a historian; he won the Pulitzer Prize for *Exploration and Empire*, but he is a Texan and not just somebody on the staff down at the University of Texas. Joe Goulden lives in D. C., but he remains a basic Texan and has done a number of important books. Willie Morris still likes to consider himself almost a Texan.

BENNETT: What about dead Texans?

GREENE: Amelia Barr was a real keen writer, among the forgotten ones. She lived in Texas for several years and was very successful as a writer. Then I liked some of the writing that was going on in the thirties. I thought George Sessions Perry was a little bit lightweight, but he was coming close to doing great Texas writing. Eddie Anderson was a damned good Texas writer. Of course, nobody even knows Eddie Anderson now. He wrote two books, and they looked like they were going to be big successes. John Houghton Allen was a good writer.

Bill Brammer wrote one book, and unfortunately it may not be as great as everybody now thinks he thought it was. But Bill Brammer then destroyed himself. The last ten years of his life I wouldn't have given you ten cents for anything that Bill Brammer could have written if you locked him in a room with seventeen IBM typewriters and then bought everything he wrote twenty-four hours a day. I wouldn't give you a nickel for it. There was nothing left of him; he was gone. Some Texas writers have killed themselves intellectually. Bill did it with pills, and anything else he could lay hands on.

BENNETT: Do you have any advice for young Texas writers?

GREENE: My advice to young writers is to become old writers, because young writers get disappointed and give up, that sort of thing, very easy. What the young writers who come to me asking about writing are really thinking about is selling. Selling has to become part of it, sure; I'm very much in favor of writers getting a decent amount for their work, but you don't do that until you've got something to sell. If you just want to be a success and a creative artist early, you'd better stick to writing rock or country and western lyrics. I think an important writer continues to write his best into old age. I'm not sure, but there comes a point when you just simply can't do as well as you used to. I may have reached it, but . . . .

BENNETT: I like to think of Yeats.

GREENE: Yeats is my hero. Not just because he was writing his best poetry when he was in his seventies but because he says things so beautifully. I used to say T. S. Eliot was the greatest poet of our day, but no question that Yeats was a greater poet. Although I yield to no man in my admiration of Eliot—I have a son named for him, after I spent a day with T. S. down at the University of Texas in 1958. My son has a letter on his apartment wall that says: "I hope the name proves auspicious. T. S. Eliot."

BENNETT: I suppose, as a former newspaperman, you write on a typewriter.

GREENE: Yes, and I can't stand "dirty" typing. If a sentence goes wrong, I start a new page. I'll do as many as fifty first paragraphs for a piece. I keep all my false starts and rejects, and I have a stack this high [*holds hand about four feet above the floor*] of bad pages. The University of Texas at Arlington has purchased some of my manuscripts and other literary remains. I told them, "Let my literary career get started first." I've never been able to write any way but by typing. I'm a fast typist, and a good typist—with the help of a little correction tape.

BENNETT: Do you work long at a stretch?

GREENE: I have a pretty good stomach for work; maybe I learned that at the *Reporter-News* and the *Times Herald*. I generally work for five or six hours once I get started. I get up in the morning, take my daughter to school, and by ten o'clock I'm at my typewriter. John O'Hara used to say he wrote till he got this peculiar pain in the small of his back. I write till I can't see.

I try to give everything at least one rewrite. I'll do a book at least twice, parts five or six times. I pencil in revisions on one draft and then do the next draft on a typewriter. I do things sentence by sentence. Sentence construction bothers me more than anything.

Usually, when I'm working on a book against a deadline, I rent an apartment. That gets me away from everybody, and nobody but my family knows the phone number, and I can sleep and eat there if I have to.

BENNETT: Your book titles are good ones.

GREENE: I always wait until the last minute to name a book. Titles aren't one of my easiest things. A fellow recently told me that he would sure like to have used *Dallas: The Deciding Years* as the name of his book. One I had trouble with was *A Personal Country*. The editors kept saying that everybody's country is a personal country. But I stuck with it.

BENNETT: How do you generate ideas?

GREENE: On nonfiction there's nearly always something historical that triggers it. On fiction—well, I've had a bunch of fictional ideas for years. Like a strong book that I wrote back in the fifties; I'm going to finish that book someday, because it expresses certain things that I feel. My fiction ideas involve a view of life I want to express. For example, there is one book I hope I live long enough to write. I've written it, but I've got to rewrite it. It is based on something that happened in Abilene, but when I write the book, it will not be set there. It concerns a man's determination to make himself; his life is going to be his own to control. I consider this an affront to God, that somebody is going to stand up and tell God what he's going to do with himself and his life.

BENNETT: It seems to me that religion is often important in your work.

GREENE: I write about religion because that was the way morality was thrust upon me. In *A Personal Country*—well, you can't write about West Texas without writing about religion. When I was young, I decided there is no way you can say absolutely that this is right or wrong. When I was ten or eleven, I looked around and saw a lot of good people who hadn't followed the fundamentalist precepts but who obviously weren't going to hell. Like Parson Willis Gerhart, a peppery little Episcopal minister. I began to pull away from the fundamentalist code. But morality is at the bottom of everything I write, the ambiguities and ironies of it. There are only three really important relationships: man to the supernatural, man to other men, and man to himself. And a man and his dog is really still man and himself.

BENNETT: Universal themes.

GREENE: Also in fiction I've been rather fascinated by men who have a flaw that they just can't overcome. They have everything else, but they have this flaw, and in the end the flaw gets them. In *The Santa Claus Bank Robbery* I believe the thing that fascinated me about the whole episode is that any intelligent person, from the first instant he read the story, would think, Here are three guys going to rob a bank, and here's how they think—and immediately you see there is no way it will ever succeed; they're just going to get into trouble. Once it started, it is inexorable.

BENNETT: John Fisher wrote that in our time the best books being written are nonfiction.

GREENE: I never have thought that was true, and John Fisher didn't necessarily think it was either. John Fisher in his last days became very bitter. He's a Texan, and he absolutely hated Texas. He was raised right on the border of Oklahoma in the Texas Panhandle. His dad ran a newspaper. I spent six hours with him one time. At first I was very much in awe of talking to the editor of *Harper's,* and then the next thing you know I was kidding him about being a Texan. He liked it, admitted it. He was a delightful man. Willie Morris introduced me to him.

I will never feel that I'm a writer until I've had at least one novel published. When you're writing nonfiction, you can come close to it, like the autobiographical detail of *A Personal Country,* and you can come close to it by interpreting other people's lives, as in *Santa Claus,* but you can't really express yourself, because you have to stop at some point, because they stop. You've got to observe this boundary, because that's where the boundary was.

BENNETT: When you were examining the *Last Captive* material, were you ever tempted to write it as fiction instead?

GREENE: Yes, I'm going to do a screenplay on it one of these days, not necessarily on Herman Lehmann's Indian life, but on his life coming back to be a white man. The Indians wouldn't have him because they said he'd sold them out, and the white men said he was a redskin.

BENNETT: How did you happen to get into writing?

GREENE: When I was a little boy, we lived in a boardinghouse up on Fourth and Hickory in Abilene; the old Central Fire Station used to be catty-cornered from us. In that same boardinghouse lived a guy who was the brother of two girls who were friends of my mother. He worked for the *Reporter-News,* and he drove a red Chevrolet convertible, about a 1928. He used to go out to cover football workouts, and one time he took me with him. I watched them knock themselves around, and then he took me somewhere else. Out by the old airport they had built some bumps—they were popular in those days, and I guess every town in Texas had a stretch of bumps. You drove your car over them, whomp, whomp, whomp, and then made a circle to come back. You paid a nickel. He took me on that thing, and, oh, boy, by the time I came back my mind was made up that I was going to be a newspaperman.

BENNETT: When did you actually begin dabbling with writing?

GREENE: That's easily pinned down. I graduated from Abilene High when I was sixteen. Before that I was talking to my grandmother one time trying to decide what I wanted to take in college. First I thought about schoolteacher and decided no to that, and then I thought about a lawyer because I knew a couple of lawyers. I didn't want to do that much, and my mother thought lawyers were immoral anyway. So my grandmother said, "Why don't you be a poet?" I thought, Not a bad idea. I had gotten interested in Stephen Crane's poetry. I began to write poetry. People would ask me what I was going to be, and I'd say poet, and they'd look at me kind of funny. In Abilene that's never a good way to open a conversation, especially when you're fifteen years old. Then I got in Selma Bishop's English class, and she assigned us to give our own ideas in a paragraph or two. So I wrote a poem. She gave me an A minus because it was late, but she said, "This is fine work; you should continue to write."

The first paper I ever worked on was in Enid, Oklahoma—the *Morning News,* I believe the name was. I took high school basketball scores on Thursday nights. Then when I was in the Navy in Philadelphia, I had every night off, so I worked for the *Philadelphia Inquirer*. I was twenty years old, but I told them I was twenty-five with seven years' experience. I had worked for about three weeks when this white-haired guy who was city editor came over and said, "Get your ass out of here; the Navy is about to sue us!"

After four years in the service I graduated from Abilene Christian College in 1948 with a degree in history. I had taken about three hours of journalism. I thought I was going to teach school. In the summer of 1947 I worked for the Coca-Cola Company here in Dallas, driving a truck, and I had bought a yellow Rolls Royce, a beautiful thing, what is called a golfing coupe, that had been parked out at Redbird Airport. After I graduated, I came back to Dallas, where my mother and father were living. I got a call from Salida, Colorado, to come teach history and Spanish. I was very enthusiastic. I could just imagine how it was, up in the mountains and everything, so I started. The Rolls Royce, beautiful as it was, had two-wheel mechanical brakes, and I stopped in Abilene to get the brakes checked. I thought that with two-wheel brakes I would really be in dutch if they weren't lined. I had an uncle who lived out on South Tenth, and I stayed with him. I finally found a mechanic named Harry Seib who would look at my car, and he called me up to say, "You'd better let me have this for as long as I need it, because if I just knock off to work on your car, it is going to cost you a lot of money, because I can't even find the bolts to take the wheels off." I said, "I don't have any money." I had twenty, twenty-five dollars. "Well," he said, "You'd better go on then." I said, "I can't go on; it scares me." He said, "Well, it's going to be a long time." I said, "Just take your time and do it cheap."

After about the first three or four days and he still hadn't found out how to take the wheels off, I told my uncle, who worked for Coca-Cola, to see if he could get me a job down at the plant. I had worked at the Coca-Cola plant before the war, so I knew bottling pretty well. I worked there a couple of weeks, and the mechanic still hadn't been able to find the bolts. I had been working there about six weeks, and I was wearing a Coca-Cola uniform—in those days the old tan with red stripes; I still have a shirt left over with my name on it—and I had gone down to Luby's Cafeteria, which was down by the Majestic Theater, and was crossing the street going north at Second and Cypress. There I ran into a guy I graduated with in the spring, and he was in law school and felt very top of the heap. He said, "I thought you graduated from college." I said, "I did." He looked at that uniform and said, "Why?"

I turned around just like that and went right up the stairs to the *Reporter-News* office. The stairs used to open there on the corner. Hal Sayles was there, but he didn't know me. I said, "I want a job." Hal said, "Did you major in journalism?" I said, "No, I took three hours." He said, "That's not enough." I said, "Well, I'm a good writer." He said, "Let's see some of it. Bring me a feature story, an in-depth feature." That "in-depth" expression had just gotten very big in journalism.

I went down and tried to buy a ticket on the Abilene Southern Railroad. It turned into a really nice little story because they couldn't find a ticket to sell me. They kept telling me, "You don't need a ticket; just get on." The train left from the freight station. You had to get there at six in the morning, and it went to Ballinger. The conductor said the only people who rode it anymore were some black preachers who rode on ministerial passes. The conductor couldn't believe it when I showed up with a ticket. I rode the train and did a story and gave it to Hal. The first thing Hal said was, "We don't use first-person stories." He told me to come back the next day, and in the meantime he read the story. When I got back he said, "I'll give you the job, but my advice is to take Salida, Colorado." I took the *Reporter-News* job at thirty-five dollars a week.

Incidentally, the mechanic finally got the wheels off the Rolls, and it didn't need brake linings.

BENNETT: You started some magazine free-lancing while you were at the *Reporter-News*, didn't you?

GREENE: The very first piece I believe I ever sold was to *Railroad* magazine [*goes to a bookcase and, after a good deal of rummaging around, produces a copy of it*]. There: "Abilene Streetcar System." I got ten dollars for it. I furnished the pictures too.

BENNETT: Did you do any free-lancing while you were running the book store, after you quit the *Reporter-News*?

GREENE: No. Well, I had some articles in *Publishers Weekly*, little things about the store now and then. But I don't think I sold anything. I had started a book, which I still intend to finish some day, and wrote some short stories—I guess, in looking back at it, I really worked pretty hard at it, but I just never sold anything. I sold a bunch of things when I was doing newspaper work. I'd just take my newspaper features and turn around and sell them. I did a full-page story one time on Doc Mead of Mead's Bread and sold it to *Southern Baker*. I used to sell to *T&P Topics* and all those. Of course, it was eight or ten dollars, maybe twenty-five. In 1957, I'm not sure what month—I had sold the bookstore, and I don't know whether I had gone back to work for the *Reporter-News* or was teaching at Hardin-Simmons—there was a little period in which I was head of their journalism department; it was a one-man department, so I was the head and also the tail—but I sold something to the *Atlantic*, which was my first prestige market. I also sold something to *Billboard* which I never did see, but I got a lot of letters from it. And I sold a couple of things to the *Kiwanis Magazine*. I wasn't making enough money even to begin thinking of living on it, but the first *Atlantic* piece paid a hundred and twenty-five dollars. It was a little humorous thing. Then in 1961 I sold them another humorous thing, and their rates were up to a hundred and fifty dollars. Both pieces have been anthologized in textbooks. I used to get calls from students who asked me about my pieces and would sort of interview me over the phone. A guy from Michigan last called about two years ago.

Then, when I came over here to Dallas and went to work for the *Times Herald*, I just was writing so much on the job that I wasn't able to do any outside writing. This old thing about coming home at night after a day at the newspaper and writing on the kitchen table—it worked for Jim Lehrer, but it didn't work for me.

BENNETT: Some writers are hyperactive.

GREENE: Jim was young, and he had me there to encourage him. I was book editor, and he'd hand me a chapter of *Viva Max*, and I'd say, "Keep going." Still, I was also working rewrite, the biggest writing job on a paper—I've won lots of AP prizes for people who didn't write the story—and I was book editor, which meant I came to work about seven in the morning, got off rewrite at two-thirty, and went back to work on the book page until about eight that night. The book page wasn't considered a job; they wouldn't even have paid if the NLRB hadn't forced them to. I finally became editor of the editorial page, but that was even more on-the-job writing.

Then my mother and father died in 1964. My brother and I were the only survivors. My parents had a very, very modest estate. We sold the house they had up there on Grove Street in Abilene, and everything was cleared. My mother was a marvelous manager; she'd have made a great corporation president. By the time we paid off the bills, I ended up with a fairly nice little nest egg of four thousand dollars. I said: "Well, I can stay with the newspaper business, or I can be a writer. This is where I've got to decide, because this may be the only time in my life I have any money ahead." So I went in to announce that on October 1, 1965, I was retiring. The publisher laughed and said, "Oh, we'll give you six weeks."

BENNETT: So you launched into writing.

GREENE: I had made a lot of contacts in the publishing world, because we used to carry a lot of book lineage, and the *Times Herald* is regarded seriously nationally. I had met Angus Cameron, the editor at Knopf who later edited two of my books.

Lon Tinkle and I were at a party at Stanley Marcus's one night that fall, and the late Bennett Cerf, who was head of Random House, was there. Lon and I got him off in Stanley's Fertility Room, where he kept pre-Columbian figurines—we'd all had lots to drink, but we were just feeling good—and Lon and I started telling him a book. We hadn't even talked to each other about it. Lon, in his very courtly tone of voice, said, "It is an epic about Texas, and A. C. will join me in the authorship." Lon would describe a section of it, and I would describe a section, and we sold him right there. Cerf went back to New York, and I thought that when the liquor wore off he would write and say, "You fools!" Then here came a check for a couple of thousand dollars. So I had made my first sale after I retired, and I was feeling pretty good. We never wrote that book . . . .

BENNETT: How did you come to write your first one?

GREENE: Well, that time Angus came around to see me about my Dobie remarks—he talked to me a long time, and he said, "When are you going to let me see your book?" I said, "I don't have a book." He said, "Then get busy and write one and let me see it." I said that I didn't know anything to write about. Right after I retired, I did this chapter, "God in West Texas." Something just triggered me, and I sent it to him. He got really enthusiastic and said to do a whole book on West Texas like that. He wanted to do photo pages, and I didn't want to run photographs, and that's why we compromised on drawings. Lon and I went up to the National Book Awards in 1966, and Angus gave me a contract then.

So I sent him the first twenty thousand words of *A Personal Country*, except that it was entitled *A Place Called West Texas* originally. Those twenty thousand words did not survive in the finished book, but that's what he gave me the advance on. That was a kind of dreamy, melodramatic beginning I wrote originally. Angus was very encouraging, like a daddy—he's actually not much older than I am, but he's retired now. He really knew the West, and he loved the West. He knew Texas, and he was fascinated by West Texas.

BENNETT: When you were in Abilene, did you know anybody who was writing outside of newspaper circles?

GREENE: Some women. There used to be a women's group working. Gwen Choate published a couple of books. I remember the Great Drouth of 1957; we were living out on Buccaneer, which was a nice little street. The Great Drouth had been going on and on, and West Texas was flat on its back. One April afternoon Gwen came over either to tell me that she had sold a manuscript to Doubleday or to have me look at a manuscript. Despite the fact that I had only been published in what you might call a few esoteric journals, I had the reputation around Abilene of being the person you wanted to have read your manuscript. While Gwen was there, it started raining heavy, and the street began to fill up with water. That's when the drouth broke, and Elm Creek got up to the bridge, and people ran around splashing and didn't care if they drowned. After Gwen left, my wife said, "Why is it you can sell everybody's book but your own?" I said, "Well, I haven't even written one." I got the reputation of being the most unpublished writer in Texas. Even after I came to Dallas. I was made a member of the Texas Institute of Letters before I had ever written a book.

BENNETT: In *A Personal Country* you mention Eddie Anderson.

GREENE: Eddie Anderson worked at the *Reporter-News*. I knew him because of the library. My grandmother was the librarian, and I'd go down to the old library and sit behind the checkout desk. Those guys didn't have any money—this was during the Depression—but they were very sure of themselves. They all knew they were going to be writers. There was a tall guy named Houston Heitchew, who was Sam Houston's great-grandson, and there was Francis Finberg, who was a poet, and Marvin Miller, a poet. Those guys were all in their twenties, and I was about ten or twelve. They would all sit over at a table, and they wouldn't shout or anything, but they would talk. They were the only people that my grandmother would allow to talk in the library. She called them her boys, but she thought they were too nasty because they used "damn" and "hell" in their books. Eddie Anderson wrote *Thieves Like Us*, which has been made into a movie twice. Robert Altman did it a few years ago, and he really botched it up. The novel was based pretty much on Bonnie and Clyde. It's a good book. Anderson also wrote one called *Hungry Men*—I think I have the only copy of *Hungry Men* still in existence. I don't even remember reading back then anything that those guys wrote; it's just the fact that they were there and were writers that stuck with me.

BENNETT: You learned that flesh-and-blood humans write.

GREENE: I was very proud of Abilene. Any time I saw a mention of it, I was proud. So if someone from Abilene wrote a book or story, I felt inspired. Max Bentley, who used to be managing editor of the

Reporter-News, had articles in major magazines. In those days the *Reporter-News* had an exceptionally good staff.

BENNETT: That's not an ordinary name, Houston Heitchew.

GREENE: Sam Houston's daughter, whose married name was Morrow, was the first postmaster in Abilene, way back in the nineteenth century, when the post office was over on Chestnut, on the south side. Houston Heitchew's mother, Maude Morrow, was Sam Houston's granddaughter, and even though she never made a great deal of it, it meant a lot to her, and she felt there was a great deal expected of them all. Houston's name was in fact Sam Houston. He spoke without any West Texas accent, and one time when I was nine or ten I said something about "William Pinn." The Greyhound bus station used to be on North Third, just east and up a little from where the library stands now. The buses all turned and squeaked and pulled around from Cedar Street to get in. When I said "William Pinn," Houston took me over to the bus station and bought me a lime Coke and made me say "Penn" fifty times. He said, "Get that West Texas accent out of your mouth." He spoke like an actor: "Penn, Penn." But it didn't do a thing; I still say "William Pinn." I did earn my first lime Coke. He was a hero to me, poor guy. Toward the end of the war, while I was away from home, he leaped out of the Wooten Hotel onto the roof of the Paramount Theater, about a nine-story drop. His mother claimed it was not suicide.

BENNETT: You went to Phillips University in Enid, Oklahoma, when you first got out of high school?

GREENE: No, Abilene Christian College. I left ACC in 1942 and went to Phillips because my mother and dad had moved there. Then I was in the Navy, which sent me to Kansas State at Pittsburg. After I got out of the Navy, I went back to ACC, and, to take some extra hours to graduate, I went over to Hardin-Simmons University at night, which is where I met my wife.

BENNETT: Any graduate school?

GREENE: I went to graduate school at Hardin-Simmons one summer. There was an ex-Abilene man, Hyder Edward Rollins, who was head of some area at Harvard. Betty interviewed him for the *Reporter-News*, and he really liked her. I never met him, but we corresponded, and Rollins tried to get me in Harvard. Harvard wouldn't take me because basically I just wanted the M.A. and wasn't going after the Ph.D. So I went to Hardin-Simmons and was always glad I did. I had Prof Bond for Browning, a terrific teacher. I didn't go back to graduate school till 1968 to 1970, when I did all my course work for a Ph.D. at UT, Austin. I was going to do a dissertation on J. Frank Norris, the old renegade Baptist preacher from Fort Worth. What a book he'd make! I still may do it. If I'd stayed another six months, I'd have gotten a Ph.D., but I decided I didn't need it. The academic world is just too nasty for me. I came up here to work for Channel 13 instead.

BENNETT: An English Ph.D.?

GREENE: No, it was in American civilization. Actually, it was ironic that in 1973 I was on the graduate-school faculty at the University of Texas, same department I didn't get my degree in. I taught a course similar to Frank Dobie's old course, "Life and Literature of the Southwest."

BENNETT: You told me once that you had some fiction published.

GREENE: Two stories ten years apart, in the *Southwest Review*. One story was called "The Fortune Hunters," and the other was "The Least Jot and Tittle." Margaret Hartley, the editor, is a very intelligent woman, and she has been handling writing for thirty years, but she seemed to believe they were nonfiction. Both are in the first person and sound like they are true. In the issue "The Fortune Hunters" came out in, Margaret wrote that it was going to be part of a book based on my West Texas experiences, something like that.

BENNETT: Preston Jones said that writers tend to cram a lot of material into their first play, usually too much. *A Personal Country* is certainly packed with material.

GREENE: I took *A Christmas Tree* out of it and expanded it. I mentioned the Santa Claus bank robbery, but I didn't really write *The Santa Claus Bank Robbery* because of *A Personal Country*. I started writing *Santa Claus* in July, 1969, and *A Personal Country* came out in September, so it was too late to pull it out, but it was just coincidental that I mentioned it in *A Personal Country*.

BENNETT: But *A Christmas Tree* was different.

GREENE: Yes, I expanded it quite a bit and took a different tack. In *A Personal Country* it was more about the tree itself and just incidentally about the family, but in the book and in the story that appeared in *McCall's* it was about the family, and I used the tree to introduce the idea. That's been a very successful little book and story. It was reprinted in England. I got paid in pounds but never did see the magazine. My agent told me that it had been translated in one of the Scandinavian countries where they observe the Christmas-tree legend.

Then Stanley Marcus did *A Christmas Tree* as a little miniature book. The original Encino edition, I believe, sold out. There was a special edition that sold out before publication—leather-binding spine in a slipcase cover and all that. I've had women's clubs in Iowa and Texas and other places write to ask if they could dramatize it.

BENNETT: You've got a minibook on the Butterfield Stage in *A Personal Country*.

GREENE: I've been right on the verge of doing a book on the Butterfield Stage several times. Then I have almost done a book on that chain of forts in West Texas. I did a series at the *Reporter-News* on the forts, and I turned up a lot of undiscovered facts. Historical societies have turned into thin-blooded academic collections. You take people like Rupe Richardson: he is a real historian; he wrote history because he loved what had happened, and he knew what had happened. Academics who are writing history now, they're writing about documents. Nobody has ever used my fort series out of the *Reporter-News* as reference in anything they write about West Texas. They just go back to the old scholarly sources and say the same old things that Rupe Richardson and Carl Coke Rister said back in the twenties and thirties. They haven't looked further. They will go to the same government documents that are cited by Richardson. They think that if they cite the surgeon general's report on Fort Phantom Hill that's the only kind of primary source. They never cite things out of newspapers, and lots of times the newspaper story will be more interesting historically, and more accurate, than the official papers. I was really amazed when I got my *West Texas Historical Yearbook* one year to see a piece on me by a McMurry student. I guess it was a paper that she gave at the meeting. She's got a fierce little paragraph in there about people who refer to me as "an amateur historian." She got very upset about this.

BENNETT: Academe is a strange place.

GREENE: I recently spent four days with Bob Hill, who is the only surviving member of the Santa Claus gang.

BENNETT: That must have been interesting.

GREENE: *The Santa Claus Bank Robbery* has become Bob Hill's autobiography. You sent me a clipping out of the *Reporter-News* by a reporter who went over to Cisco, and, of course, the people he interviewed said I had got it all wrong. Bob Hill was the only one who was actually there. He said, "You got so many things right that you had to have talked to somebody." I said, "How could I? They got killed in

1928." "Yeah, that's right," he'd say; then he'd say, "What about so-and-so? You had to interview her, 'cause I told her that, and there wasn't but just the two of us in there." I said, "No."

BENNETT: Joe Stamey, who grew up in Cisco, says you have far and away the best account.

GREENE: Sure. There were people who weren't even born then that swear they were there. When the book came out, I was sitting in the bank lobby autographing copies, sitting right there where the robbery occurred. Chuck Weeth of Sanders Book Store sold four hundred and fifty copies in a city with a total population of a little over four thousand, so we did a little better than 10 percent. James McCracken, who was president of the bank—since then he has died—was sitting there beside me. He was one of those laconic bankers. When we were getting along toward the end of the day, I said, "How would you have liked to have been sitting right here when it was taking place?" He said, "I'd rather have been standing out there on the sidewalk." I laughed, thinking he meant to be safe. He said, "We've had four thousand people tell us they were standing right there on the corner when the robbery took place—I'd rather see four thousand people get on that sidewalk than see the bank robbery."

BENNETT: You said you'd met Bob Hill. Has he come out of hiding?

GREENE: For years, through Dorsey Hardeman, the state senator, I tried to get Hill to let me come out to see him. I hadn't met Hill when I wrote the book. Hill wouldn't do it, said he didn't want to relive those old days. Well, Hill has a close relative who had some problems with his wife; she just walked out on him one day. The relative was baffled; the wife's lawyers were about to take everything he had, and he didn't have much to take. He couldn't find a decent lawyer. One night I got a call. A woman said, "Did you write *The Santa Claus Bank Robbery*?" I said, "Yeah." She said, "Does the name Robert Hill mean anything to you?" I said, "It means about as much as any name I can think of." She said, "Well, I'm Mrs. Robert Hill, and we don't know anybody to turn to but you in Dallas." She asked me to help find a lawyer. Vince Perini from Abilene got one of the people on his staff to handle it. Then Mrs. Hill—she's sixty but looks like thirty in a lot of ways—phoned me and said, "Listen, you are just one of the family now. Come out any time." I eventually went out there to spend four days. Bob's past seventy now, and his eyesight is very bad. He doesn't mind talking about the robbery. His wife, Gladys, went to bed, and he and I sat outside in a swing for hours until the mosquitoes nearly carried me off.

BENNETT: How did you hit on the idea of writing on the robbery?

GREENE: Bill Wittliff of Encino Press asked me to dream up a Christmas book that would sell during the season for several years. We were trying to figure out something, and Eliot, my son, heard us and brought in a little booklet they had published that was based on the feature series I did for the *Reporter-News* in 1957. I said, "No, that's not a Christmas story." But Wittliff said, "Wait a minute." Well, I started working on it, and I got to thinking, and I said, "Bill, I believe this thing is too big for Encino." He wasn't too happy about that! But I later did *Christmas Tree* for him.

BENNETT: A few years ago Janis Paige told me that when they did *Miracle of Thirty-Fourth Street* as a musical in New York they did great business until Christmas, but afterwards it went flooey. Did *Santa Claus* sell like that?

GREENE: No, I don't think that really had much to do with the sale of the book. It was released at a very bad time, the last day of July in 1972, which is the absolute deadest day in the book business. I think, for the book, *The Santa Claus Bank Robbery* might be a bad title; I noticed the paperbacks used to be on the racks around Christmastime every year, because somebody thought it was a Christmas story. But all the movie people say that's a great title, so we'll see.

BENNETT: Have you considered writing other outlaw stories?

GREENE: I'm really not that interested. In reading about the Santa Claus bank robbery I got interested in the people. I was interested from a historical standpoint also, but it was the people I really liked. I'm not interested in outlaws per se.

BENNETT: C. L. Sonnichsen has made a career of outlaws.

GREENE: His *I'll Die Before I Run* is a really great book.

BENNETT: Where did you get the idea for *The Last Captive*?

GREENE: Bill Wittliff wanted me to do an introduction to *Nine Years Among the Indians*, by Herman Lehmann. I'd never read *Nine Years*, and so I read it. I was working out at the University of Texas Archives, and I was very unsatisfied with *Nine Years Among the Indians*, which was obviously not written by Herman and didn't have his flavor in it. I said, "Bill, there's more to this." I went down to the state library, and they said they had a copy of another book of his. Actually, in the introduction to *Nine Years* there is a reference to *Indianology*, but I hadn't found anybody who had ever seen a copy.

Frank Dobie didn't mention it in his Southwest literature list. But the state library had a copy, and Wittliff had it Xeroxed. I read it, and it was a different approach to Herman. It had been written in 1897, and *Nine Years* had been written in 1927. Both books were shot full of errors; you could just see the errors. So I went out and did enough research on Herman to qualify for a Ph.D. on that alone. *The Last Captive* is a combination of all the things that I found out about him, and I think it's fairly accurate. We'll never know whether some of the things about Herman are accurate or not: for example, his Indian days. All we have is what Herman said. Measuring other parts against some of the surviving historical data, I think Herman comes off looking pretty good. But, after all, it was just a man's memory, and it was a memory about a time that for him was dateless, and yearless for that matter.

BENNETT: I'd hate to put together my last year from memory.

GREENE: I did a lot of extractions from Jim Gillett and some of the old Ranger stories and things. It ended up being a new book instead of just an introduction. Wittliff gave up on *Nine Years*; there wasn't any point in a new edition of it.

BENNETT: You really rewrote the thing.

GREENE: I would quote those books, and then I would say what really happened. Sometimes the books would have contradictory chapters, and I would take the account that seemed most likely, and I would quote the contradictions. In effect, *The Last Captive* is a third book about Herman Lehmann's life.

BENNETT: You have good notes at the end of each chapter.

GREENE: Or sometimes right in the middle of them. Sometimes I left out big chunks of a chapter. If I rewrote, I rewrote it on the basis of getting from one point to the next. You know: "Herman says so-and-so, and we now know it's not true, and therefore we can assume this." I had already written the book, and it had come out, before I found this copy of *Indianology* for sale, the only one I've ever known on sale.

BENNETT: I see it is all in quotation marks.

GREENE: It's a marvelous book, absolutely full of errors, almost as if someone had tried to see how many errors could be made. On the other hand, this book tells things the other one doesn't. This is where a lot of his sexy escapades came from. The title page says it is a condensed history of the Apache and Comanche nations, but on the cover it says *Indianology*. The other book says *Nine Years* Among *the Indians*, but the running title on each inside page is *Nine Years* with *the Indians*. To begin with, it was eight years. And the drawings in *Indianology*—somebody just said, "Hey, do me a drawing of some Indians sitting around a campfire or something like that." I paid a hundred and thirty-five dollars for this book in 1970, and I don't know what it's worth now, but it's worth a lot to me. Fred White turned it up; he knew I'd written my book, even though it hadn't been published.

BENNETT: Jack Holden told me once that you and he wrote a history of the Roscoe, Snyder and Pacific Railroad.

GREENE: I'd forgotten about that. I have never seen the book. I didn't even keep a carbon. I had done a couple of features on the RS&P, and I knew Don Wooten, who was president then. I really knew more about the railroad than Jack did, but Jack got us the commission.

BENNETT: He's a great promoter. He said one of the problems was finding a big event, like a train robbery, to make the RS&P interesting.

GREENE: The biggest event they ever had was a wreck, and forty years later they were still trying to pretend they'd never had a wreck. I found a picture of the locomotive lying over on its side, and they were afraid I was going to use it in the paper. "Oh, don't do that!" The wreck took place, as I remember, in 1912.

BENNETT: Did you have that kind of trouble with Dallas history? There have been no Indian wars or Confederate victories in Dallas's past.

GREENE: But Dallas has lots and lots of history. The picture book, *Dallas: The Deciding Years*, was easy to write because there have been a lot of events taking place in Dallas. It is still selling real well. I also did this little book, *A Place Called Dallas*, which is more anecdotal than anything. This young guy, Bill McDonald, did the research and writing on *Dallas Rediscovered*, and I did the introduction. It came out just before Christmas, 1978. I'm very pleased with his work. We may do a Texas book together.

BENNETT: In what order did you write the sections in *A Personal Country*?

GREENE: I went pretty much from front to back. I did the "God in West Texas" section before anything, but at first I didn't want to put that in the book, because I don't like to stick things in a book that I've already written. But I did it like that, and since it had been the basic inspiration for the whole book, it became the only thing already written that was included. The twenty thousand words that sold the book, that I got the advance for, I didn't use. They were a little more philosophical, and I went to far too much length about the influence of time. I did a very poetic piece about time—time does this and time does that, and how things change—which I finally decided just didn't have any place in the book. I gutted it. I wrote the present opening chapter after I had written other parts of the book, but basically *A Personal Country* went from start to finish, once I got into the story itself—I'd say by the time I described Weatherford.

BENNETT: The section about journeying with your parents and grandmother is my favorite.

GREENE: Tony Beck, at SMU, wanted to pull that section out to base a ballet on it. She's one of the top dance people around Dallas. I think it would make a great little ballet sequence: running back and forth to the house, and then the car . . . .

BENNETT: Didn't you have a grant to write *A Personal Country?*

GREENE: The Paisano Fellowship. I went down to Paisano in February, 1968. But I always had a hideaway. These friends of ours, Jake and Frances Mossiker, they had what used to be called a servants' quarters at back of their house, and I went out there to write. I pulled up in the driveway—had my own little gate to go back. Then when I went down to Paisano, I really did have the chance to just go right on through to the end. I finished it in April, 1968, one of those great stormy April nights—it was lightning and raining. I worked in a little room out behind the main house. I came in at ten o'clock and pitched the manuscript on the bed and said to Betty, my wife, "There it is." My wife and I celebrated with a beer. Angus Cameron was in Dallas for the American Historical Association meeting the next week, and we brought him the manuscript. Angus is famous in the trade for being slow—very, very deliberate. I didn't hear from him for quite a while. He's a very good editor in that he doesn't make you rewrite everything. In fact, it used to annoy me that he didn't make me rewrite more than he did. He got the manuscript in April, 1968, and the book didn't come out until September, 1969. I did a little bit of rewriting, and then when the galleys came out I didn't have to change them. The new 1979 edition from Texas A&M doesn't change any stories, but it does update things like the liquor law and Abilene voting wet—several things that have changed out there.

BENNETT: How did you happen to get connected with the fellow who illustrated it, Ancel Nunn?

GREENE: It was very much a coincidence. Ancel had lived in

Abilene for twenty years, at the same time I was living there, but he lived way out on the north side, and I lived way out on the south side. After I got on the *Reporter-News*, he used to read my stuff, and I had a little thumbnail picture of me on my column.

We were down in Austin in the spring of 1968, where they have an outdoor art show at Laguna Gloria, a big thing. Betty and I walked in, with Bill and Sally Wittliff. The first picture I saw when we went in the front gate was *Bright and Early Barn*, and I said, "I want to buy that." Boy, at that time we were really humping, because all four kids were at home. The Paisano Fellowship paid three thousand dollars for half a year, five hundred a month, and I didn't take much down there either, so we were very, very conservative. But I really wanted the painting; it was a hundred and ninety-five dollars. Betty said, "Let's go look at the rest and then come back, and we'll think about it." So we walked around and about two hours later came back to that booth, and it was still there. I was standing looking at it, and I heard somebody say, "Mr. Greene." I wasn't used to people in Austin knowing who I was, and so I thought it must be somebody from Dallas. I turned around, and here was this redheaded guy. He said, "I'm Ancel Nunn from Abilene." I said, "You weren't called Ancel Nunn in Abilene." He said, "No, I was called Eddie Nunn; I didn't know you knew me." I said, "I didn't." But the truth of the matter was that I knew everybody's name in Abilene. I had used their names when they were getting in and out of the hospital or when I was writing something else printed in the newspaper. We got to talking, and I said I wanted the painting but couldn't afford to pay. He said, "Pay me anything you can afford to and take it, then pay it out." I said, "Okay, I'll pay you thirty dollars, and thirty dollars a month." "Fine!" Come to find out, Ancel was so damned glad to sell it he'd have been delighted to come down a hundred. Incidentally, since then I have turned down five thousand dollars for that painting.

We were living at San Cristoval, which is about two miles as Barton Creek flows down from Paisano, a beautiful place up on a sixty-five-foot bluff above the creek, and you couldn't see anything but just lovely wilderness. We hung *Bright and Early* above a stone fireplace in the living room. Ancel was living in Harlingen, where nobody gave a damn about the arts; somebody who did might have been there, but Ancel didn't know them. He had been working as a night watchman in a compress to keep beans on the table. Ancel and his wife, Renata, drove out to Austin. He was fascinated by Austin. Bill Wittliff introduced us to Luckenbach; that's when old Benno Engel owned it.

So we all got to be friends. About this time I talked to Angus. I said, "I don't want photographs," and he said, "Let's get an artist; do you know an artist?" I said, "Yeah, I've just met a guy, who's from Abilene as a matter of fact. It would be duck soup for him." Angus said, "Send some of his work."

BENNETT: How did you happen to get into picture books?

GREENE: The Sanger Harris Department Store chain was approaching the one-hundredth anniversary of the opening of the Sanger brothers' Dallas store. Damon Webb, who ran their six or eight bookstores, wanted to do the front pages of the Dallas papers through the years, a hundred of them, in other words. I pointed out that it is very, very difficult to find Dallas newspapers before 1885, which is when the *News* came here and opened. Well, Damon wanted to do something, so Bill Wittliff came up to talk to him about a book.

About the time Bill came up, a friend of mine named Harvey Bourland—from Abilene, as a matter of fact—told us about a bunch of glass-plate negatives, a whole hoard of them that a guy had. The guy wanted forty thousand dollars for them, and that just sent Wittliff right up the chimney. But he and Harvey went out to look at them and got very excited. They were afraid to take me, because this guy knew me from television, and they thought that if they took me they would never be able to get him to come down on his price. It was a fantastic story, involving everything from midnight visits to bank vaults to incest. Anyway, one night about three o'clock Bill and Harvey came staggering in, and they had boxes and boxes of glass-plate negatives. They said, "Here they are: look through them and tell us what's history, and what's good, and what's . . . .

So I started looking through them, and, boy, there was a sensational collection. We really used only a small percentage of them in the book. Bill said, "Why couldn't we do a Dallas historical picture book using these?" I said, "Yes, except this guy obviously shot within a certain limited period. There's nothing before or after this, and we'll have to do a lot of research." Sanger Harris had nothing to do with the writing of the book, although it says, "Published for . . . ." Sanger Harris bought five thousand copies going in, and that was the extent of their participation.

I started putting it together. I went down to the library and picked up some things they had, trying to start as early as I could. I found some more pictures on my own. When I started doing historical research on it, I discovered that I was really going to have to just go back and rewrite Dallas history, because all the history that had survived was either erroneous or outdated. The Brown history of Dallas County was published in 1887, and a lot had happened since then. John William Rogers had been dead for years, and *The Lusty Texans* had been published in 1950 and 1951. Even though the historical section of *The Deciding Years* is only about fifty pages, it represents one hell of a lot of research.

BENNETT: You became a Dallas historian.

GREENE: I seem to have become *the* Dallas historian, which isn't always comfortable. I had a woman call me yesterday wanting to know what that building was that stood across the street from St. Paul Hospital for so many years when it was out on San Jacinto. She was seventy years old, and she was remembering it from when she was a girl. Her uncle used to take her over there, and he had a beer and she had ice cream. She said, "Now they called it a beer garden, but they sold ice cream." I told her I wasn't in my seventies yet, and I really wasn't even raised in Dallas. But we were able to come up with the name of the building.

Although I didn't start out to write that kind of book, everything that is known about early Dallas practically is contained in *The Deciding Years*, in one way or another.

BENNETT: Research can be fascinating.

GREENE: That's another ironic thing about Dallas history. You'd think a city of nearly a million people would have a nice historical center, but at this point I am as close to being the historical center as Dallas has, because nobody ever put it all together before. You go down to the Texas room or the Dallas section of the city library, and they can help you with what they've got, but often they don't know what they've got. Bill McDonald did most of his research at the Historical Society out at the Hall of State, but it's not collated well.

BENNETT: What is your personal favorite among your books?

GREENE: I guess *A Personal Country*. It's the autobiographical sort of thing that you always feel very close to.

March, 1979

John Graves: *A Hard Scrabble World*

JOHN GRAVES was born August 6, 1920, in Fort Worth, Texas. He earned his B.A. from Rice in 1942 and his M.A. from Columbia in 1948. He served in the U.S. Marines from 1942 to 1945. Graves has taught at the University of Texas in Austin and at Texas Christian University.

It is ironic that you can see the construction site of the first nuclear power plant in Texas from the highest point on Graves's farm, near Glen Rose. He was obviously shunning the more grandiose forms of twentieth-century technology when he bought this worn, remote farm, and he has often written about man's violation of nature.

The rock house and other farm buildings, like Graves himself, give an impression of quiet strength. "It started out just this room, and a screened porch, and a rear overhang. About that time Jane, my wife, got interested in it, and it has never quite quit growing since—never been finished either."

His study is in the northwest corner of the barn. "It's filthy, but you can look at it. Every once in a while the ladies get disgusted and go out and clean it up for me." Inside: green desk, manual typewriter, file cabinet, easy chair. Built-in bookshelves hold a lot of volumes, including Graves's own books, the *Southwest Review*, several works on agriculture. "Unless you rev up the air conditioner, it's hot as the devil in here."

In the main chamber of the barn was an upturned canoe.

Graves stands five feet eleven inches and had put on a little weight over the winter. "I'm fat and beat up." He has graying brown hair and blue-gray eyes with glasses. He lost the sight in one eye during his World War II service.

BENNETT: You got your master's degree at Columbia?
GRAVES: Yes, I never did go on for a doctorate because I really

wasn't sure what I wanted. Teaching was a fallback position; I figured a master's would let me do it.

BENNETT: Have you ever been sorry you didn't get a doctorate?

GRAVES: No. I'm not what you'd call antiintellectual at all, but I think scholarship was beginning to clutter my mind, in the sense that you are, as a scholar, at one remove from prime raw materials, and I always knew I wanted to write. One is never certain that one can make a living at writing, or what might come out. So the M.A. was just a sort of insurance against disaster. I've never been sorry about it. I've hardly ever thought about it. A number of people I was with did go on to a doctorate and got to be real scholars, and I have a lot of respect for them, but it's not essentially my kind of thing.

BENNETT: What did you major in?

GRAVES: English. I was a born English major. I've got a daughter who's the same way; she's a sophomore in college now. She was forced to decide on a major this year and went through a lot of anguish about it and finally wrote me to say she was going to major in English. That's what I told her: "You were a born English major just like me. You're stuck with it. You can't make a living at it, unless you teach, but at least you have a few quotations to meet life's disasters."

BENNETT: You've always wanted to write?

GRAVES: I suppose. Since college or so. Again, I'm a fairly realistic person, and I didn't want to get stuck with it as a way of life until I knew I could manage with it.

BENNETT: Did you start writing in high school?

GRAVES: I don't remember writing much before college. I read a lot, was interested in writing, but I wasn't active in that way until I guess about my junior year in college. George Williams is one of the old teachers down at Rice who did some writing himself; he's retired now. He was very helpful to a lot of his students. McMurtry was a student of his, and I was, and William Goyen was, and this fellow J. P. Miller—you can't say we were his products exactly, more protégés, were under his wing for a while. I wouldn't say that he wakened an interest in writing in me, but he made me see that it might be possible. I don't recall in college feeling that I was going to be anything in particular; for one thing, from about my sophomore year on, maybe longer, it was obvious that the war was coming on, and most of us were just not looking any further ahead than that. We all graduated right into service. I graduated in 1942, and I and the whole Rice football team went into the Marine Corps. Funny, I always got along well with the athletes. I liked them, lived in the same dormitory they did. Rice was a bookish place, even more so now, and they were a healthy element there. I went to a class reunion a few years ago, and I'm really not much on that sort of thing, but I happened to be in Houston while it was on. You know the sort of awkwardness that pertains at those gatherings; nobody knows what to say to the others because they've all changed so much. But the old football players and ex-Marines I could still talk to. We formed a little clot on the stairway and mulled over ancient battles and everything.

BENNETT: You used to write quite a bit for the old *Holiday*.

GRAVES: I did, at one time, quite a bit, back in the 1950s. I think it began while I was living in Majorca. I went over to Spain and lived about three years in the fifties, and wrote a piece about Majorca, the expatriate way of life there. I didn't have anybody in mind. I sent it to my agent in New York, and he sold it to *Holiday*, and after that from time to time either I'd do something for them or they'd send me an idea. Assignment sort of stuff, which I never did find very satisfying really. Not my kind of thing. I still don't, still avoid it whenever I can.

BENNETT: Have you ever worked on anybody's staff?

GRAVES: Altogether free-lancing, except for a spell when I worked for Stewart Udall when he was secretary of the interior, back in the middle sixties. It was an off-again, on-again thing, but it lasted about three years. I'd write reports for a concerted government campaign to clean up the Potomac River and make it a model for the nation and stuff like that, which didn't accomplish much, but it was instructive anyhow.

BENNETT: Tom Lea says that, except for those few years with *Life*, he never worked for anybody.

GRAVES: I've taught from time to time, at the University of Texas. When I came out of Columbia, I taught in Austin about three years. That was young-instructor stuff: five classes with about thirty people in each class, all freshman English, every pocket you have stuffed with ungraded themes so you go around feeling guilty about it. I had a first marriage that was breaking up about that time, so everything blew up at once, and I bailed out. I was in New Mexico for a while, New York for a year or so, and then I went over to Spain, came back here in the late fifties, back to Fort Worth. I really have been here ever since, outside of things like that work for Udall.

BENNETT: You taught some at TCU, didn't you?

GRAVES: That was after I came back here. I started teaching part time out there, and that connection lasted actually until I undertook the government work. Sometimes less part time than others.

BENNETT: You've published *Goodbye to a River* and *Hard Scrabble* . . . .

GRAVES: Those are really the only things that count. I did a thing for the Sierra Club on the Texas Water Plan. There were a couple of other people with stuff in it too.

BENNETT: They did one of your short stories at Encino.

GRAVES: Billy Wittliff published that "Last Running" short story. He's got one of my *Texas Monthly* pieces now that he's working up into a little book. I expanded it a bit. I haven't been very productive.

BENNETT: You've done a lot of magazine things.

GRAVES: A good bit. But somebody who is a good journalist and really going at it hammer and tongs would have ten times as long a bibliography as I have at this point.

BENNETT: Maybe not as good.

GRAVES: Some of it's pretty poor. Some of it I hope never surfaces. That year I spent in New York was kind of Desperation Alley; I figured I was going to make a start then or not at all. Actually, I had published some stuff before then. First story I ever published was when I was at Columbia, and it was sold to the *New Yorker*, which was far too auspicious a beginning. I couldn't duplicate it. Anyway, I had a grubby little old apartment, and I worked real hard. I'd write one story for "them" and one for me. There were a lot of slick magazines still functioning full blast, and, as I say, I alternated one for them and one for me. And mine were lousy! Rather horrifyingly I found I had a little bit of a knack for commercial fiction. I must have done a dozen or so in all, and maybe seven of those really crummy slick things got published. Scared me, and I quit.

BENNETT: Have you ever tried to write a novel?

GRAVES: I've got one in my trunk and one unfinished. The one that I did finish had some of the best writing in it that I ever did, but it was badly flawed, and I was too close to it, still am twenty years later, to correct it, to get it right. The other one just died. I had a Guggenheim Fellowship to do that one, but it just petered out. I still have hopes that I might do a halfway decent novel before I die, but in recent years I seem to have settled down to nonfiction. I think you can do more with fiction; the greatest potential is there, but something about me and long fiction has not so far been compatible.

BENNETT: What are you working on now?

GRAVES: Mostly magazine stuff. These *Texas Monthly* things. We don't have any formal arrangement. They seem to take just about as much as I send them, up to one a month. For the last couple of years there've been seven or eight a year probably. The editors are very gentle and don't monkey with the stuff much. But you do edit yourself to some extent when you're writing for any publication; you know what their slant is, what their readership is largely like. Those pieces, even though they're fairly honest, don't for the most part have a lot of depth to them. But they're fun. Every once in a while one comes out; I finished one up this morning. The pieces will make a book before long, I think. I've got sixty or seventy thousand words of them now. I would like to monkey with it a while longer, and fit them together a little bit better, and do some rearranging.

BENNETT: *Texas Monthly* has been great for this area.

GRAVES: I think they've done a lot of good. At times any magazine will seem to be sort of parodying what it thinks it has become, but by and large *Texas Monthly* does pretty well. They're a pretty good, fresh, bright bunch of young people—I started to say kids; anybody under forty is a kid to me now. William Broyles has been there right along, but some of them have shucked out for other realms. Broyles lost three to Jimmy Carter. Ann Barnstone, with whom I worked mostly, decided to devote more time to motherhood. I don't think there have been any upheavals or firings.

BENNETT: How do you generate ideas?

GRAVES: One reason I haven't been very prolific is that I'm not very generative. Things generally have to slap me in the face. I have never developed an orderly approach to the business of studying out something to write. It's like a nail sticking out of the wall: you walk past it for six months without seeing it, and all of a sudden it tears your shirt as you go by. Every once in a while something will slap me in the face; thank God it does. Sometimes, in between times, you get a desperate feeling that it never will again. One trouble that I've always had is exemplified in this place, and messing around with cows, and building things. I have a tremendous amount of irrelevant interests that have nothing to do with writing. Fortunately they generally turn to subject matter.

One of those people who was on the original *Paris Review* was Peter Matthiessen, and he was up there with Udall briefly at the same time I was. He was there to help Udall with his own books, but we spent a good deal of time visiting together, and I was talking one time about something, you know, that I had gotten off into. He said, "You ought to write a book about that." I said, "I didn't take it up because I wanted to write about it." He said, "You should never waste research." All of a sudden that put a new dignity on my messing around with bees, or my grapevines down here, or building a house. That's all research! And back in terms of these *Texas Monthly* country-oriented things, I have a pretty good excuse to keep on messing around. There's an old rule among stonemasons: you never lay down a stone once you pick it up; you find someplace to fit it in the wall; otherwise you'd go nuts trying to find something that would fit.

BENNETT: Are you a Thoreau fan?

GRAVES: Anybody with my interests is, to some extent. I have some reservations about him. I've never felt I was duplicating Thoreau. That's just something people wish for: the Texas Thoreau.

BENNETT: You have to come up with something when you're writing a review.

GRAVES: I think probably old Bedichek would have come closer to being the Texas Thoreau than I ever have. He was really a naturalist, which I'm not. I dabble in natural history; I dabble in history. That's one reason I got away from reviewing books, in that as a reviewer you get typed by what you yourself have written. Depending on what editor is involved, I am typed either as a southwestern writer or as a natural-history type, and that's the kind of books I get. One trouble is that both of those are rather small worlds, and you don't make enough dough out of reviewing books to go around making enemies on it. I don't like too many books that I read, and if I say what I think, which is about the only reason for doing anything that doesn't bring in much money, all I've done is to make enemies. Hardly anybody reads the bloody things. I quit.

BENNETT: What was the genesis of *Goodbye to a River*?

GRAVES: I came home in the late fifties without really expecting to stay here. My father was sick, so I stuck around for a while—for good as it turned out. During that time I was sort of renewing old familiarities, and I was hunting and fishing and was running around on the Brazos—fixed up an old canoe. A friend of mine had a project for moving some old log cabins into Fort Worth to put them in the park; they're there now, and the school kids visit them, and the ladies spin cloth for the kids. At the request of a friend I did some historical digging on those things. At any rate, without being an economic endeavor, it was all just going in that direction. When I decided to make that trip, mainly because I wanted to, I justified it by getting it underwritten by a magazine. But by the time it was over, there was a great deal more than just a magazine article there, and I just went ahead and wrote the book.

BENNETT: You started out with *Sports Illustrated*?

GRAVES: They furnished me with—I don't know what you call that—an advance or something. The thing wasn't sporty enough for them. It ended up being published by *Holiday*.

BENNETT: Do people around here know that you are a writer?

GRAVES: I guess so, those that know me. I don't strike a very high profile—go to the feed store, see two or three friends in Glen Rose. They don't really care. This country is not what you'd call a really literary place. I guess that if I were the sort of writer who snatched up characters and situations from around me I might get into trouble. McMurtry has never been on very friendly terms with Archer City, although they were greatly complimented to have the movie made there.

BENNETT: How did you come to write *Hard Scrabble*?

GRAVES: I put in so much time—over a dozen years or so—down here rebuilding this old place and trying to get it in order and make it halfway functional, that I decided to take Peter Matthiessen's advice and not waste research.

BENNETT: I envy your skill as repairman and builder.

GRAVES: I've made lots of mistakes, but if you try for strength, mistakes don't make much difference. It was a lot of time. Sometimes I wish I'd just kept on hunting and fishing instead.

BENNETT: There must be a lot of little things to keep up.

GRAVES: I'm working around to a solution to that. I've gotten a kind of removed attitude toward some of these things. Certainly if you've got three fields full of oats at the right stage, they have to be baled. But something like the bees: they ought to have been looked into every two days the last three weeks. It's their busy season, and they're building up honey, and I haven't had time, and I don't care. You get to where you just don't give a damn, in a healthy sort of way. I've known a lot of old country people, and I'd go out to their place and think, God, how can you live with a fence like that? Now I've got fences just like that, and they don't bother me. And cows, you can worry as much over cows as you want to, but a certain amount of that worry doesn't do them any good. They're going to have their calves. If they are heifers having first calves, you really should keep an eye on them, and most of the time I do. But my main line of activity is writing. It was just recently that I decided that. It's been a great relief.

BENNETT: There are very few things we have to do.

GRAVES: I sometimes think with great relief that if I just sat here and stared out every day, everything would go to hell, but it wouldn't matter. It doesn't make any particular money for me anyhow. But I like practically everything there is to do here.

BENNETT: How did you come to write your part of *The Water Hustlers*?

GRAVES: That was an idea broached by a fellow named John Mitchell, who was then head of Sierra Club Books. I guess I undertook it because I had so recently been doing that work for the Interior Department. I was really up on hydrology and the ins and outs of the water bureaucracy at the time. Up in Washington I had worked with some of the best people in the country in those fields, so I had already done a great deal of groundwork. What I did was all right, I guess, but the state water plan collapsed. Essentially any polemical writing is devoted to an evanescent problem. If it's solved, it disappears, and if it's not solved, it goes away. Polemics are self-destructive in that sense. They're not very satisfying.

BENNETT: Which book did you most enjoy writing?

GRAVES: I can't say that I enjoyed doing any of them. There was a very fine old Spanish poet, Juan Ramón Jiménez, who died in exile in Puerto Rico—won a Nobel Prize before he died. He had a set of maxims that were very fine pithy little bits of advice to himself, and one of them says, "Let us seek the great pleasure of having done." I've often thought about that. It's wonderful to have done something, but writing is not any fun, at least it's not for me, and I don't know many people who think it is. I know a lot of painters and sculptors who enjoy what they do, but they've got a tactile element, and materials that are fun to fool with. It ain't fun to fool with a typewriter and a piece of paper. It's miserable to fool with ideas. If it turns out halfway like you want it to, then it's fun; in fact, there's a period of euphoric illusion when even if you didn't do it well, you think you did. I guess there is some occasional pleasure in writing, because I know actually, sometimes in there, when I think I'm being funny I'll chortle. But I guess that's just trying it out on myself. I can't say it's fun.

BENNETT: Did you change "The Last Running" any when it was published as a book?

GRAVES: I don't believe so. I went over it. I may have, you know, a comma here . . . .

BENNETT: What is Encino coming out with now?

GRAVES: A thing I did about dogs. I called it "Blue and Some Other Dogs." *Texas Monthly* always changes my titles. They have a kind of context of humorous titles that dovetail with each other, so I don't even count on them using mine, but when I publish my things in a book, I'll put most of mine back on them.

BENNETT: Will you revise it?

GRAVES: Some, just a little bit. It ran awfully long for *Texas Monthly*, about fifty-five hundred words as they ran it, and there wasn't any question of sticking in two or three anecdotes that I had originally put in. So I will put them back for the book, where length doesn't matter.

BENNETT: If students could only observe professional writers. Is there any way students can be taught to write?

GRAVES: I spent quite a bit of time in the classroom on the theory that they could be taught, but I was never sure. You get some good products, more in terms of promise than achievement.

BENNETT: Students who could write before can write better, and those who couldn't still can't.

GRAVES: No, but they can read better. I often thought of that as an important side benefit, and for the bulk of them the main benefit: having looked at writing from the inside. They're going to be more appreciative of literature in general than they would have been.

BENNETT: It wouldn't be wise to turn them all into writers.

GRAVES: You're not going to turn too many people into writers anyhow. That's too painful an existence. Used to, at the end of every year, one or two or three or four kids would come around, individually, and seek you out sort of conspiratorially, and say, "What do you think my chances are of getting to be a writer?" You can't answer; you don't know. I ended up with what I think was a fairly truthful formula, which was: if they had to write, they were going to write whether they were good or bad, and if they didn't have to write, they were lucky, because only compulsion would carry anybody through the period of apprenticeship, and disappointment, and hard, unrewarding labor, and everything else that goes with it. I think that'll work for any art, unless you're a Mozart. The rest are going to drop out along the way, and probably be somewhat more perceptive for having had the urge.

BENNETT: Do you have any advice for young writers?

GRAVES: No, I used it all up in the classroom. If they have to, they will, and if they don't, they won't. There's so little really good that comes out of any age that they're getting into a vast lottery. I do suspect that the forms have changed. An awful lot of talent has gone into writing movies that once would have gone into prose. I don't think that the novel and nonfiction prose of quality are going to disappear at all, but I think they are going to shrink back to the kind of discerning audience they had before the Victorian middle class started making cultural heroes of writers. The big money right now is in movie writing; it's not from book sales.

BENNETT: Students make movies in lieu of term papers.

GRAVES: Billy Wittliff with Encino Press has been doing great with scripts. He's practically a gentleman publisher now; he just does it when he feels like it. Billy's thirty-six or thirty-seven, and we've been friends, I don't know, a long time. Four or five years ago he showed me a couple of scripts, and it turned out that for years he'd been getting up at four or five in the morning for three hours of writing before he went down to the press. They started getting interested in them in Hollywood and buying options on them. The only thing of his that has actually been made was a TV production that Johnny Cash did last year. It was kind of botched, but they're good work. In the process of that he was out in Hollywood, and they gave him some other scripts to doctor, and he turned out to have a special aptitude for that. He's back and forth out there now all the time. He's doing a Willie Nelson show now.

BENNETT: When do you write?

GRAVES: Mornings, when I'm fresh. The times are past when I could stay up all night on something. I think one trouble I've had with novels is that I work best in a spurt. Just get hold of something, and it gets hold of me, and I'm afraid to turn loose because it's going well. Articles and short stories and that sort of thing can be done more or less in a spurt, and I have managed to temper that to the extent that I can work on something for several days without losing it. But I used to be afraid to turn loose, just stay up fifteen to eighteen hours until I was through with it.

BENNETT: Do you set yourself regular hours?

GRAVES: Yes and no. I'm here by myself a good deal of the time, and I don't go so much by clock time as by how I feel. If I have stayed up real late reading the night before, or if an old movie came on the box and I was seduced into going to bed at one o'clock, I feel it is more profitable at my age, knowing a great deal about the way I function, better to sleep till eight the next morning and get up fresh and get over there by nine or nine-thirty than it is to get up arbitrarily at six and be there by seven-thirty or eight, which I ideally would like to be. So it will vary in that fashion somewhat, much less if I'm working on a longer piece of work. A real pattern gets into it then. But I think half the time when writers speak of their work habits they're speaking about what would ideally take place if everything were just right. Ideally I'd be at the typewriter by eight o'clock, and I'd be through by one, and I'd spend the afternoon in physical exercise so that I'd be tired and sleep well that night without drinking a lot of whiskey. But it doesn't work that way. Sometimes you can't quit at one because it has hold of you and you're scared to turn loose, and you end up nervously tired in the afternoon but not physically, and consequently you're messed up the next day. Usually I end up spending four or five hours over there.

BENNETT: Do you use a typewriter?

GRAVES: Yes.

BENNETT: Do you use a pen or pencil much?

GRAVES: Not much. I scribble notes, that sort of thing.

BENNETT: But you don't do the first draft in pencil?

GRAVES: No, I haven't tried that in many years. Oh, if I'm over here at the house at night and something occurs to me, I'll write down two or three pages sometimes. But it comes out quite differently from what I write on a typewriter, and when I revise it on a typewriter it's quite different from what I wrote down in longhand. I trust the typewritten thing more. There is a more direct communication between my mind and the paper through the typewriter.

BENNETT: In *Hard Scrabble* you're vague about places and names.

GRAVES: That's sort of to protect myself. I originally had some maps in there, and a couple of them remain; one of them shows where the county is in the state, and there's one that shows the farm itself. There was one in between that showed the county and where the farm is, and I looked at it and decided to hell with that; I didn't want to show where the place is. But the names: in spite of the fact that I don't write much fiction nowadays, I fictionalize quite a bit anything I write and try to preserve a certain freedom to do that. Consequently I'd rather keep the people too a little bit unidentifiable.

BENNETT: A lot of writers keep journals. Do you?

GRAVES: I used to. I have volumes of a journal over there that I hope I have the good sense to burn before I die. But they ceased rather abruptly about 1957, I think when I started writing that river book, and by the time I finished it, I was married. I think the journal served a very useful function for a long, long time. I go directly to the writing now.

BENNETT: Did you ever mine your journal?

GRAVES: I've used some of it. That's why I haven't destroyed it so far—I'm afraid there might be a rich mine of something in it. I might be looking at that journal sometime and this novel start writing itself.

BENNETT: I've been reading Arnold Bennet's journals.

GRAVES: I pity anybody that tries to read mine. A lot of it is written in tiny, crabbed handwriting, and it will be about half Spanish, part French, and some of it in a code, a shorthand stuff of my own.

BENNETT: You speak Spanish and French?

GRAVES: My French was never very good. At one time I spoke very good Spanish. I can still speak it, but it's clumsy; a lot of vocabulary has gotten away from me. There were some wetback hay haulers here last week, and I was jabbering around with them, but I'd come to some crucial point I wanted to make, and I'd forgotten the word. I used to work in the country a lot when I was a kid; there have always been wetbacks through this country, and they'd teach you all the words for things. I took some Spanish in school and later lived in Mexico and Spain.

BENNETT: In *Goodbye to a River*, you talk about a French government minister coming on a visit. My son David got hysterical when he read about the farmer putting his foot behind his neck to impress the visitor.

GRAVES: That was down in this country, and the farmer really did, too. Now there's somebody that reads my work, and he's really proud he's in that chapter, but he's a special sort of a character anyhow. Very pleased. Some people around here are very aware of what I do. One character came around one day and said, "If I'd known you were going to write that kind of a book, I could have told you a lot of stuff." His implication was that it was pretty unsavory.

BENNETT: When did you take the *River* trip?

GRAVES: Left on Armistice Day, 1957. About three weeks. I got in about December 2—a hundred and seventy-five miles. I just messed around; I could do it in a few days. I took a trip to Mexico a few years ago with some people from Houston, three canoes of us. We went down the Conchos River to where it empties into the Rio Grande there at Presidio. Runs through beautiful desert country and some canyons.

We went about a hundred and fifty miles, and nobody we could find out about had ever run it. We did it in six days. We had some hard-driving executive types; they wanted to whip the river. I wanted to mess around and talk to Mexicans. There were beautiful little old desert villages and primitive, nice people. I could have dawdled there for a month.

BENNETT: How did you happen to develop that wonderful style?

GRAVES: In the first place I'm not sure it always is. I don't know where any of it comes from. As I was saying about the Ph.D., there's a degree to which consciousness can be harmful to a writer. I could take you back and show you some things I did twenty-five years ago in which you wouldn't recognize my present style, although some things you would recognize. It's just a tone of voice that evolves. I think it comes from childhood reading and things that appeal to you over the years. I always hate to admit it, but I think one very strong influence on me was O. Henry. I read a lot of him when I was a kid, just read and reread those stories. In structure and what they have to say, there's not much to him. But stylistically he's one of the best of those nineteenth-century figures who use rather formal language for humorous effect, and I can see that in some of my stuff from time to time. If I'm trying to be funny, I start using long words. It isn't something I do consciously.

BENNETT: I notice that you use a much longer sentence than those of us who came through newspapers.

GRAVES: Yes, I'm not quite as bad as Faulkner, but I'm almost. There is not too much difference between one long sentence connected by commas and conjunctions and three shorter ones connected only by an idea. There's a flow and rhythm. The biggest trouble I have with editors—and I don't have it much with *Texas Monthly*—is commas.

BENNETT: Putting them in or taking them out?

GRAVES: Either one. If I put one in, I put it there because I want it there, and if I left it out, I wanted things to move fast right there. Editors want it to be consistent; they want it to go with some damned book of style. They get enraged, but sometimes you will set off a restrictive modifier and sometimes you won't, and there isn't any rule. There shouldn't be. But it drives them nuts. Any time I get into the hands of a new editor anywhere, whether it's a book publisher or a magazine, I can count on a real pitched battle before I make my point. One little girl copy editor rewrote *Goodbye to a River* entirely; she was helping out that poor old illiterate down in Texas. Then I was so mad I couldn't see, and I just changed everything back again in galleys and sent it back. It cost them a lot of money. Harold Strauss, who was my editor then, understood and said, "It's our fault."

But I can't tell you anything about my style, and I don't think many writers can, about their own styles. You come to know that such and such a rhythm and word pattern and so on fits the feeling that you are after at a certain point. It becomes sacred, and you don't dare tamper with it. It's got to be a feeling; it can't be a knowledge. I write and rewrite along. I can have gone over something ten times, and a certain sentence will bother me every time I go through, and I stop and look at it, and can't see anything wrong with it. Perfectly all right. I say baloney and go on. In the end just some little rhythmic thing, maybe a word of three syllables where there ought to be two or something like that. It doesn't have anything to do with meaning; it has to do with rhythm.

BENNETT: How many revisions do you put a magazine piece through?

GRAVES: I usually quit on the third complete draft. But that doesn't really tell the whole story, because I will rewrite an awful lot as I go along. I'll do, say, four pages one day, and the next day I'll go over there and redo that four before I start on what comes next. And I might not even get back to where I started out from that morning, or I may make a leap. I'd say there are two drafts that go into that partial rewriting as I go along. I wish to God I weren't that way; it's terribly slow. They said of Shakespeare that he never blotted a line. And old Faulkner turned them out, but I suspect he worried more over his books than he ever admitted, particularly his best stuff.

BENNETT: Some things he should have revised more.

GRAVES: Quite true. A great deal on the Snopeses is quite extended. Much as I admire Faulkner, and I admire him tremendously, I think the Nobel Prize went to his head. I think he got into a sort of automatic writing after that; he decided that anything that came out was okay.

BENNETT: A persistent theme of yours is the desecration of the land. What do you think of the ecology movement?

GRAVES: It's an interest in that it overlaps the sort of thing I've been doing. But I'm not much of a joiner, partly because I distrust polemics and partly because I think the writing that comes out of it is flawed. I have a tendency to watch. And I'm a pessimist also. If you're going to be a polemicist, a movement person, you've got to be an optimist, to believe it's leading to something good, and I'm not sure anyone can do anything about the situation of man vis-à-vis nature. There are too many of us; we're eating it up. Disaster might stop it, and disaster probably will sooner or later, but I find it difficult to look forward to that prospect with joy as some of these ecology types seem to do.

BENNETT: What do you think about them building the atomic reactor here at Glen Rose?

GRAVES: You can see it from right here on the hill. Well, I'd rather not live around it. But I haven't gotten into the discussion. I thought about doing so, and I still may, but there are two or three factors to be considered. Nothing's happened in this county since they used up the topsoil and the cotton wouldn't grow anymore. The only industry that ever existed around here was a little cedar-oil mill, and it employed something like nine persons. This nuclear plant is the only real industry they've ever had; they've got a four-thousand-man payroll, making up to thirteen or fifteen dollars an hour. Most people here were glad to see it. I'm not so sure they're glad now, after Harrisburg. I will watch it. I've had some feeling all along that it might not ever operate. One more Harrisburg, and I'll bet it wouldn't. Still, some of these protester kids come around to see me—I'm kind of a local character—and I say, "Hell, I wish you luck."

BENNETT: *Hard Scrabble* is about restoring——

GRAVES: Trying to restore. It would take two thousand years of absolute absence of people and of neglect to put this country back in any semblance of what it was a hundred and fifty years ago. You know that old rocky hillside you drove down getting here? If you stood on a piece of bedrock sticking out of it, and you snapped your fingers, and God put everything just the was it was a hundred and fifty years ago, you'd be up to your neck in dirt. It's all gone. They grazed it off, and farmed it off.

BENNETT: *Goodbye to a River* passively condemns the reservoir project.

GRAVES: They didn't move as fast on those as I thought they were going to move, though. At that time there were five proposed dams between Possum Kingdom and Lake Whitney, but the only one they've built in the meantime is at Granbury. They're still pushing for some of the others, but they ran up against a hard fact—the Brazos is too salty for a lot of uses. It's no good for municipal supply; it rusts pipes, and people don't like the taste of it.

BENNETT: When you took the *Goodbye to a River* trip, did you take a lot of notes?

GRAVES: Yes, in a little old three-by-five notebook, and then transcribed them while they were still fresh. I did a lot of rechecking on other information afterwards, and a lot of the research I had done before. Kids come along and want to make a canoe trip, and I give them one of my maps, so I don't guess I have them anymore, but I had topographical maps and in india ink, where the river wouldn't smear them off, I had footnotes about all kinds of things before I made the trip. I ran across some stuff I flat hadn't known when I made the trip, but not much.

BENNETT: Did you write *Hard Scrabble* straight through, or assemble it out of a lot of reflections?

GRAVES: It pretty much went from start to finish.

BENNETT: Did you write Chapter Ten, about the Old Fart, separately as a short story and insert it?

GRAVES: No, when I got to that point in the book, it sort of wrote itself. I didn't have any notion that was going to be there. You have to trust to instinct an awful lot. I need preliminary planning so I know where something is supposed to go, but if I stick too assiduously to it, I cut myself off from those really good arrivals that show up.

BENNETT: What was the dog's name on the *Goodbye* trip?

GRAVES: Watty. He's buried on that slope going down to that goat shed. I was looking for the stone not long ago; it's sunk down so far—the dirt's washed down on it—that I can't find it.

BENNETT: Just how long have you lived here?

GRAVES: We've had the place about twenty years, and this is part of the house I built in 1962. In actual living here, we've been sporadic, and I don't think you can say we live here yet. We moved down here in 1970, after my mother died in Fort Worth, and put the kids in school here. We were all here for three or four years together, but Jane has work that keeps her in Fort Worth a lot, so we finally took an apartment there, and the kids finished high school there. They come down on weekends and spend the summer down here usually. I'm in there maybe one or two days a week.

BENNETT: Texans like to believe they are attached to the soil.

GRAVES: My particular kind of attachment seems to have more in common with the midwestern agricultural thing. I'm very fond of the old ranching tradition, but it's very destructive. There are more ranchers now who introduce grasses and try to take care of things, like the Matthewses at Albany, who are damned good, responsible people. But it was originally almost nomadic—like the buffalo, eat it up and get out. And a lot of them just automatically overstock when it rains a little bit. They used to say about an old boy near here that he'd go up in his pasture and lie down on the ground and look up toward a hill, and if he saw one blade of grass sticking up, he'd buy ten more cows. But the biggest damage around here was done by little old bitty cotton farmers. All I've got left that is usable are these little flat fields where it couldn't wash much.

BENNETT: We're going to have to rearrange our thinking to scarcity instead of abundance perhaps.

GRAVES: But there's so many of us. Even if everybody started thinking right tomorrow, there still wouldn't be enough to go around. But what are you going to do about those other people? They're going to want to eat. Waste is not new with us. They've been at it since prehistory. All that Mediterranean country, there were magnificent forests, lots of dirt.

See those bees over there? They're optimists.

Old Webb was writing about that business of scarcity in the fifties, in his *The Great Frontier*. Seemed pretty far out then. Some of the counterculture have recently taken Webb up. There's a magazine called the *Mother Earth News* pushing a return to the land, but it's a young, longhaired type of return, and they've discovered *The Great Frontier*. They beat the drums for Webb about every third issue. I don't know what he'd have thought of that company, but at least somebody is listening to him. They are very holy and pious. One thing I've got against the movements: there's so damned much piety, misplaced piety, goes into them. I think they are good people, but they are so damned conscious of how good they are. I've always been conscious of how crummy I am.

BENNETT: Bernard Shaw used to go for vegetarianism, socialism, spelling reform . . . .

GRAVES: His wife is supposed to have left a good chunk of her money to a society to teach Irishmen manners. I don't know whether it's true. Martha Foley used to say that; she hated old Shaw.

BENNETT: Shaw was a terrific writer, though.

GRAVES: He retained his sense of humor, even about things he got embroiled in. These people I'm talking about don't have much sense of humor. Heavy satire is all they understand.

BENNETT: In *Goodbye to a River* the river is saturated with its own past. *Hard Scrabble* is full of the farm's past.

GRAVES: It's just my turn of mind. I suppose my retrospective tendency comes partly from having grown up in a southern background.

BENNETT: Do you read a lot of history?

GRAVES: I have, and still do. I think it's characteristic of a time like ours in which the future is rather doubtful, to say the least. It's partly nostalgia and partly a key to understanding; just wallowing in sentiment about lost worlds doesn't interest me. One advantage of a time such as this we live in is perspective. When things are breaking up, you can see a world, a society, a lot more clearly than people who were living in it when it was whole and strong. I would like to think that my interest in past things is at least that practical. I'm really not a very sentimental person.

BENNETT: Are you a determinist?

GRAVES: I am to a large degree. I've been puzzling all my life over it. I know free will exists, because I've exercised it time and again, but I think it's only a sporadic thing, showing up in the individual life from time to time. The rest of the time you're committed, you're flowing with the stream, and everything that happened before influences it. But I don't know what you'd call that, a free-will Presbyterian or something like that.

BENNETT: Have you read any of Anthony Powell's *Dance to the Music of Time*?

GRAVES: No. I come at reading very late ordinarily. Time winnows a great many things that you might have read, and it turns out you didn't have to waste your time. Just a few months ago I read Durrell's *Alexandria Quartet* for the first time, and they've been out fifteen or twenty years. They're good, quite good.

BENNETT: This project has introduced me to a lot of interesting reading, such as George Sessions Perry.

GRAVES: Perry's not bad. *Hold Autumn in Your Hand* is quite nice. He did a little frank imitation of Steinbeck's *Cannery Row*, a Brazos hobo book called *Walls Rise Up*; that's a nice little book.

BENNETT: I've got quite a stack of Texas reading left to do.

GRAVES: Time winnows them too. I'm not too well read in Texas terms; I guess I've read most of the good stuff. I haven't read all of the new, but I'll probably get at it if I live. You can lose perspective in this whole regional thing; of course, to some degree I'm identified with it. The University of Texas Press recently sent me a copy of the galley proofs of Dorothy Scarborough's *The Wind*, I assume for comment. It seemed curiously dated to me, a lot of florid prose, and you get this feeling that when you've seen one woman overcome by the Great Plains wind you've seen them all. And I had seen other ones before.

BENNETT: Sonnichsen discusses Scarborough's work in *Hopalong to Hud*.

GRAVES: Sonnichsen's quite civilized. That's a wonderful history of El Paso he did several years ago. He's very good in those feud books.

BENNETT: I was curious on your opinion of the Truitt-Mitchell feud.

GRAVES: It was right up here at Mitchell Bend. That was the only part of that book that I ever got any static about. I tried to be perfectly frank in that I was dealing with it fictionally, that I was seeing it as a symbol of the townsmen taking over control from the old ruffian pioneers like Cooney Mitchell, but I did lean on what information I could get around here locally, and I read Sonnichsen. I sided with the Mitchells really, but I was frank about it and said it may not have been this way. Well, the Mitchells are all long gone. But there are Truitts everywhere, and they are all female, and they're all family-minded, and one of them turned out to be the mother of a girl I used to go with in high school, and they all wrote letters, angry letters. One was particularly poignant, and made me squirm: an old lady in her eighties in Arizona—you remember that the Reverend James Truitt's testimony more or less convicted Cooney Mitchell and got him hanged, and years and years and years later old Bill Mitchell knocked on his door at Timpson and walked in and shot him out of his chair—this old lady was six or seven years old at the time and was standing by her father's chair when Bill shot him out of it. She wasn't happy with my version, and I don't blame her, but there wasn't anything I could say.

BENNETT: Sonnichsen modified his feud-book views when he later devoted a whole book to Bill Mitchell. Maybe he got some letters.

GRAVES: By God, if they lit on him the way they lit on me, I bet he did modify his views.

BENNETT: You've got to admire Sonnichsen's guts. He must have written twenty or more feuds.

GRAVES: And every one of them still has that kind of feeling attached to it somehow.

BENNETT: You say you fictionalize a good deal and intend readers to understand that.

GRAVES: Evidently the Truitt ladies didn't. It reminded me of a beehive; you go into a beehive at the wrong time and everything in there is mad at you. It must be very deep-seated, that old urge to keep the family name clear, even when it doesn't deserve to be. I've always been interested in the scandalous corners of family history, and who wasted his substance, and all that. There was plenty of this sort of thing in my family, as I guess there was in most others too.

BENNETT: Is the Old Fart chapter in *Hard Scrabble* all fiction?

GRAVES: Fiction. It just grew out of the air at that point. Oh, the details of his life grew out of, I'd say, at least two or three old men I have known. There actually was an old man very much like that at a filling station I used to trade with on Highway 80 west out of Fort Worth.

BENNETT: What about the old man you stayed with in *River?*

GRAVES: He was real. Particularly in the river book the day-to-day details of what happened and whom I met are pretty close to fact. There's very little rearrangement, if any. That fellow whom I called Hale was a composite. Some of the reminiscences of things about him I did with one friend, and some of them with another who actually came out there and spent a night and floated a day with me.

BENNETT: You grew up in Fort Worth. How did you learn so much about farming?

GRAVES: I grew up in the twenties and thirties. Fort Worth wasn't such-a-much as a city then. The country was right nearby. The Depression sort of froze Fort Worth on one line. There were vast areas of real estate that we could hunt on—and fish in the tanks—that nobody owned except some speculator. There were deer down in the Trinity bottom and everything else. Any city job worth having, there were ten men fighting over it, so about all we kids could do was dollar-a-day hay and harvest work out in the country.

BENNETT: How did you happen to get Russell Waterhouse to do the illustrations for *Goodbye to a River?*

GRAVES: I guess Carl Hertzog turned him up. Knopf asked Carl to design it, and Russell Waterhouse was a young architect who was living in El Paso. Carl carried his definition of design way down along the way. He selected the type. You probably don't remember, but the last chapter is just one page, back in town at a party, a little dialogue. Carl decided that had to be on a right-hand page; it had come out on a left-hand page. He spent three days going back through that preceding chapter, jamming things together to make room so he could get that one page over on the right. He's a little mad. I'm real fond of him. He's an absolute perfectionist and very, very fine at what he does.

BENNETT: I haven't met Hertzog. I had a delightful talk with Tom Lea.

GRAVES: I like Tom very much, and respect him, though I don't know him all that well. He's a rather formal personality, with some very strong convictions, and he's done some pretty good writing. What do you like best of his?

BENNETT: *The Wonderful Country.*

GRAVES: Me too, me too! I told him that two or three months ago when I saw him over in Dallas. I'd recently reread it, and it was damned good.

BENNETT: I'm sorry his recent *In the Crucible of the Sun* hasn't been put on sale to the public. It was published by the Klebergs.

GRAVES: Princely gesture they can afford. It'll hit the circuit sooner or later. Tom Lea and Dobie, you know, their relationship, which was very very close, was strained considerably by that King Ranch book of Tom's. I heard that the Dobie review hurt him badly. Dobie thought that Tom had soft-pedaled a lot of the most germane material concerning old Richard King, who was in some senses a real villainous old character, a nineteenth-century empire grabber. Actually it would have been more interesting if those things had been explored more objectively. Dobie just said what he thought in one of his Sunday columns, and it wasn't favorable.

BENNETT: Lea said he felt bound by facts and didn't enjoy writing it.

GRAVES: Now, Mr. Dobie tended to blame somebody else; he didn't want to blame Tom. I didn't know him till the last four or five years of his life, but we were pretty close during that time, and he told me it wasn't Tom's fault; they had these fellows feeding material to him, just what they wanted him to get.

BENNETT: I suppose Dobie just had nothing else to write a column about one day and——

GRAVES: No, that particular thing was very hard for him to write, because he knew what he was doing. He had a peculiar kind of dogged integrity, like people bite down on a sore tooth, and because it hurt he had to do it. He fell out with several of his old friends. It wasn't always Dobie's fault. He and J. Evetts Haley were very close at one time. Haley got so rabidly political, so conservative he's almost a monarchist, but he was a very gifted historian. That book of his on Goodnight is just as solid as a rock.

BENNETT: Who is the "H" that you dedicated *Goodbye to a River* to?

GRAVES: That is my older daughter, Helen. The other book is dedicated to the younger one. Jane, my wife, says the next book is hers.

BENNETT: Which Texas writers do you like?

GRAVES: Oh, that's one of those whipping-your-wife things. I like a lot of Texas writing for reasons I don't trust, because the subject matter is of intense interest to me, or if it's corn it's my kind of corn, like old Fred Gipson—I love his stuff, but I distrust my love for it in a sense, because I'm not objective about hound dogs in the Texas Hill Country. Hell, they're wonderful, just to start with! Before he's written a word, I'm hooked. Incidentally, by any contemporary definition of success, Fred's probably the most successful writer we ever had. I'll bet you more people, through either the books or the movies, are aware of his characters and stories than anybody else that ever came out of Texas. He was a sweet guy too, Fred. Poor old Fred died all by himself down on that little ranch at Mason. Things kind of went to pieces for him those last years.

But to come back to your question—and I am evading it to some degree. Essentially what I think is that I'm not quite as objective as I ought to be to answer a question like that. Katherine Anne Porter is undoubtedly the most realized artist that has ever come out of the state, in terms of literature, but it is hard to say whether you should call her a Texas writer. Her important stuff has a Texas background to it, but she has certainly never wanted to identify herself with the state particularly. I think McMurtry is enormously talented. I am sorry—although from my own standpoint I can understand it—that he hasn't continued in the direction that was indicated by his earlier stuff. But I think he had to get loose from Archer City. But that early stuff was pretty dern good. He has great talent with words, and great intelligence.

BENNETT: Do you think he might return to that material?

GRAVES: Yes. He indicated to me last summer that he has taken over a house on the old family ranch up there, and he thought he would be spending summers there, he and his son, James. Jamey, interestingly enough, who has been raised in Houston and Washington and all over the place, got to know his grandfather well enough before the old man died that he got interested in ranching.

BENNETT: McMurtry says that a writer must continue to write if he is to produce good things in his later years.

GRAVES: I have thought a lot about that. Anybody does who regards the sorry spectacle of American writers and their usual biographies. Europeans go on and get wiser. All writers are egomaniacs, but I still feel I have a chance to do better work than what I've done.

BENNETT: You've done good work so far.

GRAVES: But it hasn't been what I had in mind to start with. It's not bad for what it is; it's a matter of scope and of category.

BENNETT: Perhaps the success of McMurtry's first novel, *Horseman Pass by*, created problems for him.

GRAVES: Damned good novel. The movie was better in some ways than the book. It lacked Larry's use of language, though. That's why books will survive, no matter what movies do. But some things are very youthful and don't make much sense in the book, and they rectify them in the movie, rather than messing it up further, which they usually do.

People like William Humphrey I don't know about—they're really more southern than Texan in a way.

BENNETT: Have you ever met him?

GRAVES: No. Billy has, Billy Wittliff. I can't remember the occasion.

BENNETT: What about writers in general?

GRAVES: They keep popping up. Some of them, I'll like a book, and then that fellow never will write anything else. Of established writers, most of them are old or dead or European, mostly British. Anthony Burgess at his best; he's written too much, but his best stuff is superb. Nabokov I feel that way about. Most writers I really admire without much reservation are word writers rather than idea writers. They may be idea writers too, but they are people who make music out of words, and who play with language and make it do things on its own, which Nabokov did superbly, for instance, and Burgess can, too. There are a few others around.

I play with words too; one admires what one tries to do. Some great figures bore me; some don't. You're supposed to be bored by John Milton, and I think he's wonderful. I don't care what it means. It's all outworn theology, damned near. Doesn't make any difference. It just rolls and bounces off the walls.

BENNETT: Somebody has said that southern literature is what it is because every southern household contains a King James Bible and *Paradise Lost*.

GRAVES: Even if they didn't read the Bible at home, they got it at church. I've always been grateful that I grew up in the Episcopal church, where they had that old Prayer Book too. I'm not formally religious anymore anyhow, but I've got it specified that if there is an Episcopal service after I'm dead it's going to be in the old language. It enraged me when they changed it; I don't want that new stuff.

BENNETT: The new Prayer Book has created quite a stir.

GRAVES: There is a strong link for some reason in this state between the Methodists and good writing. It is astounding how many of the older generation of good or fairly good writers were Methodists. Like Dobie, like John W. Thomason. Thomason was essentially an artist. The best thing he ever wrote was a collection of stories about a Methodist minister who went to war as an officer in Hood's Texas brigade; they're stories that Thomason heard from the old folks while he was growing up down there at Huntsville. Thomason was a professional career Marine, a colonel. I never met him, but I knew his brother, who was a doctor in Fort Worth, and I just missed the colonel two or three times in the Marine Corps. He wrote for many years for the old *Saturday Evening Post*, and they had to have a whammo plot, so he botched up a lot of good material on that account, but those Praxiteles Swan stories, which were published as *Lone Star Preacher* when they were collected, were good. He has some passages in there that just turn in you like a knife. God, they're great! It's like the Old Testament and everything came together for him in that material.

What other writers have you talked to for your book?

BENNETT: Elmer Kelton for one. His books are getting better all the time.

GRAVES: I've been watching Kelton. He doesn't have to get much better to be pretty damned good. And he's a very generous-spirited sort of fellow. I know two or three young writers he's given a boost one way or another. One's a kid who's cowboying in the Panhandle right now.

BENNETT: Shelby Hearon, Preston Jones, A. C. Greene, Tom Lea.

GRAVES: A. C.'s got some nice stuff. *A Personal Country* is a good book, and *The Santa Claus Bank Robbery* is very competent. Some of his other work I'd classify as journalism. I like A. C.; we're good friends.

BENNETT: I have set up an interview with Leon Hale.

GRAVES: Leon's a good man. In that last novel of his, *Addison*, he didn't get away with something that he did get away with beautifully in *Bonney's Place*—this child of nature who makes everything better for people around him by emanations. But Leon's an awfully good man.

BENNETT: He must spend a long time writing them because they are so far apart.

GRAVES: [*guffaws*] It's a long time between mine, if that's any criterion.

BENNETT: Max Apple I thought I'd get.

GRAVES: Yes, he's a very talented man. You see, there's some of them I wouldn't even think about when you ask me about Texas writers, because the identification with Texas is not there. Apple's a metropolitan, that's what he is.

I know just about all of them. It's a very small world, and then we have this thing called the Texas Institute of Letters which if it only served to get them together once a year would be a good thing, but it does a little more than that. There are lots of interesting names around. Bill Porterfield is a very colorful fellow and writes dern well; that collection of his that A&M put out, *A Loose Herd of Texans*, will stand up well. Old Dugger if you want a good polemicist. There's John Rechy in El Paso; he's a wild one, wild hair anyway. There's Elroy Bode in El Paso, one of God's strange ones. He's published nothing but sketches, just little quiet things. Enormous talent if it ever gets loose, or maybe it already has.

May, 1979

Max Apple: *Voices in Fiction*

MAX APPLE was born October 22, 1941, in Grand Rapids, Michigan. He earned his B.A. in 1963 and his Ph.D. in 1970, both from the University of Michigan. Later he studied at Stanford. After teaching for a year at Reed College, Apple joined the English faculty at Houston's Rice University in 1970.

When we went to his home, Apple, dressed in running shorts and a loose shirt, took us back to the studio where he writes. It was a good-sized room with one bricked wall and a lot of light from large windows. At one end was a fireplace, and on its mantel stood brass candelabra, a seashell, an Indian pot, and an insecticide bomb. There were a couch and a round coffee table, a pot plant, and a clock radio. On the wall was an "Oranging Day" poster from the university bookstore and a paddle with the inscription "ZBT, to Max '62 from Fred '65."

The author wrote at a spartan desk that stood in one corner. It had a lot of yellow legal pads on it. A bentwood chair was pushed up to it.

He is a slender, muscular man, five feet four inches tall, weighing 115 pounds. He has bespectacled brown eyes, and his reddish-brown hair grays slightly in his beard. His interest in athletics is obvious from the number of times sports come up in his work, but these days he confines himself to running.

Apple sat crosslegged on the floor. "Pull up a chair. I'm just more comfortable on the floor." He talks at a pace more rapid than that of most native Texans. Many talkers leave sentences unfinished here and there. Apple's ideas come in such a rush that he often leaves polysyllabic words half-pronounced when the sense is obvious.

APPLE: You know, this interviewing is an odd thing. My gramp actually taught me an interesting thing about it. He lives in Houston with us, just a block away. When we first moved here, a woman from the local Jewish newspaper interviewed both of us. She was a nice lady, and she came by my office, and we talked. Of course, he didn't know the interview form, and so she would ask him questions about himself, and he would ask her questions about herself. I suddenly

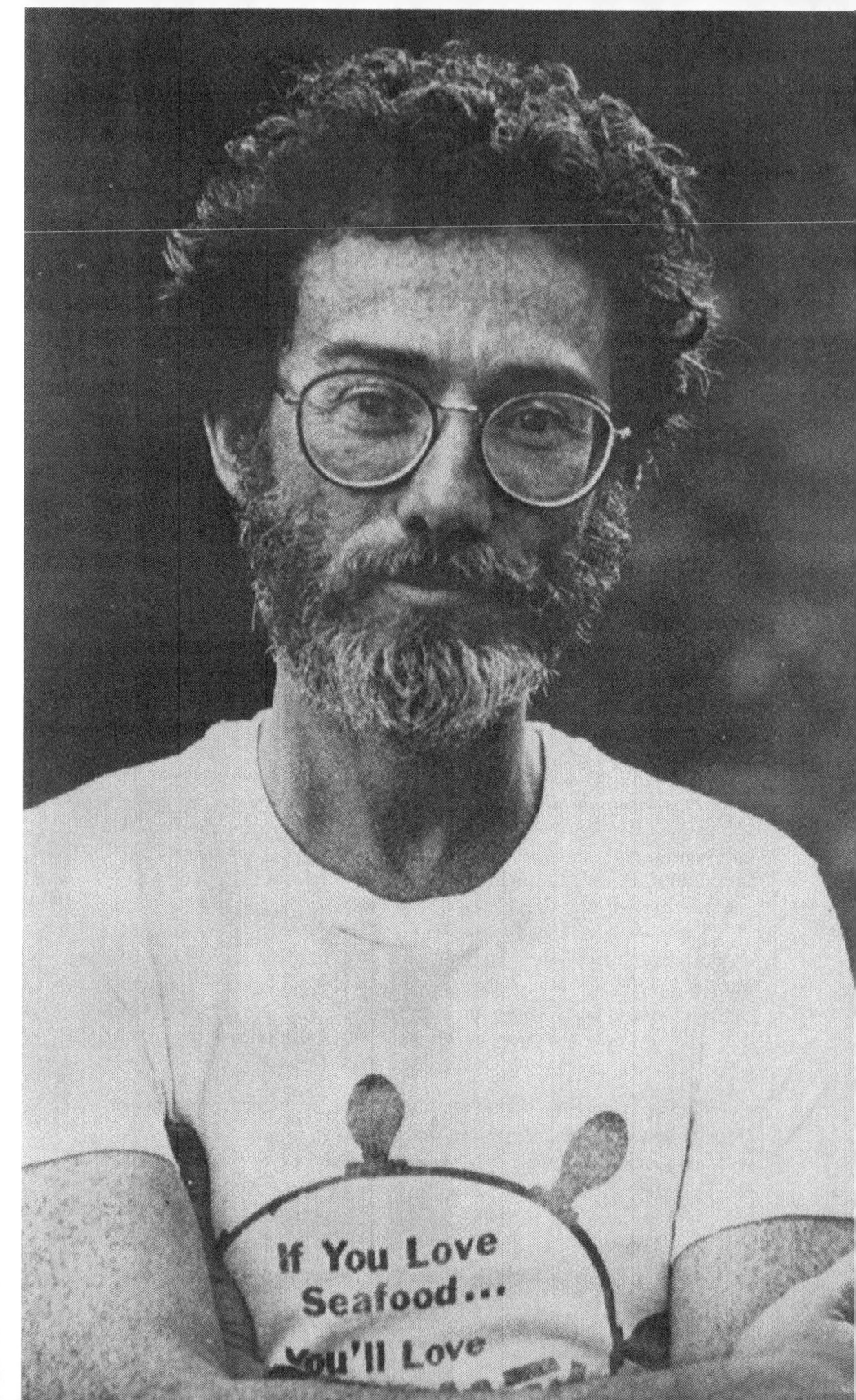

realized how right my grandpa was—that this is artificial. You know, you come here and ask me all kinds of things about myself. In civilized behavior I should ask you the same things. In fact, I am just as interested in you as you are in me, so why should we accept this kind of . . . ? You see, I've been proud of my grandpa for that: he didn't accept it. So I'm aware of how synthetic this is as we're doing it.

BENNETT: That's true. And the oddness of it had never occurred to me either. Perhaps the change of scene also made you more sharply aware. Are you from Detroit?

APPLE: Grand Rapids, Michigan. University of Michigan. I have a Ph.D. from Michigan. I spent a year at Stanford, in the writing program, '64, I think it was, after I got my B.A.

BENNETT: How did you get into writing?

APPLE: Well, you're always telling stories. I was lucky. You know Maxim Gorky's line: it came through my grandmother. I had a Russian-Jewish storyteller. I grew up with it. You know, I didn't even think of writing as being a job actually until just a few years ago, until I started earning a little money. But I always figured to be a writer, to tell stories. I didn't necessarily figure to write them, but I figured to tell them. I took a writing class in college, and I gave the teacher pretty much that same answer. You were supposed to bring a writing sample, and I had never written anything, but I just told him I could do it. He misunderstood. He took for bravado what really wasn't bravado at all. So he chewed me out, and, of course, I realized later that he was right. But I've always been a reader, interested in narrative. It just took me another generation to learn style.

BENNETT: You weren't the sort of child who scribbled novelettes in his third-grade tablet.

APPLE: I would say I never really wrote a story until I got to college. Although, now that I think of it, I remember writing some sort of stories in high school. They didn't have classes in writing in high school, but I was always good at English as opposed to other things. But I think really I tried to write a story first in an undergraduate writing class, my junior year, maybe.

BENNETT: While we're on origins, was your family name originally Apfel?

APPLE: I don't know. I think originally Applebaum, because we had relatives by that name in Detroit. You never know, the way the immigrants' names came was so haphazard. It really doesn't matter. I agree with Falstaff.

BENNETT: When did you begin to try to market your stories?

APPLE: Not really until I came here, so in that sense at least I'm a Texas writer. I did win a contest in Ann Arbor just before I left. I guess I was working back then, more seriously than I wanted to admit to myself while I was in graduate school. I never showed my work to anyone. Then I won this contest they had in Ann Arbor, the Hopwood Contest. The only reason I entered is that I had a woman who could read my writing—I don't know how to type. She could read my handwriting well enough to type my dissertation. Reasonable price. She typed it out.

BENNETT: What was the subject of your dissertation?

APPLE: *The Anatomy of Melancholy*.

BENNETT: I've intended to read that for years.

APPLE: It's good reading in bits and pieces. I wouldn't recommend anybody read the whole thing at once.

BENNETT: But you didn't start selling stories till . . . .

APPLE: "The Oranging of America" was the first story I sold. I'd had two others that had been published in a small literary magazine, only because I knew the editor and he just squeezed them out of me. I really was very hesitant to sent anything out, and if I hadn't known that I had to publish in order to keep my job, I probably would never have done it. Now it seems crazy to me, that kind of shyness or fear or whatever it is, but I think all young writers have it. You want to be public and private at the same time. I still have it.

BENNETT: There's a lot of ego involved, opening yourself to rejection.

APPLE: But that's one of the things you finally have to do. If you're a writer, you have to show it to somebody; otherwise you're a diarist or something else.

BENNETT: Where did you sell "Oranging"?

APPLE: The *American Review*. It just went out of business last year. It's a great shame it folded. That was probably the only hope for young writers to be in a national magazine.

BENNETT: And since then you've sold several others.

APPLE: Most of the ones in the collection were sold. All except one, I think.

BENNETT: Which one didn't sell?

APPLE: I don't remember the title—oh, "Noon." The one about shooting Monte Hall was not sold—the one about the shooting on the game show—the murder.

BENNETT: You call him Larry Love in the story.
APPLE: Yes.
BENNETT: What do you teach at Rice?
APPLE: I teach creative writing every semester, and whatever else they want me to teach. My specialty is presumably seventeenth-century Renaissance, but there are three or four Rice people ahead of me in seniority doing that. And I don't really want to do that now. After seven years of not teaching that, I'm not up with the criticism. I don't really care to teach graduate students now that I've gotten away from the graduate world. They're interested in publishing articles, and in the kind of specialization that I'm happy to move away from. I'm much more a generalist. One year I teach eighteenth-century novel; the next year I teach nineteenth, or the history of the story. It doesn't matter to me. As long as it's prose. I don't like to teach poetry.
BENNETT: Have you tried to write poetry?
APPLE: Oh, I tried when I was in college. I have a tin ear for it. It's lucky that I saw that quickly.
BENNETT: You don't miss mining your dissertation for lectures?
APPLE: It wasn't very interesting. Believe me, nobody will want to hear about my dissertation. As far as I know, nobody ever read it, although it probably exists on a university microfilm. Somebody said you're not really a writer unless somebody reads what you've written. So I guess if you write a dissertation, you're still not a writer. Some remarkable critical books have been initiated as dissertations, but I think they change quite a lot before they see print.
BENNETT: How do you go about writing?
APPLE: It just depends on how your life is going. When things are smooth, and I can, I try to write every day. It's like physical exercise: if you miss, if you just do it once a week, it's not going to be as good as if you do it every day, or four times a week, or whatever. So when you're really writing, you try to write every day. It doesn't have to be a lot, but it keeps you in shape.
BENNETT: When do you write?
APPLE: Whenever I can.
BENNETT: You're not one of these fellows who get up at four o'clock and scribble off five pages, fair weather or foul, like Trollope?
APPLE: No. No. I think those were more nineteenth-century habits. Most of us don't have that kind of rigidity. Trollope was a clerk or something, and he had to be at work at certain times. So many of us now are teachers, and this gives you other times. I'm not sure that's

good. I mean, after you spend a morning teaching a class or two and have a conference with a student, then maybe you've got four hours in the afternoon to write, but it's not the same. Somehow you're wiped out after that—you've got three hours, but you might as well not even try. Trollope's probably right, if you can get it done in the morning. That's the frustrating part, I think, about combining the teaching and the writing: it would *seem* that you have time to do your work. For certain kinds of work you do. For scholarly work, or you can catch a little reading, or take notes. But writing requires a certain kind of spiritual vitality that's not there after you've taught.

BENNETT: It's not there after lunch for me.

APPLE: It's not there after lunch sometimes. It's not there when I wake up, a lot of times.

BENNETT: Do you write in longhand?

APPLE: I don't type. For me, getting typed is just like getting published.

BENNETT: You don't even retype them yourself?

APPLE: No, I've been lucky. The last two secretaries in the English Department have been able to read my handwriting.

BENNETT: Your handwriting is a challenge, I discovered, when I got your note.

APPLE: That was done extra quick.

BENNETT: I began life as a newspaperman and had to type.

APPLE: I'm envious of that. Certainly my work would go much faster and would be simpler if I didn't have to go through a typist and wait.

BENNETT: Do you put your stories through more than one draft before you take them to the typist, or do you wait to see the typed version to rewrite?

APPLE: It depends. Sometimes I like to reread what I'm writing, so it's hard to say how many drafts there are. I don't usually finish it, and then refinish it again and again. I'm rewriting it while I'm writing it. It's changing itself. So I have no sense of how many drafts there are. There might be ten versions of page 16, or three versions, or I'll pencil in 16-A and XX and so on. But finally when it's done, I'll usually know it's done. Then there are no more drafts. There are a lot of drafts of individual pages or sections, but not of the whole.

BENNETT: Do you revise any after the typist has finished?

APPLE: I did with the novel.

BENNETT: How long did you take to write it?

APPLE: I worked on it several years. Usually—or until recently anyway—I was only able to write in the summers, because I was busy teaching. Then in '76, I think, I had a grant from the National Endowment for the Arts. So I had a semester off, and that was the first time I had time off from teaching. So I was able to finish then. Before I had always been in the middle of it when school started, and then I'd go back the next time, and it had changed. You're a different person the next year. Finally, when I had six months straight, I was able to bring it together.

BENNETT: You got the grant to finish the novel?

APPLE: I told them I would. Somehow I did.

BENNETT: How long altogether had you been working at it?

APPLE: I probably started five or six years before it was done. But the novel that was finished wasn't anything like the novel that was started. Everything changed. I think that if I'd had six months or a year all together to work on it sooner, I might have been able to finish it earlier. I mean, I don't think it has to take six years to write such a novel. In between, of course, I was writing stories, too.

BENNETT: When you're writing stories and teaching at the same time, do you have any idea how many words you turn out each day?

APPLE: I have no idea. The first few years I was writing only in the summers, and I wasn't writing at all during school, because it was too frustrating. When you're teaching writing, essentially you're reimagining other people's stories, and there's only so much imagination that you have per day. You spend your energy ration reimagining someone else's story and talking about it. You might just have a couple of hours that you could do something that day, but it's not going to be really good imaginative energy. So I found the two were conflicting items. It didn't seem fair, while I was teaching, to put my stuff first. In the long run there is certainly greater publicity and money in writing, but somehow you've got to face the students every hour you teach, and I couldn't skimp on them. I enjoy teaching, but I taught only half time one semester last year, and I actually enjoyed that most. It gave me more freedom than I'd had before, not having to grade freshman English papers. You know, that takes a tremendous amount of energy. I still am interested in teaching as much as ever. But the more impetus you have as a writer, the more you publish things and become convinced you have an audience, the more you are inspired to write.

BENNETT: Teaching certainly takes a lot of mental energy if it is done conscientiously.

APPLE: To return to your original question: I never keep track of how many words a day. Maybe when you type, you know how many words you do. When I write by hand, I don't know how many. I just write until it's the right time to stop. I try to keep a kind of sanity about it—three or four hours, five hours, that may be all that you can do. I have a family; I always want to spend time with my children too. But you carry writing with you. It's working when you're not.... Your imagination is going when you're off. That's the strange thing about it. That's why it's good if you can come back the next day and the next and the next, because your imagination is working when you're not.

BENNETT: What fiction writers do you think influenced you?

APPLE: I think influence is really when you're a kid. I think John R. Tunis, who wrote the baseball books—*High Pockets, The Kid from Tompkinsville* .... He's a wonderful writer, as I remember. Those were about the Dodgers, I think, but he didn't call them that. *The Boys of Summer*, that group, the Dodgers of the late forties or early fifties probably. I read almost exclusively sports books. I had two older sisters, so I had the Bobbsey Twins too and all that stuff. But I was never, even as a kid, very interested in mystery stories. I've never read a detective novel till this day. For a while I went through science fiction, but all that stuff was about the eighth or ninth grade. The first real book that I remember reading was *Les Misérables*, in the ninth or tenth grade. I loved that. I remember one thing that was so wonderful was the character that I thought was lost forever in a sewer or prison, and then one hundred pages later, there he is. I think that was primitive, but I was understanding what the rhythms of fiction really are. Then years later, in graduate school, I learned the word "circumstantiality." You know, that's the way the world can work, and I've always been fascinated by that. I remember thinking how terrific it is that a writer can do that, can fool you, can make you think the character is all gone, and then there he is back. The great changes that life weaves through a novel. And I read, at a fairly early age—late high school and early college—a lot of the Russians: Tolstoy, Dostoevski, Chekov. Isaac Babel I love—his short stories. But I think by then .... Well, I guess those are still influences. But I'm sure that doesn't show up in my work. I guess that's it. I wouldn't say that any of my contemporaries that I admire are influences, because your style is formed when you're young.

BENNETT: You're writing extended monologues, and your prose is very witty in the eighteenth-century sense, and you're using the names of real persons. Some other writers doing this are Bellow——

APPLE: I haven't read Bellow's recent stuff, so I don't really know. I don't think he is. Coover is using real names. Doctorow: he modeled *The Book of Daniel* on . . . . And he used some real names in *Ragtime* too.

BENNETT: Bellow is not using real names, but he is using extended monologue.

APPLE: Yes, he does use monologue. Phillip Roth uses it very well. Every writer just looks for a voice. Those years I was experimenting on my novel, I have third-person sections. That was just the right voice. I wanted a certain energy, and I had trouble getting it. More and more I'm using first person, and I don't know why. It's much easier to write in the third person. Just technically, as a writer, you have a much greater range in the third person. But there is a certain kind of energy that I want.

BENNETT: Someone you may not be acquainted with who is very good at first person is Raymond Chandler.

APPLE: No, I haven't read him. You mean the detective books. No, but if it's that charged first-person voice, I probably would like Chandler.

BENNETT: His cynical spokesman gives the books a wonderful consistency of tone.

APPLE: I think that's really all a writer can hope for, that he has a tone that he's comfortable with. Of course, I don't work with a plot or outline or anything. The voice carries it.

BENNETT: You don't work with an outline?

APPLE: So you don't know what's going to happen. If you're not comfortable with that voice, you're in trouble. It's all experiment; it just goes along. If I were working a highly plotted story, and I had an outline and knew what was going to happen, then I guess it wouldn't matter so much. You could have a less persistent voice. But for me that's the whole thing; the tone is everything.

BENNETT: I realize the writers using these devices aren't borrowing knowingly from one another. It seems to have flowered. Have you read Anthony Powell?

APPLE: No, the *Music of Time* series. I actually haven't. Does he use that first person?

BENNETT: Yes. His central character, Nick Jenkins, is writing a book on Robert Burton, by the way, and so you'd probably be interested.

APPLE: I'm sure Burton was .... I don't know if Burton would be an influence on me. I think that I was probably too old already, but now and then I notice that I have great lists of things, and I'm sure that comes from Burton. He too had this wild voice. He thought he was writing an Aristotelian book, straight seventeenth-century Aristotelian, but of course the book is nothing like that. He gets going, and he wonders about everything in the world. So I guess there is some consistency, although it seems very arcane and academic, that I selected a book like that, when my own fiction seems so rooted in topical America. Essentially he was rooted in topical seventeenth-century England. For example, he wondered if people in Russia hibernated all winter—things like that.

BENNETT: Did some other writer suggest your practice of using real names?

APPLE: No, it was just pure accident. Obviously I'm comfortable with it. I'm just not consciously aware of it as a device or technique. It just worked.

BENNETT: Did you know much about Howard Johnson when you wrote "The Oranging of America"?

APPLE: I didn't know anything about him, and the publisher made me put a disclaimer in, at the end of that story. If I had known him, I suppose I couldn't have written it. I had never even stayed in a Howard Johnson Motel that I know of when I wrote that. I guess that's just another sign that I'm interested in America. You know, I get a lot of this stuff from having read various critics about my work. An author is in a kind of stupor; you don't know what you're doing. You do it, and then other people tell you that it's all this stuff. That's the nice thing about getting published: then you don't have to worry about what you're doing. But even in my stupor, I guess I know that I'm interested in the way America works—you know, motels, supermarkets, the kind of cultural mix we live in. It's hard not to name names and places. There's Howard Johnson and Holiday Inn and Coke. We're so much a brand-name society that it seems to me dishonest not to use the real names.

BENNETT: I see what you mean. It's not only the characters, but it's Gatorade and——

APPLE: I think all writers now are doing that. I remember in Eudora Welty's stories Jax beer used to come up. That's one of the first things I wanted to do when I came to the South, was to have a Jax beer. I knew that exactly from Eudora Welty.

BENNETT: Part of the landscape.

APPLE: I think a writer has to be rooted in things, so my rooting may be somewhere—Michigan, Texas, you know—because of my grandmother, even eastern Europe—Russia or Lithuania—some great mix of things. The more specific you are, the more rooted. So I'm rooted in the names of America, people, places, and things. For me it works. I think that when I first did it I didn't know anybody else was doing it. If other people are doing it, I think they are doing it for the same reasons—it would be my guess, not as a conscious device, but just because it's a way to get hold of something so amorphous. Our society just moves away from you before you can grasp it; it's not the nineteenth-century world. Who knows how long there will be Howard Johnsons, how long before that's a historical artifact? But that's just a long-winded way of saying that you don't know what you're doing, when your imagination takes over and a voice speaks. I recently talked to Doctorow at a conference in Berkeley, the first time I'd met him. He read from his work a thing that he had thrown away, not used for his new book that he said he was almost finished with. Anyway, he works much the same as I do. It didn't surprise me, because I feel close to his work. He just starts, and he doesn't know where he is going, and looks for a voice, and plays with words. I'm just guessing, but I think that a lot of these writers that you mention as using this monologue technique—I think that's the way they do it.

BENNETT: Edmund Wilson says that Anthony Powell's work is impromptu.

APPLE: You can't put too great a stricture on your imagination; otherwise it's not imagination any more.

BENNETT: Tom Lea says he works on a book in the same way he works on a mural, making a detailed plan first and then reproducing it on a larger scale.

APPLE: Lea is a realistic writer. Again I'm guessing, but I would say that a realistic writer must keep his eyes on the outside world. The world that I'm dealing with is the world of my voice. Maybe that's another reason, psychologically, why I tend to use real names: that somehow brings my voice into the real world. Somehow it's always evanescing, floating away, indistinct. I don't really feel in charge. If I can root it with real names, it helps.

BENNETT: Have you had any trouble with libel laws?

APPLE: No, but my publishers have. In fact, they insisted on that disclaimer. A lawyer wrote that; I didn't. I guess they worry about that. I've never felt that I've written anything libelous. I don't, for one thing, know those people. I don't think I would knowingly be libelous. I like my characters.

BENNETT: You don't show them in a bad light.

APPLE: No, and I make them up. And if you use a name that's public, it should be all right. I guess that you can't do that with a private name. With a public figure you have some latitude.

BENNETT: I talked with a woman who was confused over whether your short stories were fiction or nonfiction.

APPLE: Yes, it surprised me. I hear that too. I think it's partly because people in this country are not used to reading fiction. The more talk I hear from publishers, or observe the best-seller list, the more that impression is reinforced. People read to get information. Television now provides the entertainment. I mean, they don't think that these policemen on television exist in real life, or this really happened in the movies, but somehow the book seems to hold the truth. Maybe it's just the way schools propagate learning. And it's a great loss! Because of the fun of fiction, the entertainment of it, I don't like the solemnity of people thinking . . . . I've faced it too, and I know exactly what you mean. They think a book has to be true in a factual sense.

BENNETT: Then there's the celebrity novel such as Maugham did about Gauguin, or Thomas Hardy.

APPLE: That exists, I think, at the more popular level. The Harold Robbins novels are the ones that are apparently about Howard Hughes or certain movie stars. I don't really feel that stuff is like mine. My characters are made up; I'm just using the names. I'm doing the opposite of what they are doing. I'm using the real names, but the characters, the events, everything is fictional. In fact, I don't think—everybody always asks me about it—but I'm not aware that the names really matter much to me.

BENNETT: You don't pick your favorite people?

APPLE: No, no. The Howard Johnson thing, for example: My wife worked for a while as dean of a beauty academy, which is a strange job. That was when I was unemployed, before I got a job at Rice. She was supposed to recruit high-school girls for a career. It was the only job she could pick up at the time. Anyway, that beauty academy met in an abandoned former motel. It wasn't a Howard Johnson's Motel. This was in Ann Arbor. Somehow I began thinking about it, and I just started writing about that beauty academy. It was a strange job, and a fellow was running a pot-and-pan emporium selling utensils to newlyweds in the basement of the building. And the beauty school was just a strange thing, you know, and I thought I would write about that—the people involved in it. I wrote a couple of pages of kind of realistic description of it, and suddenly, about the third page, there was the whole opening of the Howard Johnson story. Somehow the motel triggered it, when I was not a bit thinking of writing about Howard Johnson. I wasn't a bit in control of it, and once it started going, it just went its own way.

BENNETT: It's a peculiarly effective device. With a name like Howard Johnson—everybody's heard of him, but nobody seems to know much about him. Now if it were Mohammed Ali, it would be different.

APPLE: Yes, I didn't think of that. I'm sure that's part of it too, probably. So many things are just named after somebody, and you wonder if there ever was such a person. Is there really an Earl Scheib of the tube? They stick a smiling face on signs. You know these people probably exist. Everything gets so big in this country, franchises and big businesses, but things start with people. And fiction writers are interested in people.

BENNETT: When you used J. Edgar Hoover in your novel, you chose a well-known person. But I suppose most of us don't know too much about Hoover.

APPLE: And I knew less than most people, in fact. So the Hoover that I made up was my Hoover, whatever he did.

BENNETT: Have you found out anything about Howard Johnson since you wrote "Oranging"?

APPLE: Not really. But every once in a while someone will send me a clipping about him. I guess he has a son who really runs the business, and someone will send me a clipping of a business article that's actually quoting my story.

BENNETT: Are you curious about him?

APPLE: People think I'd be really interested, and I'm not. Once I finish the story, I'm not really all that interested. I'm no more interested than a carpenter who has finished a table. You hope it's good and that they like it, and it's done as well as you can do it, but it becomes a public thing. I'm interested in other people's work, the way someone might be in mine. That's part of what happens to you when you become a little bit public: you answer other people's questions about things you're really not interested in.

BENNETT: Still, writers talk more rewardingly than, say, actors. As a journalist I've often quizzed actors, and they are very talkative, but frequently they don't have anything to say.

APPLE: My guess would be that actors would be much more difficult, because in acting your only substance is yourself. At least a writer has this other thing, which may be only an extension of yourself, but .... I like to talk to people who have other things to talk about than themselves too. I would think an actor would be about the hardest type to interview.

BENNETT: What was the chronological order in which you wrote the *Oranging of America* stories?

APPLE: Gosh, I don't even remember. I'd just guess. The first one was "The Oranging of America." Let me see that copy of it. The second was probably "Selling Out," which is second in the book. The editor put these in order, but I think that was second. "Noon" was probably third. Maybe "Vegetable Love" and then "The Yogurt of Vasirin Kefirovsky" and "Understanding Alvarado"—no, I'm wrong. "Alvarado" was before the food stories.

BENNETT: Before "Vegetable Love"?

APPLE: Yes. Then maybe "Inside Norman Mailer" and "Gas Stations" and "Real Estate," and I think the last one was "Patty Cake, Patty Cake." That was the one written shortly after Ford became president. I was from Grand Rapids, and everybody was asking me questions about him. I didn't really want to talk about it, and so somehow my imagination got rid of that as a subject. I was always surprised by that story: I didn't mean to be coy about who the character was. I called him G. R., and it seemed that everybody would know who it was, but a lot of people told me that they didn't guess. I didn't intend that. It was just a kind of lucky accident. You get effects that you don't count on.

BENNETT: Those may be the best kinds of effects.

APPLE: I'm sure there's some Georgia writer doing the same thing about President Carter. Just trying to escape talking about Carter all the time. Everybody in America is interested in public figures. I mean, I'm not particularly interested in Ford. I'm interested in politics, but I was no more knowledgeable about Ford than anyone who came from Wisconsin or Idaho. So my imagination was forced to work.

BENNETT: How did you come to write "Vegetable Love"?

APPLE: For a while my wife and I had a little vegetable shop. It was the porch of an old building. We were just walking by one day—it was a block from Rice—and a fellow was opening a tiny shopping mall he had made from an old house. He said he had just the porch left. So we decided to do it—go into business. I had just sold "Understanding Alvarado," and so with the few hundred dollars we went into business the next day. We had a little vegetarian health-food shop. I didn't realize how skimpy the profits would be when we were selling herbs and spices and, you know, a few dried beans. Really it was almost an eighteenth-century store rather than a nineteenth-century. I figured I'd get rich. But it was nice. Our little girl would play up there, and my wife enjoyed not being so isolated in the house with the little kid. But we didn't make any money. We were making a hundred percent profit. But when you sell an ounce of marjoram, say, and make a hundred percent markup, if you sell it for ninety cents you just make forty-five cents. We were paying a hundred dollars a month rent, and we figured if we were making three dollars a day we were breaking even. We closed up when we made three dollars a day. Three dollars a day! We did it for almost a year. My mind was on vegetarian food at that time. I don't know exactly when I wrote the story—sometime in there. Again, not that I knew so much about vegetarianism, but that people would think that I did. I was a skinny guy with a beard hanging around a health-food store, and it was like they figured I'd know something about Gerald Ford. So you kind of make it up.

BENNETT: Is Kefirovsky meant to be Velikovsky?

APPLE: Immanuel Velikovsky, yes. I changed that one. The editor of the *Georgia Review*, John Irwin, said that I should change it, although I think everybody would know it's Velikovsky. I had never really read Velikovsky's stuff, but he was in the air. I knew his theories without having read them, in a popular way.

BENNETT: He has collected some disciples in recent years.

APPLE: I think that story came very much from being at Rice, from being around scientists all the time.

BENNETT: Velikovsky seems to be becoming more respectable.

APPLE: I guess so. I don't really keep up, but now and then you see a big ad for a new book on him. I think he has as many detractors scientifically as he does admirers. But I had fun writing that story, imagining scientists.

BENNETT: How long do you labor over a story?

APPLE: No set time. Sometimes you put a story away a while.

"Vegetable Love" took me a year. Not constant writing, but I wrote a part here, a part there. I never knew where it was going, and so I would wait, do other things in between. Others have come very quickly. The Norman Mailer story I think I wrote within two weeks maybe. That one seemed to come quickly. It just varies. I think with a story the quicker you can do it the better off you are. The longer it lingers, the less likely it is to be a story, I think. Your imagination is always building, and it could just as well be a novel.

BENNETT: In English scholarship we have to slot writing into classifications——

APPLE: Indeed I know.

BENNETT: ——and it isn't easy to cram reality into the slots.

APPLE: We're lucky we have centuries. I'm still old-fashioned enough to do it by centuries. Now I know there are all these other tags. When I was in college, Modernism was still pretty much in, but now there are five different varieties of whatever happened after Modernism. I have no idea what Post-Modernism is, the new avant garde. But ask the question you were moving toward.

BENNETT: You have a distinct attitude toward reality. How would characterize yourself?

APPLE: I couldn't. Other people have asked me questions about it—am I consciously trying to be avant garde?—or have called my stories Post-Modern. In all honesty, I'm just trying to write. I'm moved by the great nineteenth-century writers, by Chekov or Babel, say. Those are my idols, whom I emulate. Obviously it's not what I'm writing. Maybe in the economy I'm greatly influenced by someone like Babel. In trying to write quickly, those staccato sentences. And I don't care very much for description. I think I'm wedded to short forms too; whatever I write is short novels, short stories. There is a certain speed in what I aim for.

BENNETT: But you look back to the nineteenth century?

APPLE: I've had a very conventional kind of education. Because I've gone through college and graduate school, I've read a lot of wonderful English novels and stories. So I'm of course conscious of all sorts of styles. But I think that then when you become a writer is when you find your own voice. Those things that are in your mind are not really models for you so much as they are models for the language. Maybe the only order you have is grammar.

BENNETT: Our literary forebears tell you how but not what.

APPLE: The preplay of the imagination finally becomes just play.

George Eliot and Tolstoy and all the rest of them, they become like great Tinkertoys of the past. It's a terrible image, maybe, for them, but it's finally just playfulness. Because everything is still possible for you. Otherwise you're trapped. I mean, I remember hearing—in my graduate-school days and in a lot of those years when I wasn't writing—I remember hearing teachers say things like the novel is a closed chapter, finished—that Joyce exhausted the possibilities of the novel. And I think I probably believed those things at the time. It now seems to me a terrible mistake for people to think those things. Joyce didn't exhaust it; nobody's exhausted it. Prose fiction may go other ways. Everything is changing all the time. The imagination is still lively, and living writers have a great advantage over dead writers.

BENNETT: I tend to agree with you about the last.

APPLE: You know, at moments, particularly in serious graduate-school education, you tend to forget that. You become so immersed, say, in the complexity of Joyce or the wonder of Shakespeare. Recently I've been looking into some of those writers again, handling them for the first time since I was a graduate student. I was aware, of course, of the tremendous play, the verbal fun that was going on in the middle of Shakespeare. But I'm rediscovering such things as when Hamlet says to the ghost, "Well said, old mold"—this is a hysterical line to me. I think it's really important for writers not to be scared by the great geniuses of the past. None of us is going to be a Shakespeare or a Joyce, but it's wonderful that we're not.

BENNETT: *Zip* was your first novel? Had you ever written one before?

APPLE: I had written one that hasn't been published, a novel I wrote while I was in graduate school.

BENNETT: Is the earlier novel much different from your present work?

APPLE: I don't think so. It's a historical novel about the Russo-Japanese War. I was doing the same thing, making up people and giving them real names. Long before I'd ever been aware of anybody doing it. That somehow was just the stuff I was interested in. But you can't go back to something you've done many years before. No, I shouldn't say that: I read that Thomas Mann went back to some of his old notes—what, thirty years later—and wrote *Dr. Faustus*. Maybe you can; I don't know.

BENNETT: In your fiction you often focus on characters working. In a lot of fiction you only see the characters before they leave for breakfast, or when they come home for supper.

APPLE: I'm glad you noticed that. I'm interested in the work that people do. I wouldn't say that I had consciously thought of that, or that anyone had ever pointed it out, but I'm glad you did. I hadn't been conscious of what I do in the stories, but I know that in life I'm interested in what people do. I mean, that's the essential issue: how we work. Strangely enough, one of the real reasons that I wanted to be a writer is that, in my youthful utopian socialism, I never really wanted to exploit other people's labor. Of course, now I would be happy to. And probably do—a secretary or anybody else whenever I can. Maybe that was after the fact—I wanted to be a writer, but then as one looks for things to do, writing seemed to me to be a kind of innocent capitalism. Benign capitalism. I knew what I wanted to be—not that I ever thought I would make any money. But anyway, that idea of how people work, what they do, is central to their lives and has always been a big part of them. And if you manipulate large numbers of people or masses of money, that's different. Big numbers change the way you perceive the world. Maybe that's why I show individuals.

BENNETT: *Zip* gives the reader a good feeling of what it's like to work in a junkyard. You have a stock-market story, the motel business. People really work in your stories.

APPLE: As I say, I'm much interested in business. I'm not interested in suburban fiction, those other kinds of stories you were talking about. Updike is a wonderful writer, and he can do all of that, but he has moved in a lot of directions because he's such a virtuoso that he can write all sorts of things. But I'm not interested in yet another version of the Joyce story, where the tired man comes home to have a squabble with his wife. That may be as real as working in a steel mill, but somehow I'm interested in other stuff. Anyway, personal troubles come out as you're talking about work.

BENNETT: Do you have any advice for anyone trying to write short stories?

APPLE: I would advise them just to keep writing. There aren't very many magazines that pay anything, or even that publish short stories these days, compared to what there were even ten years ago, certainly twenty years ago. Commercially it may already be a dead form. Still it seems to me that it's been one of the wonderful forms, particularly in American literary history. Some of the great Americans used it. Even now some of the most exciting writers are working in shorter forms—some of Coover's best stuff is short, some of Donald Barthelme's. John Barth has been a wonderful innovator. Jorge Borges. We're talking about some of the great figures of contemporary literature. Kafka wrote wonderful short stuff too, as well as long fiction. But then at the same time there are no places to publish them; there's no way to make money.

BENNETT: I read in some memoirs recently about a turn-of-the-century editor contracting with an established writer for six magazine stories to be published in a year. Nobody would do that now.

APPLE: Jessica, my daughter, has a poem published, by the way, in the most recent *Paris Review*. I was in Berkeley recently, and a woman came up to me to say she'd read the poem and thought it was terrific. I got as much pleasure out of that as any literary criticism anyone gave my own work. I was writing a story for an anthology that's not going to come out until 1980. This is as close as you get today, I guess, to that writer being solicited for six stories. Now and then people ask me to write a little thing. *Rolling Stone* solicited regular fiction writers to write quasi-children's stories, and it sounded like a legitimate idea. I came home and told Jessica about it. I thought maybe she'd draw a picture. She said she wanted to do her own, so I took down dictation. My son, Sam, also told some stories, and I would sit at this desk and write them down. He would be holding a pencil, and he'd say, "This little pencil tap on your head"—that was Sam's story. We had a lot of fun doing that for about a week, and Jessica did a couple of things that were really good. So I sent one of hers along with mine. I was shamed into writing a story. I don't know that I really intended to do it, but after she had written hers . . . .

BENNETT: I gather you played sports in school. Are you still active?

APPLE: When we were in California, my nephews and I tried to play baseball. I realized I'm through as a ballplayer; I can't bend down for grounders anymore. I'm a runner and thought I was in pretty good shape. I did play, and I'm still a great fan. I played second base.

BENNETT: But you still run.

APPLE: Running is, you know, middle-aged stuff.

BENNETT: How do you think of yourself as a writer? A serious writer? A comic writer? What?

APPLE: Probably comic. I don't strive for the punch line. I'm looking for the irony, in the sounds. I'm not looking for one line, the single-line comedy. On the whole I'd say I would consider what I've written comic, although I thought there was a lot in the novel that was sad.

BENNETT: Are you personally acquainted with many writers?

APPLE: A few. Writers are sociable and not so sociable. We like to meet each other, but we don't like to talk about writing too much. I know Shelby Hearon; I know C. W. Smith, in Dallas. Just at this conference this summer, for the first time, I met a lot of writers: Grace Paley and Ed Doctorow and Joe Heller. And this wonderful—Maxine Hong Kingston. Do you know her book, *The Woman Warrior*? She lives in Hawaii. Earlier I met Leon Hale at a P.E.N. conference we had in Houston two years ago—I met a lot of people there too.

BENNETT: Have you read *Humboldt's Gift*?

APPLE: No, but I met Bellow. He gave a lecture at Rice.

BENNETT: In the novel Von Humbolt feels cheated because he does not rub shoulders with writers in the republic of letters.

APPLE: I especially enjoyed being with those writers in California this summer. I would like to—just the way I suppose anybody would like to—be able to talk to other people in their line of work. Beverly Lowry lives in Houston, and is a good friend of mine too. But I realize we are pretty isolated, compared to some, just from seeing all of the West Coast writers. The few times I've been in New York, I see it is a little different. The writers may not see each other regularly, but it's nice that they do see one another when they can.

BENNETT: What are you occupied with now?

APPLE: I'm about to begin editing a book for Bantam on Southwest writers. A book of stories, from the thirties until contemporary.

BENNETT: Right up through Larry McMurtry.

APPLE: I know Larry McMurtry. He lives in Washington. He's a wonderful talker, and he had the job that I have now at Rice, before I came. He quit, I guess, after *The Last Picture Show* was made into a movie. I'm a great admirer of his.

BENNETT: Are there any Texas writers that you particularly admire?

APPLE: Well, I like Larry. And I like Beverly, and I like Shelby—just about everybody that I've met. Stylistically and in a lot of ways I'm very different from Larry, but I feel close to his writing too. Maybe it's the vein of wit. It's hard to talk about contemporaries, especially people you know.

BENNETT: You hate to say unkind things about them.

APPLE: No, if the writing is bad, I'm not interested in it. I don't want to read bad writing, and I can usually tell the things I don't like. You know, I'm essentially unacquainted with popular literature, again because I hang around universities. There's so much good stuff today, and there's still all the good stuff in the past that I'm never going to be able to catch up on. I don't have time to bother with *The Valley of the Dolls*.

BENNETT: There have been a few serious studies of pop writers.

APPLE: I'm interested in them sociologically, but not interested enough to read their fiction. You wonder why great masses of people read it, or watch police stories on television. It's actually just formula stuff. Why gothics?

BENNETT: It may be somewhat reassuring to a reader to know what he will read in advance.

APPLE: Yes, I don't doubt that. But I think there's a great gulf in American popular culture. I think if good books were as widely distributed as *The Valley of the Dolls*, they would be sold. I could be wrong. I mean, obviously the good things on Public Broadcasting television are seen. More people watch *Upstairs, Downstairs* than *Kojak*, I think.

June, 1979

Shelby Hearon: *Time, Sex, and God*

SHELBY REED HEARON was born January 18, 1931, in Marion, Kentucky. She earned her B.A. in 1953 from the University of Texas in Austin. Since the appearance of her 1968 novel, *Armadillo in the Grass*, Hearon has devoted herself to writing, teaching at the University of Texas, and lecturing.

Hearon lives in a thinly populated development just inside the frontier of expanding Austin. A platoon of hounds met us at the fence, barking, uncertain whether to lick a hand or bite a leg. Her house is a two-story copy of an 1840s German stone farmhouse. It has gallery porches, top and bottom, and a red-metal roof. Every room goes all the way through the house: "It's wonderful in the summer and kind of chilly in the winter."

Upstairs her study is a narrow room with a desk and typewriter in the center, flanked by wooden bookcases jammed with volumes. Out on the upper gallery you can see the cats, which live up there out of deference to the dogs, with whom they have old quarrels.

We talked downstairs in the living room, which is full of grays and tans. The sofa and two overstuffed chairs are covered with a nubby gray material. A papier-mâché elephant stands at one side, unpainted, the old newspapers showing through its coat of clear shellac. Black-and-white prints hang on the walls.

Hearon wore faded blue jeans, a loose-flowing big-top blouse, sandals. She is a trim five foot seven with light-brown hair and hazel eyes. Her face has had a lot of sun and is generally in motion—talking, smiling, laughing. She lights a cigarette when the thinking gets tough.

Occasionally the animal life outside interrupted our talk, a dog barking or a cat meowing, a bird that caught Hearon's eye, a cat cautiously descending a gallery support outside.

BENNETT: One of the major ideas in all your books is time.
HEARON: That's interesting; I've never really been conscious of it,

but I suppose I am rather preoccupied with time. I personally like very much to have every piece of time colored by several different schemes—calendar time, liturgical time, geologic time, personal time—so that in doing a book I probably, without thinking about it, find out where my people are relating themselves to time, by what frames they move. In *Now and Another Time* you had the woman who was on church time; you had several different time frames in there with different people. Certainly in *The Second Dune* you have geologic time. I figure out where everybody is on sex, God, and time. These are not conscious things; it's just that you have to know that about somebody.

BENNETT: The characters in your novels are glutted with time. A woman will cross a street and thinks of her mother once crossing it and wonders when her daughter will cross it ....

HEARON: I think that was quite true in *The Second Dune*. But I also think those flashes were for her an effort to relate to the world's time, more than her own generation's time. For instance, her going annually to the beach on her birthday was not so much a pilgrimage as an attempt to mark notches on time as the world saw it.

BENNETT: The same thing happens in *A Prince of a Fellow* when Avery thinks of her mother.

HEARON: Yes, laughing in that picture. Also when she goes back to the boy at the dance in the mountains of Kentucky. I think she uses the past as a warning, rather negatively, as a prod, for where she is going to be in relation to her mother in that picture. Whenever she goes back to the boy in high school, she's thinking that that was the most real thing that happened sexually. And what happened? Nothing. I think she remembers her father in a coal-mining state, and her grandmother wringing the necks of those birds, and those shirts. I think all her memories are warnings. Our way of saying, "Look, this is how it has been in the past and is probably the way it will be again, and it doesn't look good." And Minna's past is bad too. I am trying to show how within the framework of time you can break out of that.

BENNETT: Are you a determinist?

HEARON: I dislike that term already. That there is no way you will not be where you are. I'm more of a determinist than I wish I were. In theory I believe that you can escape the past. I felt that in *Now and Another Time* I've said what R. D. Laing says so well: We are all living out dreams, the dreams of others. We are all acting out parts of plays we haven't read, and in that book everyone became the unfulfilled wishes of the generation before them. When I finished that book, I thought, This is so negative I cannot bear this. I also thought, I hope New York doesn't know that. [*laughs*]

When I started *A Prince of a Fellow*, it was to deal with that very issue. It was to say, "Yes-but." In the fairy stories you're always condemned to die, and then one fairy comes up from behind and says, "Yes-but I'll mitigate that sentence, and you'll only sleep for one hundred years." A yes-but implies a feeling that we cannot help but be who we are, and I was trying to say, "Yes-but some of us get out of that. Some of us make our own selves." Maybe the reason I gave everybody a bad past was to show how Avery does do that and Minna doesn't do that. How does one do that? All of Avery's unconscious decisions are good, I thought, where all of Minna's unconscious decisions were bad. All of Avery's conscious ones weren't. You know: she was fucking the mayor of San Antonio, which you probably didn't like, but still in her mind she knows what that is and what it's doing or not doing. Avery's not pretending as Minna is with the guy in Washington that she's madly in love with the mayor. She sees something more valid when it comes along; she pursues it. Sometimes you can pull together other possibilities from what you've been given.

BENNETT: Sometimes, yes.

HEARON: I could use the cemeteries in *A Prince of a Fellow* because I felt it was a very positive book. You're not going to be weighed down by all the segregated dead people, yeah. I couldn't have put the cemeteries in *Now and Another Time*.

BENNETT: Somewhere I read you have a Kentucky governor in your background. Weren't you named for him?

HEARON: Yes, Shelby; his last name was Shelby. There are a lot of Shelbys in Texas—that's because General Shelby knocked up a lot of people.

BENNETT: Do you feel the weight of your own past?

HEARON: Oh, not in that sense. My mother also has found us the first governor of Vermont. There was also the ancestor who was hanged as an Irish rebel. You can always count on one with the other. But, yes, very much so in the psychological sense, very much in the sense that Laing was talking about. And in the whole daughter-mother-daughter way which certainly is not, we would all agree, I think [*laughs*], in the sense of family, like a lot of my people have family. But the whole social setting of *Now and Another Time*, and even *The Second Dune*, was more set in what I married into.

BENNETT: Your novels seem to have a three-act structure——

HEARON: I do think in play terms, perhaps that is true. I certainly think in theater terms; I think it is because I am very visual.

BENNETT: We once discussed a musical analogy to your work. You seem to counterpoint themes—the two divorces in *The Second Dune*, for instance.

HEARON: I do that fairly consciously, because it is a way of keeping the author from presenting it to you as black and white, as just this way. Particularly in the first person you want to make sure you're getting about ten other views of the same event. The place that pleased me most about doing that was at the end of *Now and Another Time*— and this is a very minor thing—where she is wearing a navy dress to the swearing-in. Five different people think about that navy dress. No two ever see anything the same way. That idea ended *Now and Another Time* and became the theme of *A Prince of a Fellow*. Yes, divorce may look this way today, but it looks that way if you stand here, or if you stand here.... You have to do that to make it feel like real life, which is quite ambiguous, in which there is never anything that is absolutely true because it depends on who is seeing it or who is saying it.

BENNETT: In *Hannah's House* you see it all through the mother.

HEARON: Yes, but then the daughter finally gets to make you see that the mother has been wrong all along—I think. I was the daughter in that book. At first you're seeing it all from the mother's point of view. Then I'm saying, "Don't you realize it looked like that because you're standing here? Come stand over here and look at it." This mother is a loser; she is a dreadful woman.

BENNETT: You think the mother is a loser?

HEARON: Oh, I do! Oh, she is! Oh, I liked her, but I think you had to have that other perspective on her. You absolutely had to see there was a whole other side to the story and that the daughter had led an absolutely miserable life. She was never going to please her mother— the very complaint the mother had about her own mother. Foster could never please her own mother, and now she dumped that on her daughter. You had to see that.

BENNETT: Let's talk about illusion and reality in *A Prince of a Fellow*.

HEARON: Nobody is what they seem. Minna is really a fat girl playing the piano. The mother turns out to be good after all. I was really trying to say that out loud, instead of that business about the navy dress, which is another way of dealing with determinism, because it is a way I feel you can break the pattern of living out the dreams of others, living the agreed-upon script. If you once say that black is white, up is down, in is out, then already you've escaped by simply seeing that nothing is what it seems. That is the way she got out.

BENNETT: The names of your characters seem very important to you. How do you choose them?

HEARON: I didn't know they were important. You're giving me revelations. I'll tell you an interesting story about that. They come to me wholly; they are just presented. When the character is there, the name is there. The woman in my *Painted Dresses* is named Nell Woodard. I've never heard that name before and do not know where it comes from. I was busily trying to pick a San Antonio name with society overtones, and this name would not go away. My daughter was in Sarah Lawrence, and so *Now and Another Time* was the only book she had not read as I went along. She came home at Christmas, read what I had written, wrote down the names, and went back to look up what the meaning of the names was. It was incredible. The names were just right! My subconscious had just been lapping it up. She says that Hannah is an older form of Ann, and I had of course named the daughter for her and didn't know it.

BENNETT: I've read that Georges Simenon picks his names from the telephone directory.

HEARON: I tried to do that, but they're already there. And I do think names are important to the persons who have them. In *Hannah's House* the woman's not liking her name was part of her whole crazy, disorganized personality. "Bananas" she called herself, and "Foster" she called herself, and "Beverly" she never called herself; she couldn't get a sense of identification with her name. And Avery, in *Prince*, finding out her name did have some meaning to her mother—it mattered to her.

There was a lot about names in *Now and Another Time*. The way the daughter named Sarah became like this, and Mary like that. But that was all part of living out the dreams of the past. The child is imprinted that way from the moment he or she is named. That's sort of the negative aspect of naming.

BENNETT: Were you imprinted with Shelby?

HEARON: Yes, very much, because my mother's mother died when my mother was fifteen. Her mother was Evelyn Shelby Roberts, and so I was named Evelyn Shelby. My mother's name was also Evelyn

Shelby, and so I was third in line: very significant. But I was the first one who was called Shelby. That would have been too androgynous for earlier situations. I was also very imprinted by having an androgynous name growing up. Of course, I was growing up in the heart of Peggys and Anns and Barbaras, and I liked that a whole lot. Still, I've met women named Taylor and Johnson and [*laughs*] whatever it was time for in the family. It actually gives you a good feeling that the good name is going on whether you were male or female.

BENNETT: Did you name your daughter Shelby too?

HEARON: Yes, I named her Anne Shelby, and she goes by Anne. That's her option. I also thought it was time to get back to a clearly female name. She was named for Anne Boleyn, and she likes that.

BENNETT: Have you done much magazine work?

HEARON: No, I've done some pieces for *Texas Monthly*, and one for *Redbook*, and one for *Publishers Weekly*, and three for the *Writer* magazine, and that's it.

BENNETT: Did you do some fiction for *Redbook*?

HEARON: These were all articles. No, I did what they call a novella for *Redbook*, which means a book that never got into print, is what it really means. It was a wonderful reprieve, because the book was not going to get into hardback. It is a wonderful way to recoup your losses, but probably had I written it as a novella I couldn't have sold it. I was sort of overshooting my market. I've never written any short fiction; I do not understand the short story; I was absent the day they taught short story.

BENNETT: Had you sold anything to magazines before your first novel?

HEARON: No.

BENNETT: I was looking at book titles upstairs in your study. Let me ask you about your favorites.

HEARON: All my favorites may not be up there. I don't have in my possession all the books I want. I guess my very favorites are there: Jorge Borges and Gertrude Stein and some of those.

BENNETT: How long do you work at a stretch?

HEARON: If I am doing first-draft work, I'm mostly a morning writer. Before they messed me up with daylight saving time, I would work, oh, seven to maybe eleven, a good morning stretch. Then I usually don't work in the afternoon, and sometimes I work at night. I write in longhand. In the afternoon I try to do things like type up what I've written, answer my mail, redo stuff like article galleys, or whatever. But not the alpha-waves first-draft business.

Now, working on the Barbara Jordan book, I had a much hairier schedule and was really working ten to fourteen hours a day. But again it was not first-draft work, not alpha waves, not coming from my subconscious. It was mostly rewrite, and I rewrite at great long stretches, because it helps to do the book in as much of a unit as you can.

When I'm doing, say, a third draft, which I hope is going to be a last draft, I'm pretty much working in three shifts: morning, afternoon, and night. I try to go through it as fast as I can, to get the flow and keep the tone of voice. You can't do that on first drafts, because they come from way down inside. You can only tap way down inside so long without surfacing.

BENNETT: When you're writing fiction, how many words a day can you write?

HEARON: Probably about ten pages. A lot. I write fast, and I rewrite and I rewrite and I rewrite.

BENNETT: Do you write in pencil?

HEARON: Yes. I'm thinking ... Ten typed pages—that's two thousand words, something like that. I write very fast because I find that hidden in the mass of the first draft will be what I really need to say. If I go slow and thoughtful, punctuating and being correct, I lose that. Somewhere in that flow is what I need to say; I may not know what I meant to say.

I don't like doing first drafts on the typewriter. I'll do some scratching out as I go along, or moving things down, but mostly I don't. Some things you know are just awful right at the second.

BENNETT: Do you use an outline?

HEARON: I hate answers that say, "Yes and no." I always think through the structure of the book, and then the finished product seldom bears any relation to the structure I have thought through. You have to have something to begin, to hang it on, the scenes you're going to use. So you've thought through the structure that is going to tell the story, and of course that just turns out not to be so. Yes, I work from a vague outline, but, no, it doesn't do much good. You realize, when you are working with those people in that place, that is not what would happen.

BENNETT: How many times do you revise?

HEARON: With my first book, revision meant total rewriting. The second draft had no words in it from the first. The third draft had ten pages from the second draft. I don't know whether I've gotten better or I've lowered my standards. At any rate, revision still means throwing out a lot. It is very seldom that you can rewrite just by pencil editing; that's really a cocky attitude. It always means taking the whole thing apart. Something is good, but it shouldn't be said in this place. Perhaps two women were having coffee, and I meant it to be a small thing, and it turned out they were saying something that was vital to the whole story, a theme that was going to come back, which I didn't know when I set them down to have coffee. So—I'm thinking of *A Prince of a Fellow*—I move them into a cemetery scene, because cemeteries were also a motif, and I wanted it somewhere where it was picking up on something larger. That conversation between Avery and Minna that took place in the cemetery began somewhere else, in the first chapter, strangely enough. A piece of it stayed the same. But that meant something else was placed somewhere else also . . . .

BENNETT: I've read that Nabokov wrote on index cards and reshuffled them.

HEARON: [*laughs*] A wonderful plan. His point was very valid, and he probably didn't write the whole book on them; he probably wrote preliminary notes. I can see that you would do that.

BENNETT: Have you written any poetry?

HEARON: Yes, I wrote poetry in high school. I think one writes poetry in high school because it's quicker. And you don't sit down and write a novel in high school. I wrote whatever those other things are called, character studies or themes or whatever, but I never did any fiction except insofar as they are fiction. I wrote some poetry, and it's not all bad. I guess if you're young at least some honesty shines through. I've never sent any off.

BENNETT: Your style is very poetic.

HEARON: In the sense that poetry is very condensed and very spare and a lot hangs on each word, I think that's true. I'm not sure it's true in the sense that poetry is heavily metaphoric.

BENNETT: But you have an almost musical development at times. You introduce a theme and then introduce a second theme to counterpoint it.

HEARON: I think that's right, and I feel a sense of meter or cadence, but maybe music is a better example. Because it seems to me in poetry everything stands for something else: a cat is never just a cat. That bothers me because, in a Zen sense, I like it to be just what it is and not carry the weight of a symbol.

BENNETT: Do you have any favorite Texas writers?

HEARON: John Graves. [*laughs*] John Graves is—now get this on tape—the best writer in Texas. Well, that's rather limiting, isn't it? He's one of the best writers I've ever read. Absolutely beautifully put-together words. I like Beverly Lowry's work; she's a friend of mine in Houston who has done two novels.

BENNETT: What about Texas writers who are dead?

HEARON: No one comes to mind. This must be a grave omission. Oh yes, I like Walter Prescott Webb. But I love Roy Bedichek. When I moved to Texas, I read Bedichek, and then when I started *Armadillo in the Grass*, I went back and reread some of him. I was trying to tell what the mountain laurel smells like or tastes like. That's one reason I don't like similes and metaphors: mountain laurel smells like mountain laurel. But I decided it smells like grape, actually artificial grape flavoring. Anyway, I went to Bedichek, and actually he says something about "the grapey mountain-laurel smell." Well, thank you, Roy. I checked with him on a number of things in the beginning to substantiate my impression that this is what the mockingbirds are like, or whatever—things that are very Texas things that I was not sure I had the background for. After being reinforced by him repeatedly, I quit that.

BENNETT: Do you have any advice for beginning writers?

HEARON: Well, I taught last spring, and am going to teach this spring, and so I was put in the reluctant position of giving advice to writers. I found that beginners use too many adjectives and that they speak much too generally. It was a matter of getting them to be quite concrete. They did oral histories, and that was helpful to them. They could see what makes the speech of the sixty-year-old jazz musician sound like him all the way through, and what made their grandmother in East Texas sound like her. They could see the consistency of allusion and speech pattern. The most amateur of them was still writing about a real person who, as Stein says, repeats himself all the time.

A number of them thought of writing as a gift you have, whatever that means. Therefore you sit down and exercise that gift. They did not think of it as an ongoing exercise, like jogging, which you have to do all the time. They were also attached to their own words, something which no good writer ever is. I didn't get past that; I didn't cure that.

BENNETT: Let's talk about themes in your work.

HEARON: What I mean by themes is something I'm going to use as a backdrop. I write very much in theater terms in my head. I think of method-acting the parts; I think of setting the stage; I think of the backdrops. So, when I'm dealing with the Germans in New Braunfels,

I feel in them a life denied, gritting their teeth, cinching their belts, not really liking living very much. Then I found out they actually do have nine fenced cemeteries over there, and I became enchanted with segregation in death. That also seemed to me a motif of the Germans: to segregate everybody. So here was segregation and death all rolled up into one ball. I felt the cemeteries were a theme too in the sense that Avery, in *A Prince of a Fellow*, goes to her favorite one on her way to the mayor, and she meets Minna in one of them, and papa is dug out of another one of them and replanted in another one of them—we have a number of them running through there.

BENNETT: In all your novels the heroines seem fond of out-of-doors.

HEARON: I'm not sure that was true of *A Prince of a Fellow*. I don't think that woman ever went outside in *Hannah's House*. In the first two that was very true of that natural-history-book sort of thing. The woman in *Now and Another Time* had that nice swimming place. Well, I am, and the books certainly reflect that.

I think in *Armadillo* the outdoors represented her as being more comfortable with animals than people, and I think in *The Second Dune* the outdoors represented her different way of looking at times. I'm not sure they were just nature lovers. That was probably more true in *Now and Another Time*, where they really liked the country and liked to swim.

BENNETT: Somebody said you can read a long way in French fiction and never see a tree.

HEARON: Well, I felt that way about *Hannah's House*. Small stage set to the kitchen; you see light come onto the kitchen . . . .

BENNETT: Sex is very important in your novels.

HEARON: I have to know where everybody stands on God and sex and time. Not in that order: time, sex, and God, probably. Well, I think sex is very important, not just important in my books. What actually takes place in my books is just a way of showing you where they are in their heads. I think you have to know how they see themselves as female or male, how they see other people and the interaction between male and female, because I think our first concept of ourselves is or should be as that sex. You come to consciousness as male or female.

BENNETT: Do you have any opinions on how sexual intercourse should be handled in fiction?

HEARON: No. My mother has had some unkind words with me

about the sex in *Now and Another Time*. I tried to explain that that just happened, how explicit it is or isn't, or even how much there is or isn't of actual intercourse, in the book is a by-product of the people you're dealing with. Somebody complained to me that in *Hannah's House* the woman didn't really like sex, and somebody complained that in *Now and Another Time* there wasn't really any sex. Well, this is absurd. With Foster that's not what was jamming the wires, or what was motivating her, either, and so it took a very minor place. In *Now and Another Time*, where I have the most graphic sex, I was trying to make some statements about intimacy and to use Julie and Jimmy to speak of intimacy and where it comes from and what it feels like. I didn't want to fall into the trap of having it nonsexual, which is begging the issue, or of having it impotent sex, which had offended me in *The War Between the Tates* and *Fear of Flying*. In both of those cases the woman had an adulterous relationship and the guy was impotent, which is really saying, "I'm not offering you an alternative to that marriage." I didn't like that message. If they were going to have sex, the sex was okay, because I'm saying that's not what we were talking about. We were talking about intimacy. Yeah, they do, and, yeah, it's okay. I had to have some sex that was wholly successful, chapter four in the sex manual, which was not producing intimacy, by way of contrast. That's how all that sex got in there.

BENNETT: That's also true in *A Prince of a Fellow*.

HEARON: Right, we have a little screwing around with the mayor. It bothered some of them at the publishing house, and I never could get this across: but if you don't have a little bit of screwing around with the mayor in which you're saying, okay, so this is what making sex feels like, looks like, smells like, then how can you make the point when she finally achieves a small level of intimacy with the writer? They are doing the same thing and doing it the same way, and there's all the difference in the world. When I went back to the dance in the coal-mine country, I was trying to say that that actually had been intimacy, and no sex had taken place.

BENNETT: Dr. Alan Strout used to say there would be precious little literature without adultery.

HEARON: I think so too. It's a depressing thought. That certainly was not a central theme in *A Prince of a Fellow*, but even there you've got the mayor. Certainly it could have been cleaner, and we'd have had a nonadulterous book had he been a bachelor, but it would have been a lie.

BENNETT: In *Now and Another Time* you seem to say adultery is okay.

HEARON: Oh, I'm not sure it is ever okay, but you have it as one of the two themes. You have the woman in Houston who did not have the affair, and the man in Jasper County who did not become a judge; so in the present you've got to have an affair and become the judge. Again, to use your term, which is not how I originally thought of it, I was dealing with the whole business of determinism. I was saying, "Yes, he became judge, but in a very shallow, stylized way that had none of the integrity of his father." And, "Yes, she had the affair, but she broke through the inevitability of having it, and in addition achieved an intimacy which was not in the script. Within the given, I thought you could have it two ways: you could live out the dream, and it could be either less or more than what was in your script.

BENNETT: Are you interested in this Transactional Analysis business, with its scripts?

HEARON: No, I'm very negative about that. I'm very negative about *I'm OK, You're OK*. I'm not using script in that sense, but more as a play script. Maybe that's where they stole it from, but it has come to mean something rather computerized, and I don't mean that at all. "Parent tape" and "children tape" is enough to ignite me on the spot. "You're playing your parent tape," people say to each other when they're having a big bloody fight. I know parents who swallowed that and are making miserable home situations where they used to be doing fine when they were just crazy, and their kids were kind of crazy—energy was taking place; creativity was taking place—they were not okay.

BENNETT: In at least two of your novels you seem to be saying that adultery's all right where there is love, and not all right where there is no love.

HEARON: No, I'm not. I think that adultery is adultery, that what the mayor did and what Jimmy did are not different. They may feel different to you, because nothing is the same to everybody. But to the person out here watching, they may be the same thing, and the same judgment may be passed. I'm not passing judgment in either case. You the reader may pass judgment in both cases, but in that case they both have to be treated the same.

BENNETT: So you don't condemn them.

HEARON: But I'm not sanctioning them. I don't think the novelist can sit in judgment, because then you very subtly begin to manipulate the strings of your puppet. I feel that you should care for the mayor, perhaps as much as Jimmy, in fiction, because you see all of him, where in real life you might hate him. This is one of the things fiction offers you: a charity you do not get in real life. I think the same is true of the judge. I felt very kindly toward him and felt we saw pieces of him in fiction that allowed us to have charity, which we might not have felt if we had known him.

BENNETT: Let's talk about one or two things that are not in your novels. McMurtry uses music to evoke moods, but you don't use it that way.

HEARON: No, because you can't hear it in a book. I think it is quite artificial. They're always quoting lyrics in books, and if you're not hearing it, it just doesn't do the same thing. I mean, you can always say that she put on the last act of *Il Trovatore*; well, what does that do for your reader?

The same is true of a whole lot of visual things which if you can't see them I'm not going to use them. In *The Second Dune*, for instance, the leather elephant that cost a hundred dollars. We had that elephant, we kept that elephant, we lived with that elephant—we didn't just buy a hundred-dollar toy. Visual things like that you've got to really create and show and be able to see, for them to work.

I furnish the rooms pretty carefully that way, so you can see them. We have a lot of that lacy green bedroom, and we have a lot of that living room in *Hannah's House*. Instead of just dropping in: "It was a vivid pink and orange room," or "She was really into modern art," or, "The radio was playing."

We had musical titles all through *A Prince of a Fellow*, of course. But that was not a mood device. If she was on the radio and she was playing records, you've got to know what records she was playing. And if you don't know the musicians named, it doesn't matter. If you did, it probably didn't enhance it very much.

BENNETT: The other thing missing from your novels is violence.

HEARON: I know. I have trouble in the one I'm working on now, *Painted Dresses*. This guy who is my hero, who's dying, who's a biochemist at the Menninger Clinic, has an earlier scene in which he steals his brother's girlfriend, who has a butterfly tattoo on her shoulder. They come back from their honeymoon, and his brother has flayed and roasted his dog in the yard. And I just hate that scene! I just hate it so bad that for a while I thought I couldn't handle it. I wasn't having that in my book!

In the protected lives of the nonpoor South the violence, the damage is almost all psychological—what the family in *Prince* does to the Swedish wife or whatever. There was flogging of blacks in East Texas, but we didn't witness it. And so it's a sort of unwillingness to look at that, or to deal with that, or to know it exists—that's very much a part of the culture I write about. It is an evasion of it, not only on my part but on their part. Perhaps, again, it's like a play. When you think of O'Neill's plays, let's say, no one is tortured, raped, or beaten onstage, but a great deal of damage is done by people to each other. Whatever physical brutality takes place is offstage in their minds as well as in the audience's eyes. I do notice in fiction what often seems to me like gratuitous violence. You read something like Jerzy Kosinski, on the other hand—oh, God, it's so hard for me to take! I can hardly bear it, but it is so integral to what he is telling.

BENNETT: I've been reading Elmer Kelton, and in his western novels there is a lot more violence than sex.

HEARON: That was true then. I mean, you and your horse didn't do a whole lot.

BENNETT: Occasionally a cowboy hankers for a friend's wife and is ashamed.

HEARON: Back to adultery. I think one reason you'll get adultery in what we'll call the drawing rooms is because the lives are so circumscribed, and often the adultery didn't actually even include sex. Depending on the time and culture, there might be a burning affair of the heart that lasted two generations, but there was never consummation, or one handshake, or one letter. The adultery becomes more the nonaction, which is even true of Julie and Jimmy in *Now and Another Time*, because he is killed in a car wreck two years later coming back from Little Hills. Which is very sad. Sorry about that. We assume they got maybe two weekends in Little Hills, and that's the end of that.

BENNETT: This car accident, is it in your next novel?

HEARON: No. You have to know everything about your fictional characters, the generation before they came, and for a period of years after the book ends, to know when to end the book. So, if you'd like to know what happened to any of the rest of them . . . .

BENNETT: What happened to Julia?

HEARON: Well, Julia dies of a stroke about six years later. Both of her parents died young, and so Jimmy's wife and the judge live forever. And Louisa becomes the first woman governor of Texas, and by that time she is sort of stocky and mustached and pretty hard, as you would expect. Fay goes to England and takes a cottage and has a baby by the astronomer and gets her doctorate, and finally, in about eight years, he leaves his wife, and they get married. Her daughter's name is, of course, Mary. That takes care of all those people. Flower, the one who has Jimmy and Jo's daughter, and who ran off to New York to work for a magazine, reappears in *Painted Dresses*; she is the goddaughter of my patron. And Eleanor from *The Second Dune* reappears in *Painted Dresses*. You never did really see Flower, but you'll see Eleanor again.

BENNETT: What do you think of the musical idea in Anthony Powell's *Dance to the Music of Time*?

HEARON: I think of my work more in collage terms. You paste all the pieces on, and when you get through, it makes a big picture. In Agatha Christie's murder mysteries she'll have one person who tells the truth. I learned after I read two or three that if you can spot that truthful person you'll know who did it, because what they say is true. I also feel that is a thread that goes through my books. If you're getting lots of different views of how it looked and how it was, there has to be one person who tells the truth. Since the narrator doesn't judge, you don't want it to be the narrator—which is the trouble with a lot of books. The narrator should just be saying, "Look at all this." There must be one person in your book who can be trusted to see more nearly correctly. Usually not the main character.

BENNETT: You're saying that how a person stands on sex, time, and religion makes the difference?

HEARON: On God. I think I mean literally God, and literally deity. Because what is his religion? Well, law is his religion, and education is his religion—that's another whole thing. That's called, "What does your character love?"

BENNETT: A lot of your characters very definitely belong to one sect or another.

HEARON: I think that is because it is true culturally. The arguments in *Prince*, the church fight, and all that business—very much a part of the culture over there, in which the Evangelicals don't think the Lutherans can get there. Really bitter fighting. I knew more about that. I really had to do a good deal of research on the Episcopal church in *Now and Another Time*; I really didn't know about that.

BENNETT: What is your own background?

HEARON: My parents did not go to church. I don't think we said "atheist" at that time in rural Kentucky, surely. But they were nonbelievers. My grandparents, who lived in the same small town, went to the Methodist church. My grandmother, whom I absolutely adored, was a very big and strong churchgoer. Part of that, which I did not see at the time, was that she had nine children, and it was her principal social outlet. She always won all the prizes at all the contests, at all the circles. She was a college graduate from Virginia way back then, so she was in this town of two thousand with all those children. Some of that I tried to get into the books, that church occupies a different place in different lives.

I now belong to the Presbyterian church. My daughter married this guy who went to Yale Divinity School, and he came back to be a Presbyterian preacher. He was fired from his church, but I remained a Presbyterian. I may be the last person converted to the Presbyterian church in the twentieth century. I went back and read the original—it was called the Confession of Faith, I guess—but anyway the old scary, terrifying original thing that sets up election and all those things that they are now trying to forget are in there. They are quite wonderful. Saying things like some of us are damned and there's nothing we can do about it.

Everyone in my books is not that involved with religion. Avery was not; Foster was not—because it is not in the life of some of those people.

BENNETT: But even in *Hannah's House* there is the big church wedding, and the feeling that the daughter is drawn to that sort of thing.

HEARON: That's true, although it is certainly not a large issue. I think you feel that goes with the return to the traditional.

BENNETT: A thing that pops up in your novels is the fairy tale.

HEARON: Yeah. [*laughs*] I noticed that.

BENNETT: Is *A Prince of a Fellow* a fairy tale?

HEARON: I think it is. The *Newsweek* review was very wonderful about that and treated it as a fairy tale. Said, "As in all fairy tales, . . ." and so forth and so on. I liked that.

BENNETT: Did you have any particular fairy tale in mind?

HEARON: No, my favorites are mentioned in *The Second Dune*. I love "East of the Sun, West of the Moon," and I love the one about the twelve dancing princesses—that was in *The Second Dune*, I know. And "The Seven Brides and Seven Brothers" because I think I was having something about the seventh daughter of the seventh daughter in that one, which sort of came back in *Now and Another Time*. And the one where the prince rides up the glass mountain.

But I don't think I took any of those for—except that in fairy tales you do have that confused identity, way before Shakespeare thought of it. The princess was raised on a hog farm or whatever; the prince was taken off when he was only an infant by flying birds; the stepmother turns out to be a witch. You have that theme a lot in fairy tales. So I think in that sense it's a fairy tale. Fairy tales are wonderful about the whole issue of what is true and what is not true.

BENNETT: You have a ball where the mayor gets his comeuppance.

HEARON: Cinderella's ball, and she says, "I'm Cinderella." But also in the fairy tale the ball wasn't actually that good a time. The person has to do so many arbitrary things to get to the end. I didn't labor that, but she has to go through a certain number of hurdles that the prince throws down to get there.

BENNETT: All of your books have a party at the climax.

HEARON: They took the party out of *The Second Dune*, but in the original I had the party. But *A Prince of a Fellow* doesn't end with a party—well, it is pivotal. I hadn't thought of that. We have a party in *Armadillo*, where everybody gathers to see her work. And then we had a party at the end of *The Second Dune*, which got cut out.

BENNETT: And the reception in *Hannah's House*.

HEARON: Yes, the wedding. And in *Now and Another Time* we certainly have a party, the judge's. That's wonderful! I hadn't thought of that. Well, again, you know, I think that's theater: in the third act they're all assembled there for something, so you can finally see the interaction, or so it comes to a head.

BENNETT: I thought you were doing that on purpose.

HEARON: I don't think writers do anything on purpose.

BENNETT: You seem so well organized.

HEARON: I think it's more significant if you're not doing it on purpose. It becomes rather arbitrary if you're doing it on purpose, and I'm thinking, Now what party am I ending this book with?

BENNETT: [*examining the tape recorder*] When you were taping Barbara Jordan, did you leap up every once in a while to see if the power had failed?

HEARON: Yes, I spent my whole time watching, not Jordan, but the little red light. She has a lot to say about no eyeball contact. I was trying to think if the Jordan book ends in a party. I think it does. It kind of does. I really did work from an outline with her, and when I was mapping out the chapters, I thought, I'm going to end it at the commencement address at Harvard, which had not yet taken place, which I eventually flew up for. How did I know? So that's the party at the end, and it tied up all the loose ends. Because she went to Boston Law School, so she's back at Harvard across the river.

BENNETT: The heroine of *Armadillo* is a sculptress. One of the ladies in the sewing circle in *Now and Another Time* sculpts.

HEARON: But she doesn't really do it, which is sad.

BENNETT: Do you sculpt?

HEARON: No, I don't sculpt. It is interesting that in *Painted Dress* I'm getting back to a woman who is an artist, and I think this is a really big theme for me: person as artist. I thought I did it—I question now if this is why I did it—in *Armadillo* because I wanted to pick a nonverbal heroine; I didn't think I had the ability to write about a verbal person, if that makes sense, and it would be easier to work with a nonverbal person. I think the reason I really did it was to explore the whole idea of creativity, but that would have scared me quite badly had I considered that I was doing anything that large.

BENNETT: Do you know anyone who sculptures?

HEARON: When I was working with *Armadillo*, I dealt with two different women who sculptured, and both of them equally well, although one of them has not done anything with it. The other one has gone on and is in Paris and having shows.

It's one thing to read Cellini, which I did, on the lost-wax method. But you have to know what they do in Texas today, so I had to have somewhere where I could go to a studio to taste the wax and see what wax tasted like here, what it felt like here, because it's not the same as it was in Florence. You always have to play with it firsthand. But those two women didn't do the pieces my character did. I went down to the studio to see them and see how the firing was handled. Now I'm a painter——

BENNETT: You paint, yourself?

HEARON: No, I mean in the current book. And I'm loving that. I'm going to Santa Fe to paint. My woman decides she can't paint in Santa Fe; she says the colors are wrong. Of course, coming from San Antonio, if you are in the beginning a dilettante painter, you have to make a ritual trip to Santa Fe, which she does.

BENNETT: Now, about mothers—which I've labeled a personal theme——

HEARON: I think time is a personal theme. You may have to reorganize your notes. I think I was bitten by Proust and Mann at an early age. I think time is as personal a theme as mothers. I think reality is a very personal theme.

BENNETT: What kind of person was your mother?

HEARON: I keep killing her off in books, but really she's still here, and very patient about being killed off in the books.

Well, my mother is several things. She's the oldest daughter, as I am the oldest daughter, as my daughter is the oldest, and her mother was the oldest daughter. She's from Kentucky. She does have that sense of good family, and it was important to her. Her mother died when she was fifteen. She had a younger sister, ten, and the younger sister died. First mother went to Vanderbilt, and then she finished at the University of Kentucky. My father went to the University of Virginia. They're both from this same little bitty rural town, and married after they had finished school. I think because of her own relation with her mother—because I'm very much of a Jungian if not a Freudian—I think that it all does begin back there. My father had polio as a small boy and got out of high school at fourteen anyway, having taken two years off to have polio. He went off to UVA with no money at all, and worked his way through, and made a hundred in all his classes.

Father looked up one day, and he was not doing what he should be doing, and so I suppose that was the turning point. He left Kentucky to come here in his early forties. Came back here actually. He had been here with Shell as a geophysicist earlier. He has written two books, which he did after my books. His last one is called *Fuels, Minerals, and Human Resources* and is about running out of fossil fuels. Ann Arbor pressed it.

I think from both of them we got in different ways, very much, reality distortion, which we have all in our own way solved or not solved. I think that fantasy or making movies in your head is a destructive ego-coping mechanism. Hopefully the creative person turns that into a message in a bottle which a lot of other people read, so that you're turning it into something that makes contact instead of something that keeps you from having to make contact.

One of the things that was important for me in deciding to write was if I was not good, and if I was not published, then no delusions about the little magazines or whatever. If I couldn't make it, I would quit and go into counseling. Because I think the "would-be writer," coming from where I came from, would be too threatening a life—thinking I was lying to myself, maybe that I was retreating into fantasy.

Back to my mother: She is a voracious reader, and very interested in the migrations of people, which is an interesting theme, one that I haven't really gotten into, but one that if, say, I were doing her, would be the paramount metaphor of her life. She is always finding exciting books on how the Mayans got there, all of that. She relates to us wonderfully when she is dealing with history, or when she's dealing with people out there. Intellectually we got a great deal of verbal feed-in from both parents.

BENNETT: Where is your daughter, and what is she?

HEARON: My daughter and son are too marvelous for words. [*laughs*] The fascinating thing about the children is that it's so easy to see what they got from me and what they got from Bob. And the new combinations they made from the same things. Their father is very verbal, very brilliant, is a lawyer. When you have two children of a different sex, and you have just two, you get the whole dynamics of the nuclear family. You have the Freudian attachments and the role attachments. Everything is so rectangular. It is interesting to see what they have done with that. And what they did is so much better than what we did—they're both so much smarter. I don't mean smarter as in school, but smarter as in living. And nicer. My daughter is twenty-two, she's married, and she's finishing school here. She moved from psychology to human development so she could get her a degree that was going to make her some money in child development. She went off to Sarah Lawrence and came back, and Reed went off to the University of Chicago and came back. He's now going to Austin Community College and working until he can get into the University of Texas. He's in humanities, and I don't know what he is going to be. We're all dreadfully verbal, but he is the best writer unquestionably. I don't know whether he'll do anything with it. You know, you don't want to become what your parents did.

BENNETT: You were going to tell me how you did rooms and people.

HEARON: All right. We're thinking in theater terms. When you sort of know what you're going to say, then you have to decide who best would play that. I mess around with these people and decide that these people in this general situation would be able to say that, and get all their grandparents and brothers and sisters and teachers and schoolmates—all that stuff—in my head. I steal their bodies from people I don't know. If you know the people, their personalities get in the way.

In *Hannah's House* the guy who was the anthropology professor had been somebody that I had known very, very vaguely, at back-to-school nights all the way through. I was doing back-to-school night, and I saw that guy, and I thought, I bet that's who was in my mind—you know, his body and the way he moved. Got the book in print and found out he was an anthropologist. On some level I didn't know I knew I knew that.

Anyway, I steal the bodies and have these people in the bodies and know their whole background and their families and everything. Then you have to figure where they live, both the town, which is to say the culture, and the house. It is a play set in that I don't remember doing lots of different rooms in any place. I saw the green bedroom very clearly, and I can still give you the green bedroom. I miss it a lot—wish I had it. And in *Hannah's House* I certainly remember the living room, and then, as I say, the cut on the side of the stage into the little kitchen room.

I didn't do that as clearly with the garage apartment in *A Prince of a Fellow* on purpose. That room didn't seem to be something that she really lived in, or really fastened on, or really came home to. If I gave it to you as clearly as I had it in my mind, it became that important in her mind, and it wasn't. Even at the grandmother's house, which I could draw you pictures of and give you fabric samples of, was not that relevant to her. If you were doing those as stage sets, you could do them as clearly as I saw them, and it wouldn't matter, but that's not true in fiction because you can only give so much space to things, and if you give it a lot, it's got to mean a lot. I think you have to give the setting which constitutes the outside world of the person.

BENNETT: Why did they cut out the party in *The Second Dune*?

HEARON: They felt it wrapped things up too neatly. I think they were correct. When *Redbook* condensed it, they left the party scene, so you can go back and read the party there. Yes, I think they were probably absolutely correct.

As for using parties at the end, you get everybody there, but you can, you know, end the play somewhere else. It doesn't have to be resolved at that gathering.

BENNETT: A kind of epilogue?

HEARON: No, I don't think of it as an epilogue. It was an epilogue in *Hannah's House*, but it was not an epilogue in *Prince*.

Anyway, you furnish the room, and then you have to say what is the outside world. The outside world in *Armadillo*, say, was literally the backyard and the animals. The outside world in *Prince* was more the state of mind of the Germans, more the patriarchy and the negative aspects. In *Now and Another Time* the outside world was probably pretty much what the newspapers say the outside world was, which doesn't make it any more true, just more conventional.

BENNETT: What did you major in at the University of Texas?

HEARON: In a liberal-arts program called Plan Two.

BENNETT: Were you planning to become a writer?

HEARON: No, but that's about all you could become, or you could go to graduate school. I actually went out and learned to type and was a bookkeeper, putting my husband through law school.

I was sort of a closet scientist and didn't have sense enough to know it. I think a good liberal-arts education is better for a writer than something like journalism.

I don't think I knew that I wanted to write because I was writing, so it was not something that was missing from my life—you write so much in school. So I didn't know I wanted to write until I got out, and there wasn't any writing. I thought, What has happened to my life, where is its central core, its meaning? I guess I'm saying that I never went around "going to be a writer." I'm still not "going to be a writer." I like to write; I like the process.

BENNETT: Many writers seem to find writing painful.

HEARON: I spoke to an architecture class, because they were doing a project on a center for writers and were trying to find out where to put writers. They kept using judgmental words. They would say, "Now when you get in that isolated room . . . ." "Isolated" is so judgmental. You should just say, "When I'm in that room." They were obviously so bothered by the idea of a solitary pursuit of anything that they could hardly bear it.

BENNETT: What do you think of Women's Liberation?

HEARON: I'm a feminist, yes. I think of myself as a radical feminist. I'm not sure the radical feminists would think of me as a radical feminist. One of the arguments we get into when I speak to feminist groups—your really red-chick militants—is they don't like what I do with my books, and they say I'm not a writer, which means a tract writer. Tract writing is okay, but that's not what I'm doing. I also point out to them that if you perceive the compromise that Foster is making in getting married again, then I must perceive it to have showed it to you. If you wish that Avery was not sleeping with the mayor of San Antonio, then I must understand the denigration it represents for you to feel that way. Then they get off on, "You're just giving a slice of life in your novels and not really making a statement." I say, "That may be true, but if you know that the injustice exists when you read it, maybe I more than you make a statement." Yes, I think of myself as very much a feminist.

BENNETT: Are you a member of any feminist group?

HEARON: I give money to the Women's Center, and to the Rape Crisis Center. I'm not giving that kind of time, anymore. I've done my community tithe, and I'm not giving more time. I give them money, my love, free speeches.

BENNETT: Which women writers do you particularly admire?

HEARON: Doris Lessing, Margaret Drabble. My favorite book by a woman writer is *Kristin Lavransdatter*, by Sigrid Undset. She won the Nobel Prize in 1928, if you can see a woman doing that. And it's the best book there is. I don't think of her as my favorite writer because it stands on that book; her other stuff is not that good. I think *The Golden Notebook* is pretty wonderful, and I thought Drabble's *The Waterfall* was especially good. *The Summer Before the Dark* tends to be a little tracty.

BENNETT: Do you like Cather?

HEARON: Yes, I do. I taught *Death Comes to the Archbishop* in a course, and I don't think the kids thought it was worth a shit, but I like it.

BENNETT: What about Eudora Welty?

HEARON: I like her. But I like Carson McCullers a whole lot better. I used to want to grow up to be Sylvia Ashton-Warner. And I did. Now I want to grow up to be Carson McCullers.

BENNETT: Did you learn much from Barbara Jordan while you were working on the book on her?

HEARON: Oh, yes, that was the most wonderful thing—not doing the book, but working with her. It was like a therapy, and therefore I got a lot of exciting feedback, a really good feeling that a lot had happened that she didn't know had happened and that she was dealing with a lot she hadn't perceived before. I went over my own life in my mind since I was running chronologically with her, reliving a lot of time.

We have remained very good friends. I think if we had not I would have tossed the book away.

BENNETT: How was it different from writing a fiction book?

HEARON: It was very painful—and quite revelatory in my coming to understand what fiction was doing for me therapeutically. I used to say in speeches that writing is therapy and a lot cheaper than a shrink because you have only a pencil and yellow pad—a throwaway line. I had not realized the extent to which fiction, in its way of going into your subconscious, going down into those lower levels in the Jungian sense of being where you've been before but where you haven't been yet, was very necessary to me—and was the way that I got new energy and got a feeling that the theologians call grace, a feeling of being a whole self as opposed to being fragmented, which seems absurd when I think of it, because you're fragmenting yourself into all those different fictional people, all of whom are you. Nevertheless, it worked by bringing them together in one place, in one person. All of that was missing in the Jordan project. My caring for her was coming out of a deep level, but the rest of it was coming very much on a conscious level. It felt very depleting.

September, 1978

Leon Hale: *Optimist as Novelist*

LEON HALE was born May 30, 1921, in Stephenville, Texas. He finished earning his B.A. from Texas Tech in 1946, after time out to serve as a U.S. Army Air Force aerial gunner in World War II. He has worked as a Texas A&M Extension Service assistant editor, a Humble Oil magazine editor and a *Houston Post* staff writer. He now writes a widely read daily column for the *Post*.

We talked in the vast and, on that Sunday morning, empty *Houston Post* city room, but Hale doesn't even keep a desk there. He often writes sitting under a shade tree with a pencil or in an auto pulled off the road with his electric typewriter plugged into the dashboard cigarette lighter. But mostly his intellectual headquarters is at home in "a little bedroom" about ten by twelve feet.

His desk consists of a slab door sitting on two filing cabinets. The door is unpainted, decorated only with "all the graffiti that run out of my head." His typewriter sits on a typewriter table, and Hale himself sits in a comfortable swivel chair.

"I wrote standing up for ten years," he said. "I had a nerve problem in a leg, and my doctor advised me to write standing up. He had read that Hemingway wrote standing, and maybe he thought it would make me write like Hemingway. I wrote *Bonney's Place* standing up."

There are plenty of books in the little room, ranging from a set of encyclopedias to a shelf of material on Texas and the Southwest. There are pictures of his children. On one wall there is a Texas road map, and elsewhere on the walls he has pinned bits of dialogue and similar things-to-remember.

For some reason Hale's book-jacket portrait had led me to expect him to be a small man. Quite the contrary. Hale is a lanky six footer who weighs 178 pounds. He has thick, graying brown hair and blue eyes.

BENNETT: Your books seem basically optimistic. Is that the way you look at life?

HALE: I guess it is. When *Addison* came out, I was on some talk shows around, and people kept bringing that up. I'm not conscious of it. My wife says I'm optimistic about everything, but I didn't much think I was. I guess they're right. If it's true, the reason is that it's the way I have of enduring—thinking, well, things are going to get better. I was raised that way, now that I think of it. My mother especially, she was sort of a stoic person who took a lot of hardship, and her way of looking at it was, well, don't worry, because things are going to get better tomorrow. Another aspect of this attitude of mine is that the world, and this country, and this state have already undergone so many remarkably horrid things and survived that I don't see how we can fail to think it's going to keep surviving, no matter what hits.

BENNETT: Did your father farm?

HALE: No, my dad was a kind of traveling-salesman type, and he also worked in stores. About half his time he was a clerk in a department store, and the other half he was a traveling salesman. That's what he loved most, traveling. He sold everything from overalls to, oh, counter equipment for stores, like tape machines and things clerks used to wrap packages with. He traveled a lot; that was his thing. He had an itchy foot.

BENNETT: I was delighted to find we have some things in common: we both studied at Texas Tech, and we both wrote columns for the campus newspaper.

HALE: You know, in a way it's a disadvantage to have written college humor. It takes you so long to recover from it. Like, I was a worshiper of Max Shulman. I wanted to write everything just like Max Shulman, and it took me a long time to get over it. I think I finally did.

BENNETT: Shulman hasn't gotten over it yet.

HALE: No, he hasn't. He's never graduated.

BENNETT: When did you start writing?

HALE: I guess in high school, really. When we started a little high-school paper, I wasn't editor, but I wrote jokes and that kind of stuff. I was humor editor of Eastland High School's first paper. I guess that's when I fell in love with a by-line.

BENNETT: I was humor editor on my high-school paper too.

HALE: I'm not real proud of it.

BENNETT: And I thought Max Shulman the epitome of wit.

HALE: He's one of two people I read when I was going to school—just to show you the level of my literary interests—Max Shulman and Damon Runyon. I loved Damon Runyon, and everything he wrote I thought was just great. I'd have huge arguments with my faculty members about whether that was literature. I thought it was the greatest literature in the world, because that's what I wanted to do. I still think Runyon is great.

BENNETT: About that time I discovered S. J. Perelman too.

HALE: You know, I never did get going in Perelman much. I've read him, of course. Almost everybody has. He has had a huge effect on humor writing—and on literature. Joseph Heller was in Houston not long ago, and I got to talk to him a little bit. He said that when *Catch-22*, which is really a classic, came out it didn't sell more than one of my novels has. Then one day S. J. Perelman was on a talk show in New York, and somebody asked him, "What have you read lately that you like?" And he said, "A book called *Catch-22*." That made the thing take off, just that little broadcast. Oh, it's frightening what it takes for success.

BENNETT: When were you at Tech?

HALE: I started out there in the fall of 1939, and that was a desolate place. When I was drafted, I was registered for my last sixteen hours, so I just had a semester when I went back in the spring of '46 to finish. It was an interesting place, and I had a great time there. I never did fall in love with Lubbock and that old country. I majored in journalism.

BENNETT: Did any of your professors have a particular influence on your writing?

HALE: Dr. Alan L. Strout was sort of my mentor out there, and a fellow, who is now dead, named A. B. Cunningham. Dr. Strout is very old now—I thought he was old as the dinosaurs when I was out there, but of course he wasn't. His face always reminded me of Ernest Hemingway in later years. I took everything I could under him. Dr. Cunningham taught creative writing. He had written a lot of novels, mysteries. He liked my short stories, and he encouraged me, he and Strout, more than anybody else. I always got along well with Louise Allen too; she was in journalism. Some thought she was a little bit too pedantic. I was in love with her, because she was a beautiful woman; gosh, I thought she was. The dean's wife, which was kind of neat for the dean, dang right.

BENNETT: Did you write a humor column?

HALE: Sort of. I wrote a column called "Bottlescars" for the *Toreador*. I claimed there was a typo in the heading; we thought that would be a neat thing. At that time it was popular in college newspapers to write what we called "parables" in the biblical style—you know: "And lo it came to pass," that sort of thing, applying it to current situations. A lot of people thought it was sacrilegious, some Bible people did. But I loved it. I still love the Old Testament, read a lot of it. I still get a day's work out of the Old Testament for the newspaper a lot of times.

BENNETT: Do you have a fundamentalist religious background?

HALE: I was raised up by a staunch pillar in the Methodist church, my mother. My father, I always suspected he went to church to please my mother, but I can't be sure about that. I grew up in the front row, sang those "Living for Jesus" and "Old Rugged Cross" songs. Sunday school, prayer meeting on Wednesday nights; preacher came to dinner a lot of times. But not I'm not really churchy. I mean I'm not a member of any denomination.

BENNETT: Did you sell any short stories when you were at Tech?

HALE: Not really. I used to write short stories in longhand and send them to the *Saturday Evening Post* when I was in school. Of course, I never sold. As a matter of fact, I never did much break into the magazine market, certainly not the national magazine market, except for a little case or two. You could stretch a point and say I sold to the national magazines. I sold to a lot of local ones and state magazines, and I got a little thing going with a couple of trade publications—did some short fiction. I'm one of the few guys that ever sold fiction to industrial publications, because they didn't buy much for years. But I never did much enjoy figuring that magazine free-lance deal. Too much work for a nickel.

BENNETT: Television hit magazines hard.

HALE: I used to be a worshiper of the *Saturday Evening Post* when I was in school. That's when, shoot, eighty percent of their editorial matter was fiction, and my huge ambition when I got out of school was to write short stories for the *Post*. Never made it.

BENNETT: I have a few rejection slips from that direction too.

HALE: I've got them from the old *Liberty* magazine, from *Collier's*—it's a pretty standard pattern.

BENNETT: What industrial magazines have you been writing for?

HALE: I haven't done it for ten years now. I quit this paper for a while and went to work for Humble Oil editing a house magazine. That's the way I got my contacts with the industrial publications here in Houston, and I wrote for several of them for, I guess, fifteen years. Really, they were paying better than the other magazines that I could sell. They'd write you a check with the corporate strength of an Exxon or a Tennessee Gas behind them. But I got tired of it. When I started trying to write books, I quit.

BENNETT: Paul Horgan says he wrote several novels before one was accepted for publication. Did you?

HALE: No, I would have got discouraged and quit long before that. I don't have a completed manuscript that's unpublished. I've written three books, and I've been involved in the production of two or three others, such as writing the text for a sketchbook or an art book. And everything I've done has been on contract, just like building a chicken house. Didn't sell so much, but published.

BENNETT: With a little break, I think your novels should sell quite well.

HALE: It's such a long shot though. Oh, they'll make a little money. *Bonney's Place*, over the years, has made a good deal, but it came so slowly, over a period of four years. It was like getting a Social Security check for a hundred dollars a month. We've had offers on the film rights for *Addison*, but that's the only way now . . . .

BENNETT: Apparently it's difficult for a story to make it all the way to film production.

HALE: Tell me about it. You know, I was naïve enough to think when they bought the film rights to *Bonney*—that's big talk!—that they were really going to make a movie. So I went around telling everybody, "Hey, they bought my book, and it's going to be a movie." I told them who was going to be in the film and where it would be shot. That was eight years ago, and the first frame has not been shot. But that derned thing resold not long ago, and the people with the film rights got paid more than I got for it. So it's still alive.

BENNETT: I gather that raising the money is the trick.

HALE: There's no doubt about it. They tell me the tax situation now is such that people with money can drill oil wells and other things to make more. But—and this is secondhand information—they say old John Wayne spent three years here in Texas trying to raise money for *The Alamo*. John Wayne!

BENNETT: I would think *Bonney's Place* would make a good stage play.

HALE: Some people here wanted me to try that. I'm going to try a play, I think, when I get the projects I have going now cleared away. I never have tried a play. I'm pretty good at dialogue, and I believe I could write a play. That sort of interests me: the idea of people running around on stage saying my words. I bet that would be a kick.

BENNETT: What are you working on now?

HALE: Nothing, really, other than a daily column. I've got a book project that I promised to do, a friendship deal. I'm old enough to know I oughtn't to promise things like that. Oh, I've got two or three more books in me that I could write without doing a whole lot of research. But I don't know if I'll ever do them. I guess I will if I live long enough. There's one—the thing that I do here at the paper that's most popular is nostalgia about old hometown stuff. I think at times I overdo it, and I may be getting a reaction out of a small percentage of the readers. But I think it's the best stuff I do, and I'm going to write a book with that. That's five years off, though, from being finished.

BENNETT: Have you started it?

HALE: I've been working on it for twenty years. Sheaves of notes, bits and pieces hanging on the walls. I don't see how anybody ever says how long it takes them to write a book. That little old thin book (*Addison*) that I wrote on a year's contract, that I wrote on weekends and nights when everybody else was out playing, it has been in my head for thirty years. When do you start working on a book? When they ask, I just go ahead and say, "It took a year." Then they always know somebody that wrote one twice as long in six weeks that sold a million and a half copies.

BENNETT: Some writers crank it out pretty fast.

HALE: I'm a great admirer of Michener. Not so much his writing ability, although he's good, but the way he's made an enterprise of himself. I understand that on *Centennial* he had only two full-time paid researchers helping him. Fantastic! Gol dang, his are not books, just monuments. He's a workaholic; a good little old day's work for him is two thousand words.

BENNETT: How much do you write a day?

HALE: When I'm working on a book, I try to get six pages a day. I'm talking about a day's work, not after supper. A lot of guys do that, I understand, after supper. But I'm slow. And I did this book differently, did it in pencil for the first time. I liked it, with a yellow pad sitting under a shade tree. I didn't have to have a lot of materials sitting around me. Then I transferred it myself onto the typewriter, and I ended up typing the manuscript myself. A lot of it from that first pencil version I was able to keep; that's the first time I've ever been able to do that. I usually rewrite a page four or five times.

BENNETT: You wrote on a typewriter before.

HALE: I always said I couldn't think except on a typewriter, but I've found out different. You know, when you're in the daily-news business it's ridiculous to use a pencil. One time I went down to Mexico City. I was going to stay ten days to do a magazine assignment and my daily column, and the first thing I did down there was lose my reading glasses in the airport. I can see without them, by holding everything way out there. What I did was write the column with a pencil for ten days, in great-big letters where I could read it. And I found out that I could get by with a whole lot less rewriting that way, going slow and thinking about what I was saying a little bit. That gave me the idea, and I've liked it. I still don't write the column that way; I use the typewriter. But I did the book that way.

BENNETT: Have you taken time off to write your books, or have you done them nights and weekends?

HALE: I do them on vacations. For *Addison* there, I used all my vacation time here at the *Post* for a year. I've been around so long I get four weeks' vacation, and it took it all, and weekends and nights. I didn't work just constantly, but I had to work pretty hard because I'm so slow.

BENNETT: In all the composition took about a year?

HALE: Yes, I think I had a contract for fourteen months, but I'll say a year, because there were months in there that I didn't work on it at all. I've never written a book that I don't decide about halfway through that it was a bad idea anyway and to hell with it, and just chunk it away and quit. Maybe not for six weeks, not even think about it. If anybody asks if I'm doing a book, I tell them no. Then it's the newspaper reporter in me that makes me go back to finish. Because of the deadline. I'd never do anything if I didn't have a deadline. Everybody talks about what inspires you. Shoot! Deadline is all that inspires me, just like sending in my income tax.

BENNETT: You worked for Texas A&M a while, didn't you?

HALE: For a year and a half after I got out of Tech, a press-agent type job. I'd go around interviewing the scientists and all up there and write stories and send them out to the papers. That's where I got hooked up to this *Post* outfit here: they saw one of my pieces of copy and hired me. This paper has been awful good to me. I'm lucky, I think, and I'm one of the people in this world that found their little place. You're familiar with the Peter Principle, where everybody tends to rise one step above his capability. Well, I have not been a victim of that. One more step—if they were to make me city editor, I'd have that trouble. I'm happy where I am. I write about what I want to write about. A third of my time is spent running around, but it's not hard travel. I used to fight it pretty hard and set up interviews, two or three a day. On this little trip I just got back from, I didn't do a single interview, just took part in a couple of little old things. But every good thing that has ever happened to me professionally has been a direct result of my connection here, doing a column on a big metropolitan daily. And doing a column is a heck of a kick. I don't need books to satisfy what craving I have for recognition. It's just that I can't live with only it, on a newspaper salary. I'm sitting right here in the middle of a city that has one point seven million people, and in theory I get a shot at them five mornings a week.

BENNETT: I meet people who love your column and don't know that you write books. You don't push your novels in your column?

HALE: No, they wouldn't like it around here, and anyway that would not be professional in my view. I write sometimes about writing books, but I've never one time printed the name of one of my books in the column. There are circumstances in which I might print the title of one of them, but I can't say, "Okay, folks, everybody run out and buy *Addison* because I need the money."

BENNETT: In your first book, *Turn South at the Second Bridge*, what you've obviously done is stitch together some of your better columns.

HALE: I'd say ninety percent of the material in that is based on stuff that I gathered my first ten years around here. It's classified by all the libraries as folklore. I didn't know it was folklore at the time; I was surprised to hear it. I wasn't sure I knew what folklore was when I wrote it. It won an award at the Austin Writers Roundup, in '65, I think, and I was surprised to find it won in the folklore category. I was rereading it the other day, just kind of backing up, and there's a lot of stuff in that book that doesn't exist now, that I can't find now in these little old places. It makes me feel good that I recorded something that was disappearing, and got it down.

BENNETT: I'm sure you had to write a lot of transitional material.

HALE: I really worried about it, and it ended up that I didn't do as good a job of transition as I should have. But it's all rewritten; none of it ran just like it was in the paper, except for direct quotes.

BENNETT: What was the reaction of the persons you wrote about in the book?

HALE: I haven't had any objections, not one, from any of them. As far as I know, I got either no reaction or a favorable one. There may have been bad feelings in some cases I didn't hear about, but I didn't get one ugly letter. Now I get ugly letters about my novels. Nice little old ladies write about my language and that kind of stuff.

BENNETT: I'm often shocked at what some people are shocked at.

HALE: Every day. You know, especially over here in the Bible Belt country, they really say some ugly things about my novels and try to make me feel bad. But I've been through it a couple of times now, and it doesn't bother me anymore.

BENNETT: Do you get many like that?

HALE: I can't say I get so many, but I do get some that are pretty poisonous.

BENNETT: In your column a couple of days ago, you wrote about a physician who takes his fiddle to the hospital and plays. It would be quite easy to make fun of fellows like that. But you never do; you always take their side.

HALE: Shoot, yeah. I want people to do whatever they're having fun at, because I enjoy watching it. I think it is a great thing for a doctor to play the fiddle. He's not hurting anybody, and his priorities are in the right place. When the phone rings, he goes off and sets a broken arm; he doesn't let them suffer. I think the unique and bizarre is what we look for.

BENNETT: You're good at finding those things.

HALE: I'll tell you, I've got an awful lot of help. You bet. I couldn't find it without help. I've been around here a long time, and I've developed a set of contacts. I don't mean to say that I've got dozens and dozens of them, because there aren't that many of them that know what I'm looking for, but I've got friends who call me and say: "Dr. Roy Lee has a jam session every Wednesday night when he's at the hospital on Red Bluff Road." And I chase down a lot of bum leads too.

BENNETT: It sounds like a great job.

HALE: I've always thought it would be the best job in the world if the pay was a little better. I wouldn't want any better job.

BENNETT: The best jobs never pay best.

HALE: I have a strange attitude about money, I guess. I've never ever asked for a raise in my life. Not one time. I've always felt that if I was working for the right people and doing things right they would give me a raise if they could. Lots of people think that's a weak position, and it may be.

BENNETT: Do you fictionalize much in *Turn South at the Second Bridge*? John Graves told me he fictionalized quite a bit in his books.

HALE: No way. All the people in there are called by their right names, and whatever they say or do is whatever they said or did. John surprised me on a couple of things like that. I always thought the best thing he ever wrote was in *Hard Scrabble*, about that boy dying, holding onto John's hand, talking about the red dirt of Mississippi or somewhere, during the war. I told John so at the time—it was one time a lot of us were dead set on deciding who the best writer in Texas is, and John's always a candidate for that honor. And he told me it was fictionalized.

BENNETT: Of course, there's obviously a fictional short story in the middle of *Hard Scrabble*.

HALE: I fictionalize in the column sometimes, but I do it in such a way that anybody with half a cup of brains is going to know I'm doing it. And the ones that don't, they don't need to know.

BENNETT: Have you ever thought of doing a second book of columns?

HALE: Yes, it wouldn't sell anywhere else, but it would sell maybe twelve, fifteen thousand copies around here. And if it was done in a quality paperback where it could sell for less than five bucks, it might sell twenty, twenty-five thousand with proper promotion. I've been kicking the idea around. I may do it myself, just get it printed.

BENNETT: Shaw published his own plays.

HALE: I wouldn't try it on any other kind of book, or anywhere else. I'd have to have somebody who would go around to see that it's in the bookstores and all. I don't want to sell it myself. That's something I've never done, sell my own books.

BENNETT: You mean autograph parties?

HALE: I've done that. You have to do that. I mean, I'm not one of these guys who has a bushel of them in a trunk and, "How about buying my novel at eight dollars ninety-five cents plus tax?" That's the way you lose friends. A lot of people do; some people are good about promoting their stuff, and I guess I'm a little weak on that. I've had some real sweet autographing parties down here, when this *Addison* came out, oh, man! You know, lines. Then I've had some that were real bombs too, and that's about the worst feeling there is. You advertise that you're going to be there, and nobody comes. One of the things I refuse to do is sit behind a table in a bookstore with a stack of books and a pencil in my hand waiting for somebody. I just won't do it. I go to the back, or pretend I'm one of the clerks. I've even sold books, other people's books, cookbooks.

BENNETT: I've had some experience selling books printed by the college.

HALE: Gosh dang, selling books! It's just pure promotion. I'm convinced that one of those big New York publishers could take any book and sell it if they wanted to. Look what's been on the best-seller list, for heaven's sake, the past year—*The Book of Lists*. Of course, what I'd like is for *The Book of Lists* to be off and mine to be on.

BENNETT: How was critical reaction to *Turn South*?

HALE: I think it's fair to say it was good, but it wasn't widely reviewed. Here in the state it was good. I don't remember a really negative review. I mean, what are you going to say bad about a harmless little book like that? I do remember one negative comment: somebody said it was too folksy.

BENNETT: How did you come to write *Bonney's Place*? Did you decide you were going to write a beer-joint novel?

HALE: No, after I'd been running around doing what I do for a living, I came to know several individual beer-joint operators who were people sort of like Bonney. And I came to admire them for their standard of values, for the good that they do, because they do an awful lot. The folks that are sitting around judging them are almost unanimously putting them down and condemning them as people that are spreading alcoholism and degeneration. I saw so much good that went on in these people. They remind me of Damon Runyon characters, and that's what I love in them. There's good in everybody. They're eccentric, and they're not degenerate, these people that hang around beer joints, not necessarily. So I took about ten of these guys that I know and kind of rolled them in one and got Bonney. He is my character. There is one person that is more like Bonney than any other, at a place where I used to hang around a lot, but I don't think he ever read the book. Because he never asked, "Is that me?" Or said, "That reminds me of myself." In fact, I never have had any of my people, my characters, do that. Maybe they do recognize themselves, but they don't mention it.

BENNETT: I suppose it is something like looking at a picture of yourself. You feel that you look different.

HALE: It's really not them either, because by the time you get through shaping them the way you want them, they probably can't recognize themselves.

BENNETT: There is a strong sense of place in the novel. Is it based on an actual place?

HALE: No. I had a location in mind, because one of the places was in a certain spot up here, and I would see that place in my mind when the action was going on, but it doesn't exist. People ask me: where is Bonney's place? One of the things that pleases me about that beer-joint book is that I've got letters from thirty-two states, people writing and saying, "Isn't Bonney's place in so-and-so in that state?" And that pleases me, because that was what I was trying to do. One of the places that I did write quite a bit out of is the little town of Glen Flora, which is about an hour's drive down this highway right here, Fifty-nine, down the coast. It's called Scheller's Place, and we have a party there once a year, around Christmastime, to kind of celebrate because Scheller's Place is still there, and it's a good thing. If you're ever down here you ought to come join us, in December, two days after Christmas. Free beer and piano playing, song singing. They invite a lot of people that I love, and it's really a special time for me.

BENNETT: What about other people in the novel? Rose-Mama? Norman Akers?

HALE: I've known people like them is all I can say. I can't say that I just made them up. Rose-Mama, I've known women like her. I've been to her house; I could take you to her house. I see houses beside these country roads every day that are just like her house, and I see her out there in a bonnet fooling with the cow. She's out there, real, no doubt about it. She's a big, overgrown, loud-mouthed gal, with a real strong character. She lives in a million women; well, maybe not a million. All the other characters are pretty much the same way.

BENNETT: So you've known all these characters.

HALE: I used to say that I never had just flat made up a character, until I wrote this little *Addison* book. I felt at first, even after I wrote it, there were a couple of those little soldiers in there, Addison's buddies, that I just made up because I wanted them to be that way. But that's not true really. I've known people like that. I don't see how you can make up anybody. I guess minor characters you do, where you just need somebody sitting by the door when your main character walks in, to say something to them.

BENNETT: You got some adverse criticism of *Bonney's Place* on the bad language?

HALE: Locally here. The critics, now, are a lot more sophisticated than to expect missionary-society language. That complaint comes from local readers of my column that expect me not to cuss or drink beer, or to ever go to a beer joint. Nice little ladies. I've had them send it back to me and tell me to flush it down the sewer where it belongs. Philip Roth's book *Portnoy's Complaint* came out about the same time, one of the nastiest books I ever read, and so I'd tell them to go get that and read it. I sold a lot of books by Roth that way.

BENNETT: Do you answer people who write that way to you?

HALE: I make it a point. I have never been able to answer all my mail, but I always answer the critical ones, because I enjoy it. I feel like I need to defend myself. When somebody writes me a real flowery letter, that's pleasant and makes me feel good. I save the prettiest ones, you know, so in my old age I can sit around and read what a great fellow I was. By far the heavier part of my mail over the years has been kind. But there's a certain type of person, evidently, that I just rub the wrong way. They hate the way I look and sound. I'm a cornball, and they don't understand why a metropolitan newspaper would pay a guy like me to write that crap. I sort of enjoy it, being criticized once in a while. Just so they don't get too close to the truth.

BENNETT: Did you get a contract on *Bonney's Place* before you started?

HALE: Yes, just the standard way. I submitted a sample chapter and an outline. I got a year's contract and a little old advance.

BENNETT: Did you use the sample chapter in the finished product?

HALE: It was the first chapter.

BENNETT: Did the novel get much national attention?

HALE: Not too much. It got something *Addison* didn't get, and that was twelve lines in the *New York Times Book Review*. There's the feeling among a lot of authors that if you don't get reviewed in the *Times Book Review* then you ain't gonna cut it. There may be some truth in that. The thrust of the *Times* review was that it's a nice little story written thirty years too late. In other words, that it's old-fashioned. I don't know, it could be right. Overall I got nice reviews. But, shoot, good reviews don't sell books. Good reviews help. I didn't say that right: favorable reviews don't sell books; good reviews do sell books, good thoughtful reviews, not necessarily favorable.

BENNETT: Bad reviews probably hurt, those that really pan.

HALE: When our movie critic says it's a really rotten movie, I'm not going to pay three-fifty to get in.

BENNETT: For several of us the death of Addison came as a shock. Have you had that reaction much from other readers?

HALE: Yes, everybody. It is common for people to say that they didn't think it was necessary for him to be killed off. And a couple of reviewers thought it was a little too abrupt, that I didn't set it up good enough. It may be valid criticism, I don't know. But he was doomed from the start, and I thought that it was even pretty obvious.

BENNETT: Looking back, I found that you left little clues.

HALE: All along, all along. Even in his dreams, nightmares, he was seeing his death. In fact, I even went back and dropped things in so it wouldn't seem abrupt. I felt he had to die right from the start to emphasize the main point: that such a person can release from his character such an impact on other people in a short time. I thought that his dying would emphasize that premise. The editors of Doubleday didn't give me any problems on that.

BENNETT: The overall plan of the novel is fairly plain.

HALE: The criticism of the death didn't upset me. The only one that upsets me is when people say that it's a man's book. Hell fire, it's a love story. The next biggest character in it is Sarah, even though she doesn't appear in the tent in West Texas. A lot of people, including Evelyn Oppenheimer on the *Dallas News*, supported me on its being a love story, a woman's book even more than a man's. But some of my best friends say, "Hell, this is a man's book, an army book. The reason I didn't emphasize the army aspects of the book is that I didn't want it to be classified as a military novel. These damned publishers are hell on categorizing things. I didn't even tell where the characters were or what they were doing for a long time, hoping the reader would get interested in the story. Finally saying that, hell, these guys are out in the desert in the army, but by then my hope was that the reader wouldn't care, that the reader would be interested. I did shed a few tears over that book, and not all of them for Addison dying.

BENNETT: You softened the impact of the death. A woman I know read through the death a few pages without actually realizing he was dead and then went back to see if he really died. Did you do that intentionally?

HALE: Yes, I didn't want to have him knocked over and twisted head over heels out of the jeep by that bullet. It is just where it ended for him on the road. I don't know why I did it that way.

BENNETT: Were you ever in a West Texas military camp?

HALE: Addison was suggested to me by a guy who lived in Chicago. I was in Yuma, Arizona, in 1943, in the Army Air Corps gunnery school. We stayed out in the desert. This was really out in the sand, not that greasewood like you have in West Texas. We stayed, I believe, thirteen weeks, learning how to shoot a fifty-caliber machine gun out of an airplane. We lived four to a tent, those tent shacks with the concrete bottom and the wainscot-high wood frame with canvas top and screen door. I was twenty-one or twenty-two, and there were two other guys who were younger than I was. Then there was this guy; I don't even remember his name now—Fred something. He was like thirty, and he was married, and his wife was in Chicago, and he was just sick in love with her. This was the first person I'd ever studied who was in love, and he taught us in that tent what it meant to love a woman. He missed her so bad that, in order to take the edge off his not having her there, he would talk to us about her. Not to the extent that Addison did, about the sex and all.

We started putting little notes in his letters to his wife, and she would write us little notes back, like in the book. She was pregnant too. That's the first time I ever had any interest whatever in a pregnant woman, other than I knew by then it was something to avoid, not being married. She would write us about the first day the baby kicked, and we got all excited about it out there in Yuma, Arizona, about a baby kicking in a woman's stomach in Chicago. Then, like happens in the army, one day we were just all gone, and I never heard from him again. That baby would be—what?—thirty-seven. I've often thought what a keen thing it would be to go try to find it, and try to find that guy. That's where the story came from. That guy had a huge impact on me. I knew him only thirteen weeks, but he taught me things, not just about babies and love, but a lot of good things. He was kind of fatherly to us, and he would go into town with us, like Addison did his gang, and keep us out of trouble. He gave us lectures about whorehouses and things like that. Hell, he did a lot of good.

BENNETT: You were young and impressionable.

HALE: I was a green twenty-two. I had never been out of West Texas. The others were even greener and dumber than I was. Fred went off in one of those B24s like the rest of us did; he might have been killed. When *Bonney* came out, I was in Chicago to be on the PBS Book Beat show, and after the show I was sitting in O'Hare Airport, waiting on a plane to come home, and I couldn't help but look in the crowd for Fred's son. Fred was a distinctive-looking guy, and I could imagine what his son would look like. I just assumed it would be a boy, a man. I didn't look for a girl. At that time the story had been knocking around in my head for thirty years, and it was a story I could do without a whole lot of research.

BENNETT: He makes a strong fiction character, and that may be the reason you have difficulty with his death. There is a death in *Bonney's Place*, but the character is minor.

HALE: Sam Hobbs, the old drunk.

BENNETT: It doesn't strike deeply. Now if you had killed Bonney....

HALE: I wouldn't dare kill Bonney.

BENNETT: How did you get Bonney's name?

HALE: I got it off a Texas road map. I get a lot of my names off Texas road maps. His full name is Bonham J. McCamey. Bonham is Sam Rayburn's old home. McCamey is out in West Texas. I didn't think I was doing it in *Addison*, but there is an Addison near Dallas and Fort Worth, a little suburb. Trinidad is where my wife, Ellen, is from, Trinidad on the Trinity River up close to Corsicana; he's a Chicano, a Latin. Booker, there's a Booker. McKavett—Fort McKavett.

BENNETT: I've never heard of that naming system.

HALE: I look at road maps a lot, and I love them. A map's as good a place as any, because you've got every name, every culture that was ever here and had any influence on what Texas is now. The names are on there, the place names, some of them not towns but creeks and mountains.

BENNETT: Did you have any particular Texas place in mind for your setting for *Addison*?

HALE: No, it's just one of those ridiculous farflung outposts like Pyote or Marathon. I gave it the name Spanish Wells because Spanish Wells is not on the road map. I just wanted it in Texas. Really the place is not all that important. I needed four guys in a tent in an isolated place. I even started out with them on a ranch and not even in the military, but I couldn't think of a situation that I could live with that would be better than the army. How am I going to get one from Alabama, one from Pennsylvania, and one from Arizona all together in a tent? The army is the only way, just about.

BENNETT: What kind of published criticism did *Addison* get?

HALE: It's been overwhelmingly favorable. That doesn't mean it's necessarily good, but a lot of really nice things were said about it. And the bad ones have been really bad, from people who just didn't like it anyway.

BENNETT: Why did they dislike it?

HALE: One of them was highly critical of my killing of Addison, that it was too abrupt and not set up. His remark was that evidently my deadline came due, and I just ended the book. I worked so hard to keep it from being that way. Another old gal said it was a good idea for a book and the message was good enough, but that I was just totally ineffectual in the telling.

BENNETT: Perhaps they didn't read it very well.

HALE: I don't know. You can always tell when somebody reviews your book off the dust jacket; the only good thing about dust-jacket reviews is that they are always favorable.

BENNETT: At any rate, *Addison* attracted some hostility, which *Bonney* didn't.

HALE: A lot of my friends don't like *Addison* and won't talk to me about it. People that love you don't really like to tell you that you've done something they don't like. One of the best friends I have saved *Bonney's Place* as a film property at a time when nobody was interested in it by borrowing money to buy the film rights. He thinks *Bonney* is the greatest book ever written, but he just didn't like *Addison* worth a damn and has never said one word about it, good or bad.

BENNETT: Do you see many writers here in Houston?

HALE: I don't see writers very often. Of course, I'm a member of the Texas Institute of Letters, and I was on the board of directors up until this last meeting. I go to the meetings, and that's where you see everybody. Some of us decided that at meetings everybody really ought to be required to wear name tags with a list of credits, so we could put on our glasses and see what each guy had written.

BENNETT: What about here in Houston?

HALE: I seldom do. We've got people here who write books, like Jack Donahue, one of our ex-managing editors, who writes mysteries. Beverly Lowry writes novels, and Max Apple. Five or six Houston novels came out this year.

BENNETT: I'm surprised by how many writers Texas has. I discover a new one every day.

HALE: They're all over. My old friend Martha Ann Turner at Huntsville, for instance. She taught English, Southwest literature, for years and years. She's retired now and working on her twelfth book. They are published by outfits like Shoal Creek in Austin, but she's made quite a contribution overall. She's good, too, a historian, knows how to put things together, a hard worker. But she's not widely known. There's John Thomason, who, I feel, was the best writer we ever had in Texas, but not one person in twenty has ever heard of him. And listen, he was nationally known.

BENNETT: A. C. Greene called my attention to Eddie Anderson's

Thieves like Us, which was recently made into an Altman movie.

HALE: Did you ever hear of Jewell Gibson, who wrote a hell of a fine novel, right up here in East Texas, called *Joshua Bean and God*, which was on the best-seller lists?

BENNETT: Sam Pendergrast told me about meeting her, and I vaguely remembered the title.

HALE: Fine title. You know, the best title I've heard in a hundred years was Elmer Kelton's *The Time It Never Rained*. I think that could have been the great Texas novel. I don't mean that I could have done it better, because Elmer is really fine. But I think the publishers should have seen the potential in that story, because, God, it was great. I blame the editors. I've known Elmer a long time. We haven't been close; we've just crossed trails every once in a while. I saw him in Dallas not long ago, had breakfast. I'm a great admirer of his, because he's the real article, nothing phony about him.

BENNETT: Do you write the titles to your novels?

HALE: There's a give-and-take about it. They didn't like *Addison* at first. My editor up there thought that I should have some provocative three- or four-word phrase, but I was hung on the one word so long, from the first, and I just had to fight for it. They try to keep you happy, unless they think there's some real bad reason for a title not being used. Same way with your grammar, and your commas and semicolons. I had a hard time with them on my cussin' in *Bonney*. I've got this theory about terms like "goddam," and I use a little gee because it's just an expletive. So some copy editor up there very carefully went through and changed every one of my "goddams" into "God damned." And there were a lot of them. We had to thrash that out, and reset a lot of line of type. With experience you learn to anticipate these things and tell them in advance. They may argue about it before it gets into type, so you won't have to reset so much. That's one advantage of staying with the same publisher: they get to know your ways. On the other hand, it bothers me about Doubleday being so big. It's easy to get lost in the shuffle.

BENNETT: I wonder how many books they do annually.

HALE: I think it is something like a thousand. That means that every working day they've got to come out with five or six books, and you're just one of them. One morning your book comes out along with four or five others. It's a huge event in your life, and for all I know, at the publisher's it might not be as important as a coffee break. You've got to have a break, some way, a huge break. But, listen, it happens.

BENNETT: In our time, whose work do you like? Graves?

HALE: Oh, I don't like everything John does any more than he likes everything I do. He gets wordy sometimes, Ph.D.-sounding. But I love his *Goodbye to a River*. And I love Larry King when he comes back to Putnam, and I think he's written the Texas tongue better than anybody else. Are we talking about Texans only?

BENNETT: Anybody contemporary.

HALE: My favorite contemporary passage is that description by Ray Bradbury of a foghorn, and why it was invented, and how it sounded. It's the most beautiful thing. It's in a short story about how the foghorn calls up a monster from the deep.

BENNETT: What about young writers?

HALE: We've got a lot of good young writers here in the state. The way that realization came to me is that the last three or four years I've been on the judging panel for the Stanley Walker Award, which is administered through the Texas Institute of Letters. Some of that stuff that comes in is so good that, man, it'll make you want to quit. There's some great writing in two or three of these little city-type magazines which are springing up.

BENNETT: Anybody come to mind?

HALE: Someone I should have mentioned earlier, before we started talking about the younger writers, is Ben Green. He's dead now, of course. I remember the first one that came through the newsroom here, *Horse Trading*, and the book editor asked me if I wanted to read a Texas book to review. I just loved it. It was just so refreshing I couldn't believe it. I made a point to know him after that book, and they finally took him into the Texas Institute of Letters. He had a lot of strange things in his background which were talked about. I don't know if any of them were true; I don't care. He left us some really good old books, you bet. And, you know, we've got a guy right now doing some interesting books, old Bill Brett over in Liberty County, on the edge of the Big Thicket. He's a genuine guy, a real old cowboy, and he's got a wealth of material in him.

BENNETT: I gather you don't see other writers on a regular basis. Writing is a lonely business.

HALE: That's one of my problems: I always welcome interruption. And I wrote my first two books with two kids hanging around my feet, hollering for a drink of water or soda pop.

BENNETT: You write at home?

HALE: Right now I've got one room of the house. I could work up here in the newsroom. They'd give me a desk and telephone, but I don't want up here. Once in a while I'll come up here to write a column because a deadline's got me, and I just use somebody else's desk. I've always written with my home life and my work all mixed up together, and it's not really good.

BENNETT: I read somewhere that Bradbury wrote on a pay typewriter in a public library.

HALE: I do the column in a lot of strange places, on the tailgate of my station wagon, or under a shade tree. With all this computerized typesetting, I have to use an electric typewriter and special paper, but I've rigged up now where I can use the electric typewriter off my cigarette lighter. It takes twelve volts of DC current off the battery and steps it up and makes AC out of it. Of course, I can't stay too long without running my engine a little.

BENNETT: I've been trying to learn to use the visual display terminals which reporters write on now.

HALE: I used to say that when I had to use an electric typewriter I'd just quit. But they said I had to use an electric typewriter—and I didn't quit. I needed the work. I was one of those who put their elbows on the keyboard when they were thinking, and these IBMs just explode if you do that. Smoke comes out.

BENNETT: Have you ever tried radio or television?

HALE: I was on radio for a while. For three or four years I had a little old country-boy radio short going. We sold in Abilene and Amarillo and Lubbock—at one time we were on twenty-six stations with pretty much the same kind of junk I do in the column. I was living in Bryan at the time, and I'd go down there once a week to record five programs, and they'd stick commercials on it. It got to going pretty good, but it took a great big gasp one day and rared up and fell over dead. I never have known really whether it sold as well as it did because it was any good or because I had a master salesman peddling it. I've suspected the latter, because after he ran off, it never did go again.

BENNETT: Have you written any poetry?

HALE: I play around with it. I enjoy it, for fun. I write what I call a poem in the column every once in a while.

BENNETT: With rhyme?

HALE: Got to have it. Well, I do some of that blank stuff sometimes, making fun of it. I've got a calico cat at home that writes poetry; she does a column about every six months or so, as often as I think I can get away with it. I stole the idea from *archy and mehitabel*, of course. I have a sister who is a pretty good poet: Maifred Hale Cullen. She lives in Fort Worth. She has done a couple of poetry books, but she didn't get much recognition.

BENNETT: Becoming famous as a poet is doing it the hard way. However, Paul Foreman of Thorp Springs Press told me that his poets carried his business when he first began. He recently published a novel he had written.

HALE: Anybody that would publish his own novel—I'll tell you, that's faith.

June, 1979

Preston Jones: *In the Jaws of Time*

PRESTON JONES was born April 7, 1936, in Albuquerque, New Mexico. He earned his B.S. from the University of New Mexico in 1958 and his M.A. from Trinity in 1966. He joined the Dallas Theater Center in 1960 as actor, director, and, later, dramatist. His *Texas Trilogy* of 1974 brought him international fame. He died September 19, 1979, after becoming ill ten days earlier.

Almost all of Jones's professional life took place in the Dallas Theater Center, a southwestern holy place of drama designed by Frank Lloyd Wright and further sanctified by the great teacher-director Paul Baker. It is a compact, five-tiered building in a lushly wooded park area of the city's Turtle Creek section. Jones wasn't particularly localized in the building and borrowed the office of his wife, actress-designer Mary Sue Jones, for our conversation. The office, which Ms. Jones rates as assistant administrative director, is a geometric trapezium worked in beside a hallway; it measures roughly ten by six by eight by five feet, with a desk built in. Jones wrote with a pencil, which allowed him to write on a park bench or in a wing of the stage or, most often, on the dining table at home.

Jones was a six-footer with 185 pounds spread over his big frame. He had brown eyes and graying black hair. When I first met him the previous spring, he had a bushy mustache, but at the time of our talk he had shaved it off for a role in *The Devil's General*.

One can get only a dim impression of Jones's conversation from the written word. He was a man of the theater, and his voice was full of meaningful shadings, pauses, and tonal modulations. No Basin Street saxophone player ever produced more expressive sounds. His face spoke also. Jones often left sentences unfinished in a grammatical sense, but the weight of their intelligence was never in doubt when you were sitting across from him.

Jones died shortly after the successful Dallas production of *Remember*, the play he was revising at the time of our conversation. But *A Texas Trilogy* remains his best-known work, and his determination to follow it with other significant writing gives a poignancy to his closing remarks.

BENNETT: You have said that time is the enemy. What do you mean?

JONES: Well, it comes up again and again. I'm just fascinated with it, with time, with the effect of time on human beings. To me it is the greatest mystery in the world. I can't get over it. I've always been interested in people, and I can't imagine . . . .

My daughter came to visit me for the first time two or three weeks ago, not more than a month ago. I hadn't seen her for fourteen years—I'd lost contact with her mother and the family and that sort of thing—and my daughter was filling me in on happenings. I couldn't believe her. I just sat there. All that had happened over this relatively short period. People had died; people had gone away. It fascinated me.

A great friend of mine in junior high and high school and all the way through college—when we were kids we were just scared to death of that boy's father. He wasn't a mean or vicious man; we were just afraid of him, both of us. He was a very dynamic man, very outgoing. He was an engineer and built things, and he was a strict man. The two of us boys were very close. So when I went to Santa Fe many years later, his family had moved there, and I went up to visit them. My friend wasn't there, and the father welcomed me, said, "Come in and have a drink." W-e-l-l, here I am, a grown man, and I was very—I was very uncomfortable. Here I was a little kid again, you know. He said, "Have another one, Preston." Well, gee, I don't know; am I allotted? Yeah, yeah, yeah, he was talking, blah, blah, blah. It's an odd feeling. Time and its effects fascinate me. I don't know what it is . . . .

BENNETT: Why do you call it the enemy?

JONES: Because it just upsets me horribly to see how it erodes. Physically. My mother, for instance, had a stroke several years ago and is in an old folks' home. She doesn't live *now*; she lives back in 1960 or something. I've seen people who—and this is what's funny—they were probably my age when I was a kid, and I see them now and they are a little doddery, maybe in their seventies now. I can't get used to the fact. It's a religious thing too, I guess. Why did this happen? What did it do to us? Then, of course, here comes the next generation, and I'm sitting here worried. My daughter comes and throws it off like it's nothing.

BENNETT: I understand that you used to live in Colorado City, Texas.

JONES: My first wife was from Colorado City. I was there on and off for several years. In '59 or '60, when I had finished school at the

University of New Mexico, I was waiting to come to graduate school—not here in Dallas, but at Baylor in Waco, which at that time was connected with this theater here—and I took a job at the State Highway Department there in Colorado City. I worked that spring and summer and lived there in town. Before we went to Waco.

BENNETT: Your description of Bradleyville has the ring of truth.

JONES: I knew quite a few people there. My daughter and son and ex-wife and her husband still live there. I must get back one of these days. The last time I was in Colorado City was just before we went into production of *A Texas Trilogy* at Kennedy Center. The set designer came from New York, Ben Edwards, and he wanted a look at West Texas. So we hopped in the car and went, oh, gosh, everywhere. We went to San Angelo, Big Spring, Sterling, Colorado City, Sweetwater, Haskell—so he could get an idea how to do the set. We had a pretty good time. He is originally from the South.

BENNETT: Did you study theater at the University of New Mexico?

JONES: I originally took a degree in speech, in secondary education. I taught a semester in high school at Tucumcari, New Mexico. Before that I had taken a few courses in drama and done one or two plays. I got interested in drama late in college, but I was too far along to change horses, so I went ahead and finished in speech. Then Eddie Snapp told me if I'd come back to the University of New Mexico and do the shows, he'd arrange a graduate school. I went back to Albuquerque and took another year, just straight drama. I was interested then in directing more than anything else. Eddie Snapp had gone to school with Paul Baker at Yale, and so he recommended Mr. Baker very highly, and sent in things here, and I was accepted here. Then the Highway Department, then Waco. I only went one semester at Waco, and then Mr. Baker brought me up to the Theater Center, and I've been here ever since.

BENNETT: Was that about the time of the battle over *Long Day's Journey into Night*?

JONES: That was in '63, and I came in '61. I was in kind of a bind. There were three of us who had finished all our master's requirements except our theses. We transferred to Trinity, and the graduate dean let us have all our hours. So I got one degree from the University of New Mexico and the other from Trinity. I jokingly tell people that I was expelled from Baylor.

BENNETT: Did you have anything to do with *Long Day's Journey*?

JONES: No, that was a student production in Waco. I don't believe any of our people here were involved, no.

BENNETT: Did Tucumcari whet your interest in theater?

JONES: No, it was really just a semester. I was considering going back again, but I went back to the university to go through the cap-and-gown thing so mother could see me, and at the president's tea I ran into Eddie Snapp, who made this offer. I packed up very quickly from Tucumcari.

BENNETT: The thing that originally got you interested was being in a couple of plays?

JONES: The very first play I was in was called *Such Sweet Sorrow*, written by Pauline Snapp, Eddie's wife. It was just a thing where I saw a notice on the board, went over, and tried out. I knew several people in the drama department. I was in a fraternity at the time, and I used to write little skits for them every year. The other show I did for the department was *The Lark*. When I went back from Tucumcari I worked in *The Rivals* and *Abe Lincoln in Illinois* and *The Adding Machine* and I don't know what all. Then I worked in a little theater in another place, and I did *Green Grow the Lilacs*.

To show you how small this business is: I did *The Visit* and *Green Grow* with a fellow named Bill Pappas, that I was in school with. In fact, he was in the very first play I ever wrote, a one-act play at the University of New Mexico, through the playwrighting class. They took the three they thought were the best and produced them. It was called *The Eye of the Beholder*, which I think is a very good title, but I understand there is a book out now with the same title. Well, it was kind of fun. Then we went our separate ways. And two years ago I was doing a play of mine called *A Place on the Magdalena Flats* in Santa Fe, and my lead was the same one, Drexel Riley, who played it here. Then he couldn't go, and we were going to do it again, at the College of Santa Fe, and so they said, "Oh, we know an actor by the name of Bill Pappas . . . ." So he played my lead up there, with a twenty-year or maybe more span between the time he played my two shows.

BENNETT: I gather you've actually been writing a long time.

JONES: Well, off and on. I wrote that little one-act play.

BENNETT: You wrote those fraternity skits.

JONES: That's not exactly—well, I guess you'd call that for the stage.

BENNETT: Did you do anything like that in high school?

JONES: No, nothing. I guess I've always been interested in writing. Somehow people have got the misconception that I just sat down and started writing these plays, and that's not true. But when there's five or six years between efforts, maybe even more .... The next serious writing I did was on my thesis.

BENNETT: What did you write your thesis on?

JONES: I adapted a novel, *The Night of the Hunter*, which Charles Laughton had made a movie of. My thesis was that this selfsame novel could be adapted to the stage as well as the screen. The thesis was mainly geared to the Dallas Theater Center. There's a river scene, for instance, where the kids go down a river, and I was going to use the revolve. It's still around somewhere, and I'll have to look at it one of these days. I also had to write a prerequisite play.

BENNETT: Have you ever tried to write anything outside the theater? A novel?

JONES: No. No, I have many friends who are novelists, but I have trouble writing descriptions—it bores me. I guess that's being in the theater so long. I'll give you what setting I want, but I know full well that set designers will take it and do with it what they want. In this new play of mine I just say—it takes place in a motel room—and I just say, "The play opens in a typical Holiday Inn-type motel room in a western American state in the year '76." I say there's a double bed, bedside table, desk, this sort of thing. Unless it has to be really specific; for example, in *Knights* I talk about the flags, where they are, and the cross. But I think being a novelist would be very difficult because you must do the description.

BENNETT: Some of them don't know where to stop.

JONES: Thomas Wolfe. I grew up in college with Thomas Wolfe, or rather grew up with his novels.

BENNETT: Did you do any acting in Colorado City?

JONES: There was no place to do it when I was there. I understand there is a theater there now. The opera house. I don't even remember it, don't even know exactly where it was. I guess it was shut down or something then.

BENNETT: How long do you write at a stretch?

JONES: It depends on where I am. When I start with an idea, I like to finish it. Only one time have I started a play, gone to something else, and then come back to it. It didn't work very well. I just about have to concentrate on what I'm doing, or it gets to be a mishmash. I was a little upset with myself on that play. That's not to say that I don't rewrite a play many, many times, but I like to stay with the same project until I get through. I'll write sometimes all night, and sleep, and work all night again, until I've got the play down. Then I go back and work again.

BENNETT: So you do a lot of writing at night.

JONES: It's a habit I acquired when I was doing a lot of acting here at the theater. I'd do a show, and then go home and work. I'll work all night long sometimes. Which is kind of good, you know, if you've got the chance, because the phone doesn't ring; there's no noise or anything around. I get a lot more done. This afternoon I'm just going over what I did last night.

BENNETT: Do you have any trouble sleeping after these sessions?

JONES: No, I'll sleep late, then hit it again. Some nights. I can't do it every night. And I can only do this when I'm not working on a show, of course.

BENNETT: How long does it take you to rough out a play?

JONES: It depends on the play. A week. Two weeks. It's hard to say, after you've had one, two, three, four, five, six plays done, since '74. Everybody says that's pretty fast, but to me it doesn't seem so. Then too I work on the play while it's in rehearsal. I'm lucky that way: I don't have to go with a completely finished product. For example, with this play, *Remember*, I'll go ahead and check in with my actors at today's rehearsal and show them what I've got for them. We'll read over again. And then we'll just talk about it. Other things come up, and I'll take that back home to work with it. That was basically my idea on this play; that's the way I wanted to work it. Other times I'll come in with the completed play, and then, as things happen in rehearsal, things are changed around, or I'll find that I've overstaged something. I hear the actor, and it's done, and I think that's a very important step in playwrighting—where you hear the actors.

BENNETT: That must be a great advantage.

JONES: Yes, because I tend to overstate. I mean, I'll make the point, and then I'll make it again, and then I'll make it again, because it's just me listening to myself. But then when I hear the actor . . . .

BENNETT: Do you know how many words you write at one session?

JONES: No.

BENNETT: Well, how many pages do you generate, between something and something?

JONES: Very difficult to answer. I just can't put a number on it. Sometimes one, sometimes a bunch.

BENNETT: On the first draft, do you use a typewriter or a pencil?

JONES: I don't type at all. I just write it out in longhand. I have a typist who works for us. She does my correspondence and all my plays.

BENNETT: Do you plot in detail before you begin?

JONES: Usually, I'll start with me. It may be just an idea; it may not be a whole plot. For example, with this play, *Remember*, I was in Santa Fe with a play of mine, and a whole bunch of friends got together, ex-fraternity buddies I hadn't seen in a while. They came to see the show, and afterward there was all this talk: "Whatever happened to so-and-so?" and, "Hey, remember the time we did this and that?" It got me thinking about different things. The play isn't about a college reunion or anything like that, but I started thinking about the play then.

I decided for my lead to use an actor who was coming back to town, in order to use some of my experiences there. He runs into an old girl friend who happens to be in Santa Fe who is married to somebody else now. I thought, That's kind of interesting, and I'll keep thinking about it. Then when I sat down to work, as I went along, other things occurred. When you start feeling the play snowball, then you know you're on the right track. The hard part is making that first breakthrough; then it becomes easier. A lot of playwrights I know, and novelists and other writers, will make an outline, but I do not. I tried that once. I threw it away and went back to what I was doing, because as I was thinking of the next step in the outline I was thinking to add onto A and not B . . . . I decided to heck with it.

BENNETT: How much revision?

JONES: Oh, boy, lots!

BENNETT: Before rehearsals begin, do you put it through several drafts?

JONES: At least four. In some cases seven.

BENNETT: Do you let your typists type it and then revise?

JONES: She doesn't get it until I'm satisfied. It's all written like this. I don't know if it's a bad habit or not, but if I start to revise I have to start back at point A. I can never say to myself, Scene one is great; scene two is bad—I'll start on scene two. The minute I start on scene two I think, Oops, I should do something in scene one. So I'll go all the way back, and this means completely rewriting the play. That's when it gets tedious. You want to yell at people and tear your hair.

BENNETT: Do you like to write?

JONES: I love to.

BENNETT: Do you like to revise? Or do you prefer first draft?

JONES: I kind of like to revise. It's really kind of fun to do. It's tedious, and it's the hard part, but you run into a few things. Like here just today I fooled around and wrote what I thought was kind of a funny speech. I'm glad that happened. Had I not been revising it and fooling around with it, it wouldn't have happened—the play would have gone without that speech. Of course, there comes a point when you've got to stop and say: "Hold on now, Preston. You can't sit around and revise all the time. You've got to move on." Once I'm satisfied, I give it to Jo, and she'll type it, and then I'll have it read.

BENNETT: Read? How is that done?

JONES: In the theater. Sometimes in our company, our meetings, we'll read new plays. I'll Xerox off a number of scripts, and then we'll read it. But in the case of *Remember*, Mr. Baker and I decided to go ahead and cast it and then read it, because, for one thing, all the actors in it are around in their forties; so it's silly to hold open auditions. I didn't write it for anyone special here. We're in the process of reading and rereading now.

BENNETT: You've already had your reading, and you're still working on it?

JONES: Oh, sure. I'm doing big revisions of this play, but I knew I would. It was way too short when I presented it the first time. I sent a version off to my agent, and she read it and said what she thought, which was basically what I wanted to do with it also. I said: "Well, here's the first copy; just see what you think. If you think it's absolute rubbish then I'll go out and start on something else, but otherwise I'll stay with this."

It occurs to me that the only time I ever successfully worked with an outline was when I converted *Graduate* and *Lu Ann* into a screenplay. That one I had to. I was taking scenes out and putting them back in; here it was written, but to combine the two . . . .

BENNETT: Do you have some nibbles on it?

JONES: Oh, yes, but I haven't signed anything yet. They're being very cautious, which is fine with me. I'm in no hurry. It would be terrible to rush into production on that. So many things torn up that way.

BENNETT: Do you have any advice for young dramatists?

JONES: No.

BENNETT: That was quick.

JONES: I'm just funning. I remember John Steinbeck won the Nobel Prize, right during the Cuban missile crisis. When the television news came on, it showed the Cuban crisis. Then this interview with Steinbeck, this deep voice. [*mimics*] They said, "Well, what were you doing when you heard about the Nobel?" "Why, I was watching that missile business." "Do you have any advice for young writers?" "No." It was funny.

I can only talk about playwrighting, naturally, but I tend to think—this is my own experience, now, and to a lot of people it won't mean a thing—but I think that the place to learn how to write plays is to be in the theater. I think it is very important that I've worked in different parts of the theater: acting, directing, you name it. I don't mean you've got to drive the Theater Center truck to be a playwright, but I think it's very important that the fledgling playwright works in the theater so he knows what he's going into. You find out what you're going to be working with. People send me plays, and I simply can't read all of the plays that I get, but most of the plays that I get and that I see by new playwrights tend to, number one, overuse the facility, and, number two, put far too much into what they are doing. It was also with me the same thing. It was with this play I wrote, prior to writing the thesis play. I put their entire lives into this one play. I could make about six plays out of that. Everything was there; it was burdened down. I think that when you act in plays and direct, you learn not to do this. You learn by working with the words of other authors, and by getting out there and actually doing things. You learn, Hey, I'm putting too much in here. I think you'll find for the most part that playwrights who have acted before will write more for the actor.

I try to stay away, for example, from mechanical devices. About the only time I've used one was in *Knights* with the flashing cross. Because I know from experience that sometimes the gun doesn't shoot, and if that's a high point of the play, well, you're in trouble. Regardless of your dialogue. You can have beautiful dialogue, and the tape-recording truck doesn't show up, and there you are.

I think actual stage experience is very important. I've talked to several groups around colleges—I was at Penn State, Ohio State, Texas Christian University, and, you know, not too many places—and stressed experience. It's not mandatory, God knows, because the students sit there and poke people at me who've never been around the theatre, and that's fine. But I think experience is important.

BENNETT: Are you involved in every production at the center?

JONES: Personally? Usually one or two a year. As an actor? I simply don't have time. I perform in my own play, in *The Texas*

Trilogy, simply because I've done it before. I took a role in this current play because I had worked with the director, Harry Buckwitz, and he asked me if I'd do it. But I haven't done back-to-back shows like I'm doing now in, oh, I don't know how many years. I try to do at least a show a year, because I think for me it is good discipline.

BENNETT: Do you also teach here?

JONES: No, I don't. I never have.

BENNETT: How do you select the names for your characters?

JONES: That's very difficult for me. Important for me too, the names. For some reason, for me, the names have to ring true. If they don't, I can't do anything with the character. I'll combine names of people that I know. I never pick out a person like a name out of a hat, such as John Figgleman, because I don't like to base a character on a particular person I know.

BENNETT: Your names are quite good.

JONES: I think it's important they should be. I ponder a lot about names. Sometimes if I get the right name that will start opening up doors to the character for me. I make lists. Sometimes, when you see an original manuscript of mine, you can see where I scratched it out and put somebody else, and scratched that out, and another name, and combined these two, and tossed that one out too.

BENNETT: Do you use name books or anything of that nature?

JONES: No, no. I've known enough people. I can always come up with—or I try to—the right name. That's important to me. It is right now in this new play. I'm hung up on a name for the old girl friend. It'll come to me; I'll get it. I've got one now, but it doesn't sound right.

BENNETT: Is there any particular way in which you generate ideas?

JONES: The first two plays, *Lu Ann* and *Knights*, they're plays I had thought about for a long time. When I started *Lu Ann*, I invented the little town of Bradleyville. After I had done that I thought, Aha, that's a perfect setting for this *Knights* play that I'm going to write. Then in the third play I knew the character I wanted to write about was the colonel. *Knights* and *Lu Ann* had already been produced before I wrote *The Oldest Living Graduate*. I was watching television, Channel Thirteen, and one of the schools here in town, a Catholic school, Ursuline Academy, was moving from its old location to a new one. And they introduced this lady—said she was the oldest living graduate. I told my wife, "That's kind of sad; that's not a bad title." That's where I got the title for that show. I just incorporated a little bit of that idea into *The Oldest Living Graduate*, the school moving and that sort of thing.

BENNETT: You've already said that you often incorporate suggestions made at rehearsals.

JONES: Oh, certainly, yes, and that's fine with me. In no way am I the type of author who says, "This is it; now you stay with that." That's ridiculous, that is absolute insanity—with a new play.

BENNETT: Do you continue to work with a good show, which already plays successfully, like *Magnolia*, for instance?

JONES: No. It was very interesting the second time we did it here, because when I went to New York with the shows, we made some revisions in *Graduate* and in *Lu Ann*. Not too many. *Knights* never changes much; it's just too difficult to do. But when I came back, the cast wanted their old way of doing it. So I said, "Well, okay."

BENNETT: Which version was in the printed edition?

JONES: The printed way was the Washington production. What happened was that it was published by Hill and Wang first, before New York. There are some things I wish weren't there, but there they are.

BENNETT: Are there other Texas writers you admire?

JONES: Oh, gosh, yes. John Graves and A. C. Greene, among others. I'll tell you some I admire very much are the fellows who write those columns, John Anders and Dick Shedd. There are some gems in those things, and I'm always amazed that they do it day after day.

A marvelous author from Texas, who has written one of the funniest books I've ever read, is Bob Flynn, in San Antonio. The book is *North to Yesterday*, an absolute masterpiece. I think that somebody is going to rediscover it one of these days and take it right to the moon. A beautiful book. Another is a book called *A Street Full of People*, by Winston Estes. He lives in Washington now, and he looked me up. We had a nice talk. I was staying at the Watergate. He sent me a copy of his book, and I just love it. It's a dandy. And, of course, McMurtry. I met him briefly in Washington. Seems like everybody is in Washington right now.

BENNETT: Then there's D. L. Coburn.

JONES: I know Don very well.

BENNETT: Is *The Gin Game* his only play?

JONES: It's enough.

BENNETT: Any other southwestern dramatists?

JONES: There's not an awful lot of us, I'll tell you. Some young playwrights that I don't know personally are coming along now. A very good writer, Sam Havens, from Houston, a very good playwright. And Oliver Haley is from Texas; he's had several plays in New York.

BENNETT: How did Coburn come to write *The Gin Game*?

JONES: He and I were doing a commercial—or I was doing a commercial, and Don was the writer. That's when we first met. And Don's a big baseball player too; we had that in common. We were out at the lake somewhere. So I was talking about what I did, and what he did, and that sort of thing. There was a one-man show at the Theater Center called *Diary of a Madman* that Tom Troupe was doing in our little theater downstairs. I believe he told me he'd never seen a theater play before, and I said, "Come and see the thing." Well, he just got enthralled with it. He came about a dozen times. He came up to me when I was just getting these plays on, and he said he had a one-act play that he had finished. And I told him, well, if he possibly could to extend it into two acts, because there was no market for one-act plays. So he said, well, he thought he could. [*big laugh*] He did.

BENNETT: And that was *The Gin Game*?

JONES: Yeah. So, that's my advice to a young writer: if you can change it to two acts, okay.

BENNETT: Are there any of these plays you particularly admire?

JONES: Don's. I like *The Gin Game* very much. I like *A Different Drummer*, by Gene McKinney, one of the first shows I did when I came to this theater. I'm crazy about Glenn Smith's plays—*Curious in L.A.* comes to mind. Glenn has been writing a lot longer than I have, and his plays are just now beginning to really start doing things. He wrote *Home Away From* that my wife Mary Sue was in off Broadway in New York. He has a new play that I understand is very, very good that follows *Remember* on Down Stage Center. To me, pound for pound, maybe Glenn is the best of the current playwrights.

BENNETT: More broadly, what twentieth-century dramatists influenced you?

JONES: The greatest was Thornton Wilder, of *Our Town*. Oh, boy, anybody who could write a play as good as that! I was in it; it just tore me to pieces. It's not one of those things where I sat down to write a better play than his. Then there was Arthur Miller's *The Price*, which I think is a beautifully done play. In fact, whenever I get bogged down, or messed up, or discouraged, then I go back to read it, not to steal anything, but just to see the beautiful way he sets things up. It's just a marvelous piece. Well, I'd include quite a few—you see, I've done many, many, many shows.

BENNETT: Have you ever read William Archer's book on playwriting?

JONES: I have read no books on playwriting. Oh, I remember reading a few when I was in playwriting class. Let's see: *How Not to Write a Play*.

BENNETT: Many books on writing aren't much good.

JONES: Writing is such an individual thing. Probably what you're doing in these interviews is the best help. Because then a person can see many different viewpoints.

I was very interested in reading Hemingway's letter to Fitzgerald recently. It was in the *Saturday Review* or something. I like letters. Anyway, Hemingway said when he ran into trouble was when he tried to describe a scene he didn't know. Faked it. Bang! Exactly what happened to me with *Magdalena Flats*. I had a suicide scene, and I didn't know anything about suicide, so I just went ahead and faked it. It didn't turn out very well. Also he said another thing. He told Fitzgerald that only a fairy would deliberately sit down to write a masterpiece. I thought of having a big sign with that on it put up in the dining room where I work. I'm not a huge Hemingway fan; I've enjoyed some of his books, not all. But I enjoyed that.

BENNETT: I'm a little confused by the chronology of *Texas Trilogy*. They are not like *Mourning Becomes Electra*, where three plays follow in sequence.

JONES: We've done them chronologically.

BENNETT: The way you wrote them?

JONES: No, we broke them up. We start off with the first act of *Lu Ann*. We do it by year, don't you see. They've done it in Wichita Falls too, and a couple of other places. It works fine, all in one evening.

BENNETT: How long does it run?

JONES: Well, *Long Day's Journey into West Texas*, we had dinner in between. They did the same thing other places. The only problem I see is that we have the death of the colonel, and then we have two more acts of *Lu Ann*, and the death is hard to follow. I worried about that, but it didn't seem to hurt anything here. When I wrote those plays, I wrote them specifically so that they would stand up by themselves. I was being practical, thinking maybe I could sell one out of the three. But what ties the trilogy together is not any one character—there is no one character appearing in all three—but it's the town. In our case here we played to the point where the colonel is going to the meeting, then the meeting, and then he comes back. In New York we did them in rep, but it doesn't matter where they are in the book, when they are printed as three separate plays.

BENNETT: There is no time lapse in *Last Meeting*.

JONES: No, that's a false break.

BENNETT: Shaw has a couple of plays like that. Somebody has called them "long one-acts."

JONES: They've done that with *Knights* too. It's really longer than a one-act, though. I put that break in there because I've been in this business long enough to know you've got to have a break. I've seen that too somewhere else, where they stop and start again in the same place. But when we do them all together, then we don't put in the break at all. When we do *Long Day's Journey into West Texas* we just run *Knights* straight through.

BENNETT: Did the audience come in the afternoon for *Long Day's Journey*?

JONES: No, they were out at two. Seven to two, or six to two, something like that. There were several intermissions.

BENNETT: *Lu Ann* reminds me of Arnold Bennet's *Milestones* in its treatment of time. Did you have any specific model in mind?

JONES: With *Lu Ann*? No. The person gets older as the play goes along. I had to do it in acts, and ten-year periods seemed to me the right breaks to make. Not fifteen, or twelve and a half—they'd be all the time looking at their programs. I didn't know I wanted the cycle to go all the way around when I started.

BENNETT: Do you consider *The Oldest Living Graduate* a tragedy or a comedy?

JONES: A little of both.

BENNETT: How should it be played?

JONES: All my plays should be played just as naturally as you possibly can. I don't think in any of the plays there is a setup where *this is a comic situation*. It will be funny if it's just played. The worst production I ever saw of one of my plays—I'm not going to say where; it wasn't in Texas—was when they went at *Knights* like a complete caricature, and it just exploded. It was so wrong that I was about to climb under the chair. Everything was blown way out of proportion. There are a lot of throwaway things in the play. I like to throw something away and move on to the next line, and they'd land on those time after time. For example, the initiation: some of the guys take it very seriously. Not all the brothers are serious, but some are, and it's much funnier when a guy who can't read or is really having trouble with it—you know, instead of horsing around with it. If everybody is horsing around, it's not funny. What is funny is when L. D. says, "All right now, do it right." Or when Milo says, "This isn't right, you know; everybody has got to be standing up or sitting down, one of the two." That's funny. You don't want to camp on this stuff. The same with *Graduate*. Randy Moore plays it so beautifully because he plays it just pow, pow, smoothly, and this makes it much more poignant when you hit the end. I've seen colonels try to camp on his telephone conversation with the minister, but it loses something.

BENNETT: You've taken up the career of a cheerleader. Have you read Ralph Keyes's *Is There Life After High School?* or Coleman's study of the social structure of the high school?

JONES: No, but they sound interesting. Here's something I'll read you in this play I'm working on. This fellow is talking about a friend of his who was a big shot in high school. He says: "The trouble was that we graduated. So long high school and hello college. This fellow couldn't hack it, couldn't make the grade. He flunked out, and so he went home, put on his high school letter sweater, placed his prizes, trophies, and pictures in a neat pile on the floor, and then hung himself. Hung himself! That's right, hung himself. For him high school was his entire life: love, honor, career, happiness, everything."

BENNETT: Coleman and Keyes divide high-school students into "innies" and "outies."

JONES: My little bunch were "middies." It's funny, but lately I'm hearing from all the people I hadn't heard from in years. We're having our twentieth high-school reunion in June—or maybe twenty-fifth. I'm torn whether to go or not. Now I'm interested; I'd like to see them, find out who are the superachievers, and who were and aren't now. Like my character in the play, I don't know who went from school to nowhere. Some innies never really learned to compete, really, and when they hit the really biggie guys at college, it was a whole different story. Things started to turn around right there, just in that one-year stand. So now the outies were becoming presidents of fraternities and that sort of thing . . . .

BENNETT: Some high-school football stars were surprised.

JONES: I didn't play at all. In those days we played single-platoon football. You had to be a pretty big boy. I played baseball and basketball. When I grew up, a friend of mine sent me a picture showing our bunch—we had a Hi-Y group—and we were a mixture of everything. There was the first-string guard on the team, and the guy who was a chess champion. We were a weird bunch. When we were seniors in high school, we refused to attend the pep rallies; this is '54

I'm talking about. There were enough ballplayers in our little bunch that we weren't destroyed by irate jocks.

BENNETT: In *A Texas Trilogy* in particular you examine all kinds of time.

JONES: I think you're more aware of time in little towns like Colorado City. In theater I don't think of things as much in years as in theatrical seasons. In fact, I'll have people ask when I wrote a certain thing, and I'll say, "What play was the Theater Center doing at that time? When I get the two together, I'll tell you what year it was."

I think that being in the theater gives you a younger outlook. With this theater you're working with young kids all the time. When I got together with those ex-fraternity brothers of mine in Santa Fe, with one exception I thought, My God, here I am with a bunch of old men. It upset me with myself, that I wanted to talk about the good old times, and have some beers, and sing old fraternity songs—and they didn't. I left with the feeling of an absolute idiot. Geology professors and whatever, they were quite compatible with each other, don't you see, but not with me.

An interesting phenomenon of the fifties is that, well, I can't think of but maybe two of my close friends who married right out of college and stayed that way very long. These friends that I met were working on, say, marriage number three. One of them had gone up to four. And here I am, in this crazy business, and Mary Sue and I have been married for twenty years, and just one wife before that, so I don't count at all. Consequently some of the people I know have grown kids and little tiny ones too. I think it had something to do with the Victorian climate of our college, the University of New Mexico, in those days. In this order they would graduate with their engineering degree, get their lieutenant's bars in ROTC, get married, and go away.

BENNETT: The happily-ever-after didn't follow.

JONES: I would venture to guess that the exceptions were the ones who stayed together.

BENNETT: Is *Knights* about time?

JONES: Not as much as the others.

BENNETT: It's about the effect of time on the lodge.

JONES: Yes, but not as much individually. They talk about the old days. L. D. says, "Boy, back in the old days we were great." And one of the members is the colonel who really remembers the big days, but all he remembers is getting drunk and throwing up all over the place.

BENNETT: But *Lu Ann* is about time. Critics have said that's the weakest of the three, but in a lot of ways it is the most interesting.

JONES: I was worried about that play when it went out. I thought everybody was going to want to be the colonel, because that was very popular. But I've found that *Lu Ann* has done very well—very good reviews on *Lu Ann* from around. Once again, it's how you go at it; the *Lu Ann* lead is very important.

BENNETT: It is a plum for an actress.

JONES: It scares a lot of actresses. They are afraid of either the first act or the third. I think that might have happened to us in New York. I think Diane Ladd was a little bit afraid of that first act.

BENNETT: How old was she?

JONES: Late thirties, I guess, and that first act scared her a bit.

BENNETT: You have a generation time problem with *Graduate*.

JONES: That always comes into it. The colonel has a long speech in there, remembering back . . . . The only reason he keeps this one piece of land, which is important, is so that an old man can have a place to remember on, which I thought was kind of fun.

That is really not as specific as the effect of time on Lu Ann, but it is times changing. That is different from the effect of the progress of time on an individual. You can either change with time or not change, but it still marches on. I've got a line in the screenplay where she talks about Skip. She says he's been walking around at the bottom of an hourglass until the sand is finally enough to go over his head. I thought that was a kind of fun thing: he lets it pile up until pfff.

BENNETT: Have you ever gone into the opinions of formal philosophers on time?

JONES: I put together a speech one time once for a class. I was very interested in the writing of Calderón de la Barca: *Life Is a Dream*. Being a Catholic—I have a Catholic background—I was always fascinated and skeptical and awestruck at the same time about mysteries. Perhaps that's why you have so many Catholic and Jewish writers: the religion is of such a structure that you start pondering this and then you find yourself pondering the whole human experience. Only lately has that really come home to me.

One thing I'm blessed with is a good memory, and I remember vividly when I was in high school we were going by the college campus and one of my sisters said, "Hey, look at those kids." I remember, gosh, they seemed to be huge adults to me. Now they just look like kids.

BENNETT: Do you think of yourself as a realist or a naturalist?

JONES: Probably more realist than naturalist if you want to use those terms. If you can find a thing between the two . . . . I think in this country far too often writers get pigeonholed. You try to step out to do something else, and, "Oh, Preston Jones can't do that because he is a realist." I got an awful lot of flak on a comedy I wrote. I thought the comedy was funny, and what upset me a little was that the criticism I got wasn't that the comedy wasn't funny but that what I had written was just pure out-and-out comedy. So why not? Write the criticism on the play's merits. One of the magazines went so far as to say I was just pulling wool over the public's eyes, that I was just messing around. The audience seemed to have a good time and laughed. That happens too many times. Neil Simon tries to write a fairly serious play, and he gets clobbered for it.

BENNETT: Or Woody Allen and *Interiors*.

JONES: What you first come out with does it, and then there you are. It's a hard mold to break. Nobody really wants you in that vein. "Write us another *Magdalena Flats*." "No, I don't want to." "Oh, yeah, write one."

BENNETT: You fool around a lot with a decaying small town——

JONES: That's just in the trilogy. In *Santa Fe*, I deal with Santa Fe. And *Magdalena* is mostly about the ranch, not about the town.

When I first came to Dallas from Waco, I would go through Italy and Milford and that way around—now we've got a goodie that passes Hillsboro and passes them all. But the last time I made the trip I took the old way, and I was shocked. Stores all boarded up. So I used that kind of image for Bradleyville. Colorado City isn't all that bad. That decay interested me. You remember: he says that the bypass has gone around, and it's true that either you move to where the bypass is or that's it.

BENNETT: What do you consider your literary goal?

JONES: To build up a body of sound work. It's fascinating to me to do this screenplay. I'm not going to get into that business, but it's a different medium, and I think I'm going to enjoy it very much. I'm signed on now as the screenwriter, and I'm looking forward to it. The business is at a contract-signing stage with my agent in New York. You know, I needed publicity, and I've got it, and it's going to enable me now to do things other than the theater. That's exciting to me.

BENNETT: Is Colorado City close to being Bradleyville?

JONES: Not really. I set the plays in that area. I didn't want to call it Colorado City, because I'm not writing about Colorado City. I'd lived there, and I wanted to be really specific about where people were going, and so I thought I'd use Colorado City's locale and another town name, because I wanted to make up the town myself, which I did. I made a map, and I've got a place where the colonel lives, and Main Street, and .... I just made it up myself. But I had the locale of Colorado City definitely in my mind. You talk about going to Big Spring, which I think is fun, or San Angelo, or Abilene. A guy says, "I lived in Abilene and got transferred here." I stay with a specific place for the same reason I do with a specific character.

BENNETT: Are any of your characters based on specific people?

JONES: No, not really.

BENNETT: Did you have anybody specifically in mind with the colonel, for instance?

JONES: No.

BENNETT: Do you write with certain actors in mind for the parts?

JONES: No, never. Especially myself. I'm very bad in my plays; I think I am.

BENNETT: Which character did you play in the *Trilogy*?

JONES: L. D.—Henderson Forsythe did him in New York. I copied his performance as much as I could. I told him that. Now he's really hit it big with *The Best Little Bleep in Texas*. We were kidding about that. No, I definitely don't write with an actor in mind, because it seems to me that would limit you horribly.

BENNETT: Bernard Shaw did.

JONES: Well, that's all right. Somebody might accuse me of it, because some of the actors here fit so well in the parts. It has occurred to me that I might do it, but I always get rid of the idea. It's just not good business. Your character has to be done by you. I wouldn't even for Mary Sue. Then your character has taken on a wrong dimension, don't you see. It's wrong. I'm glad Mr. Shaw isn't around to disagree with me.

BENNETT: Shaw was trying hard to get his plays produced. So he wrote roles for Ellen Terry, Henry Irving——

JONES: I can understand that.

BENNETT: Did you enjoy the time you lived in Colorado City?

JONES: I really enjoyed it.

BENNETT: Were there many people there your age?

JONES: Not really. Mike Hammonds was a good friend, and we would go fishing. He was older than I was. My only other real buddy there, besides the guys on the Highway Department, was a fellow named Chili Black.

There's a funny story about Colorado City. The weekly newspaper there had a contest which was designed to encourage the people of Colorado City to shop in their hometown, instead of going to San Angelo. What you did was write a little poem about how much easier it was to shop there and why you did that. First prize was a ten-year subscription to the *Colorado City Record* or a bag of groceries at the Pick and Pay, something like that. A blue-plate dinner at the Dairy Queen . . . .

BENNETT: Did you enter it?

JONES: Every time the paper came out.

BENNETT: Did you win?

JONES: I would write these long epics. I thought they were great. And a guy by the name of Joe Earnest beat me every confounded time, a lawyer there in town. He was writing these small things, and I was writing these massive . . . . He'd be first and I'd be second, or he'd be first and I'd be third. I never met him, never saw him. Well, years later I was in Midland, when they were going to build their new theater there. I understand it is finished now. Well, for their dedication play they were doing *Graduate*. Actually *Graduate* was then under option, was then playing in Washington, but I got my producer to let them do it. It wasn't going to hurt our Washington audience. So at this dedication we were all standing around in the Petroleum Club, having a drink and looking at the model of the new building, and yak-yak. A guy comes up to me and says, "I brought something for you," and he handed me an envelope. He says, "It's some clippings that I cut out about you that I had seen if you hadn't." I said, "Thank you very much," and I looked later at the return address on the envelope: Joe Earnest, attorney-at-law. "Well, I've been wanting to meet you for years." When they asked me later to give them a talk, I told them that story about Joe Earnest. It turns out that he is one of the guiding lights behind the theater at Colorado City and a great theater buff—went all the way to Midland, goes to Dallas.

BENNETT: Is *A Texas Trilogy* a hard act to follow?

JONES: Yeah, it really is. Frankly, I'm getting a little tired of it now.

BENNETT: But you've got to follow it.

JONES: Oh, you bet! It's something that has to be done. But I don't know that I'll ever have the freedom that I felt when I wrote those first plays. Ever again. I'm just a lot more critical of myself, and I feel that with the two that follow, *Magdalena* especially—I'm still working on *Magdalena*—I was overly critical about myself, overly specific, and I didn't just let the action go like it's supposed to go. I won't lie to you; it's difficult. It was years and years ago I did those. Well, it hasn't been all that long, three years, two years, with the big hoopla about it. I don't want it to be my—like the fellow in *Long Day's Journey* with *The Count of Monte Cristo*; that's all the father did. Really, my *From Here to Eternity*.

BENNETT: You see writers who are paralyzed by that first success.

JONES: My wife, bless her soul, got this book for me on the man who wrote *Raintree County* and the man who wrote *Mr. Roberts*, and she made sure I read it.

BENNETT: Your situation here at the Theater Center should help.

JONES: That's right. And I'll use the other doors this has opened for me, not only in my writing but in my acting. But, thank God, I'm getting tired of the *Trilogy*. I'll go on and do something else.

February, 1979

Elmer Kelton: *Racial Friction Out West*

ELMER KELTON was born April 29, 1926, in Andrews County, Texas. After serving in the U.S. Army in World War II, he completed his B.A. in 1948 at the University of Texas in Austin. He joined the *San Angelo Standard-Times*, where he was farm-and-ranch editor until 1963. Then he became associate editor of the *West Texas Livestock Weekly*. Kelton sold many western stories to magazines before he turned to novels.

Elmer and Ann Kelton live on quiet Oxford Street, near the university in San Angelo. Back in his study there are books everywhere, all kinds, but most concerned with the American West. Originally twelve by fifteen feet, the study has been expanded to a depth of twenty-five feet. "Before, I had books boxed up, and in the garage, and up overhead endangering the ceiling. Even with all this, I'm going to have to make some half-height island shelves to put in this open area. I've got close to three thousand books."

At one end of the room on a desk stood a big standard electric typewriter, its keys looking well used. Against a wall was a stereo with plenty of records, a mixture of western, pop, and grand opera. His favorites: *La Bohème*, Gene Autry, Bing Crosby.

Kelton is five feet nine inches tall and an unflabby 180 pounds or thereabout: "I haven't had nerve enough to check lately." He wore a nonwestern shirt, cardigan sweater, slacks, and cowboy boots. He still has most of his brown hair. He has worn glasses over his blue eyes since he was eleven. Rimless glasses. "Very old-fashioned, but I like them."

For a West Texan's, Kelton's words come rapidly, although all the Gary Cooper pronunciations and speech figures are there. He is a modest man, a little shy about talking of art. His conversation is full of wry, understated humor.

BENNETT: You've always been a West Texan?

KELTON: I went to high school at Crane. My father went to work for the McElroy Ranch in 1929. He stayed on that ranch thirty-six years.

BENNETT: How did you get into writing?

KELTON: Well, I don't know how far back to go with this. I've always wanted to write, ever since I can remember, just about. My mother had been a schoolteacher, so she taught me at home, and I was reading by the time I was five. I started making up stories when I was still a kid in grade school, writing stories in my notebooks. I always enjoyed English in school, writing themes and so forth. I was doing sort of amateurish fiction stories even in my high-school days. I read almost everything that came to hand, in the beginning, that was in our school library. I guess I've got a larger library here right now than my school had, and I read just about every book that was on the shelves there, whatever it was. But I always kind of leaned toward westerns because I had grown up in that atmosphere. I loved to read Dobie, Will James, Zane Grey, all those fellows, from one end of the spectrum to the other in the western field.

BENNETT: When did you start submitting material for publication?

KELTON: I started actually writing and submitting material when I got back from service. I still had about a year and a half to go at the university, and I started writing stories and submitting them, I guess, during that time. I'd written two or three while I was still in service. And I tried them; you know, they didn't sell, but I tried them. Then I got back after the service and took a couple of correspondence courses in writing. At the university I took a course in feature writing—I majored in journalism. I had one so-called writing course at the university, which wasn't much. I've got more out of my correspondence courses and my own study than I did out of that. But I began trying to analyze stories in magazines and break them down for myself, to try to determine how they were put together and what made them work. Then I'd try to do the same thing with my own stories. I wrote, I guess, twenty-five or thirty stories and finally sold one my senior year in the university. I sold it to a western pulp. And at the same time I sold a piece that I had done in a feature-writing class to a restaurant magazine. I got forty dollars for my feature and fifty dollars for my short story, and I thought I was on my way to wealth and fame. I didn't know how long it was going to be before I sold that second short story. I guess it was six months to a year before I hit another one.

BENNETT: Whom did you sell the first one to?

KELTON: *Ranch Romances*. It was one of the leading western pulps. Pulps were good training ground for me, and I wonder sometimes where young writers today get a chance to earn while they learn, which the pulps gave us. They don't have anything quite of that nature today to start on. You start at the top, and just stay in there until you either make it or give it up.

I started selling pretty consistently after a couple of years. I began to get the feel for it, for what worked and what didn't. Within three or four years I was selling just about everything I had time to write while I was working here at the *Standard* as farm-and-ranch editor.

BENNETT: How long were you with the *Standard Times*?

KELTON: About fifteen years.

BENNETT: And it was six months before you sold your second?

KELTON: Possibly longer. I remember that the first story I sold as a senior came out in the magazine shortly after I came to San Angelo to work. I can't remember exactly when my second story sold, but it had to be at least six months later than my first one. But the lady who edited the magazine took an interest in me, and even though she sent the stories back, she'd write letters telling me what was wrong with them. Some I could patch and some I couldn't, but she gave me some really worthwhile advice. Really, in a way, that was almost as good as a writing course, because it was professional.

BENNETT: Were you married then?

KELTON: I married after the war, while I still had one semester left at the university. I met my wife, Ann, overseas while I was still in the service. She's Austrian, and she came over here in the summer of '47.

BENNETT: Did you sell quite a few stories before you tried to write a novel?

KELTON: I did. I didn't try to write a novel until the pulps began to die out in the early fifties. My agent, whom I had had for several years, got after me to try a full-length novel. He could see the pulps were going, and he kept after me to try to switch to something else that would survive. I wrote my first novel, called *Hot Iron*, oh, about '52 or '53. I started it as a long novelette for a magazine and just expanded it. It was published, I believe, in '55.

BENNETT: Was it published by Ballantine?

KELTON: Yes, Ballantine. They did all my original paperbacks except one. They've quit publishing westerns, so I've had all my rights revert to me on those books. Ace Books is beginning to reissue some of the early ones.

BENNETT: Many of your early books have short titles. Do you title your books?

KELTON: I'd say, over the years, I've published something like twenty-three or twenty-four books; about half of the titles that have come out are mine. Sometimes they changed them up some. *Hot Iron*, for instance: I wrote it as *Running Iron*, and they decided nobody except people in this country would know what a running iron was, so they changed it to *Hot Iron*. A year or so later another book came out with the title *Running Iron*, so somebody else didn't worry about it. Doubleday has used all my titles, and those have tended to be a little long for some reason—and a couple of my pseudonym books I've had as Lee McElroy: straight westerns, in the Double D series, both hardcover.

BENNETT: Your last three were serious novels.

KELTON: They were intended to be. Of course, *Good Old Boys* was a little more humorous, at least on the surface. In a way it is a sad story, at least on the second level.

The Lee McElroy novels are more or less action-type stories. Let's say that one of them was pretty strongly historical and one was more of a western farce. It started out to be serious, but the character took it away from me and ran with it. It was a humorous piece.

BENNETT: And you've continued to write these action westerns even after you began writing serious novels?

KELTON: I'd say I've done two or three since then. I enjoy them for a change of pace. Doubleday wanted some. I did, I guess, fifteen or sixteen for Ballantine. They were sort of semihistorical, most of them, but still basically action-oriented stories. I did the one called *Massacre at Goliad*, which is very strongly historical, about the Texas Revolution, and then I did a sequel to it which took up the first few months after the revolution, *After the Bugles*.

BENNETT: It seems to me that you've tried to give a serious theme to most of them. You have a little more leisurely development in your intentionally serious novels.

KELTON: In those last you have more time to develop character, history, and color. The story line may not be that much different, except that the emphasis is more on character and the social aspects of some of these things than it is on the action.

BENNETT: They say that characters in English novels tend to be eccentric while those in French tend to be typical. Your Charlie Flagg seems to me to typify a certain type of rancher. Is this intentional?

KELTON: I'm not sure I completely get your point. I like first of all to have individualists as characters. I like individualists. I've grown up around a lot of them. I try to have people who more or less live by their own standards. Of course, their standards are set by the way they've grown up. Charlie had some strong ideas about the way to live, and about independence, and about personal dignity. He didn't sacrifice independence or dignity either one to help him get through this drouth. Hewey Calloway is a little different type of character, and yet he has some kinship to Charlie Flagg. He is also an individualist and wants to live his life by his own lights.

BENNETT: What are you working on now?

KELTON: A thing that's turned into a massive piece of work, far more than I envisioned when I started. *Reader's Digest* ran *The Good Old Boys* in their condensed books. Then they wanted me to try a book about the black cavalry. There were two black regiments, the Ninth and Tenth Cavalry, and then there were two black infantry regiments. At one time, during the early seventies on up to the end of the Indian wars, most of the troops, say from noncoms down to privates, stationed across this whole part of Texas were black. This was particularly true here at Fort Concho, and of course it was true up in Fort Griffin, and at Chadbourne when it was operated after the war, although mostly it was just an outpost.

I worked up a fictional narrative about a black trooper, a private. I always write mine about the average people, the little people down at ground level have always interested me most. I never have been able to write a book about the great tycoons or the land barons; I just somehow can't relate to them.

So, I'm doing this about one black soldier, following his adventures at Fort Concho, and I'm paralleling it with a Comanche Indian who is more or less his counterpart. And on down to the end of the Indian time. There's a confrontation between the two: they come together at the beginning of the book, and they come together at the end of it, although they are not aware of one another as individuals. It's turning into a seven- or eight-hundred-page manuscript. I intended it to be three hundred and fifty or four hundred, but when you start out, you begin to build character, and you sort of do it your own way, and it just goes on and on. I'm nearly finished with my first draft; I have maybe another seventy or eighty pages of rough draft to do.

BENNETT: Do you intend to cut it down any?

KELTON: Where I can. But, other than just editing, I think I'm going to send it to them in the long version and see if they faint. I've already warned them that it's a lot longer than they wanted. Doubleday has contracted it; *Reader's Digest* has an option on it. It may be too much book.

BENNETT: Has anybody done a movie from any of your things?

KELTON: Nobody has come up with any serious proposals. I did have one group which went so far as to do a treatment on *The Time It Never Rained.* And they had a scriptwriter, good one, lined up, and even had a star more or less tentatively lined up, but they couldn't raise the money.

BENNETT: Do you work an eight-to-five day at the *West Texas Livestock Weekly*?

KELTON: Pretty much. I stay in the office Monday through Wednesday. We put it to bed on Wednesday after lunch. Then I get out and travel Thursday and Friday, and sometimes Saturday, gathering feature stories for it. We're taking a two-week break over the Christmas holidays, and so I just came back night before last from about eight days in Oklahoma and Kansas doing some feature stories. That's a little longer trip than I can normally make in a two- or three-day run, so I had time.

BENNETT: Do you own it?

KELTON: I have a small interest in it, but a fellow named Stanley Frank is the principal owner. My writing is a sort of sideline to that, and to the other jobs I've had previously.

BENNETT: When do you find time to write?

KELTON: Make it. Saturday and Sunday mostly anymore. I work nights some. I took work with me on this trip. I was working on my Indian chapters right at the moment, so I took along some research books that I had on the Comanches. I had to lay over last weekend up in Oklahoma, so I had all day Sunday to sit there and work. I guess I roughed out about twenty pages over the weekend.

BENNETT: How long a stretch do you work?

KELTON: Oh, two or three hours. Then I get up and do something else a while and then come back to it. It's harder to get one started, and it's hard to keep my interest level up in the beginning. It's tough to get one rolling, but sometimes after I get the momentum going, I'll sit down, and it sort of flows out, and I'll spend long hours at it. I'll stay at it as long as it's coming easily. I won't break up a winning streak. When it starts getting really tough, and I feel that maybe I'm straining a little for it, well, then I'll quit and do something else. I don't ever want it to be strained and mechanical.

BENNETT: So you work mostly weekends and at night then, two or three hours at a time.

KELTON: I don't have the discipline anymore that I used to have. I guess you give up some things as you get older, and that's one of them. Back in the early years I'd work almost every night at least a couple of hours. The *Standard Times* used to have six-day weeks, so mainly I'd just have Sundays to work on it. That's a tough grind, and it takes away from your family some. It's just one of those things, a sacrifice that you and your family both have to make if you really want to be a writer, a serious one. I have never been able to make enough income off fiction writing for a real living; I've had to do something else for a living.

BENNETT: There aren't many who do.

KELTON: I know a lot of the western writers, and very few of them are full time; most of them do something else just like I do.

BENNETT: You write mostly with a typewriter. You never use a pencil?

KELTON: Not often. Occasionally, if I'm out on these trips, sitting in a motel room at night, and don't have a typewriter with me, I may have some thoughts I really want to get on paper, and I'll sit down and do them in longhand. But, by and large, I do it on typewriter. My writing is not fast enough to keep up with my thoughts.

BENNETT: Do you outline?

KELTON: Basically the outline is in my mind, and always subject to change. Often I'll do about a third of a book and then send that third and an outline or projection of the rest of it; I'll go ahead and get a contract on that basis. But very often they're so slow about the contract that by the time they get it to me maybe I'm halfway through the rest of the book. A time or two I've finished the book while I was waiting around for them to come around with the contract. Which is fine! The outline that I send them is only tentative. I always let my feelings guide me as I write. If a character takes the story away from me and runs with it, that's fine. A book seldom ever follows the original idea exactly.

BENNETT: But you don't put the whole outline on paper first?

KELTON: To a degree I may. I have thoughts that I don't want to let get away from me, but by and large it's in my head.

BENNETT: Your books have pretty good sized casts.

KELTON: I'll usually sit down and work up character lists. I seldom ever just sit down and start one without having lived with the characters in my mind for a year or two. I'm usually working on one and thinking ahead on a couple more. This novel I'm working on now: it was presented to me, and so I didn't have time to develop the characters like I normally would. Hewey Calloway—I had him in mind for twelve or fifteen years roughly before I ever wrote the book. *The Time It Never Rained*, very much the same way; I was formulating that while the drouth was going on.

BENNETT: You have some great names. Hewey Calloway really fits, and Charlie Flagg——

KELTON: I give a lot of thought to character names. That is, if they're major characters. Some I have to make up as I sit down to write; as these transient characters come in, I have to maybe stop and work up a name that seems to fit. There is no great formula for that; it is just a sense of what seems to fit that character and what sounds good.

BENNETT: Georges Simenon picks his names out of the telephone directory.

KELTON: I get some of my minor characters out of that book. I make a point not to use the full name. I'll get maybe the last name out of one part and the first name out of somewhere else. I have one of these books of baby names too, and I'll occasionally, when I can't think of something, go flip through that book. I have a feeling for how names fit together, first names and last names. I try not to use names that sound alike, or main characters whose names start with the same letter. The reader might confuse the characters. Minor characters: you know, there aren't enough names, or enough letters in the alphabet to keep you from having some problems with them.

BENNETT: Your novels are very visual. For instance, Hewey bathing at the windmill.

KELTON: I try to work very much in visual scenes. I don't like the transitional things any more than is necessary to carry you from one place, or maybe carry you through a time span to put you down into another scene. I like to work it out just as if it were on screen or on stage, with people actually doing something and saying something, and convey the story through that. It works better for me that way. Rather than just narratively tell about it.

BENNETT: Have you ever done any work in drama?

KELTON: No, I haven't. It's just a format that works for me. I'm a movie buff, and I've studied the way movies do it, not in any formal way, but I've watched the way they play off a scene, and I kind of get a sense of what works and what doesn't. I think the reader can visualize it better that way. I like to let the dialogue characterize the people as well as carry the story forward.

BENNETT: How much do you revise?

KELTON: Lots of times what I call a first draft is, at least in certain parts of it, maybe a third or fourth or fifth draft. I may rewrite a passage as I go along until I'm fairly well satisfied with it. Then usually one major redraft, and that's about it.

BENNETT: Do you retype the whole thing when you do it?

KELTON: Usually. Then I always type my own submission manuscripts, and I'll give it another going over when I do that. I especially cut. When you sit down and do it all from beginning to end continuously, you get a better feel for rhythm and for excess than you do when you're sitting down here writing two or three, or maybe eight or ten pages at a time, and then stop.

BENNETT: Do you try to do those on weekends?

KELTON: Yes. Really I enjoy that part more than I do getting the first draft down, because when you finally put the polish on it, you can see the story come to life. I like to do as much as I can at one time.

BENNETT: Do you have any advice for beginning writers?

KELTON: The main thing that I tell them is that the time to start is tonight. I was asked to talk to a college English class two weeks ago, and I told them that: "Don't put it off." I started writing even in grade school and really got serious with it before I got out of college. I think if I had waited much longer, by the time I had a family and job and all these other calls on my time, I might not have stuck with it. I see a number of people who I'm sure could have been better than I am, I'm sure, but they gave up. They just let it slide. It takes a lot of dedication to begin with and just an awful lot of hard work.

Too many people expect to be too successful too soon. They forget that if you are going to be a doctor you have to study for—what?—six or eight years. If you're going to be an attorney, you have to study for five or six. Even a veterinarian. A lot of people think that all you have to do to be a writer is sit down and write one story and you're on your way. You've got to pay your dues, your apprenticeship. Chances are you won't sell anything you write for two or three years.

BENNETT: Do you have any favorites among authors? You once mentioned Hemingway.

KELTON: I've read a lot of Hemingway's work and like him. But I hate to go into this business about favorite authors, because I'll forget the one I like best sure as anything. I'll talk about western writers a little bit more. Of course, J. Frank Dobie was my idol when I started, and I was always a little shy of whether Dr. Dobie would have approved of the stories I was writing for the pulp magazines, or even my first western novels, for that matter. But maybe he would have liked *The Good Old Boys* and Charlie Flagg, I don't know.

BENNETT: He might well have liked some of the others too.

KELTON: I had a letter from Frank Goodwyn, who was one of Dobie's protégés back early. He sort of liked what I did. He studied under Dr. Dobie, and I guess Dobie helped him on his first book.

Of your more commercial man-of-action stories I always liked Ernest Haycox and Luke Short. I studied Luke Short quite a lot when I started, because he had such a vivid way of putting a story on paper, and his characters were always well developed. His people always acted completely in character, and I particularly liked him. Then there's some contemporary ones. Ben Capps of Grand Prairie is, I think, a very good western writer of today. I think he has been underrecognized. Gosh, it's hard to list them without leaving some out.

BENNETT: What about other Texas writers?

KELTON: Well, I sort of like Larry McMurtry's work, some of it. I don't agree with his viewpoint, but I like the way he puts his stories on paper. I'm sure he would have seen Charlie Flagg from a completely different angle. I've read his *Horseman Pass By*, *Leaving Cheyenne*, and *The Last Picture Show*. We're not all supposed to agree with each other, or we'd all be doing the same things.

Tom Lea, by all means Tom Lea. I went by and just presented myself to him last summer. I was out at El Paso for a writer's convention. He's not a joiner or anything like that, so he didn't come over, so I just went out to his house. I took all my Tom Lea books along and got him to sign them for me and gave him a copy of *The Good Old Boys*. I got a very nice letter from him, and he sent me *The Wonderful Country* and signed it. I had a paperback of it which I had used up; I didn't have the nerve to take it out there for him to sign when he did the others. *Wonderful Country* doesn't really have a whole lot of plot, but it is so beautifully written, in the characters and the scenery, that the country all just comes alive.

I've liked what I've seen of A. C. Greene. And Frank Tolbert; I don't know if Frank writes much in book length anymore, but I've read some of his, like *The Staked Plain*, that I've enjoyed very much. And also a couple of his nonfiction works I have.

BENNETT: What about Prescott Webb?

KELTON: Oh, yes! Dr. Dobie, Prescott Webb, Roy Bedichek, Mody Boatright: to me those fellows are sort of put up on a pedestal by themselves. I studied under Dr. Boatright. By the time I got my prerequisites in to study under Dr. Dobie, he had left. But I took Dr. Boatright. It was a good course, extragood, and I enjoyed it very much, getting to work with him. Those fellows are unique; nobody else has done quite what they've done. And probably shouldn't try. I know I don't try.

I started out copying after other people to some degree, until I established my own style. Since then I try not to copy after anybody else. I've had people tell me they know my style, but I don't know my style. I don't want to find out; I might ruin it if I knew what it was. My agent says he can recognize my stories from the first page without my name on them, but I don't know how he does it.

BENNETT: Many of your books have a racial theme.

KELTON: It's not in them all, but it has run in a lot of them. Because it's here, you know. If you do Texas history, you cannot separate racial problems from almost anything you want to write about. From the beginning, with the first settlers in Texas, there were the conflicts with the Mexican people and the conflicts with the Indians.

BENNETT: In the book you're working on, you're still working with this.

KELTON: Of course, with Charlie Flagg I was trying to tell something about the more or less modern racial thing, and how it had developed to that point, between the Mexican and Anglo people. If you do a story about the ranch country in this part of the world, that's just part of the life. If you ignore it, pretend it doesn't exist, you're not being true to the subject.

BENNETT: The only late work in which I didn't find anything of that nature is *The Day the Cowboys Quit*.

KELTON: At that time and in that place, there wasn't any real— there weren't any black people much at that time, and what few there were stood pretty much intermixed. There were maybe a few wagon cooks and so forth. The only Mexican people had probably already pretty much pulled back to New Mexico. There were a few Mexican sheep men who had drifted over out of eastern New Mexico, out of that area east of Santa Fe. They had established some plazas there in the

Texas Panhandle—Romero and two or three other communities were basically Mexican sheepherder communities. But they had pretty well gone out of the picture by then. Because they didn't own the land, or have any lease on it; they just used it. Because it was there. Most of those people had traded with the Comanche Indians; they were Comancheros before they were sheepherders in the Panhandle. So when the Comanches faded out, they came in with their sheep flocks. But there really wasn't any place there for racial conflict, because it just didn't develop in that country. When you write about this area from here south, then the racial thing has to be part of it. Even in *The Good Old Boys* I touched on it with Julio.

BENNETT: Yes, I went back and discovered a number of paragraphs about Julio's problems.

KELTON: And about Hewey getting the best of it even when they shared the room in the barn. Hewey got the iron cot, and Julio had to settle for the canvas one. The color line had to be observed even in that situation. That was just the way it was.

BENNETT: Until I read *After the Bugles*, I didn't realize it went back to the Texas Revolution.

KELTON: It was there as part of the buildup to the revolution. There was just a conflict of two cultures that really couldn't mix; they were oil and water. They haven't completely mixed yet. But in those days they were very much alien to each other.

BENNETT: It's all through *Manhunter*.

KELTON: I based that to a degree on a real incident. There was a fellow named Gregorio Cortez who was caught up in that sort of situation. I used that for a takeoff, although I didn't follow it a hundred percent.

BENNETT: You're very evenhanded with both Anglos and Mexicans. Do you know many Mexicans?

KELTON: Yes, I've been around Mexican people the bigger part of my life.

BENNETT: Do you speak Spanish?

KELTON: I'd like to say yes. I've studied it, and I've worked with it a little, but I'd have to say the very best I have is a pidgin-type Spanish. It's very poor. When I get down in Mexico, I can speak enough that I won't starve to death. And I can usually follow the gist of a conversation; I won't get it in detail.

BENNETT: Do you have any Mexican friends around here you see socially?

KELTON: Not really close friends. As a boy growing up, I was around a good many, and I know quite a few casually. I knew a good many at the university, and as a livestock reporter I get out on these ranches with the Mexican ranch hands a whole lot. Even though I don't know them individually, I feel a certain empathy there. I've known a lot of wetback people over the years; came to work for people I knew, and so forth.

BENNETT: *Wagontongue* deals with blacks.

KELTON: That's really the only one I've done, other than the one I'm working on now. I haven't grown up around black people that much, or been that much around them during my life on intimate terms. I guess you just have to kind of put yourself in other people's place when you write a story.

BENNETT: Were there quite a few black cowboys?

KELTON: Oh, yes, they were very much a part of the cattle industry in this country. There were a lot more of them, probably, than the literature would suggest. Mexican cowboys too. Of course, you would expect Mexican cowboys from here south. But there were just lots of black cowboys too.

BENNETT: Race is a big thing in Faulkner. Have you read much Faulkner?

KELTON: Not much. Out in the country where I grew up the black people stood apart a little bit, and then again they were more or less part of the community too. They weren't as numerous as, say, in East Texas. I guess there was just a whole lot easier attitude toward them. Maybe they didn't accept them on an equal footing, but they accepted them.

BENNETT: You mentioned that your viewpoint differed from McMurtry's.

KELTON: Well, he chooses to look at the darker side of life. I guess I do too in a way. I sort of felt that way about *The Good Old Boys*. It was a sad story to me, because this was the passing of time, and this fellow couldn't have lived and done what he did ten years later. That's the point of the ending of it too: he was trying desperately to live it all just one more time, and you knew that he was not going to really succeed in it, because it just couldn't be. Of course, we've got his kind with us today, but they're driving trucks and working in the oil fields. They're driving cars instead of riding horses, but they've got that character about them.

BENNETT: I've known country printers like that, and an old World War I comrade, a painter and cook, who used to visit my dad.

KELTON: Sort of like my old man, Boy Rasmussen. He was real. I moved him back thirty years, but I knew him when I was a kid. He would come to my grandparents' place just like he did in the book, and he died the same way. He was picked out of life, and about all I did was change his name and move him back in time a little way.

BENNETT: How did you happen to choose Lee McElroy as a pen name?

KELTON: The idea came from Steve, my number-two son. My dad spent thirty-six years on the McElroy Ranch at Crane, and then for a good many years he had the Lea Ranch leased for some cattle of his own. I was kicking it around with Steve one day, trying to think up one, and he came up with the idea of combining those two ranch names. The only thing was that the Lea Ranch was L-e-a, and the editors arbitrarily decided to make it L-e-e because the other sounds like a woman's name, and there is still a male-chauvinist attitude toward women western writers. There's this old thing about B. M. Bower, who was popular back in the early days, more or less a contemporary of Zane Grey, wrote *Chip of the Flying U* and a lot of books that sold beautifully. Until finally, after twenty or thirty books, the word got around that B. M. Bower was a woman: Bertha M. Bower. Her sales dropped pretty dramatically after that, because people wouldn't accept action stories by a woman. That's been a scare thing with the publishers ever since.

BENNETT: Are any women writing them now?

KELTON: Yeah, quite a few. There aren't many in what you'd call the action field per se, but there are several who at least border on it—Jeanne Williams, who at one time lived in Abilene.

BENNETT: I knew Jeanne.

KELTON: I have copies here of a couple of her novels. Not exactly western—more what I'd call "bosom-and-blood" type of books.

BENNETT: She used to be married to John Creasy.

KELTON: I knew him slightly. He used to attend the Western Writers' conventions. He was the only one who'd come to them and take off several hours every day to go back to his room and write. I think he was the only one, other than a few who were trying to sell something to an editor and were doing a little polishing work to show them. Creasy made a point to every day—rain, shine, or whatever—to write so many pages.

BENNETT: Did he write any westerns?

KELTON: Way back he did. He wrote them before he ever came over here and saw the West. He was always a little shy about talking about them very much. He said he had one passage where a coyote was flying noiselessly over the prairie on silent wings; he thought a coyote was a bird. A few details like that got by him.

BENNETT: There seems to be some violence in all your books.

KELTON: To a degree. Well, *The Time It Never Rained* doesn't have any real violence. It has a suicide. It has a fistfight between the boys at one point.

BENNETT: Yes, and the fellow who attempts to rape the girl.

KELTON: But it doesn't have any true violence. *The Good Old Boys* doesn't really have any violence in it per se.

BENNETT: Except where he ropes the car and causes a wreck.

KELTON: The fistfight there on the river, too. That car thing came about—there's two or three stories about these old-time cowboys roping smokestacks on train engines. Really that's what I had in mind: this fellow getting off on a wild stunt and roping a smokestack, but it has been done a time or two in fiction. I know it was done in real life in Midland; a fellow just escaped being killed by the fact his rope broke. But I decided to have him rope a car, and that helped the plot because it gave me a chance to let Hewey's impetuous nature get his brother hurt. Hewey has to take over his brother's duties then.

BENNETT: Have you had any personal experience with violence?

KELTON: I've been in the infantry in the war if that counts. Otherwise, no.

You know, the cowboys I grew up around were a very nonviolent bunch of people. I never saw, in all the time I was growing up, a real fistfight that amounted to anything. As much of a fistfight as I ever saw was over here at the *Standard Times* parking lot one day between a couple of *Standard Times* employees. About the biggest fistfight I ever saw in the service—I saw a few pretty good shenanigans—a fellow at Christmastime over in Austria drank too much. This old boy was a big fellow, and he got a hatchet and was trying to catch this other kid that had insulted him some way. He'd have killed him if he caught him. But he couldn't.

BENNETT: I nearly saw a shooting one time. I really got out of the way.

KELTON: You did? I had a few shots fired my way, but it wasn't personal. They were trying to kill me, but it wasn't personal.

BENNETT: Do you feel violence is a necessary ingredient of life and books?

KELTON: In a historical context, the type of stories I've written, it would have been there. You could write a lot of stories in which there wouldn't be any violence, like *The Good Old Boys*, which had nothing of a drastic nature; nobody got killed or anything. I think that any type of story that you write with conflict between people always has a potential for violence. It depends on how deep the conflict and what the nature of it is. When you're writing these historicals where you have people clashing, and each side is on God's side, the potential for conflict is there. If you'll study history, it existed.

I've tried not to overdo the violence in my books. I've tried more to stress character than just riding and shooting. Where the violence came, it was an integral part of the story. I've tried to skim over the violent parts, not to write a really bloody scene. I guess I follow the old Saturday B westerns: they can have an awful lot of shooting going on, and the worst thing anybody does is grab his shoulder. You didn't see people, like they do in these movies, bleeding to death in technicolor on a wide screen.

BENNETT: How do you go about handling violence in the novel?

KELTON: I always try to build up to it. I don't just suddenly jump it at you without warning. I use the buildup as a suspense thing to heighten tension. In *The Day the Cowboys Quit* I kept the threat of violence a big part of the way through, but really the violence never does show up. It is muted when it comes. The one death in that book occurs off scene; it has already happened when Hitch rides up. This book I'm working on has some violence in it; you know it has by the nature of the thing. But I'm not going to have them agonizing in death for two or three pages.

BENNETT: Do you normally put violence at the climax of a book?

KELTON: It depends on the story, where it fits. In *The Day the Cowboys Quit* the only death was probably two-thirds of the way through. There was a big confrontation toward the last of the book, but no shooting. You have to build a story, but the climax doesn't have to be violent.

BENNETT: The trial was really the climax in that novel, although the confrontation between Hitchcock and old man Torrington in the street is good.

KELTON: Yeah, that's the point at which the most violent scene could have occurred, but I pulled the fuse just in time.

BENNETT: In a straight western would you have put some shooting there?

KELTON: If I had been writing an old-fashioned powder-burner, I might have.

BENNETT: Your books seem to be getting a little more serious all the time in handling these things. Did you one day just write a manuscript which tipped over into another class, and your agent said that this could be a hardback novel?

KELTON: It was my decision to try the hardback. I had known this Doubleday editor for a good many years through the Western Writers' conventions, and he had asked me two or three times if I couldn't do something for his publishing house of a little bit more serious nature. You know, not what you'd call a shoot-em-up-type western. I'd been making my Ballantine books increasingly serious anyway over the years.

Ballantine was a unique paperback house. Basically it was a man and his wife, and they were looking for something different from what all the others had. From the very first they encouraged me to do more history, more character, less violence. That's the kind of book they liked to publish; it happened to be the kind I liked to write. I couldn't have done that for some of the other paperback houses. Ballantine was very liberal about this. In fact, a time or two they just almost didn't take a book of mine because it was a little too much of the old-fashioned type. Mrs. Ballantine once wrote me something like—paraphrasing Jesus—go forth and sin no more; we'll take this one, but let's don't do this again. It was a semihumorous book with quite a little action in it, and she didn't like the book much, but she took it. It sold about as well as the rest. Ballantine has merged with a conglomerate. The Ballantines haven't been with the firm for several years now.

BENNETT: Your first serious novel, *The Day the Cowboys Quit*, is closer to the old powder-burners than the other two.

KELTON: *The Day the Cowboys Quit* is, to a degree, a true story. The characters were different, and, of course, some of the scenes were fictional, but the basis for it is fact. In real life there might have been more violence than there was in the book. You can't always convert life directly into fiction; as a fiction writer you have to keep it plausible and logical.

BENNETT: Someone said that the era of the cowboy lasted only about forty years. As you say, they're driving trucks now. What is it that so fascinates people about that era?

KELTON: Partly it's fact, and partly it's fiction, what we call the open-range-cowboy period. We still have cowboys today. We've got ranches and people who work on them, and to some degree they are spiritual descendants of the old open-range cowboys. I still know more people in that trade than almost any other. But in some ways they are very much part of the modern scene too: they watch Johnny Carson on television. They are kind of ambivalent in a lot of ways toward the old and the new.

But I think people have tended to overromanticize the old-time-cowboy period. I have always tried to show that the cowboy's life was basically pretty hard and very often lonely. It did have some rewarding aspects, and one of them was the individual freedom he had. He could always saddle up quick and ride away if he didn't like where he was. Probably it was easier to do then than it is today. Everybody today is saddled with a certain number of things, and in those days a fellow didn't have anything, so he didn't lose anything when he left. The cowboy period that Gary Cooper talked about in that great television special began, oh, in 1870, more or less. It took a few years for the way of life to develop, and it lasted into this century. I imagine that forty years is not badly off. There was still a strong flavor of it in my father's time, and still a little of it when I was a kid. I knew a lot of those fellows as old men who had been cowboys in what you'd call the heyday of the cowboy period. I listened to a thousand of their stories when I was a kid. I still feel like I belong to them more in a way than I do to this so-called modern life. I feel more attachment to then. Time goes off and leaves me in certain respects. I'm having a hard time adjusting to the '70s, and I dread the '80s and '90s.

I grew up in the '30s and '40s, you know, and everything I do and everything I believe has a basis, at least, in that period and in the years before that which set that foundation.

BENNETT: Dr. Alan Strout used to say that there would be precious little literature without adultery. But you don't have much sex in your books.

KELTON: No, I guess I've never done enough basic research. I just don't feel comfortable using that element to any great degree. I usually suggest it where it needs to be at all, but I don't go into explicit scenes.

If it doesn't fit me, if it doesn't feel comfortable, I just don't use it. It's a part of life, but it's not the only part. From a lot of literature you get today, you'd think it was the only thing that mattered. It's like the violence: I just don't like to overplay it.

BENNETT: There is some sex, in *Manhunters*, for instance.

KELTON: There's a little, more or less by suggestion, in *The Time It Never Rained*. Even by suggestion in *The Good Old Boys*. What there is, however, is just a suggestion. I think we're probably beginning to move away from that a little bit, and I won't have as far to move as a lot of them.

BENNETT: Religion seems to obsess some Texas writers. But not you.

KELTON: I touch on it a little bit. All my characters are believers, but they're not what you'd call big Bible-thumping believers. Charlie Flagg believed more or less because of nature. He saw it, and he believed in God because he could see him all around. For that matter, so did Hewey Calloway. But it wasn't a big issue in their lives; it was just part of everyday life. They didn't make a big scene or anything.

I grew up in a family in which my dad never went to church, although he believed, and my mother went to church every Sunday. As kids we went to church and Sunday school most Sundays, unless we had some work that couldn't be put off. Especially as time went on and war started and labor was hard to get, you had to work a lot on weekends when you could get schoolkids to help out. I think this is even truer today than when I grew up. I'm a backslidden Methodist. It's just never been a big issue with me. I believe, but I don't have to go to church every Sunday and testify to it. Like some of the cowboy characters, I can look around everywhere and see God and his work. I think a lot of formal religion today is probably overformalized and isn't basic enough.

BENNETT: Some Texas writers—I think particularly of McMurtry—use a lot of country-western music in their novels. I can't recall music in yours.

KELTON: Of course, the only really contemporary book was *The Time It Never Rained*. In that I had Charlie with a bunch of old Jimmie Rogers and Vernon Dalhart records, but really there hasn't been that much place in my books for it. I'm trying to think if Hewey Calloway—I had some sheet music in the parlor of that ranch house, and I lifted those titles off an ad I found in a 1903 *Standard Times*. One of the stores was selling sheet music, and I lifted some of the most outrageous titles that I could pick.

I have a story in mind that I'm going to do someday which might border into that a little bit, but it won't be much. I have an old character who is a kind of country fiddler, and a great fan of Bob Wills, since I am also. But it's not a major part of the story. I think the others use a lot of that music just to set the scene; that's part of the country scene and part of the contemporary Texas scene.

BENNETT: McMurtry told a group of us, "Country-western music has been the background music of my life."

KELTON: It is in my case. When I was a kid, one of the things I remember first was one of those old morning-glory speakers. We were in a line camp on the McElroy Ranch, before we ever went to headquarters. Dad bought a radio and climbed up to put the aerial on top of the windmill tower, and all he listened to were the stations from the Mexican border, XELO and XEPN and so forth. Then there was National Barn Dance, and as Grand Ole Opry came along, why, we listened to it. I used to go to an old-time dance occasionally with fiddlers and guitar players, with the kids. I still like country music.

BENNETT: The men in your books have quite a bit of trouble with courtship.

KELTON: I probably did too. A lot of these fellows, particularly the old-time cowboys, grew up in a more or less bachelor atmosphere, and they were self-conscious around womenfolks. This came from a time when there weren't a great many women out here, particularly in the open-range days. Maybe the ranch owner and the foreman had wives and families. As the farmers began to move in, they brought womenfolks. But these cowboys spent so much of their lives where there weren't any women that they were very self-conscious around them. My old drifter was that way in real life, as well as in the book. He was scared to death of my grandmother, for good cause.

BENNETT: Boy Rasmussen. Hewey Calloway is not too forward either.

KELTON: The cowboys I knew as a kid, by and large, were awkward around women. I was. I guess I inherited that.

BENNETT: Hugh Hitchcock in *The Day the Cowboys Quit* was backward with Kate.

KELTON: I believe it; I haven't read that book in several years. I forget a lot of character names. I usually remember my major characters, but the rest of them get away from me. But the awkwardness was just a trait that came from those times. Always you borrow from yourself, and I was awfully shy growing up. I was fully grown before I could talk to a woman without blushing a little and so forth. I didn't have any sisters. My mother was the only woman around.

BENNETT: You have a number of novels with Mexicans and Anglos, blacks and Anglos—I don't like that term "Anglo," by the way——

KELTON: I don't either, but it seems to be the only—what are you going to say, "gringo"? The Mexican people don't seem to use that term here. If you catch them off guard, well, it's likely to be a really contentious term, such as "gabacho."

BENNETT: But another of your contrasts is older and younger persons. The old Ranger and young Ranger in *Manhunters,* for instance. Do you sit down and say, "I need a contrast here, two strong men"?

KELTON: I always try to build characters who contrast to each other, and particularly characters who may have a conflict. That doesn't necessarily come out of age; it might come out of other things. I like every individual to be an individual, so the reader doesn't confuse one with the other. You have more reader interest if there is a conflict between characters, but I don't mean it has to be violent. It may be like the age conflict between Charlie Flagg and his son, two different viewpoints based more than anything else on their age. In *Manhunters* the old man was trying to prove that he still was a man. His conflict was not so much with the young Ranger, because the younger man recognized it too, but with society at large.

BENNETT: It seemed to me that *The Time It Never Rained* paralleled the Book of Job. Did you feel that?

KELTON: I didn't plan it, but I became more and more conscious of it as I wrote the book. It just worked out, just gradually seeped into my consciousness that here was Job, updated. The main thing was to show his tenacity, that Charlie had certain principles that he lived by and would rather die than compromise to any serious degree. I've known a lot of people like that. Their honor and dignity were worth more to them than anything else.

BENNETT: Do you base your characters on real persons? What about Flagg?

KELTON: Charlie wasn't any one person; he was a composite of a good many people. My mother thinks he was my father, and to a degree that's valid, but not altogether. He did things my father hasn't done. I borrowed from a bunch of old ranchers I've known over the years. Charlie is a character in his own right, but you nearly always borrow from people who are real. Very seldom have I picked up somebody bodily and used him unchanged.

BENNETT: I believe Charlie Flagg's wife, Mary, is from a German-settled area in the Fredericksburg section. The first time I telephoned your home, there was your wife speaking with a German accent. I thought: here's something . . . .

KELTON: There's a little bit of my wife in Mary, and a little bit of my mother in Mary, and a lot of Mary is just fabrication.

BENNETT: You borrowed this business about keeping him on a diet?

KELTON: I did borrow that from Ann. My dad was always heavy, and my mother fussed about it, but she always fixed him the very foods that made him that way. That's the only thing she ever cooks, even yet. She cooked all the starchy stuff; she fussed about him eating so much pie and cake, but she always had two more in the oven waiting for him. But Ann has been a little more rigorous with hers. She just denies me those things for a long period of time by not fixing them. I spent a lot of time in the Hill Country over the years. I know a lot of those German people, and I empathize with them, I guess from having spent thirty-odd years with Ann.

BENNETT: Do you speak any German?

KELTON: Yeah, I speak a lot better German than I do Spanish—pidgin German, Austrian dialect. Ann didn't speak any English when she came over here. I can follow it pretty well.

BENNETT: Which of your novels do you like best?

KELTON: I like *The Time It Never Rained* because it was the most personal one I've ever done. It was the nearest to real people and real situations that I've personally lived with and seen with my own eyes. *The Good Old Boys*: I had a whole lot of really the same feeling about that. To some degree I borrowed from my grandparents and from my father on that book, and from a whole lot of cowboys that I knew. *The Good Old Boys* has got to be a close second. Then *The Day the Cowboys Quit*: my grandfather cowboyed up in that part of the country just a few years later than the events of the story, but not much. He worked on the XIT before he was married, and this had to be in the late '80s or early '90s. So I had a family kinship with those.

BENNETT: Which of your paperback originals do you like best?

KELTON: *Massacre at Goliad,* because I used more history on that. I have a feeling for Texas history. Then *After the Bugles* was the same people, more or less, the ones who survived the first book. I carried them over and added some more characters. Then I did a little book called *Horsehead Crossing,* which took place partly here in San Angelo. And *Manhunters*; that was my last, and probably all in all my best paperback. Then, of course, I have an attachment to the first one, *Hot Iron,* because it was the first one.

BENNETT: You like a base of historical fact. When was the *Day the Cowboys Quit* strike, and was it about employees owning cattle?

KELTON: 1883. Cattle owning was at the bottom of it. A lot of it was the intrusion of the eastern factory mentality. It pushed into a way of life these cowboys knew. They were trying to hold back time, but neither side really won. The big ranches won in a sense, but everybody lost in the long haul. The losing strikers stayed in that part of the country in towns or on their own little ranches and over a period of several years became the dominant political force. Economics and a couple of hard winters broke a lot of the big ranches. The cowboys tried to hold back time at one period, and the ranchers tried to hold it a little farther down the line. Neither one could hold it. Maybe that's the theme of a lot of my stories: that you can't stop change. A new group of people trying to do something different, and the opposition that is natural. It's just a natural basis for fiction: change and resistance to it.

BENNETT: The drouth was certainly a big change.

KELTON: It was a watershed as far as the ranch industry was concerned, and I've been close to it all these years. It taught some lessons that badly needed to be learned about range management. It wasn't all bad, the way most wars bring some good things too. Ranching has never been the same.

Of course, I was already off the ranch when the drouth came along. I was mainly off because I didn't have the cowboy ability to stay on it. If I had been a good cowboy, I'd probably be out there right now, working for two hundred and fifty dollars a month for somebody. I didn't know when I was well off.

BENNETT: Do you do research specifically for each novel, or just read widely?

KELTON: I read fairly widely when I can. But usually, when I'm working on a project, I concentrate all the specific research for that project that I can. I have no idea how much work I've done on this cavalry book, how many books I've bought, how many books I've borrowed, how many notes I've taken. There's always a certain amount of tangent material that you pick up along the way that, sooner or later, will evolve into something else. I haven't read all the books I've got in this room, but I know pretty well which one to pick up to find a specific item. I can do a big part of my research with books I already have on hand. At least I can get enough bibliographic material here to give me a start.

When I'm working on a particular project, if there's something I need to any great extent, I'll try to buy the book. If the book is out of print and no longer available, I'll go to the library and make Xeroxes of it, so that I have it for reference. I made Xeroxes of Carter's *On the Border with Mackenzie*. There wasn't one to be had anywhere.

BENNETT: Do you go to Austin for research at UT?

KELTON: Sometimes. And to Texas Tech for the Southwest Collection. Between UT and Tech they have just about all the southwestern history books that have ever been printed, I guess. At UT the Barker Collection has a Xerox machine handy. I usually go to one of them and get all the material I can handle in, say, half a day's time.

December, 1978

Frances Mossiker: *The Method of Madame Mossiker*

FRANCES SANGER MOSSIKER was born April 9, 1906, in Dallas, Texas. She graduated from Barnard College with a B.A. in 1927 and has studied further at the Sorbonne in Paris. Mossiker conducted radio programs in Dallas in the 1930s. Her first book, *The Queen's Necklace*, in 1961, established her as a talented writer.

Spiritually, Mossiker lives in seventeenth-century France, but her corporeal twentieth-century self lives on the tenth floor of a well-kept apartment building in the Turtle Creek section of Dallas. Outside the door of her suite is a poster portrait of Napoleon, a personage with a large role in two of her books. Inside hangs a picture of the necklace that blighted Marie Antoinette's reputation. We went into an airy, light-filled sitting room to talk.

Elsewhere in the suite Mossiker has converted "our fourth bathroom" into a compact study with desk, electric typewriter, and bookshelves. She jokes about "a bathtub full of books," but all bathroom fixtures vanished in the remodeling.

The study opens off her bedroom, which is furnished in the Louis XV mode. Many of her books are shelved there also.

Mossiker is a carefully groomed woman, trim and attractive. She is one inch over five feet tall: "I'm proud of that one." Her wide, lively eyes are blue. She talks charmingly, laughs a great deal, pauses in the middle of sentences while running the front and rear ends of them breathlessly together. When she agrees, she often does it with two or three long yeses, which finish with a lot of "ess-hiss."

After our talk, she let us glance through her notebook, which bulges with details for the work she is now writing.

BENNETT: Your books on old-regime France remind me of an incident when I was in college. A group of us used to lunch together and argue about this and that. One day the question came up: What historical figure would you most like to have been? Ruth Todasco had the most interesting answer—Madame de Rambouillet.

MOSSIKER: I wouldn't decide with her, but she must have had her reasons.

BENNETT: Which person would you choose?

MOSSIKER: Maybe Madame de Sévigné, because I so admire her style. I like the period she lived in. I like her metier; I like her way of life. She didn't end up on a guillotine. It was an uneventful but very pleasant way of life. Certainly, of all the persons I've described, I'd prefer her to any of the others. I don't have the makings of a Madame de Montespan. I had trouble identifying with Josephine, although she was beautiful, attractive, and I enjoyed doing her book.

BENNETT: You probably find her too limited intellectually.

MOSSIKER: Oh, very. Little education, of course. She made a great effort to learn botany, and she learned the *Almanach de Gotha* from end to end because she wanted to know who was to be addressed as what and who was to be preceded by whom, but she didn't really have a great intellectual curiosity. She was a limited woman.

BENNETT: Maybe we ought to start with easy questions.

MOSSIKER: I'd like that. Warm me up.

BENNETT: Tell me about your education.

MOSSIKER: My grandfather was one of the people who brought Miss Hockaday to Dallas, and so I attended with Miss Hockaday. Then I went to Smith. An early marriage—in those days you might not finish Smith, and so I was expelled. I went to Barnard to finish. But Smith seems to be my alma mater. I love it—that's where I got my junior Phi Beta Kappa—although Barnard took me in, for which I should be much more grateful than I am. I have studied in France at the Sorbonne and various places. Occasionally. Last year I went down to work with people at the University of Aix, with the man who was the greatest living authority on Madame de Sévigné. So I think education goes on forever.

BENNETT: What was your major at Barnard?

MOSSIKER: French and Romance languages. My mother's family lived right outside Strasbourg, and so I spent much time with them always. I grew up speaking French. Otherwise, I don't think I would have tackled them.

BENNETT: Was your mother French?

MOSSIKER: No, she was born in Mississippi, but that was her family, and people were very close and maintained contacts. I had German governesses and French governesses, and I grew up speaking French, so I stayed with it. The family name is Geisenberger, which is

Alsatian. One of the great uncles had been a career soldier under Napoleon and had become a captain, which was as far as a Jew could go under the Napoleonic Code. He had all the medals from every campaign. So my whole feeling has been for the French branch of the family, and I just love everything French. I love traveling there. Last night some friends of mine said they were going back to the Orient—glamorous. I find myself just going back and back and back to France.

BENNETT: Are you working on a book on Madame de Sévigné?

MOSSIKER: Yes. Yes, I think my contract with Knopf says I will deliver it next year, but I'm never made to feel bad if I'm six or eight months late. I think the only time my editor ever became really insistent was when I had been working on *Pocahontas* for five or six years and had not finished it. He said, "We *are* going to have this for the Bicentennial Year." And I did finish it in time for publication in '76. Otherwise we've never had any set-tos about time. It always takes me four or five years to do research. Oddly enough, I was really just ready to start writing last week, and—whether this was psychosomatic or not I don't know—I fell and broke my wrist. Or rather a bone in the wrist is broken, but when I went to see the doctor, he did think within two weeks I could use the typewriter.

BENNETT: I've only read a few of Sévigné's letters.

MOSSIKER: I think it is interesting that in England she is so well known, but England has never seemingly developed that interest. One reason may be that she doesn't anthologize well. What I hope to do is to tell her story in her own words, to let her and her letters bear the burden of the narrative as much as I possibly can, because I think this is much the better way of giving a sense of marvelous diversity.

BENNETT: Isn't that the "Mossiker Method"?

MOSSIKER: It's the one I'm going to try this time. I'm going to give her life, and the setting, and then try to fill the things in. Incidentally, I don't know whether you've noticed this marvelous thing that's happening at UT Dallas and the university at Austin too—this new American Literary Translators Association. I think it's wonderful that for the first time there's going to be a directory of American, of international, translators. I feel that this is a very important part of my work. I would never dream of letting anyone translate a line for me. I think it's just integral to the personality. Sometimes I could reduce my working time if I did, but I don't do it.

BENNETT: You capture the difference in personalities. You manage the effect of a good novelist—various distinct persons speak in your books, but somehow the tone of the novelist is also present too.

MOSSIKER: I struggle hard to do this. The voices are so different. The use of phrase, the use of vocabulary, the use of humor. It's a personal thing with each writer I use, and I feel I must try to translate the way it comes about. The only thing I've done that hasn't been in French history and therefore involved translation was *Pocahontas*. I loved doing it, but I'm glad to be back in my own bailiwick.

BENNETT: How did you happen to choose Pocahontas?

MOSSIKER: I don't know. It was some sort of obsession. I had to do it. In fact, I was at that moment under contract to Doubleday to do one of that history series that Gunther had been sponsoring. I was to do the one on the Bourbons, and I just suddenly developed this thing about Pocahontas. It caused a terrible brouhaha at Doubleday, when I wanted to exchange Pocahontas for the Bourbons. When they finally agreed, I decided I had to go back to Knopf, to my own dear editor, and the whole thing had to be unwound again.

BENNETT: Writers often identify closely with their subjects.

MOSSIKER: You talk about identifying with your heroines, and the woman who'd rather be Madame de Rambouillet. Madame de Sévigné and I, well, I keep finding parallels. In the basics, her writing—I'm not claiming any similarity, that marvelous style and so forth—but there are so many things that are almost uncanny. For instance, she is so against bleeding, the common remedy of her time, and she said she simply had no veins. And I have no veins. I keep running across one thing after another like this. If I believed in reincarnation . . . .

BENNETT: Do you believe in reincarnation?

MOSSIKER: Yes, I do. But not in the sense that Taylor Caldwell does. She was on the *France* in '71 when I was on board, bound for Africa. Actually I was going to Africa to get to Saint Helena. I had finished the Napoleon book, but I still wanted to see the rock. We got there, and there was some sort of tidal disorder; we couldn't go in. There we sat, for four or five hours, Jamestown in view and the French consul waiting for me on the quay, and we couldn't ever get in. We turned and left and went on to South America, and I'll never get back. Anyway, Taylor Caldwell was aboard, and she had just done that regression through hypnosis which she felt was a perfect attempt to establish an identity with this other person, this other incarnation. But I do think one identifies with one's hero or heroine, or else it doesn't really come off.

BENNETT: You have a vague feeling about reincarnation.

MOSSIKER: Oh, no, I have a very real feeling about it. To me it's the only sensible explanation of the injustices or justices of this life. Or, rather, we continue to take with us what we have done with our minds and spirits. How did we get off on this? But I do, I really do.

BENNETT: When did you begin writing?

MOSSIKER: Too late. Too late, I feel. My editor keeps saying that you don't start until you're ready, but I feel there are so many things that I would love to do that I won't get around to. I have another book on the way, a young-adult book I'm about five years late delivering; I just don't seem to be able to get around to doing them all. It was late in life, 1961, with the publication of *The Queen's Necklace*. I had done radio scripts previously, and a few magazine pieces, but mostly radio.

BENNETT: You did that here in Dallas.

MOSSIKER: Yes, I did a five-day-a-week woman's-world program. And I did a book review for the *Dallas Morning News* early on, back in the '30s. The woman's-world program was fun because I did everything with it—fashion, female visitors to town, news items, books, movies, plays. It was an amusing program to do. Then I found out that I couldn't travel with my husband enough, that I would have to stay home to do the program, because I did it as well as wrote it. So I gave it up, and then I started thinking about writing and came up with *The Necklace*. I was so lucky in that I ran into Robert Gottlieb, who is now president of Knopf and was then with Simon and Schuster. He must be one of the few great editors in the business today.

BENNETT: Did you do the radio show only in the 1930s?

MOSSIKER: Yes. Then I remarried, and I didn't start writing until the '50s.

BENNETT: The type of book you write must take an immense amount of research.

MOSSIKER: Everything I've done has taken me four to five years before I start writing. Then it usually takes me about a year, because by then I'm organized and have all my material organized and my chronologies in order. That's the way I like to work.

BENNETT: You mentioned you'd done some magazine work.

MOSSIKER: Nothing really that was important. Just here and there, and occasionally. I can't remember anything important enough to register with me. The *Saturday Review*, something or other. That wasn't the way I wanted to go.

BENNETT: Then it takes you about five years to do research for a book?

MOSSIKER: Oh, I suppose I could rush it more, but I enjoy it so much. This to me is the delight of it. So often I'm asked the questions: "How much research?" "How do you know when you've done enough research?" It seems to me that it has to be to the point where you are totally at home in your period. You have to know the street songs, and which cafés were popular, and what the styles looked like. Until you have that feeling about it, I don't think that you can really bring it to life. You know how much research that one does that serves no purpose except that something it creates in oneself about one's subject.

BENNETT: You actually listen to the music of the period?

MOSSIKER: Oh, I do, and I love to see the architecture, wherever it is still standing, as happily in France it is still standing. Someone said that one of the best biographies of Shakespeare was written by a man who never went out of the New York Public Library. However, I certainly knew Josephine better because I knew her Malmaison house, where she loved to live better than anywhere else. I find that to see the places is very meaningful. Madame de Sévigné, for example—every place she lived is still there. I went to her chateau in Brittany; so many of her letters were from there. The Comte de Ternay occupies it. His family took it over from her family right after her death: bad debts. Even the alleys that she arranged and described and named are still just as they were and have been maintained that way. It gives you a feeling you cannot get unless you have seen it. The day I got there was a rainy, foggy Brittany day. The Comte de Ternay is in his late seventies or eighties, and I guess he could tell I was going to be quite disappointed if we could not walk through all those alleys of which I knew every name and turn. He wheeled up his little Jeep, and we put an umbrella over us, and in a Jeep in the rain we were able to cover miles of the paths. Research can be heavenly.

BENNETT: You obviously look at many paintings, judging from the illustrations of your books.

MOSSIKER: Tracking the portraits in this particular book is a problem because there are so many of them. I try to find all the portraits, particularly those that are mentioned and are meaningful. Then you have to travel for documents many times. For *The Necklace* I needed the trial records. They had never been printed in extenso. That was something I had to go to Paris for, and I did find those in the archives.

The Method of Madame Mossiker 211

BENNETT: When do you write?

MOSSIKER: When I'm writing, I try to write at least four hours a day, and I can't pull myself away from the typewriter when I'm going well. It's always a question to me whether to say, "I'm going to stop here because it's going so divinely that I can't wait to get back to the typewriter tomorrow morning;" or whether to just write as long as it's flowing. I do try to write regularly, and mornings are definitely my time. It seems that one has somehow frittered oneself away by the time the day has gone on too long.

BENNETT: John Graves tells me that he sometimes writes at night.

MOSSIKER: But then John has all those farm chores to do.

BENNETT: You try to write at least four hours a day?

MOSSIKER: I do. I do. One doesn't always achieve what one plans, but unless there is an emergency of some sort, yes. I cut off my phone, and someone else will answer it in the kitchen or somewhere. If there's a fire, they can tell me.

BENNETT: Do you use a typewriter?

MOSSIKER: I do. I do. I remember Frank Dobie had originally written with a pen and then he went to a typewriter. At the end he had gone back to a pen.

BENNETT: Leon Hale says he likes a pencil.

MOSSIKER: I just can't. So often when I'm on a ship—we've done quite a bit of cruising—I think, This would be such a wonderful time to write. But something doesn't happen between me and the pen. Whereas that contact with the typewriter keys just makes prose jump, come alive.

BENNETT: Do you translate as you need a passage, or do you translate the material in advance and work it into the text?

MOSSIKER: I think I'll talk about *The Necklace* again, because when I started doing *The Queen's Necklace* I had no idea what I was going to do with it, and my husband was concerned, because I had been doing all these years of research, and I had not been very well, and he thought I might be building up such a terrible disappointment for myself if I found no one was interested. I didn't know a human being in publishing. So I suppose I had translated about half of the memoirs, and I went to New York with what my editor calls this unpaginated, untranslated mass. I had really translated only a third when I took it to him. I did the rest later. Now, with Madame de Sévigné, if there's a passage that simply stirs and delights me, I fiddle with it. I can't resist. But I am going to try to wait until I begin organizing it, because I don't yet know just how much of what letters I will be using. You know, this thing is three volumes of onionskin paper, thousands of letters, so that I must control myself. I think I'll do the same thing I did before with the memoirs, which is simply putting it together first in the original and then translating as I see what I need of each piece and where.

BENNETT: Do you translate from English to French also?

MOSSIKER: When *The Necklace* was bought by Julliard in Paris, they asked if I would like to turn the English back into French. I said no. I adore the French language and have such respect for it that I wouldn't. I would not care to translate English into French for a French audience. And the strangest thing happened with this, because I had no idea that France would buy the book when I was doing *The Necklace*. This had just never occurred to me. I took snippets and pieces of memoirs and journals here and there, and translated the excerpts I wanted, and didn't keep exactly where they came from. Then when they bought it, they wanted the original French text, and it was a jigsaw puzzle. I did my best to tell them where each piece came from.

BENNETT: I had run across the "Necklace Affair" in Carlyle and other places over the years—it was a real eighteenth-century Watergate—but it seemed terribly confusing. You make it quite clear.

MOSSIKER: Oh, I'm glad. I'm glad. Although certainly the final answer has never been given. I was so glad when the publisher ended it with a question mark, because it has never been proven. There have only been deductions, as you'd like to make them.

BENNETT: Each of those characters justified himself in his memoirs.

MOSSIKER: That was when I really became excited, when I knew that everybody had written it in the first person. Where else do you have that, except maybe Watergate now? And it is the same thing: who trusts what they say?

BENNETT: It is like a Pirandello play.

MOSSIKER: I think so often we don't know the truth ourselves, particularly with things we remember. Your memory may be true to you and not be true to the fact at all.

BENNETT: Do you use an outline when you write?

MOSSIKER: Yes. Yes.

BENNETT: Do you revise much?

MOSSIKER: Yes. Yes. Yes. I do most of it as I'm working, and then I revise only when something comes up editorially that we think should be changed or moved. Usually we have talked out format so well that I don't have that problem. When I was doing *Pocahontas*, I went off on this tangent about the corn culture in Central America, and my editor said, "It's a lovely chapter for a magazine, but there can't possibly be a corn-culture chapter in *Pocahontas*." So there is revision that you weren't always expecting.

BENNETT: But you don't sit down and retype the manuscript from one end to the other?

MOSSIKER: No, No. It seems to me that I do my retyping while I'm working. That doesn't mean that when I get to the eighth chapter there might not be something in the fourth chapter that I might think should be handled another way.

BENNETT: Do you have any advice for young writers?

MOSSIKER: Start very young. Start young, and read voluminously. It seems to me that taste can only come from wide, wide reading. So they must read and write. What else?

BENNETT: Do you have any difficulty projecting yourself into a different period?

MOSSIKER: No, I live there most of the time. When I first started writing *The Necklace*, I had been very ill, and the project was an escape hatch. It was just a beautiful century to go away to. There's something about the rhythm of that life and the elegance of it. You know, I'm glad I'm alive now and not under one of those lovely *ci-gît* ["here-lies"] tombs, but it was a beautiful century to live in. Talleyrand said that anyone who did not live before the French Revolution did not know the sweetness of life. But we could say that about anyone who didn't live before World War I, or the Civil War, or World War II. Every move we make is moving away from elegance, and service, and the rhythm of life that I loved. We can see that our way of life has changed, and not for the better. Even the elegance of hotels, or ships. When I think about the *France* finished and done, it hurts me; that's the last of the great liners, and it was just a glorious experience to travel on her. No, I like going to another century.

BENNETT: What writers have influenced you?

MOSSIKER: Proust and Henry James. I'm not sure, and that's a terrible admission. But I do love Proust and James; maybe that's why my sentences are so convoluted. Proust was mad about Madame de Sévigné. His grandmother had a copy of Madame de Sévignés letters which has been put out—where did I see it?—somewhere in France.

She was very meaningful to him, and he felt she had an almost Impressionist method of seeing and writing which intrigued him no end.

BENNETT: I haven't read enough of her to judge.

MOSSIKER: She's been so little talked about here. The last translations were done in the 1920s—about 1925—with the three-hundredth anniversary of her birth. There was a Somerset Maugham–prefaced edition, and another one by Violet Hammersley, but in most of them the translator wasn't even named. They were such clumsy, poor translations, which was all the reader had to go on. It wasn't something that would capture people's imagination. I hope I am going to present her as I would like to see her presented, as attractive as she is, and as modern as she is in her viewpoint. She was quite a feminist in her own sense, although she wouldn't have recognized the word.

BENNETT: Aside from Proust and James?

MOSSIKER: Well, I do like a number of French seventeenth-, eighteenth-, and nineteenth-century writers, but I would say the two writers who influenced me most are Proust and James. Roger Shattuck—did you know Roger when he was at the University of Texas?—he did one or two beautiful Proust studies.

BENNETT: Do you read Texas writers also?

MOSSIKER: Of course I read my friends. I loved Frank Dobie. Walter Prescott Webb I admired extravagantly, knew and liked and admired. Larry McMurtry is an excellent writer. Larry won the Texas Institute of Letters Award for *Horseman Pass By* the year I won it for *The Necklace*, which was '61. I was on a panel at TCU with John Graves and Larry McMurtry when they were both teaching over there. So I have known and admired Larry for a long time. And A. C. Greene; I think his *A Personal Country* was marvelous. And John Graves; I think his *Goodbye to a River* may be the best thing that ever came out of Texas. Except Dobie. I loved Dobie; I loved him as a friend and as a writer. *Apache Gold and Yaqui Silver*, I thought, was wonderful. I interviewed him for that woman's-world program I was doing when that book came out, and that was the beginning of a friendship.

BENNETT: When I interviewed Tom Lea——

MOSSIKER: Oh, I love Tom Lea! I think *The Brave Bulls* is just great.

BENNETT: ——we discussed his illustrations for *Apache Gold*.

MOSSIKER: They were marvelous. I thought *The Brave Bulls*

illustrations were just beautiful. Speaking of research, as you know, the iconography is the responsibility of the author, and that's another reason for all the research on the books I've done, especially in France. I went through all the available photographs, architectural and portraits and what-have-you, because I always have to supply them. The publishers wouldn't know, as I would know, what was pertinent and what was there. The Bibliothèque Nationale has a marvelous department that has nothing but engravings and things like that. You just go in there, and they bring you these huge folios with whatever you're looking for.

BENNETT: Do you do your own photography?

MOSSIKER: All those libraries have their own photography and Xerox and so forth. Then there are the marvelous places like the Bettman Archives here, and there are French ones where you can find so many things. So you spend a lot of time there, too, as well as the Bibliothèque Nationale looking for engravings and glossies.

BENNETT: Where do you find the music?

MOSSIKER: So many of the things are operatic, and you can get recordings of those. Then once in a rare while something will actually be performed that you are especially interested in. Not often; usually it will have to be recordings. In the event that's not available, you may be able to get hold of the music and find someone to play it for you.

BENNETT: Do you play an instrument?

MOSSIKER: No. Do you?

BENNETT: No. Music is often mentioned in writing about the French Revolution.

MOSSIKER: Yes, and so many of the revolutionary songs are hard to find, the "Ça Ira" and so forth. Of course, that they're still doing. And happily "The Marseillaise" is still with us. But most of them you do have to track down.

BENNETT: What about the influence of other biographers? Lytton Strachey?

MOSSIKER: I read *Eminent Victorians*, but it has been a long time. I think that he had a certain facility, that he was an extremely interesting writer. He did a lot for biography in his time.

BENNETT: Some of his disciples in particular have been accused of a certain smart-aleck attitude.

MOSSIKER: That's always easy to do. I hope I have a certain irony, but I think I come at it straight. I'm excited about the century and period, and I don't try for a mocking tone.

BENNETT: Had you ever considered such a thing?

MOSSIKER: Oh, well, sometimes you think you could do a terrific satire about a whole period. It's there waiting for you, but you could do that about anyone. No, I just approach it as a marvelous period in history. The other has not been my cup of tea.

BENNETT: Do you think of yourself as a translator?

MOSSIKER: I'm happy to join this American Literary Translators Association, because I think we've come a long way, baby. Earlier the translator wasn't even named, as I said. P.E.N., which I belong to, has begun emphasizing the role of the translator. But I'm certainly not primarily a translator; I hope I'm a biographer and doing a certain historical narrative. I'm always amused at lectures, where they almost invariably introduce me as a historical novelist. I don't really mind, because if I have so hewed to the line of fact and it still has the mood of a novel and reads like a novel, I've succeeded. I don't see why history can't be entertaining as well as enlightening. That I try to do. If you're going to hold the interest of the reader, and take him into a period he doesn't know at all, you've got to make him comfortable and make it attractive to him. I think narrative flow is important.

BENNETT: What was the genesis of *The Queen's Necklace*?

MOSSIKER: The necklace affair has always fascinated me. Carlyle, Dumas—every history of France always has its chapter. You can't have not been conscious of it. When I suddenly found out that the first-person narrative was there in almost every instance, I just couldn't believe it, and that just galvanized me into action. There it was: "*I did*," "*I said*," "*I thought*." You just can't beat that when you're telling a story. Of course, if I hadn't had this facility in French, if I hadn't been able to work with people in France and translate, I don't think I would have been able to do it. DeGolyer had some letters from one of the Russian czars that were fascinating documents, and I toyed with that for months. I read them; they were mostly in French, and only the pornographic passages were in Russian. But I realized when I started looking at research that most of it was in German, and my competence in German is really no longer there. Either German or Russian, and I just realized that I couldn't do the research. So somebody has those beautiful letters when they want them.

BENNETT: Madame de la Motte is a wonderful character.

MOSSIKER: Madame de la Motte de Valois, yes. She was definitely a Becky Sharp.

BENNETT: Did you identify with her?

MOSSIKER: I thought she was fascinating. Whether I identified with her I don't know, but she was most entertaining, and certainly not trustworthy, but delightful, charming, bitchy.

BENNETT: Of the various contemporary accounts of the affair, who wrote the most truthful?

MOSSIKER: The Cardinal de Rohan's Jesuit secretary, Georgel. I think he tried to tell it as straight as he knew it. And Beugnot I believed, and I thought his sense of humor was delicious.

BENNETT: Did you feel Beugnot was embellishing on his connection?

MOSSIKER: Again, everything that you remember takes on a different tone. Oh, I think he did embellish, but there are certain things that have a ring of truth in them. You learn to catch that note, and I caught the ring of truth a great deal in his account. Even the Countess de la Motte: you couldn't believe her, but certain parts of her narrative she had to make jibe with what everybody already knew. I just had to decide which little pieces I was going to take and which to reject. What I tried to do was to let them tell it, and then let the reader decide, because I felt that was just the only way to deliver it.

BENNETT: Watergate also brought down a government. Do you feel there are any real modern parallels with the necklace affair?

MOSSIKER: No, not really. We've had many, many women who've been hussies and impostors, but not like this particular incident. For instance, the great importance she placed on her royal ancestry, and this part of her story I believe. The French court genealogist did give them the pension because the connection could be established. This particular situation is unparalleled because she had this relation to the royal house.

BENNETT: Michelet and some others have felt there was actually a sinister connection between Marie Antoinette and de la Motte.

MOSSIKER: I never believed that. I think that she made it up out of whole cloth. I do think that they induced the cardinal to believe that. The sad thing about it was that Marie Antoinette's reputation was such that people were ready to believe it.

BENNETT: Michelet wanted very much to believe it.

MOSSIKER: Because he was so antiroyalist, yes, as I am. I am sure that I was one of those people who sat knitting around the guillotine. I get positively livid about the whole thing, and I know Michelet was too.

BENNETT: Michelet writes beautifully.

MOSSIKER: Yes, oh, yes. I love him dearly.

BENNETT: I've been intending to reread him for some time. And Carlyle.

MOSSIKER: But I find Carlyle is so little read now. Only J. Frank Dobie and I. He adored Carlyle, and he decided that he and I were probably the last two people left who did.

BENNETT: Did you have any difficulty getting such a long work published, more than six hundred pages?

MOSSIKER: It must be close to that. Today they'd want eight hundred, wouldn't they?

BENNETT: Publishers want longer things?

MOSSIKER: I understand they call them "laid back," whatever that means. They're laid-back books I read, and the longer the better. People want to just immerse themselves. I'm reading St. Aubyn's *Edward VII*, which I think is a splendid book, and it's really big and fat. But, did I have trouble getting it published? No, I was very fortunate. I walked into New York and met this editor through a friend of mine, whose daughter had gone to school with him. As he said, all he needed was a book from the friend of a classmate's mother. Then, after reading it, he accepted it within three days.

BENNETT: Is this the man you spoke of as "my editor"? Have you been with him since?

MOSSIKER: Yes. I thought I could leave him, and I did go to Doubleday and sign a contract. He was simply livid. He had offered to do a joint publication with Doubleday, which they had never done, and they turned that down. That was when Maggie Cousins was at Doubleday, and Ken McCormick was a marvelous gent. But I knew I had to go back to work with my editor. So they let me out. And I've stayed with him the whole way. I'm not bragging; I'm just saying it makes it easier. I was just very fortunate. I had never had an agent until about three years ago, and my editor said, "What do you need one for?" She is the doyenne of New York literary agents, Monica McCall, and a lovely Englishwoman, but the reason I went to her was that someone had gone to Simon and Schuster for movie rights to *Napoleon and Josephine*, and by then Bob Gottlieb had gone to Knopf. Well, nobody even bothered to let me know, and they wouldn't give him my address. I decided that with things like that going on I'd like an agent. I really don't know that it served any purpose, but it's tax-deductible.

The Method of Madame Mossiker 219

BENNETT: Where did you come up with the idea for your *Napoleon and Josephine*?

MOSSIKER: That was my editor, who said there had not been a good biography of Josephine in at least twenty-five years. I had always been enchanted with her. So that was a very happy suggestion. *The Affair of the Poisons* was my own idea. Then I did Josephine in a young-adult book called *More Than a Queen*, which I had a good time doing. There were no strictures.

BENNETT: What age were you writing for?

MOSSIKER: They said, "Whoever you think you are telling it to, just tell it."

BENNETT: They didn't ask you to use a vocabulary of twenty-five words or anything like that?

MOSSIKER: The only thing they asked me to do was to shorten my sentences and paragraphs. Possibly that's a good suggestion anyway.

BENNETT: Quite a sacrifice for a fan of James and Proust. I had some difficulty in obtaining a copy of *Napoleon and Josephine*.

MOSSIKER: I'm proud of it; I like that book. It's now in print, I'm happy to say. *The Necklace* is not in print. I must write one of those secondhand book places in the *New York Times* where I get a lot of things and try to rake up a few copies, because even my foreign copies are all gone. These universities, where I have placed all these materials, have wanted all the various foreign editions and paperbacks.

BENNETT: Have any besides *The Necklace* been translated back into the French?

MOSSIKER: Yes, *Napoleon and Josephine* and—before you leave, I would love to show you the foreign books. It is so interesting to see how differently the national genius expresses itself. My books have gone into Swedish, Spanish, German, French, and I always feel that it's almost like being apotheosized, being translated. It's a rare experience, and I love it. The only one I couldn't check at all was the Swedish, which I don't know.

BENNETT: What about the genesis of *The Affair of the Poisons*?

MOSSIKER: Again, this had just been one of those affairs that French history is full of, and it intrigued me because it was so full of black magic. This whole underworld in Paris, of abortionists and black magicians, was such a contrast to that Versailles court, which looked so beautiful, and then you realize that so many of these women were going to get love philters. I found it fascinating. And the whole system of punishment.

BENNETT: You must have had to dig deeply into the justice system of the *ancien régime*.

MOSSIKER: Yes. Yes. And the iconography. The dust jacket of the book is by a contemporary artist showing all the various hideous forms of torture and execution. It was an interesting case, a sordid case. I always think the underside of the glorious side is interesting to check into.

BENNETT: Montespan is an interesting figure.

MOSSIKER: And having always loved Madame de Sévigné, I had that insight into the era. She talked so much about the Affair of the Poisons.

BENNETT: Did I misinterpret a hint in your book that Sévigné wasn't averse to an affair with Louis XIV?

MOSSIKER: It was primarily that there was a possibility that her daughter had been singled out for his attention. She was a little too old herself, but I think Madame de Sévigné was susceptible to his grandeur, because he overwhelmed everybody who came into contact with him. There are some passages, which some of her more critical friends point out, where she just fawned. You can understand it. Anybody would have, because this man was life and death, and favor and glory were in his hands. We have no comparable head of state. I can't blame her for her adulation, although she sees very clearly, too. In her letters to her daughter, she must be careful because of the surveillance of the mails. She has codes . . . .

BENNETT: I've always wanted to read the letters.

MOSSIKER: Wait! Wait until I get the galleys. Don't read any of those awful translations that are around. Unless you read French.

BENNETT: I have found her French difficult.

MOSSIKER: Well, she's a little much. She's taken me into Provençal. I've become fascinated; I'm translating a Provençal poem. She adored Provençal words, and Brittany names, and she would roll them on her tongue.

BENNETT: I looked for a good translation of her letters recently when I read Chesterfield's.

MOSSIKER: I've only read anthologized Chesterfield letters.

BENNETT: But everyone in that era wrote a few good letters.

MOSSIKER: The tenor of hers is so constantly beautiful, flavorful, imaginative, graceful. Each one is like a beautiful poem. I hope I can bring them out that way.

BENNETT: In much of your work you use the method of voices, with each person speaking for himself, but in *The Affair of the Poisons* the narrative dominates. Why?

MOSSIKER: Because the voices were lacking. I always use them when I can; I think there is no better way of telling it. Now again with Madame de Sévigné, I will light a background so that when she comes on she's placed in time and society. But then again I hope to turn it over to her.

BENNETT: The voices method works very well for you.

MOSSIKER: Maybe I gravitate to cases where it will.

BENNETT: Still the Affair of the Poisons is typical material for you, because you like to explain something not thoroughly understood. The last reference I remember to it was when I picked up E. T. A. Hoffmann's *Mademoiselle de Scudéry.*

MOSSIKER: They were fairly good friends. Scudéry always sent Madame de Sévigné copies of her most recent publications. The thing I find so interesting about Madame de Sévigné is that I genuinely don't believe she had any idea that her letters would ever be published. She was talked about in her day, and people loved her letters, and read them aloud to one another, but I don't think she had any feeling that this correspondence, which is so personal and contained so much that she would have considered shameful about her daughter and son-in-law's financial ruin, and the expediency to which they were reduced— I know she never dreamed the general correspondence would see the light of day. Yet while other people slaved their lives away writing for immortality, she achieved it and loved the writing of it.

BENNETT: Were any of the letters published in her lifetime?

MOSSIKER: No. No. Shortly after her death. Not from her granddaughter's cache, but from her cousin to whom she had written. They were published among other beautiful letters of the period, because they put great stress on letter writing, as you know.

BENNETT: Some of them did write for publication.

MOSSIKER: All the manuals of letter writing. Letter writing was used for many things — letters of compliment, letters of condolence, letters of recommendation. The letter was so necessary in that society.

BENNETT: *Pocahontas* was quite a change for you, in scene and to some extent in method.

MOSSIKER: Yes.

BENNETT: You evoke the period very well.

MOSSIKER: It was a difficult one, I think, to evoke—shadowy and remote. But I was satisfied with what I had done, which isn't always the case. My editor thought it was a good book.

BENNETT: Did you consider modernizing the Elizabethan spelling?

MOSSIKER: We certainly talked about it, but I thought there was a definite flavor there, and I hated to lose it. I think there's no difficulty in understanding. Some people would rather it had been in plain twentieth-century English, but I thought it was integral to the expression and that it affected the whole sentence structure. It was a different way of writing. I'm so glad we kept it.

BENNETT: I gather you had some trouble finding hard facts.

MOSSIKER: There certainly isn't the documentation there is in French history, but there were a number of journals. All of the people with that expedition wrote voluminously. Then I was forced to go to anthropological sources for the ways of the people, which I just adored doing. I went to linguists in the anthropological departments to try to reconstruct the speech, and I used every possible method to authenticate what I formulated. A lot of it I did here at SMU at the Department of Anthropology, and they were very helpful. Of course, reading, reading, reading. All the Virginia people were marvelous to me. I worked about ten days at Williamsburg and Jamestown, working with the foundation at William and Mary, with a number of people who have been outstanding on the Virginia Indian scene. I talked with them about things they hadn't mentioned in their writings. I remember that no one had written that the women smoked, I mean the pipes. So Dr. Frank Speck, with whom I talked, said he would have to check, that he had never thought about it. He couldn't remember anyone, except one chieftainess, a female chief who did pass the pipe of peace. Otherwise he did not think women partook, because they were not allowed even to plant the sacred weed. That was the only thing they did not plant. Discrimination again.

BENNETT: You mention her seeing women smoke in England.

MOSSIKER: Shocking, yes. But the family line among the Indians was through the women, matriarchal.

BENNETT: I suppose we know a lot more about Pocahontas than we know about Shakespeare. I always feel sorry for the fellows who write biographies of Shakespeare.

MOSSIKER: It hasn't stopped them though, has it?

BENNETT: What is your opinion of the character of Pocahontas?

MOSSIKER: She was a very strong woman, and a very fascinating woman in that she could have made that transition. I could never figure out her motivation. I don't know how anybody could renounce everything—gods, language, people—unless she had some sense of what this other world meant. No, I found her a very interesting character, and I thought her disappointment in Smith's affection was poignant, and I thought her adaptation to the other world was just amazing. Hard to do. You know, defying her father. I thought the father-daughter relationship was exceedingly interesting, all sorts of overtones and undertones.

BENNETT: What did you think of Smith?

MOSSIKER: I thought he was a blustering braggart, and it took that kind of man to have gone and done what he did. He really held the colony together. I don't like his relationship to women. He tells about all those women in the far reaches of Turkistan and God knows where. You can't follow all those wanderings east of Istanbul and to the Russian steppes, and, oh, there are women who are mad about him! One bought him as a slave and fell in love with him. Oh, yes, he's quite a ladies' man and fancies himself as such. Married the nun. Then I thought his last lines were so poignant, that he had not even an acre of land in Virginia, had no children, had no wife, had no dogs, had no cards—he didn't gamble. His whole life had gone into this, and I found it very touching.

BENNETT: With a fine irony you point out that he finally achieved fame as a writer after all the other had slipped from his hands.

MOSSIKER: Wasn't that funny? And he never intended it that way. Of course, it wasn't as a writer; it was the narrative, the adventure. But he did make it live, and his reputation came that way.

BENNETT: You mention the difficulty of turning the Pocahontas story into a play, because the climax tends to come with the Smith rescue in the first act.

MOSSIKER: What do you do after that?

BENNETT: You overcame that very well by making her appearance at court the high point.

MOSSIKER: I tried to. It's interesting that an option has been taken on my book for a musical. I don't ever count chickens before they hatch. All I know is that I have the check for the option deposited, and I met the entrepreneur, the producer, when I was up in June. He's a man who stands very well in the theater, is highly respected, and has access to money. He has a feeling that the whole trend of the musical play on Broadway has become operatic rather than musical comedy. He feels that *Pocahontas* would be a great opera. I've always felt it had balletic tone; I could always see it danced. In fact, somebody wrote me from Boston who wanted to use it as a ballet, and thought my description of the scene had been balletic, that you could follow it as choreography. One hopes something will come of it, but I won't put any faith in it until it develops. *Napoleon and Josephine*, as I said, they tried to get for a movie, but they were frustrated. Then BBC did the whole book two years ago in twenty-five fifteen-minute segments. They have a very popular program called "Story Time," five days a week. So you never know what is going to happen, which keeps it exciting.

BENNETT: A question just occurred to me: Does Pocahontas ever speak herself? Is there an authenticated sentence she spoke?

MOSSIKER: Only what Smith says she said to him in England. I think there was the ring of truth in that, because it was not flattering to him. It was a reproach, and I thought I heard her voice.

BENNETT: That's the only one, isn't it?

MOSSIKER: The only one. You only see her through other people's eyes, and hear her through other people's ears.

BENNETT: The central figures in all of your books are women.

MOSSIKER: I think I understand women better. I don't seem to feel competent to analyze the male psyche. It has always been the heroine rather than the hero that has attracted me. I feel that these people are all so difficult to understand. I have been talking with analysts and psychiatrists about Madame de Sévigné because her relation with her daughter was so complex. It became popular at the turn of the century with the Freudian viewpoint to inquire whether it was an incestuous love. It was excessive, and she uses the word "passion" constantly, which is a strange way to refer to maternal love. But it is so difficult to understand people, and I feel you can't write about anybody until you've come to some sort of terms with what they were and thought and wanted and meant.

BENNETT: Aside from Sévigné, do you have any other plans at present for books?

MOSSIKER: I have something I started as a young-adult book, and it changed as it came along. If you've ever heard of a Byzantine gothic, that's what it's going to be. A friend of Josephine's cousin went with her to the fortuneteller, which begins my *More Than a Queen*, and she was told that she would be kidnapped by pirates and end up in a palace and that her son would be a great ruler. Sure enough, she was abducted on her way home from the convent in France and ended up in the sultan's harem in Constantinople, and her son did become Mahmud III. We just have wisps of information. I started to do it the other way, and I decided, no, that I wanted to do it as a romance. When I finish Madame de Sévigné, I'm going to try that. I think it will be fun.

BENNETT: I'm sure there are a lot of other historical scandals awaiting you.

MOSSIKER: Yes. One I'm yearning to do for young adults is the story of the children in the temple—Marie Antoinette's two children and the last days. I would love to do the Duchesse d'Angoulême, who did get out finally, and came back with the Restoration, and led such an embittered, dreadful life. I would also love to do a biography of Madame Vigée-Lebrun. I think she was a fascinating woman for her time. She left her husband to go kiting all over Europe, painting in all the courts. Everywhere she went she was acclaimed. A marvelously interesting life. I'd like to do them one after the other. I have vaguely researched all of them, and would like to do more.

BENNETT: Your writing is a little like conjuring ghosts.

MOSSIKER: That's a good line, a very good line.

September, 1979

William Goyen: *A Poet Telling Stories*

WILLIAM GOYEN was born April 24, 1915 in Trinity, Texas. He earned his B.A. in 1937 and his M.A. in 1939 from Rice University. He served in the U.S. Navy in World War II. Afterward, while writing and supporting himself as a waiter in Taos, New Mexico, Goyen met Frieda Lawrence, the widow of D. H. Lawrence, who in turn introduced him to Dorothy Brett, Mabel Dodge, Tennessee Williams, and Stephen Spender. Soon after, Goyen, with a girl named Dorothy, traveled to London, where they stayed with the Spenders and met Cyril Connolly, Elizabeth Bowen, Rose Macaulay, Edith Sitwell, and others. Critics acclaimed Goyen's first novel, *The House of Breath*, in 1950. He has since written successfully in many fields, taught, and worked for a publisher.

Although it was a mouse-gray winter day when I talked to him in New York, Goyen was in good spirits. "This is a wonderful snowstorm we're having. It's quite thick, and I'm glad of it. I'm just here for a few days from California. The snowstorm is quite a gift. I was out early in it, in Central Park. It's lovely."

Goyen and his wife, actress Doris Roberts, now live in Los Angeles. He visits Texas these days—writers' conferences, friends, his mother, who lives in Fort Worth—but he has lived elsewhere most of the time since World War II.

Goyen is exactly six feet tall and weighs 165 pounds. "I'm a light man. If I eat a lot, I may weigh one hundred and sixty-eight, at worst seventy." His dark hair is now well mixed with gray. His eyes are brown. "We call it 'hazel' in Texas. You call it 'hazel' whenever you aren't sure of the color." For some years he has worn glasses while working, and he now wears them all the time.

BENNETT: Have you been writing this morning?
GOYEN: Yes, I have, since five o'clock. I generally start around four-thirty or five. I was sitting here just dozing, because I generally

sleep from about eleven to twelve. That's about as far as I can go, that five or six hours. Then I still have a good part of the day to do other things, revise and rewrite, but generally I don't. I let it go then. Once I've done that much, I generally just go away from it.

BENNETT: That's a long stint of writing.

GOYEN: Oh, boy, it is! But I love those early hours, no matter where I am. Wherever I've been.

BENNETT: In your writing you seem to be mining your unconscious. Of course, all of us do to some extent. Do you find the early hours best for that?

GOYEN: Yes, I do. I just get what I get then. It comes to me. That's my time.

BENNETT: How many words do you normally write each day?

GOYEN: Not a great deal. I'm not a fast writer. It seems like I am, but you can see in the history of my work—well, it's short fiction isn't it? I just go slowly. I would say maybe, in longhand, sometimes ten, sometimes fifteen pages, all over the place, and that's what I get. God knows what it takes to get that. When it comes, it just comes out. But I'm slow, and I may get up and read a little, or look at photographs or paintings, or I don't know what. I'm not over the manuscript that long. I rarely type. I hate the typewriter, and I don't type until the handwritten manuscript gets illegible from revision because I write all over the place.

BENNETT: Do you retype your own manuscripts?

GOYEN: And then I retype in order just to get another version, another draft. I make many drafts. I just can't stop revising; I'm a heavy reviser. Then finally, from what I get there, which is half-typed and half-handwritten, I get a typist to do it for me. It's always a chore and a problem, because it's always hard to read. I have never been able, except in those very early days, to type the whole thing myself. The main problem is that I keep revising as I do. I really can't leave it alone. I finally just have to abandon it, let it go that way.

BENNETT: Roughly how many words do you get to a page in longhand?

GOYEN: Let me guess. I don't even know how to guess. I write fairly small. Have you any idea what's normal?

BENNETT: My handwritten pages type out about what my double-spaced typewritten pages make.

GOYEN: Yes, mine do too. That's about two hundred and forty or fifty words to a page.

BENNETT: With lots of revision.

GOYEN: Yes, and I generally just write straight ahead; I don't go back. I go on from where I am each day, which I love to do. It's like somebody literally telling a story: "Where were we when I left off?" Just going right on, so that I really don't look back, for several reasons. If I do, I get caught back there revising, and it becomes too fine a work too soon. It must be like chiseling a sculpture; if the sculptor does too fine a work too soon on what's big, heavy, gross work, then it's out of balance somewhere. I should imagine that he has to do all different phases of gross work, and then finer and finer and finer detail. There is a question of proportion and balance. What odd habits we have.

BENNETT: Do you use an outline of any sort?

GOYEN: Very rarely. I generally get an outline from what I've written. That's kind of in my head, and comes to me as I'm writing. Outlines are generated, generally, by the work I'm doing and not beforehand. I just don't really know that much in advance.

BENNETT: Do you know the general direction?

GOYEN: I know the general direction, but I like truly to go with what's happening. I just write out a situation or event and see where it leads me. When I've done that, I'm able to go back and, even though I'm still writing ahead, give it some kind of outline or structure. If I get really bogged down and lost, then I will make an on-the-spot outline, but rarely have I worked from a general or grand plan.

BENNETT: Do you begin more with characters then?

GOYEN: That's right. I begin with the characters, and my search a lot of the time is for an event. It is often within character that I see story. The teller has always interested me almost as much as the tale. And, of course, the listener interests me too, because attitudes of listening—that is, the way in which people listen—really fascinates me. You can see how it would be hard to outline that.

BENNETT: Do you envision a certain audience you're writing for?

GOYEN: Rarely do I do that. There's always a listener, of course, and I'm just not very sure who that is. I'm sure that I am listening, you know. Really I am both teller and listener. I really do listen. I really do hear the tale when I'm writing it, and then I write it down and hear it again that way. That's the way we heard stories in our childhood; we heard stories going all the time. So we were really listeners before we tried to tell the stories again: "Let me tell you what my uncle told me when I was a boy" When we decide to *tell again* is when the writing starts, for me anyway.

BENNETT: Are your characters somehow related to real persons, perhaps something like the old lady Arnold Bennet saw in the restaurant who set him off on *The Old Wives' Tale?*

GOYEN: It has worked both ways. Very often I have worked from somebody that I've seen on the street. Even then that person is connected somewhere, or gets connected eventually to somebody I knew well, or was around. That gets very specific for a little while in the process of writing, and then I lose it again. You know, then it broadens again away from the specific. For me, it almost becomes fable; it almost becomes larger than life. Often it does. I don't intend that, but that's what happens, and I kind of like it. I'm glad about this. I really prefer writing about people who are a little larger than people really are, than about the really detailed person per se. The photograph doesn't interest me as much as the impressionist painting. I didn't know this while I was doing it, but I see, now that I've done a certain amount of work, that this is what has happened. I'm just talking from hindsight, looking back. At the time it just seemed so much like a gift to me, writing and what comes to me. It's just a seizure, you know. I just love that; it just takes me, and that's what I have to do. It gets hold of me. It's really kind of like making love—you know how we are: suddenly it comes over you. It's the natural thing; nature works through art as well as through propagation. You've just got to have it, you've got to do it, and that's when it happens, and it is a compulsion, but a wonderful feeling most of the time, and a lot of pain too.

BENNETT: Do you have any specific way of getting names for your characters?

GOYEN: There again, they just sort of come to me. I like to leave myself open to names. I suppose nothing ever really just comes to us; that's such a mystic way of talking about things and perhaps is not grounded in fact. I suppose always somewhere there is a real objective correlative for the thing that comes. It is objective, and it's not the internal image so much. So surely there are names close to those it seems to me I've made up, names that have been in my life. I hear names; I love names. Names are character for me very often. I've been writing about a woman named Johna, which is a name I like. I heard someone speaking about his wife, whose name was Johna, not long ago at dinner. Later I thought, that must be Juana—that it must be Mexican or something Latin. But Johna! What a marvelous name! It's probably a Texas bastardization of Juana.

BENNETT: Do you overwrite and then cut back on later drafts?

GOYEN: I do. I do. When I talk to young writers, I make them do it, especially when they tell me they can't. One should just go for broke, just go crazy, and then one can always throw it away. One rarely does. Or just cut back, and take what is still living there; the rest is all kind of costume. I love to let myself go, because who cares? I am writing for myself; I know that. If it's any good, then it'll please me, and that's bound to please a certain number of other people.

BENNETT: I suspect even Harold Robbins does it.

GOYEN: Yes. So I go at it like that and then cut back.

BENNETT: How should a reader approach your work? What kind of expectations should a reader have?

GOYEN: I want them to come to it expecting to find someone who is trying to write at his best and to write seriously. They should expect to find a writer who is carefully and honestly trying to tell about something that has meant so much to him that he has taken time to put it down within certain traditions and with a fairly old language. It is a serious endeavor, a piece of work. To say that to a reader outright, of course, is to make him say, "Oh, rubbish!" On the other hand, I think we can help readers by saying, "If you read this, you will meet a man who has had a genuine feeling about what he was writing." And with that, making a second one-A priority for me, is really wanting to tell a story that holds and that somebody would want to go on hearing. That's my pleasure too.

BENNETT: You have some good yarns to tell.

GOYEN: This one I'm writing is even more so. It is so outlandish that I can't believe it. I'm up every morning at four-thirty or five to write this outrageous thing that I'm writing. But I truly love it, and I'm just about through. I've shown it to my publishers. I thought they might nix me, because it is as far out as anything, but they are very much taken with it, and feel it ought to be longer, which has quite thrown me. I never write long things. But that was encouraging. Indeed, I came home and started; I've been rewriting and adding to it. This visit to New York, I came to sit with them and see what they thought about this little novel. It really is enlarging, and I've just let my head go, and I'm having a ball listening to it.

BENNETT: Is it as wild a yarn as *Come, the Restorer*?

GOYEN: I think it is. It's called *Arcadio*; that's the name of the man, who is a Chicano—I guess that term's okay, but I still call them Texas Mexicans. I grew up with them, and they're wonderful people and part of my whole upbringing down there in South Texas. Arcadio is a Texas Mexican. He just tells his story. He's sometimes like Mr. de Persia in *Come, the Restorer*, except that I believe he's gone him one even better.

BENNETT: Is the new one set in Texas?

GOYEN: It's set in Texas, and he's sitting under a railroad trestle that I remember out in East Texas, an abandoned trestle, one of those old trestles that goes over what used to be a river, and there's no river, and there's no train. It's really a relic of the whole past, and under it sits this man who tells a kind of fantastic story of himself. I just love it. He's escaped from a sideshow; he's at large, so at large he tells the story. I'll just tell you that little bit. I've never talked much about it, but I'm full of it this morning, or of Arcadio. He's got me. He's got me.

BENNETT: You write principally in the mornings. Does it bother your wife or upset your homelife much?

GOYEN: You see, it's worked out so well. She's a night lady. She's on the stage, or rather now she's out in California making television. Nighttime is just her time and not mine, so that when she's on stage, she's not in bed till two o'clock, or at least after one, and I'm just about to get up. I have about two more hours after she gets there. Then she sleeps till noon, and I'm through; I've done my day's work. We come together that way, you see. Everybody is used to my going to bed early. If I have night activities, then they know that I grumble and that I'm always asleep at the dinner table or wherever. So it has worked out just beautifully. I think writers and actors are a good combination. Our combination has really been good.

BENNETT: I made it a point to watch your wife on *Angie* this week.

GOYEN: I watched it too; I'd just got here. I just love her; she's so wonderful. Love her! She's my favorite actress. I'm not too fond of television, but I put up with it. She's such a wonderful stage actress, and she's made a couple of beautiful movies too. It's a fanciful kind of life that she leads, and I love it. Part fantasy. She's made-up half the time, and I like that. I don't know that I could have a wife who's always unmade-up. For an old East Texas boy, that's pretty good, to get him a wife with full makeup. Wigs on a lot, lashes.

BENNETT: In your home in California do you have a study where you work?

GOYEN: Well, a new thing has happened to me. I work in a little office. I've never done that before, because here in New York we have this large apartment where I'm sitting right now, and I've always had a wonderful workroom far off from the rest of the house. We brought up a little boy in this house; he's twenty-two now. Other people were here—Doris with her parties and her theater. I've always had my workroom in back. But California is a very different style of life. We have a big old Spanish house out there which is surrounded by a community of houses—you know, a neighborhood. In New York you don't know what a neighborhood is. In California people really don't mind calling in a window or knocking on a door, the way they do at home in Texas. But I'm not used to that when I work. So it occurred to me a year ago to take an office down the hill, near Hollywood Boulevard and Vine Street. It is there in an old bank building, up on a top floor, in the back. It's just a little room that is absolutely mine, surrounded by people who are walking around with papers in their hands, whatever they are doing. I don't hear anything though; it's right smack in seedy old Hollywood. It's just wonderful. I begin work at home, because I don't much want to go down there at that hour, up at four-thirty at Quebec Drive, working back in a sittingroom in our house until about seven. Then I get ready and go down to the office.

BENNETT: Does anybody there know what you're doing?

GOYEN: They haven't a clue. I wouldn't dare let them know, and they just don't ask questions. I'm surrounded by what look like porno movie offices. There's one with a telltale name, and it says "Casting" on the door. I just let them go on with their business, and they don't bother me. Sometimes I'm there quite late at night. I have all my books there, and I read. I never dreamt I would have this kind of thing anywhere, certainly not in Hollywood, California! They're out there doing television series, and all that other awful stuff they do. To write a book is unheard-of there. A book is just a foreign element. I feel really hidden. No one else is doing it. It's true fantasy, true isolation, true hiding out.

BENNETT: At Rice what were your degrees in?

GOYEN: I took a B.A. and an M.A. there, quite a long time ago. My M.A. was in comparative literature. I was caught up in three literatures—Italian, French, and Spanish. I truly love Spanish literature, and then I was kind of led off into German literature as well. I really did eat it up. I spent three years working on my master's degree and had a wonderful time. I thank God I did it.

BENNETT: Do you still speak all those languages?

GOYEN: They're there. I read without any problem, and I guess I could write without any problem, but if one doesn't speak it, you know how we all get. I'm in Europe a lot; we go fairly often, because we love to do that, and so I can use it and kind of brush it up and see where I am. Mainly I learned those languages in order to read literature.

BENNETT: Was your bachelor's degree also in languages?

GOYEN: Yes, I had done all my work in the languages. What I finally wrote my thesis on, oddly enough, was Shakespeare. His theater. Not so much on his plays as the theater itself, the public, the populace. Shakespeare's audience interested me. I was able to use a lot of cross-reading. I elected to do that because I wanted to write plays then. Only after that did I delve down deeply into classic and medieval literature.

BENNETT: Did any of your professors start you on the path of good writing?

GOYEN: Well, I was so young that I was turned out of the creative-writing class at Rice, which was probably the best thing that ever happened to me. The man teaching what was called creative writing was George Williams, and he became my dearest friend. He's retired now. He just felt I was too young, but I nevertheless went to their meetings and read my work—I was writing then. The next year he wanted me to come into his writing class, but I had no room for that because I now was heavily a scholar. He did become an influence on me, a truly poetic influence. He showed me Irish literature—Yeats and Synge. And modern British poetry, Eliot and Pound and Auden. So he was a great influence on me there. He gave me models, showed me books, and encouraged me to write, and through the years has been a great friend to my work. I think he was the only one there who really cared about me, because Rice is and was then a very scholarly place, and anybody who thought seriously about writing and letters was sort of encouraged to go somewhere else.

BENNETT: Yet three of the writers I've talked to went through Rice: you, John Graves, and Larry McMurtry.

GOYEN: John and I, I believe, were classmates. He might have been a year ahead of me.

BENNETT: What writers influenced you?

GOYEN: Gee, that's always hard for me to answer, because American writers, contemporary writers, don't really interest me. I just can't read them. I don't know what that means or why, but I can't. They're my friends, my contemporaries, like Styron. But I can't imagine writing a book like *Sophie's Choice*. There's nobody, and I just feel out of the stream with them, and that's okay with me. I don't feel a part of this whole thing of American writing somehow. Nobody's ever known, if they paid any attention to me, where I am. I'm not a Southern writer, although a lot of people insist on calling me a Southern writer. I don't feel close to any group; I feel an outlaw, and that's all right. The people I truly love are poets like Ezra Pound. People are always surprised when I talk about Pound. He has shown me a great deal, and I suppose helped me find in these later years something of a way of looking at things, maybe even stylistically helped me to write. I don't know. But I feel that's true about Pound and Eliot and poets in general. Lately I've been reading again the stories of Flaubert. When I first read them with George Williams at Rice, they gave me a whole way of looking at writing. Such wonderful stories. I've been reading "St. Julien," the one about the hospitaler who massacred animals. Wonderful, wonderful, wonderful. And Balzac and Hawthorne and the nineteenth-century writers, European and a few Americans.

BENNETT: Did you ever meet Pound or Eliot?

GOYEN: I met Eliot. Eliot had read *The House of Breath*, which was shown him by Elizabeth Bowen. I finished that book over in London, and I was vulnerable to some of those people. After I came back here and the novel was published, Mr. Eliot was at the University of Chicago, and I happened to be there for one winter. So we came together, and I went and sat and had tea with him one afternoon. It was terrifying. I think I still had on orange shoes; you remember we used to wear those old shoes in Texas, and orange is the only color I can think of to describe them. I felt very hicky and country, even though I had been in London that time. He just scared the hell out of me. I just listened, and I sat there with him, and it was an experience for me. I had just read his *Four Quartets*. I love his short poems, all of them. I know people are now doubting him again, and he's called phony, but I don't care. I know my feeling for him, which came early.

BENNETT: I read *Prufrock* years ago, when I was in high school and it knocked me off my feet. I didn't know what it meant——

GOYEN: That's right. I didn't either. But listen, it touched us, didn't it? There was an elegant, well, desperation is what I should say about it. It is quite easy to read as poetry, which surprised us because we must have had the idea that reading poetry is hard to manage. Here was a man writing quite simply.

BENNETT: He somehow shows us.

GOYEN: Then, you know, I loved Balzac. He just cleans my mind out, and I read him, read him, read him. Sometimes in French, or if

I'm too impatient I just read him in translation. But, oh, how I relish him! Those writers are the ones who have a hold on me, and that's where I go when I read.

BENNETT: Have you read any Texas writers?

GOYEN: I know McMurtry, and he's okay for me, more than any other novelist of my generation in Texas. It's so photographic, to my mind, but that's often what he means to do—photograph a place. I can get just so much of things as they really are when I read him that I can't go on. On the other hand, I admire him for just that: that he shows me what is and leaves me with a feeling for it, and that's what I like about his books, a kind of tenderness and melancholy there. McMurtry's admirable. We're as totally unalike as any two Texas writers can be, but I like to read him, and I admire him. Graves is a wonderful writer too. I admire his clarity and his strength and his good sense. I've always liked his writing; I wish there were more. Those two I really care about. I was at Rice reading my work when Apple was finishing his first novel, and we got to be chums and talked a lot. That novel is very strange, but I understand the tradition that he writes in, and think it's good. He's a gifted and a serious writer, and I look for major work from him.

BENNETT: Do you know Shelby Hearon?

GOYEN: She's a gal I meet when I go down there to those writers' conferences, and she's just full of beans and terrific. *Armadillo in the Grass* was quite a performance for a first book. In this last one, *Prince of a Fellow*, I felt her style has got *New Yorker* tough and hard. But she's caught a way of life. She has a real sense of the writer's craft and work. A talented woman whose strong work is ahead, I believe.

BENNETT: Preston Jones?

GOYEN: I got to meet him—he and I had the same literary representative, Audrey Woods, who is a wonderful friend to my work and still at that agency where I've been twenty-five years. I got to meet him through her once here in New York when his play was running. Then I met him in Paul Baker's theater in Dallas. We're so alike; we just got along warmly. I think his plays are brilliant; they really are alive and honest and loving too. I feel he had a lot of work ahead of him.

BENNETT: Tom Lea?

GOYEN: I met him with Dobie and all those people, when I was young.

BENNETT: What about Donald Barthelme there in New York?

GOYEN: I'm so fond of him. He's delicate—would anybody use such a word for him? I have some difficulty understanding his vision at times, and I believe there's a danger for him in lack of variety, in getting repetitive. I believe he'll freshen and elaborate. But he's superior to Vonnegut and Barth and all those—I just can't hear them. I haven't a clue as to what keeps firing them up. Their trap is cuteness, oddness, sophomorism, I feel. But Barthelme is a poet.

BENNETT: What about dead Texans? Dobie?

GOYEN: You just couldn't help liking Dobie. He was always around there when I was young. I've read a good deal of his scholarly stuff; he discovered some precious things on Texas folk and folklore. For me those other men, Bedichek and Webb, they were wonderful, those old pioneers. They were really like my forebears, you know, as I was growing up, like my ancestors. Their work on Texas history, Texas folklore, myth, nature—the whole thing truly fed me and enriched me. I'm indebted to them; I'm glad to be in that tradition. I hope I am.

BENNETT: You know Margaret Hartley.

GOYEN: Oh yes, what a beloved friend she is. She and Allen Maxwell have published a whole lot of my work in the *Southwest Review*. I love Allen so much, too. Both of them are the dearest Texans to me, and have been close to my work all these years.

BENNETT: Many critics have found your work interesting.

GOYEN: Robert Phillips has just published a study of my work. And there is what I believe to be a fine one being written by a young Frenchman, Patrice Repusseau, who is the protégé of my old French translator, Maurice Edgar Coindreau, who is now nearing ninety. This young man's book will be translated. He was at Rice University—came there one year on a fellowship to research my work there in the Fondren Library. That's how I met him. He has finished his research, and it's brilliant. There was Clyde Grimm at the university at San Marcos, who finished the first complete checklist and bibliography of my work just before he died two years ago. It was such a loss for me. He had become a dear friend, and he had done really in-depth work on my writing. He really cared, and he found wonderful things that showed me what I didn't know, and he documented carefully. And I am grateful for the Phillips book. He's a friend, and a scholar of my work, with surprising insights.

BENNETT: What sort of person was Frieda Lawrence?

GOYEN: Just a wonderful great big huge piece of a woman. She was a very simple woman in her style of living and in her feeling for life. She was peasantlike, although she was a baroness and a woman of distinguished lineage, and of fine upbringing. She just lived a dirt-bottom life. That's what I lived, and that's what she taught me. I went right to her when I met her in Taos in 1945, and I lived around her until she died in 1956. I did not leave her really until I buried her. I was there twelve or fifteen years, and she just really got me started after the war. She helped me find a whole way of living, and I was able to write while I was around her. D. H. Lawrence didn't have much to do with it. I didn't really come to read Lawrence or get any sympathy with his work for a long, long time. I have to admit that it's been only in the last three or four years I've begun to read his stories, and of course they're beautiful and show me a lot. I just stayed away from him. Who wouldn't have, living there, with those cult people around? I was vastly turned away from him. I was writing all that time, my first novel, *The House of Breath*, and I was totally obsessed. I didn't want anybody else. You know that I'm writing a long memoir about that time in my life, Taos and Frieda, an autobiography. I've got a whole chunk of it done, but I've been very careful about it. Frieda is the pivotal figure of the whole thing.

BENNETT: Is this the book, *Six Women*, which Phillips says concerns Frieda Lawrence, Margo Jones, Mabel Dodge Luhan, Dorothy Brett, Katherine Anne Porter, and a former landlady of yours?

GOYEN: It used to be *Six Women*, but I'm about to change that title because it has grown and moved away from the original concept. That concept is still there as the ground, but it has become larger. There are also lots of men in it now. Six women and five men, or whatever. Still, Frieda is in the center. She is the listener; I mean that I'm telling the book to her and reminding her of a lot of things, hoping that she'll remember, and telling her some things that happened after she went away.

BENNETT: I gather you had a problem with writer's block while you were at McGraw-Hill.

GOYEN: Yes. Who wouldn't have? It was a marvelous experience for me, and they were fine people to me. They respected me and gave me full leash to do what I wanted to with new writers. I did a lot of things there in five or six years, as it turned out to be. They asked me to come for a few years to help build a list of fiction. I got so involved with writers, wanting this one and luring that one, as an editor, that six years passed. And I was totally dry. It made me ill; I was quite ill then and for the next five or six years it was a bad period. I came through, and all is well again, but it was a bad, long period. You see, nine, ten, eleven, a lot of years that were a blackout. It's not lost, and we know that something is always happening, and I'm writing out of that lost time now. So that's okay. But it was a long, bad time.

BENNETT: Were your commentaries on Willa Cather and Ralph Ellison from those years?

GOYEN: They were from earlier years. Even then that was about the best I could do, and that was hard. I regretted I couldn't do more. I loved the Willa Cather one; that was an inspiration to me. And the Ellison one. There might have been three; I'm not sure. But those two meant a great deal to me.

BENNETT: Cather is terribly underrated now.

GOYEN: Yes, she is. She'll be found again. The company that published those little books is gone, and they are way out of print.

BENNETT: I gather you graduated quite young from high school.

GOYEN: Very early. I went to Rice when I was sixteen. I was so terrified and young, and so bound to Texas and to that place and to my family. I was so pushed under that it took me a long while to come up. Obviously God gave me the war to free me and mature me. That's a cliché, but it gave me a chance to grow away from everybody, out on the Pacific Ocean, so I wouldn't be in anybody's way, because God knows it is a terrible process. God just stuck me way out there.

BENNETT: What sort of high-school activities attracted you?

GOYEN: I belonged the last year to the dramatic club, and there I found an expression of myself. Alas, I had the strangest role. There was a play written by a man there, an original play, and I had the part of a seventy-five-year-old man, with all that stuff in my hair, and a cane, and trying to be bent. That was my sole expression.

BENNETT: One thing that seems to obsess you is religion and Christ figures.

GOYEN: I see that now. I didn't when I was writing.

BENNETT: Did you get a generous dose of religion when you were growing up?

GOYEN: Yes, I did. We were Methodists, revivalist Methodists. I had that around me always, and it was one thing I held on to. I wanted even to be a minister, a preacher. I planned to do that when I was about fifteen; I was so tormented by everything, sex and art and music. I thought the only thing to do was to renounce it all, before I had even begun it. Poor thing. And go off as a missionary. Indeed I went to a summer conference, an indoctrination, to be a minister. But I was too wild with the world. It was no good; I was already in trouble, you know, with the world itself. But that trouble has always been there! Then during that very bad time at the end of McGraw-Hill and after, when I was ill and went down to the bottom, I started. The last year at McGraw-Hill I began doing a lot of reading and thinking about writing a life of Jesus. It finally occurred to me that it was not to be that sort of thing at all, but a little handbook, a little pocketbook that I finally wrote. That marked my breakthrough. I began to come up after that. Now, Arcadio, the narrator in my new novel, reads a great deal of the Spanish Bible and quotes a lot from it. It's the only way he gets through, because he is a true sensualist. So again I'm able to draw on the Scriptures, which mean so much to me.

BENNETT: Are you active in any church now?

GOYEN: I'm not. I'm not. I'm discouraged by churches and by groups, and so I'm not a member of any church at all.

BENNETT: Many of us trickle in at Easter and at Christmastime.

GOYEN: Yes, I always do that at Easter and Christmas. And I love studying the Scriptures. I take courses; I've taken a couple of courses in the New Testament. I love scholarly study of it.

BENNETT: Sex is a major theme for you. You're interested in sex in all flavors.

GOYEN: Torment of passion, the sexual threat and obsession, people whose struggle is as much sexual as spiritual—I've written as often about these as I have about the spiritual turmoil in human beings. And what I've found is that the turmoil is the same. Arcadio is a hermaphrodite, and this duality produces a bitter turmoil in him. This tension is balanced only by Jesucristo, by the figure of Jesus.

BENNETT: You also seem to be interested in ecology.

GOYEN: Very much so. I grew up in the fields, by a river and trees. My family were all poor, and their job was to cut down those trees at a nearby peckerwood sawmill. I just lived in terror of there being no more woods, no more river, and sure enough there aren't many woods, and the river that I loved is nothing; it's dry and gone. The Trinity River there where I lived is nothing, vanished. The Rio Grande in New Mexico where I lived for the longest time has vanished there; there's a whole tributary of it gone. That's closely related to what we've talked about in human nature: its barrenness and fruitfulness. The destruction of nature is very personal to me, and the greed which does it is enraging.

BENNETT: Your work is quite musical. I gather you were interested in music when you were young.

GOYEN: I was. I wanted to write music very much, and I had a natural gift for it, for playing piano by ear and all that. I wanted to study music. My first ambition was to write opera and ballet, really a ludicrous ambition for this boy sitting in a house among sawmill people, half of them alcoholics, dope fiends, and all, killing each other—and the revival going on, my God! I wanted to write a ballet, and had begun several by the time I was fourteen or fifteen. I was closer to Liszt than I was, let's say, to Chopin, but something of each. But I liked them all. Wagner, Brahms. But what was important was what I felt, and it was a great disappointment to me that I was not able to study music. But it's okay.

BENNETT: You have written scores to some of your plays, haven't you?

GOYEN: Yes, and I've written a lot of little songs. But I still have felt very inhibited with music.

BENNETT: Did you listen to the Metropolitan Opera broadcasts?

GOYEN: When I could get the baseball people off the radio, or even the hillbilly music. I liked that too, however.

BENNETT: You liked hillbilly music?

GOYEN: I loved it. I loved those Lightcrust Doughboys. I grew up with them, and that's true, wonderful music. I began to see when I was out there on that ocean, when I began to grow up during the war, that it was the music of my boyhood. It was the homesickest music I knew. I just died when I heard it, thought of it even.

BENNETT: Did you envision a novel when you began the writing which became *The House of Breath*?

GOYEN: I didn't really know. It was so deep in me and so personal that I thought I would die from the feeling. I began writing it just in the order in which it was published. There was a little magazine, now defunct, called *Accent*, published by the University of Illinois, and in it were published my first pieces, called "Three American Portraits as Elegy." They were of Aunty and Folner and Granny. They were written in the ship. It was all little farewells to them, and I thought it was the end of the whole thing. It was just pure, pure homesick memories, and wanting to honestly document their lives. So it grew, and more people came in, and it began to take on a shape of sorts.

BENNETT: An atmosphere of secret guilt seems to permeate the novel. Did you purge yourself of this by writing it?

GOYEN: To a great degree. I don't really believe that art purges, however, as much as it enlightens. I think what it does is to free us of one layer of whatever emotion is there, guilt or fear or whatever, only to take us down into another layer, so that we have deeper insights. No confession in the world ever made anybody okay forever, I think. So the purge isn't eternal. We're the children of Adam, and so we're never saved altogether. But each piece of work that I've got through, that I've accomplished—I won't say "finished," but "accomplished"— has taken me into a deeper insight, and a richer one, and a certain kind of freedom, because I believe the deeper the insight the more freedom we have—the less bound to life experience, and to all these emotions and fear and guilt and time. It does free myself of a family, the guilt of a family, and the confusion of where I belong. And frees me of place: there is no greater bondage than place—it truly breaks our hearts to see it destroyed or leave it, to have to leave it, choose to leave it even. All those things were operating on me then. Also the discovery of sexuality, of a very deep, rich, confusing, and elaborate kind of sexuality to be discovered through these people. All nature became just an expression of that elaborate and fertile sexuality—the river too, all those things.

BENNETT: It's terrible to be sixteen, isn't it?

GOYEN: Oh, God, it's a ball, and especially to have been us! We're constantly freeing ourselves, trying to break the bondage of those things. Art for me is just those successive stages of freeing myself, so that I'm more in control of my expression. But not purged or saved.

BENNETT: Even your books of short stories have a unifying feeling about them.

GOYEN: I know this afterwards, and I see. One does connect a little body of work. In this connection he begins to see either the unity or lack of it, and it helps him keep going, gives him something of a frame or of a design. Then we have to break a view. This time I think I'm going to go deeper with Arcadio than I've ever gone.

BENNETT: You moved from Trinity when you were very young. Did you feel you wanted to return to Trinity when you were growing up?

GOYEN: Yes, yes. Always. Yes, always.

BENNETT: What was the genesis of *In a Farther Country*?

GOYEN: That book came truly out of New Mexico, out of living primitively in that strange part of the world in my own adobe house that I built, just really in the earth. It made me quite deranged some of the time, that haunting landscape, and I tried to find a way to save myself from it without having to leave it. I was that woman Marietta McGee-Chávez. I had gone to live for a year in New York on West Twenty-third Street, which is the ugliest place, really a hell street. I lived in a loft there, right smack in the middle of it. The feeling of hovering between the New York reality and the unreal enchantment of the mud life in the desert in that strange part of the world, that feeling led me to write a really quite autobiographical book.

BENNETT: Is Marietta a figure close to Boy Ganchion?

GOYEN: She's such a mixture. She's probably closer to Arcadio. She was half-Irish and half-Mexican, and she was the warring of the two halves—which we all are, which I always feel myself to be. My life seems to be made up of trying to pacify those two warring halves, whatever they are. She's part Boy, and part Swimma, the girl who ran away. And part hellion too; she's got a lot of Mr. de Persia in her. She wasn't just a silly, dreaming woman. She's really an absurd woman. But she has the gift of being able to make that perfect, ancient kind of stitch that I love, the colcha stitch handed down by the generations. I kept her in the tradition.

BENNETT: What was the genesis of *The Fair Sister*?

GOYEN: There was a little story first. That truly came from a black cleaning lady who cleaned for me just for a little while. She told the original story about her sister who had run away from home and was obviously a young whore, really a young gal out in the world; the sister was much more radical than in the story. She didn't really tell me as much as she'd tell herself. She'd be talking to the vacuum cleaner while she cleaned a very small apartment. That's what I heard. My soul, I believe her name was Savata too! I've never had much conscience about using real names, and that name was so wonderful.

BENNETT: Probably she hasn't read your novel.

GOYEN: I guess she hasn't. Later my editor, a brilliant man at Doubleday where I was for a little while, loved that little story, and one day he said: "There's a lot more to that story than you've told. Why don't you write more? I'd love to see it published."

BENNETT: Did he like the novel?

GOYEN: We laughed week after week as I'd bring it to him. I had a ball writing that; I loved it. The movies have been on that twenty times, trying to make a film out of it, and so many people have tried to make it a musical. Somehow they always run into black problems. Diana Ross and Pearl Bailey, all through the years, Sammy Davis Jr.—

but it's still not too easy to be black and make black movies and plays.

BENNETT: What was the genesis of *Come, the Restorer*?

GOYEN: I was truly in heaven writing that most of the time. I was obsessed with the figure of a man who used to come through our little town and literally restore. He came periodically, and he restored my grandmother's photograph. They were enlarged photographs, you know, that hung on walls in those big old frames. My family would go up in the attic and bring down things for him to do. He was a magician, a magical kind of man to me. Also I saw an enormous sexual figure as a huge symbol of the fertility of the world. I think I overheard stories of his making out with women of the town. For a young boy who thought he would never leave the place, you see what it was. He came to me as a savior and a holy man. This grew and grew in my head for many years and suddenly came up to the surface. I don't know what brought it to there. I was here every morning from four. I found a Shubert Symphony—No. 1—that I had never heard in my life, but I just picked it up in a record store, and I brought it here. It just was the story, and I played it every morning for two years as I wrote about Oil King and Mr. de Persia and their escapades. It's Houston in there. It came together like a fairy tale for me.

BENNETT: Everything in the book seems to have two sides, a sexual side and a religious side.

GOYEN: That's what I'm caught on, I guess. Don't you see that in life around you, and feel it in yourself? I felt it so strongly in the man Jesus, which could drive me out of many a town if I were to proclaim that, but still he is one of the most sensuous men I ever read about or envisioned. To imagine that body on him, the problems he had, just made me like him. That helps me through a lot of days. It all gets mixed up in people like Mr. de Persia and Arcadio and Marietta, and all these people that got into my head.

BENNETT: Are you ever going to publish *Half a Look of Cain*?

GOYEN: Well, it's such an odd book. It's told by a man who turned out to be ninety-six years old—that's what my editor figured out—but that was his age at the time of the story, which appalled me, and I didn't know what to do about that. It's not a far-out book, or surreal, or any of those things, but there's a gap in it. I really cannot bring it together. Maybe it's supposed to be left with a hole in it.

BENNETT: I really liked the part you published.

GOYEN: Many people have told me that. I just haven't been able . . . .

BENNETT: There seems to be a return to *The House of Breath* material with the flagpole sitter.

GOYEN: There is a return, literally a return, at the end.

BENNETT: Have you known a male nurse somewhere whom you based the central character on?

GOYEN: I don't believe I have. His name is Curran, and the name of the man who ferries the dead across the River Styx is Charon. That was a mythological figure who haunted me, and so I attached the whole thing to that.

BENNETT: Have you studied mythology a good deal?

GOYEN: Not a lot. It's just part of me, and a very natural way of looking. I'm not a classics scholar, but what I know is just absolutely used to the hilt.

BENNETT: Have you read Frazier?

GOYEN: A long, long time ago. I was a sophomore, I think, and it was too soon for me. *Come, the Restorer* is a very popular book at universities, and they just mob me when I go around. A lot of the very bright students ask me about *The Golden Bough*, but the book had nothing to do with the surface of my consciousness anyway.

BENNETT: You didn't publish an early novella called *The Well* either. Are there other books you haven't finished?

GOYEN: There's one other that I can recall. *The Well* is a New Mexico story, and so is the other. It's called *A Vision of St. Eustace*, and it was about the strange red-dirt desert and the Mexican people there. It was a long, complicated thing, and I guess I just didn't have the heart to go on with it. Or it was too soon for me. It had wonderful things in it, as I remember.

BENNETT: How successful have your plays been?

GOYEN: They've never had a long run or been a commercial success, but they've always been an oddity. People don't forget them. I wouldn't do them again for anything. It's the most terrible, the most terrifying experience. I won't even go near the theater when my wife's playing very much. I feel maimed out in front of all those audiences, and people, and actors, and directors. Your work's in the hands of those people, you know. I love the theater and always thought I wanted to write for it, and may again—who knows? It's terrible for me, because I have never been able to let a play alone. I was in there every night revising, and I couldn't understand why they wouldn't let me put in new lines, sometimes a whole new act. I'm a reviser, and I saw things .... My plays are going to be published, incidentally, by Black Sparrow Press.

BENNETT: Will both versions of *The House of Breath* be there?

GOYEN: They are distinct. That was a strange experiment that the Trinity Repertory Theater in Providence did with *The House of Breath, Black/White*. This brilliant director, Adrian Hall, a Texan also, had the idea that the same character could be played by two persons, one black and one white, so that one could see that we're all the same. It was an odd concept, and there were always twice as many people on the stage, half black and half white. It was overwhelming, it was so wonderful, the set and such talented people. Sometimes very very moving. It was magnificent, as was that one at the Circle-in-the-Square earlier. People have asked me to do it again here and there, but I just couldn't ever go through that. On the other hand, *Aimee!*—the one about Aimee Semple MacPherson—was a huge success in its own way, in that repertory theater in Providence. It played on and on for four or five months, and filled the house, and people loved it.

BENNETT: It was a musical?

GOYEN: A play with music. And with a whole lot of music; I wrote all the songs, about twenty-three. Many people have wanted to do it too, and offered me a lot of money to go back into it and make it like a Broadway production, but I've run as far as I could.

BENNETT: *Aimee!* is drawn from material different from that of the other plays, isn't it?

GOYEN: The others are part of one big body of stuff. It really begins with "Rhody's Path," a story about a snake getting loose at a revival, which I saw; that happened to me when I was a boy. The handler fell dead, and the people fled, and the snake got loose. They hunted the snake all night and found it and killed it, which was a terrifying thing to see. You know, Oil King was the very man, except he was now an independent oilman I had known in Texas, too. *The Diamond Rattler* really is about that man again, who converts himself through that snake, but he doesn't die. *The Possibility of Oil* is really about Swimma, from *The House of Breath*, coming home in her middle age, because she hears there's oil on the land. *Christy* and the two *House of Breath* plays also go back to the Charity material.

BENNETT: Have any of your plays been done in Texas yet?

GOYEN: No, nothing's been done in Texas.

BENNETT: Maybe we should get Paul Baker into action.

GOYEN: Let him do it. Don't let me come near it.

BENNETT: Do you have any other work in progress?

GOYEN: I have a bunch of stories. I see a book of stories coming, if the publishers care about them that much. There are about ten stories that I've been slowly trying to make right, and I don't think any of them have been published. I can't seem to get them right. I'll just have to take my time with them. Some of them won't work out yet, but we'll see.

December, 1979

Larry L. King: *Turning On the Memory Machine*

LARRY KING thumbnailed his life for me: "I was born January 1, 1929, at Putnam, Texas. Raised a farm and ranch boy. Moved to Midland, Texas, in 1942 when my father began work for an oil company. Went to high school. Worked in oil fields, as postal letter carrier, in Kansas wheat harvest. Joined the Army at seventeen. Entered Texas Tech briefly, disenchanted quickly, left. Newspaper reporter Hobbs, New Mexico, and Midland and Odessa, Texas. Aide in Congress ten years. Been a free-lance writer since. End of story."

King and his wife, attorney and literary agent Barbara Blaine, have a new daughter, Lindsey Allison King, which kept him in Washington. At his suggestion, I sent questions. Jacky English of the Folger Theater Group, which staged *Kingfish*, recorded his answers on tapes light years ahead of mine in quality. His house is "about a block and a half directly behind the Library of Congress, which means we are almost the same distance from the Supreme Court and about four blocks from the Capitol Building. Right here on top of the hill. It's an old house that I imagine was built about 1890 or 1900, but it was completely renovated two years ago." Where does he work? "I'm sitting here in the room now, looking out at the Library of Congress. The back of the house faces the Library. I use a room that's all windows on the second floor. I can also see a piece of the Capitol." Later we talked directly and I poked into his earlier answers with a few more questions.

The first time I saw King was some years ago in a newsroom when ... *And Other Dirty Stories* was published. He's a big, blackbearded fellow, a quarter inch over six feet tall by his own measurement. "I weigh right now about two hundred and twenty-five, which is twenty pounds too much. I'm getting a bald spot on top of my head. Blue eyes. I've always had bad eyes, and my right eye is especially bad. I wear black hornrims with a right lens that looks as thick as the bottom of a Coca-Cola bottle."

BENNETT: You've said that you reassessed your goals because of the trauma of the Kennedy assassination.

KING: At the time that Kennedy was assassinated in 1963, I had been working on Capitol Hill for about nine years. I originally left Texas newspapers to work as an administrative assistant in Congress: one, to get out of West Texas; two, because I had a really long-standing interest in politics; and, three, for the money. I was starving to death on Texas newspapers, and I could simply do better working in Congress. But I came here with a goal of working three years and then going off to write full time. One thing and another happened, including three children, and I couldn't find a writing job that paid as much as the political job, and so I got stuck.

I had been here nine years when John F. Kennedy, whom I had grown to know a little bit while he was in the Senate and worked for and with in the '60 campaign, went down to Dallas and got killed. It happening in Texas was a great trauma for me in some way. And I had been very unhappy in my job and in my personal life. A few days after all that happened I began to reevaluate my life, thinking: John F. Kennedy was young, he was forty-three, he was the President of the United States, he was rich and he was handsome. Now he's dead. But at least he got what he started out to get. They cut it short, but he got there. The corollary was: I've never done a God-damned thing I set out to do, and I'm going to set out to do it. I'm going to quit politics, and I'm going to quit the wife with whom I've long been disenchanted, and I'm going to begin to write. I'm going to start over. I'll sink or I'll swim, but, by God, I'll have tried.

BENNETT: How did you get into writing?

KING: I always wanted to write. It's the earliest memory I have, really, about ambition or setting a goal. I don't really know why, except that my mother read to me a lot when I was a child, and I'm told that from the time I was eighteen months old, before I could talk well, I would toddle across the floor dragging a book behind me by its cover and making gestures that I should be read to. My mother taught me to read long before I started school, and by the time I started, I was already trying to write stories. Under the influence of Mark Twain's *The Adventures of Tom Sawyer*, I set out to write a book called *The Adventures of Hap Hazard* that lasted for about four printed pages on a Big Chief tablet.

BENNETT: Did you have any good teachers, or perhaps a salty old editor, who encouraged you to write well?

KING: One of each. I had a teacher named Aubra Nooncaster. Mr. Nooncaster came to Midland, Texas, when I was in high school, as our football coach and also as our English teacher. We assumed—all the football players did, since we were deferred to in all things—that like most football coaches he would be primarily interested in keeping us eligible and would have a snap course. We enrolled in English thinking we would get automatic A's and B's. Mr. Nooncaster, it turned out, took English and literature much more seriously than he did football. Nearly everybody on the team flunked. I tried to fake it for a while, along with the other football players. Mr. Nooncaster would read a poem, and say, "Drake, what does that mean to you?" And Drake would say, "It don't mean nothing to me, coach." A pained look would cross Mr. Nooncaster's face, and he'd say, "Edwards, what does it mean to you?" Edwards would say, "Shit, it don't mean nothing to me neither, coach; it's silly." Finally, about the fourth person he would ask would be me, and I gave him the same sort of answer. About the third time this happened, he looked down and said: "I hope never again to darken the door of a schoolhouse after this year and be exposed to so many mindless people. Class dismissed. I'm sick of you." Everybody jumped up to leave. He said, "Not you, King." He closed the door and said to me: "So-and-so's father is rich and owns a hotel, and so-and-so's father is rich and owns a ranch, oil wells, whatever. Your father's not rich. These other guys can go through life brainless if they want to, but you're never going to go anyplace unless you learn something. I'm not going to put up with this from you." This impressed me very much. After that we would sort of sneak away from the rest of the football team and read stories and poetry and talk together. I still stay in touch with him, send him all my books and stuff. He lives in Pampa; he retired from teaching about five years ago. I'll never forget him.

Then there was a guy named Brad Carlisle on the *Odessa American* in the early 1950s, when I was a very young newspaper reporter. Although Brad's only four or five years older than I am, he was many years advanced in terms of knowing about writing, and everything else. He graduated from Oklahoma A&M, and I was a high-school dropout. He was very salty, very tough, and made me get it right. He taught me a hell of a lot about writing, and about integrity about writing. He's an editor on the *Banner* down in Nashville, Tennessee. I still stay in touch. I thought so much of him indeed that I named my only son Bradley Clayton King.

BENNETT: Were there any memorable teachers at Texas Tech?

KING: Hell, I was only there about thirty minutes. The coach there wanted to recruit me for the football team when I got out of the Army. I told him that I wanted to be a writer, but when I got there, they wouldn't let me take any journalism my first year. So shortly thereafter I dropped out of Tech, became a newspaper reporter, and never went back.

BENNETT: How long do you write at a time?

KING: There's really no way to say that. I tend to write in clusters and bunches, especially if I'm doing something under deadline. If it's a magazine article especially, I will put it off to the very last minute and then work virtually night and day for a week or ten days, whatever it takes, and forget to eat or bathe or anything else much. I don't have regular work habits. I wish I did, but considering the fact that I like to socialize a lot and drink a lot, I have to work my work in around my social schedule. Some people say I'm underpublished, and that may be the reason.

BENNETT: How many words would you say you usually write in a day?

KING: I write from zero to five thousand, depending on my mood and what's happening. No real pattern.

BENNETT: Do you use typewriter or pencil?

KING: Typewriter almost exclusively. I might make a few notes in pencil. When I'm out interviewing, I use a pencil for all my notes. Once I actually sit down to write, it's strictly a typewriter. I like to see it in front of me.

BENNETT: How much do you rewrite?

KING: I can't be exact. I work on each sentence until I'm satisfied with it and go on. I may rewrite one sentence nineteen times, and the next sentence eight times, and the next sentence three times. When I'm lucky, one sentence just once.

BENNETT: Do you use an outline?

KING: I loosely form in my head where I want to go with a piece, but I've never been an outline person. I consider writing rather an act of discovery, and I like to let it sneak up on me.

BENNETT: Do you keep a notebook?

KING: Sort of, and sort of not. The only thing I've ever kept long notes on—and tried to do it day by day, or at least once a week summarize—was when we started working on *Whorehouse*, and I had a vague notion that just maybe we might get lucky, and I thought even if it didn't and we failed it might make a pretty good book. So I kept a journal all the way through the production, and I intend to do it again when we make the movie this year. When it's all over, I'm going to write a nonfiction book called *The Whorehouse Papers*, which will be subtitled *The Making of a Broadway Hit*. Had it failed, it would have been subtitled *The Making of a Broadway Nonhit*, I suppose. But I used to keep more journals when I did a lot of journalism. I kept a notebook and wrote down observations and whatnot as they came to me and as I traveled around. A thought would hit me, and I'd grab a piece of paper to jot down a few words. I'm not as meticulous about it as I used to be. That's largely because I'm not writing much nonfiction any more. I'm working more now in plays and movies.

BENNETT: Do you have any advice for young writers?

KING: Yes, read all the time you're not writing.

BENNETT: What writers have influenced you?

KING: There have been a lot. I guess the first one was Mark Twain. When I was six years old and had whooping cough, my mother bought me *The Adventures of Tom Sawyer*, which to the best of my knowledge was the first *real* book, other than Big Little Books and funny books, that I owned. She read that to me several times. As I got a little older, I fought my way through it, and then got *The Prince and the Pauper*, and another Tom Sawyer book, and later *Huckleberry Finn*. I think Twain was the most American of all American writers, and he's continued to be an influence on me. I particularly like *Life on the Mississippi* and his autobiography, which was put together by an enterprising publisher, who went through all his other works and picked out autobiographical chapters here and there. H. L. Mencken, who was wrong about many things but wrong in a funny way, was a very early influence. I always read a lot of Faulkner from the time I first heard of him when I was young. An old fellow named H. Allen Smith, who died a couple of years ago, and who was a very popular writer in the 1930s and 1940s, was a funny man. His best-selling book was *Low Man on a Totem Pole*. I got to know Mr. Smith in his later years when he was living, in some bitterness, in Alpine, Texas, having come through Alpine once during the beautiful part of the year, hunting season, with all the trees turning on the Davis Mountains, and he thought it was a wonderful place. With no more investigation than that he went back to his home in New York state and sold out and moved to Alpine. Then he said he found out that nobody in Alpine read, that everybody there considered his work woman's work, that everyone took offense at anything he wrote that mentioned Texas. He did not come to a happy end down there, but anyway he was an early influence on me too. Then there was a Texas journalist who was killed in a dispute: Brann. They called him Brann the Iconoclast. He published newspaper articles, and one of my most prized possessions is the thirteen volumes of his collected writings. They're very rare now.

BENNETT: What forms have you written in? Poetry? Short story?

KING: I have not written any poems, except as a joke. I can't write poetry. I tried to write short stories when I first began to try to sell, back when I was a kid in the Army, and I sent them off to *Esquire* and a lot of magazines that are not even extant anymore. And received back nothing but rejection slips, so I kind of gave up on the short story. Every time I try to write a short story, it creeps out into a novel, and generally it turns out there's not enough for a novel, but I can't get it in a short story. So I've worked in nonfiction; I've worked in novels; I've worked in plays. I'm working with Pat Oliphant, the cartoonist, in, of all things, a comic strip. We're doing one called *Toby and Company* which is supposed to be the first adult comic strip ever. I suspect we'll get seven hundred papers to take it, and six hundred and fifty cancel the first three weeks because they get so many complaints.

BENNETT: Tell me about your connection with the *Texas Observer*.

KING: When it was founded by Ronnie Dugger and a few other young Texas liberals, I was a young Texas liberal working in Congress for a fairly conservative fellow I was trying to change to liberal. When it came out originally in the mid-fifties, I read it all the time. I couldn't write much stuff under my own name, but I would give tips to Dugger and later Willie Morris and other editors on what was going on inside the Texas delegation in Congress. Then when I left the Hill, I began to publish regularly in the *Observer*, did for four or five years, until I got to where I needed more than the thirty-five dollars an article that they paid. But it's a good thing, and I'd like to see it keep going.

BENNETT: Are you still really interested in football?

KING: More than I ought to be, I guess. I played it a long time; I like it a lot. It's kind of like chess and war, a combination of both of them. I've noticed that my work production drops off, literally, about forty percent during football season, because I spend so much time watching the games. I know football is not a serious pursuit, but some folks collect coins or write operas or whatever they do for hobbies. I watch football.

BENNETT: You've written a lot about it. You use a lot of autobiography in your nonfiction and poke fun at yourself. Is that some sort of reaction against writing public-relations handouts?

KING: I don't think so, really. I always poked fun at myself, even back when I was writing public-relations stuff. I would write a lot of fake PR handouts about the congressman I worked for and inject some poking-fun-at-myself stuff in there. One of them got mixed up with the regular ones, and they printed this quite insane thing down in Texas—unfortunately, as the congressman saw it, but much to my hilarity and glee.

BENNETT: You've read a great deal. Do you read as much now as in the past?

KING: I read all the time when I'm not working, just about. Like writing, the reading comes in spurts and bursts. If I'm out drinking and partying, I'm not likely to come in at three o'clock in the morning and grab a book, but I imagine I read at least three books a week. Even in my drinking weeks I'll read one. Sometimes I'll read six. I read everything, fiction, nonfiction, politics. I read a lot of sports too, and I am rather addicted to spy thrillers. Now and again I'll read a good book. One of these days, when I have a free six months, if I ever do, I would like to write a little spy-type thing.

BENNETT: How about tough-guy detective stories?

KING: I have never tried to do one of those. A few years ago an editor, then with Atheneum, asked me to try to write a modern-day Sam Spade detective story set down in Houston. I didn't know Houston that well, and at the time I couldn't go down there. So I didn't. I think Gary Cartwright might have written one for him, or started one.

BENNETT: What spy-book writers do you read?

KING: Well, John le Carré; Frederick Forsyth, who wrote *The Dogs of War*; Ken Follett, who wrote *Eye of the Needle*—those are the three names I recall. I don't pay much attention to who the author is because half those guys write under pen names.

BENNETT: From reading Lon Tinkle's book on Dobie, I gather old J. Frank when young felt that writing might not be quite manly. Did you have any problems with that?

KING: I really never have. I think an older generation did. H. Allen Smith said everyone in Alpine thought he did, quote, woman's work, end quote, as a writer, and this seemed to bother him and seemed to bother Tinkle. But they're considerably older than I am. When I came along, there was not any sissiness attached to it, no.

BENNETT: I've discovered that Dobie and John Graves and others fictionalize some in their nonfiction. Do you?

KING: I think that all nonfiction writers improve dialogue a little bit, improve scenes, maybe invent a little bit. I do it, and I think most of us do. If you'll look at nearly everybody's nonfiction pieces in magazines, they're too neatly tied up. There are never any questions left, or ambiguities. You've got to work hard when you're out there interviewing people to tie everything up; you're bound to forget two or three things you wanted to ask, two or three things you wanted to cover. Then when you're writing your piece, you realize, Dammit, I can't get hold of this person again, and I need to deal with this question. So you might tend to invent a little bit of dialogue or a little bit of scene that will tie it up in a neat package. An honest writer will tell you that. Once, teaching down at Duke a few years back, I was asked this question by a student. I gave much the same answer. That day we had a panel of writers and editors, and all the other writers hung their heads and didn't say anything. An editor began to rant and scream that if I worked for him and faked anything at all in a story I'd be fired. I said, "Thank God I don't work for you, and thank God I left newspapers long ago. We're talking about a higher form of art than newspaper writing."

BENNETT: What is your technique with interviews?

KING: I'm not doing interviews any more, I hope not for a long time. That's work for a younger man, I think. You have to spend an awful lot of time with people, at least I do in my technique, in order to capture them, to get some picture of them, to get whatever you're seeking. It's time-consuming and takes a lot of energy, and if you don't need the money, it's not a thing you want to do. When I did it, my technique was to hang around them a long time until they'd begun to accept me as part of the scenery and would begin to talk to me without realizing who I was. That's a little bit deceptive, but it's also terribly effective. It takes a lot of time. It can't be done by a newspaper person who is working against a daily deadline. But if you're working in the magazines, and you're willing to hang around them long enough—it may cost you a little money—and they like you, and of course you do everything you can to ingratiate yourself with them, then they'll begin to volunteer stuff. Then they'll begin to respond to questions, if you don't push them too quickly. You'll wind up getting a hell of a lot more, or at least I do, than if I sat down with a list of questions and began to ask them if they slept in the nude or whatever. It's simple: I wear them down.

BENNETT: Do you use tape? Memory? Take notes? What?

KING: The only time I ever used a tape in my life—because I'm an idiot about machines—is the time I was out with Louis Armstrong, the great old jazz musician. He talked so fast, in such a beautiful rhythm, and had so much music indeed in everything that he said, that I realized after an hour or two with him that I couldn't get it down fast enough. I would miss a lot, and to miss him was to really miss him. So I aborted that interview, rented a tape recorder, and laboriously taught myself to use it, clumsily, on that one story. The rest of the time, no. I don't like tape recorders; I like to take my own notes. I worry so much about the machine, since I'm so bad with them, that I spend all my time fretting about the machine instead of the person. I won't hear him, I miss the nuances, or I don't see what the person is doing. When it's just me and a pencil and my memory and the person, I can concentrate.

BENNETT: Can you shoot your own pictures if you have to?

KING: Good God, no!

BENNETT: Who is the person whose profile you most enjoyed doing?

KING: The one I just mentioned, Louis Armstrong. He was such a great old dude. This was at the Steel Pier in Atlantic City, back it must be about 1971. I went to spend a week with him, and he was simply so fascinating, and would sit up with me all night long drinking and telling such great stories and putting on a fine display not only of showmanship but of warm human qualities, that I just loved the old man, and I stayed with him a month instead of the week that I had planned. Willie Morris, who was then paying my salary as a contributing writer at *Harper's* magazine, called me and said, "Come on, get off the road." I stayed with Armstrong much longer than I usually do simply because I enjoyed him so much. Economically, of course, the more time you spend out on the road, the more money it costs you, especially if you're being paid a flat fee, as we generally are as magazine writers.

BENNETT: Who was the person you least enjoyed doing?

KING: It's a tie between Nelson Rockefeller and Johnny Unitas. Rockefeller, when he was governor of New York and was thinking of running for president in 1967, granted me a week with him. He would wink and slap you on the back and whisper to you and give you the impression while you were with him that he was giving you all this great confidential information. Then, if you did any research at all, you would realize that he had said in public at least nine times every Goddamned thing he told you. He was really deceptive. He wouldn't allow a private interview; that is to say, he always had a man with him, other than myself, and generally it was a fellow who took down everything he said, whether he coughed or whatever, on a little machine like court reporters use. I said to Rockefeller one day: "Get this damned fellow out of here—this machine is bothering me—and let's sit and talk." He had the guy leave the room and was very nervous. Two minutes later Rockefeller said, "Excuse me," and left the room. He brought the guy back and explained that because he was a controversial figure and in politics and prominent and had money, et cetera, that he always had to have every word he uttered or anybody said to him. Well, a guy like that is not going to tell you anything, because he doesn't say anything that's worth a shit. So I wrote a bad piece, and it was not a pleasant experience being with him.

The other hard interview was Johnny Unitas, Hall of Fame quarterback for the Baltimore Colts. I spent several weeks with him, trying to find out what made him tick. He simply—and he had every right to do so—said: "Look, I'll talk to you about football, anything you want to know about football, but what's in my private life and what's in my head are not any of your business, and no business of your readership. I'm paid to play football; I'll talk about football." I agreed with the guy. I've never understood, quite frankly, why people from all walks of life will let journalists come nosing into their business, and make them say things eventually that they don't want to say, and reveal them as inferior to what people think they are. So I agreed with Unitas that privacy is privacy and that one ought to guard it more carefully than most people do. But as a writer, trying to get inside somebody's head, that makes a tough assignment.

BENNETT: You've had a lot of experience in politics. Has it dampened your faith in democracy or liberalism?

KING: I guess it has dampened my faith in human nature more than it has in those things. I spent ten years working in Congress. I met some good people there, some hardworking people, but by and large most congressmen and senators are interested in themselves. Too many of them, whether they are liberals or conservatives, get interested in the perks of office, the privileges. They'd like to be called "your excellency" and wear robes and crowns, I guess. They don't work as hard, most of them, as one would have them do. They are not as thoughtful as you would like to have them be. Many times the bells would ring for a vote in the House of Representatives, and I would watch the congressmen run in their respective doors—the Democrats in one particular door and the Republicans in another—and in each case there would be a party functionary standing by the door, so that as these people would go by, the functionary would say, "A yes vote is a Democratic vote," or, "A no vote is a Republican vote." Many of them would go in to vote on bills having no more information than that.

As for liberalism, I've gotten older, I've made a little more money, and therefore I'm probably a little more conservative than I used to be. I'm perhaps more of a realist; I know we can't solve the world's problems as easily as I once thought we could. I've not lost faith in liberalism so much as I've lost faith in the fact that we can effectively within the government bureaucracy do a damned thing much that we set out to do. I used to think that you could throw a lot of money at the poverty program or whatever and before long you wouldn't have much poverty. I no longer believe that is true, for many reasons, but one is the bureaucracy. Nothing much gets done. Congress may enact very noble bills, and somehow they get watered down and perverted, and people will either misapply them to the extent that they actually steal money, or they will just get bogged down where bureaucrats use it as a way to just do something today and hold it where they won't have to take on a new project tomorrow. You finally wonder how in the hell anything gets done. So it's not so much in the system or ideology but in the people, that's where I've lost faith.

BENNETT: Did you know Bill Brammer?

KING: I knew Bill very well. When I was a young assistant on the House side of the Capitol in Washington, Bill was one of Lyndon Johnson's employees. He signed on as a speech writer with Johnson, and, like many people who did that, he wound up doing nine hundred other things. He had developed a fairly jaded eye about politics and Johnson, although he loved and was fascinated by Johnson. He wrote a novel called *The Gay Place*, Brammer did, while he was working for Lyndon Johnson, and it was one hell of a fine book. Quite obviously his governor in the thing, Arthur ("Goddam") Fenstemaker—because he said "goddam" so much—was based on Lyndon Johnson, very much so. I watched Bill as he wrote it, and talked about it with him two or three times a week, and indeed had the pleasure and privilege of reading some of the early parts chapter by chapter as he wrote it. Bill died a couple of years ago now and never produced any other work. A great disappointment. *The Gay Place* ended, if you will remember, with the death of Governor Fenstemaker. The governor had a brother, Hoot Gibson Fenstemaker, who had been a sort of ne'er-do-well and good-time Charlie but who nevertheless was interested in politics. Lyndon had a brother named Sam Houston Johnson. Bill started a second novel called *Fustian Days*, which opens with Hoot Gibson Fenstemaker deciding to run for governor to succeed his dead brother. I read about a hundred pages of that, and it was going really well. Then Bill got some sort of writer's block that he never got over the rest of his life. He also started a long book on Lyndon Johnson, nonfiction. I was around him, and he had just page after page after page of notes and observations. I read a few of those and thought they were quite good. Somehow he never finished that or anything else.

BENNETT: Why are so few of the articles in your collections primarily about politics?

KING: Because political articles are so perishable. When you write about politics for magazines, you write about issues at the fore in a given moment, or about politicians who are at the fore in a given moment. When you go back five years later to cull your pieces out for a collection, then you see that the politician is now of limited interest, and the issue is no longer of interest at all. I've a new book coming out in the spring of 1980, called *Of Con Men, Outlaws, Whores, Politicians, and Other Artists*, that has more politics in it than any other I've done. But the truth is that political writing usually will not last long.

BENNETT: How do you approach writing about a place like Putnam?

KING: When you're writing about home and roots, you just turn on the memory machine. I make notes quite a bit, when I'm sitting around in idle reverie, and I think of an incident that happened to me as a child in Texas, and that leads to another incident, and so forth.

BENNETT: How did you become preoccupied with race?

KING: I don't know that I am preoccupied with race. In 1971 I wrote *Confessions of a White Racist*, which traced my progress growing up in a racist society, in Texas and in the Army, and then into Congress, at Harvard .... Just about everywhere I've been I've run into certain forms of it. It's a bad thing, and it's a thing not many people had ever written about in America, and I thought our racism ought to be covered. I think it was a pretty good book. But I don't know that I'm preoccupied with race. What probably triggered me in part was a unique experience I had in the Army. I went into the Army when I was seventeen, and up until that point the black and white troops had always been segregated, and the black troops always had white officers. When I was eighteen or nineteen, a year maybe before Harry Truman integrated the military services in a worldwide policy for the first time, he picked out six small units and carefully made them half black and half white. I happened to be in one of those, at the Signal Corps Photographic Center, where the Army made its training films. So for the first time I was thrown in with black people as, quote, equals, end quote, and began to see them as quote, humans, end quote, for the first time.

BENNETT: Was that what set you to work on *Confessions of a White Racist*?

KING: No, I didn't write it until years later. Then the funny thing is that I set out to write the opposite of what I wrote. Willie Morris and I were drinking one afternoon in New York, and, both being from the South, or at least from Texas, we shared some attitudes. We were talking about race and all the hostility that had come to the surface. Black anger was mostly what we were talking about. I told Willie I was going to write a piece entitled something like "They Call Me Whitey." It was going to take a sort of wounded, injured tone that here as a white man I had always been interested in race, and from the time I was in the Army and began to associate with blacks socially and know them as individuals I had tried to be a good fellow. Now I resented all this stuff coming out. I sat down to write that, and it just didn't work. I couldn't make a good enough case for what I had done. When I considered that I really hadn't done much—and I considered myself enlightened—I began to examine events from the other side and see and understand. I went back and did a lot more reading on what had happened racially in America. So when I sat down to write what I thought was the truth, the real truth got in the way, and I wrote a different book.

BENNETT: What do you think the United States should do about its racial problems?

KING: There's no answer to that. I thought it was weird that, when *Confessions of a White Racist* was reviewed in the *New York Times* by a good writer from the South named Walker Percy, he ended his review on a note that Mr. King provides no solutions. He wanted me to solve the racial problem in America. I can't do that; if I could, I already would have.

BENNETT: Do you feel strongly about women's equality?

KING: According to my daughters and my wife, I do not feel strongly about it. I guess I must plead guilty to not being as concerned about that as I have been about race.

BENNETT: Do you feel strongly about homosexual rights?

KING: Again, no. I want homosexuals to have their rights, but I have never crusaded about it. Race is the only thing I have crusaded about, and I'm giving up crusading—that's a young man's job.

BENNETT: The issue of black rights is central for *The One-eyed Man*. What specifically set you off on that novel?

KING: It's funny how that happened. It was based on a little deception—that seems to be the story of my life. I had loosely thought of writing a political novel, but I had never really tried to do that. I had, however, tried to write a couple of other novels. One was about the captives in Korea who refused repatriation. When I was a young newspaperman in Odessa, a fellow named Claude Bachellor of Kermit was one of those fellows who refused to come back from Korea. They called them "turncoats." I think he was finally tried and sentenced. Well, I got to know him a little bit, covering the story, and got to know his family, and I tried to write a novel about that. I didn't know how to write very well yet in those days, and I also was handicapped by never having been to Korea. So that didn't work out. I sent it around to publishers, and nothing happened. Then I tried another sort of autobiographical novel about a young newspaperman, and nothing much happened to that. A published writer named Warren Miller, who had written some fairly good books, had seen my novels and a couple of other things I tried to write. Warren told Bob Gutwillig, who was an editor at New American Library, that he thought one day I would be a publishable writer, so Gutwillig wrote me a letter asking if I had anything he could see. I didn't, but I wanted to, and so I sat down and started writing him a letter telling him that I was writing this political novel. As I wrote the letter, I invented the plot; I wrote him about four pages. I got a letter back from him immediately saying, "If you can write the novel like you wrote the letter, then I'll make you half rich." I went on with the novel, and it turned out to be a Literary Guild alternate selection, and made me about forty thousand dollars, which is not bad for a first book.

BENNETT: Why did you pick state politics for *The One-eyed Man* when you've had so much experience with national politics?

KING: Because I got interested in state politics when I was seven or eight years old, and paid much more attention to races for governor and the Texas Legislature for many years than I did to national politics. In 1952 and 1954, for example, I did a lot of volunteer work for Ralph Yarborough when he was running for governor of Texas.

BENNETT: Are any of the characters in *The One-eyed Man* based on real persons, particularly Blanton?

KING: Cullie Blanton? He's a lot Huey Long. He's a little bit of Earl Long; he's a little bit of Lyndon Johnson. In fact, he's probably just a little bit of every sly old Machiavellian southern politician that I ever knew. A few other characters in that book are loosely based on some people that I knew, but they're mainly composites. Anything you write, whether it's fiction or nonfiction, is based on somebody. However, if you write fiction, you'll go outside the basic ingredients of any one person for a character to make that person your own. You're going to have awfully bad fiction if all you do is take one person and put that person through fictional paces.

BENNETT: Where do you get the names of your fictional characters? Phone books? Baby-name books?

KING: None of that. I don't know. I just try to think of something suitable. Sometimes I try to name them so that the name will indicate something about the person. In *The One-eyed Man* the protagonist, the fellow who tells the story, is the governor's public-relations man and dog robber and lackey and aide, much as I was in my political career. So I named him Jim Clayton, because Clayton reminded me of clay, and clay reminds me of earth, and this is a very earthy story with earthy experiences. I don't know if it meant a damned thing to a reader—probably it didn't. I don't really think about the names of most of my people that much. I don't know where I get them from. I just put together sounds, words that sound plausible. I don't really try to do the Charles Dickens thing of making everybody's name sound like the character is.

BENNETT: Do you have any other unpublished novels in your trunk?

KING: I've got a novel that is maybe half done that I put aside a few years ago to work on *The Best Little Whorehouse in Texas*. It's a novel called *Emmerich Descending*; Emmerich is the man; it's very autobiographical. At the time of the story he's about forty-two or forty-three years old. He drinks too much. His work has not produced in his career what he hoped it would, and every day he goes a little deeper down in his personal life, so much that it becomes a travesty almost. A lot of black comedy. I got about halfway through that book before I put it aside to do *Whorehouse*, which has been, as you know, a huge success. And I've gotten involved in other projects. But I want to go back to that novel because it shows the dark side of a writer's life, the dark side of anybody's life. My man in the story happens to be a writer because I'm writing about me, and it was maybe the lowest period of my life. I want to write that before the good times get to rolling so much that I forget how it was.

BENNETT: What are you working on now?

KING: A few months ago a fellow named Ben Z. Grant, who is representative from Marshall, Texas, got in touch with me and said he had the idea for a one-man show about Huey Long. He invited me to be his partner. So we produced it here in Washington in the summer of '79, a one-man show called *Kingfish*. Since then we've talked to Mike Nichols, who is thinking about buying it and turning it into a musical. So shortly I'll start working on turning that into a musical. And Pat Oliphant and I are starting the *Toby and Company* comic strip.

BENNETT: Whose writing among contemporary Texans do you like?

KING: John Graves just does a tremendous job. His *Goodbye to a River* is wonderful. His *Hard Scrabble*, about working this farm he bought a few years ago, is just magnificent. Larry McMurtry, who wrote *The Last Picture Show* and *Leaving Cheyenne* and any number of books, is very good. I like the work of Bud Shrake—Edwin Shrake— especially a novel he wrote a few years ago called *Blessed McGill*; nothing much happened to that novel, and something should. A. C. Greene wrote a fine book in *A Personal Country*, and he and I are talking about working on the screenplay for his *Santa Claus Bank Robbery*, which I also like. Dan Jenkins is a really fine comic writer. I liked *Semi-Tough* a hell of a lot, and I can hardly wait for his new novel to be out. It's about these two middle-aged old gals who grew up in Oklahoma and moved to West Texas. There are a couple of young guys whose work I've liked in the last few years: Max Apple, who wrote *The Oranging of America*, and Max Crawford, who wrote *Waltz Across Texas*.

BENNETT: Among dead Texas writers whom do you like?

KING: I guess we've all got to go back to J. Frank Dobie, who was the first modern-day Texan to become known throughout the nation as a writer. O. Henry was before that, but we're talking about modern Texans. I like the work of Bill Brammer, and I like Brann. Preston

Jones was a magnificent playwright who died tragically a few months ago, hell, in his early forties. I thought his death was a tremendous loss to Texas letters.

BENNETT: How did you come to publish your collections of essays? There are a lot of magazine-article writers in the world, and not many are invited into hardback.

KING: I believe Willie Morris suggested the first one. I had done a number of pieces for *Harper's*, and I had done a number for some other publications. About 1967, Willie said, "Larry, you really ought to go through all those and cull out the best ones, because some of those pieces ought not to die." I went to my then publisher, NAL-World, and they were not very excited about it, saying that collections didn't sell, nonfiction and all that. I got pissed and threatened to leave their publishing house. So they published it rather reluctantly. There's an irony there. I had written some new material, bridging, and I got Willie Morris to look it over when I got galley proofs. Willie said, "Larry, it's a kind of disaster; you'd better get them to edit the new bridging material." I called the editor, and he wasn't interested in the book, I guess. He said, "Well, God damn it, it's not worth doing; it won't sell." I said, "Well, it's my work, and I think it's worth doing." He said, "If Willie said that, get Willie to edit it." I said, "Willie hasn't got the time." He said, "Well, by God, edit it yourself." So I did. I kept it about four months. Then I didn't hear anything from my editor until one morning he called, he woke me up, being real friendly. I said; "God damn, what happened? I must have got a rave review in the *New York Times*." I was making a joke, but that was exactly what had happened. I changed publishing houses after that book and went to Viking, where they encouraged me to bring out that second nonfiction collection. The Viking attitude is more literary, and they want good writing even if it doesn't make expenses. They asked me to bring out this new collection too.

BENNETT: That's a great piece on your dad.

KING: That's my favorite piece of anything I've done. I don't think I'll ever top that one. It's bad to think that in a certain sense you have your best writing behind you, but I was very proud of how that came out. It came closer to saying what I felt and meant than any piece I've ever done.

BENNETT: It's a great tribute to the old boy.

KING: I still miss him.

BENNETT: How did you come to write *The Best Little Whorehouse*?

KING: It was a total accident. Originally I wrote that as a nonfiction article for *Playboy* magazine, and I took my three thousand dollars and my expense check and went on. Then two years later an actor named Peter Masterson, who was on Broadway playing in *That Championship Season*, happened to run across a two-year-old dogeared copy of *Playboy* with that article in it. He didn't know me, but he knew Carol Hall, a woman in New York who's originally from Texas and a friend of mine as well, and he had her call me to ask if the three of us could get together to talk about turning this into a musical comedy. I laughed. I'd never seen but about three musicals, and I didn't like two of those. I didn't know anything about doing it.

When I met with them, I said, "You guys go ahead and do this if you want to, but I don't know anything about this form of art or whatever the hell it is." Pete said, "You're the only writer here." I said, "I really don't want to write it." And we go back and forth. Finally, he said, "Go home if you will, and write the part maybe where the madam of the whorehouse is laying down the rules to a new girl who is applying for a job." I went back and turned that into the first scene and decided, Hey, I can do this.

BENNETT: Any future theater projects on your agenda?

KING: Nothing right now beyond *Kingfish*, although I've always had in mind that I want to write a straight play, not a musical or one-man show. The play will be about my family. It will hopefully be Eugene O'Neill with a lot of black humor.

BENNETT: How did it feel playing the lead Sheriff Ed Earl Dodd on Broadway those two weeks that Henderson Forsythe was on vacation?

KING: It felt real strange. I thought it would be a real kick to be standing on a stage and hearing people laugh at my lines as I delivered them, because I had sat in the theater many times and felt a great satisfaction in seeing people laugh or be quiet or respond as I wanted an audience to respond. So I thought it would be a double kick to be up onstage and have that happen. You know what? It doesn't happen. You get up there, and you're not the writer anymore. You're the actor, and you're that character, and all of the laugh lines you get are really technical holds, so that you're thinking what you do next and who comes in next and what to do if they don't come in on cue. You're really just up there in a technical situation, and there's no satisfaction at all as a writer. Then there was the song. The only time I have ever sung in public was when my loved ones begged me to sit down in bars. Suddenly I had to sing "Good Old Girl," in which the sheriff talks about his secret affection for the madame who operates the whorehouse. Fortunately this song was written for Henderson Forsythe, who can't sing very well either. Now Henderson won a Tony for his acting and well deserved it, but he's not going to run Sinatra out of town. So the song wasn't that difficult for me to sing, because it's about half talk song anyway. It's hard to mess up, but I never got over my fear every night of having to sing that song. I was never afraid of acting, because I had acted in Army training films, and I had acted in community-theater stuff and at Actor's Studio in New York a little. But the singing scared me, and I never got over it.

BENNETT: Did you do any of your community-theater acting for Art Cole at Midland?

KING: I did, as a matter of fact. I was in *A Streetcar Named Desire* for Art Cole in about 1953, I guess. He has a great organization. I remember when he came there in 1945. I was on the high-school debate team in Midland, and we had a debate at a civic luncheon the day Cole came there to be introduced as the new director of Midland Community Theater. Then I was in a couple of things in fairly small roles. The big one was *Streetcar*, where I played the guy who lived upstairs and fought with his wife all the time.

BENNETT: You said you did some work at Actor's Studio?

KING: Only when we did *Whorehouse* over there. We started developing it there, and for a while there was a role in it that we called the Old Nester—he was just an old country guy who sat around the barbershop and the café and the sheriff's office cracking wise and using colloquial expressions. I played him. We finally wrote him out of the show. Then one night Henderson Forsythe couldn't make it, and I played the sheriff and did all right. So later they asked me to do it on Broadway while Henderson was vacationing.

January, 1980

Tom Lea: *The Book as Art*

TOM LEA was born July 11, 1907, in El Paso, Texas. He studied two years at the Chicago Art Institute and then began a career as painter and illustrator. In World War II he was a war artist for *Life* magazine. His first novel, *The Brave Bulls*, brought acclaim, and he has continued successfully both to write and to paint.

Lea's ranch-style home is "on the east side of the mountain" in El Paso. We walked through, past his magnificent full-length painting of his wife, Sarah, past rooms lined with books. We crossed a strip of backyard grass to his studio, a trim building about fifteen by twenty feet inside. The easel of Lea's old master in Chicago, John Norton, stood at one end of the room with a painting of a horse's head locked into it to square the frame.

Lea's typewriter sat on a big drafting table. Lining the walls were cabinets, files, and the like.

"These things are building in on me; I still don't have any place to store my stuff, which was one of the reasons I was glad to give some of it to the university. These two chairs were in my father's law offices from about 1912 till he died in 1945. This was his rolltop desk—I had the rolltop taken off—and this was his other desk in that office. Victoriano Huerta and several other of those Mexican guys sat in these chairs."

Wasn't Tom Lea, Sr., a friend of Madero?

"Not so much a friend, but he knew him. He was a pretty good friend of "Maximo" Herrera and Pascual Orozco. Orozco was the first guy to revolt against Madero, and Huerta got Villa to actually lick him."

Lea stands five feet seven and a half inches tall. "I wish I was taller; I'm the short guy in the family." He weighs 175 pounds. He has graying brown hair and brown eyes reinforced with trifocal glasses. He speaks forcefully, with a deep, manly voice, and his sentences take classic form without any special effort.

BENNETT: You write standing up?

LEA: Yes, writing is nothing but a projection of my painting. I've never painted sitting down.

BENNETT: How long do you write at a stretch?

LEA: I really rewrite a chapter at a time. The only way you can measure how long I write is the hours I put in trying to get a single paragraph. Which is long, long. I'm not a fluent writer, and I have to struggle to do it piece by piece, rather than making an overall rough draft and then polishing and cleaning and fixing. I have to have it about right as I go along.

BENNETT: Is that the way you paint?

LEA: I paint with a careful preliminary study or design. That's obviously a habit from my procedure as a mural painter, where you have a certain area and you design forms to function for that area and to say what you want them to say in that area. The mural is an enlargement of a preliminary design that you already have on a piece of paper or in your mind.

BENNETT: Therefore you write from an outline.

LEA: Usually. I have to have that preliminary overall design. I can't start somewhere and see where the road leads. It leads too many places that I haven't taken care of when I started. I don't just write to be writing another book. the only reason I set out on one of these journeys is to get a certain place, where I will have seen a certain thing and tried to show it to the reader.

BENNETT: I gather many persons don't. E. M. Forster didn't know where his novels were going. Didn't Picasso improvise a lot?

LEA: This is how he did it. But, you see, I work in isolation without a group of friends around me who do anything at all like what I do. My friends are all citizens engaged in more ordinary pursuits than writing a novel or painting a picture. I consciously stay away from arty circles. I tried that for two or three years in my very young life, my salad days, living in Santa Fe. The art colony is nothing for me. Neither is the daily backscratching session with people who are also writers and also painters. Whatever nourishment I get is from people living their lives in the ordinary world.

BENNETT: I suppose there may not be too many people who write in El Paso.

LEA: Oh, there are a bunch of them.

BENNETT: Do you use a typewriter?

LEA: That's my third or fourth rewrite. By the time it gets to the typewriter, it's practically a printed page. I work on little scratch sheets that look like hell, and with a stub pencil, so nothing will look nice. With painting, part of it is a performance that has a nice appearance. That has nothing to do with writing good prose. It looks like hell. It's how it fits in your mind, not in your eye, that makes it.

BENNETT: So you struggle along with a stub pencil——

LEA: If I get three pages a day, I'm doing fine, on an old sheet of scratch paper, using the back, and it will take me all day to do that. Some days I'll start in the afternoon to rewrite, starting with the first page I've done. Then I might go back to what I wrote yesterday, and then see, Why, hell, that's not right. So I'll start rewriting what I did yesterday, and it will take me two days to get onto what I've done today.

BENNETT: You wait until you're pretty far along before typing it?

LEA: I try to rewrite it so it's fairly legible before I put it on the typewriter, and then on the typewriter I can see how the bulk, the paragraph, goes, and how it sits there. The great problem I have, I think, is that it's too easy for me to write conversation, and as I grow older, I've grown more and more interested in trying to say everything I can with conversation. I'm not thinking of ever trying to do a dramatic piece, where you write only speaking parts, but I'm trying more and more to make what the man says what I want to say in the book.

BENNETT: Your descriptions are great, but you had a great deal of that conversation approach in *The Hands of Cantu*.

LEA: The thing I'm working on now, that's keeping me so long—I've been on it for several years—is even more just conversation.

BENNETT: What are you working on now?

LEA: I absolutely refuse to say anything about it. I said too much about it three or four years ago. Then I reread what I had written and threw it all away except the opening chapter. Now I've thrown it all away. It's about something that happened in Mexico about the year '18 or '19, in northern Mexico. Country people. No English in it; I have to hear it all in Spanish.

BENNETT: It is never a good idea to talk about whatever you're writing.

LEA: You can talk a thing to death. You see, I have no confidence of having professional training as a writer. I'm thoroughly confident of what I'm doing as a painter, because I know what the hell to paint, and I know how to look at it. Still, I never paint so that the final thing is what I wished I could do; I just finally have to quit and say, "This is the best I can do." But with writing, I didn't start writing until I came home from World War II. I had written long captions for paintings that I did during the war for *Life* magazine. And I wrote a little account of thirty hours in combat that Carl Hertzog printed after the war, that made me feel I was missing a whole area. I came home tired, and I decided I'd let the painting rest a bit. I decided to see what I could do about writing, not just writing a book, but writing about a particular thing. That was bulls.

BENNETT: You wrote about fighting bulls, and *Life* didn't like it.

LEA: Didn't like it at all! You see, that's the only time in my life I ever worked for a company, when I worked for *Life*. I worked for them for nearly six years and had a great time. The experience of World War II was the most vivid thing that ever happened to me.

BENNETT: You had a couple of rather narrow squeaks.

LEA: Don't talk about that.

BENNETT: You use a good outline of what you're writing?

LEA: Yes. That's what's wrong with this thing that I'm working on now. I've had two or three outlines, and I've had to discard them. The minute I throw away the outline, I have to start again on page one. You have to know where to begin. When I started *The Brave Bulls*, I knew the first line, and before I could go on I had to know the last line. This is a mural painter at work; you see the whole area so that it all flows the way you need it. That's the only way I can work. And I'm not successful at it. Still, I refuse to believe that if I could just read the right technical journal I would know exactly how to do this. It all has to come from your guts, you see.

BENNETT: And you always rewrite a lot?

LEA: Sometimes I get a page that needs almost no rewriting at all. After I've rewritten, I come back sometimes because the first one is better. Other times I rewrite half a dozen times at least. In this thing I'm working on now, some of the conversations I've rewritten a dozen times. Of course, as you rewrite you drift away from your initial impulse, your initial motive, and you have to watch not to be carried away into something else. So I probably do it all wrong, you see, but nobody is going to tell me that except myself.

BENNETT: As a former journalist I have a hard time rewriting. The emphasis was on getting shut of it quickly.

LEA: I had a newspaper friend for many, many years named Marshall Hale. He died about three years ago. I was very familiar with how he had to work down there at that office, and I never could understand how he was able to deliver the amount of good writing that he delivered.

BENNETT: What advice do you give young writers?

LEA: I feel that I'm not really qualified to give advice, because I started when I was over forty, and it was a projection from something else I had done. I'd earned a living as a painter since I was nineteen, when I quit the Art Institute in Chicago, and was very proud of my self-sufficiency as a practicing craftsman who could make a living out of his craft. Gee, some of my friends said, "This guy has spent almost a year now writing a novel, and he doesn't know a darned thing about it." I said, "No, I don't, but I'm going to write it." And I did write it. I'm proud that I went on to a new adventure. I think for a kid who wants to be a writer the only thing I could say is: "Don't ever want to write a book; want to write about something. And if the something isn't burning in your heart and mind and guts, don't even try."

BENNETT: It's quite a jump from painting to writing.

LEA: I'm extremely conscious of how things look—that's my profession. I can understand the direction and flow of forms, the luminosity of the particular tone, the value to light and dark. I see those things automatically. This is a matter of eye, and a mind that is trained to read what the eye says. With writing it's a totally different thing: it's what you hear. When you're there with the stub pencil in your hand, the main thing is, What does it sound like? It's not beautiful typography; it's not fine illustration. This is why it is so particularly fascinating to me right now to be writing a book in which not one word is said in English, and I have to hear every word in Spanish—the feel, and the kind of life that sound produces.

BENNETT: But you're writing it in English, aren't you?

LEA: Oh, sure.

BENNETT: You're translating what you hear.

LEA: I'm translating these people's lives, not only their tongue. Every man that's trying to write is a poet. Poetry is the use of words in a lyrical way. I suppose when you understand one of Einstein's equations, it is lyricism. My son is a mathematician, and he says it is.

BENNETT: When you go through a long problem, and it all works out——

LEA: The balance, yes, the music. You can always recognize that poetry thing, that quality of how it sounds, in the inner ear and in your mind. It's so often just an encounter that you suddenly make that you can't devise at all. The word suddenly fits with another word, and there's the sound of poetry. But if you get off on this idea of we'll-make-it-pretty, then you become a poetaster.

BENNETT: You've read about Flaubert taking all day to find a word.

LEA: I can't read French, and I wish I could, because he's the only one I know of who's that strong on the thing, and I'd like to see if it really affected me the way it must have affected Flaubert. I think Joseph Conrad had some moments like that: the right word almost slew him, trying to find it.

BENNETT: Conrad is wonderful.

LEA: You bet! It just burns me up, all that critical folderol. Conrad and Kipling are such dead ducks. Writers are fashionable or unfashionable.

BENNETT: I've been reading a writer who is even deader: Arnold Bennet.

LEA: Now there's a man who used great discrimination in how words went together, tremendous balance.

BENNETT: Your writing might be called naturalistic.

LEA: I leave an awful lot out. Maybe expressionist—I would call it that in painting.

BENNETT: A writer has to leave a lot out.

LEA: I'm perfectly willing to chop a scene just like that, not to make a bridge ....

BENNETT: How do you get the names of your characters?

LEA: I don't know how I pick names, except that they have to sound right.

BENNETT: Do you recall how you happened to choose Martin Brady or Luis Bello?

LEA: I don't know how I did that.

BENNETT: Do you ever change names in the middle of what you're writing?

LEA: No. This book I'm writing now, I've changed the title of the book itself from the name of the man who I thought was the central character, and now I find that he is not. So I changed it from Juan to Maclovio. You see Maclovio very infrequently. It's more in use in the Argentine than in Mexico. One of Villa's generals was named Maclovio Herrera.

BENNETT: Do you choose your titles, or let your publisher pick them?

LEA: Oh, no. The title is a part of what I'm trying to say. Lon Tinkle wrote, in *The Making of an Ample Mind*, about one time when Dobie tried to get me to change the title of *The Brave Bulls*. We were all drunk, and he was quoting Sir Walter Raleigh. Well, you get all enthusiastic, but when you sober up, the best thing to do is go ahead with what you originally intended. I take great pleasure in the titles of my paintings. This over here is only the preliminary proof of a color reproduction they're trying to do up in Connecticut of a painting I did last year; they haven't got the color yet. But the name of it, in which I take delight, is *Grace Note in a Hard World*. The titles of my books are even more carefully hewn.

BENNETT: Then you don't follow the practice of calling a painting *Study No. 1*?

LEA: Well, you know, that's a certain kind of mind. They want the painting to say everything, and the title is simply a label for classification. I like to think of it as something more. Actually, the impulse of *The Wonderful Country* came from that phrase out of old Captain Gillett's *Six Years with the Texas Rangers*. The title was the way the book was born, asking myself if I really knew how wonderful old Gillett's country was. I'm saying, Yes I do; this is how it must have been."

BENNETT: You've told me how your painting affects your writing....

LEA: And how my writing affects my painting is that I can't paint while I'm trying to write.

BENNETT: You can't?

LEA: No, it's two different worlds, that of sight and that of sound. It has to come from something very deep, and those two wells don't flow simultaneously. They cannot for me. Of course, the illustrations I make after the book is done, that's just icing on the cake. They are a projection into a slightly different dimension, and I hope they deepen the meaning. But if I had to depend on them .... One of the things that burned me up worst was some guy, reviewing *The Primal Yoke*, said he wanted to point out to me that I couldn't depend on chapter heads to make my book. I wanted to poke that guy, and I would have if I'd been in the same town.

BENNETT: Then you make the illustrations after you've written the book.

LEA: You see, working with Carl so long, I design my books too. For instance, when we had the black-and-white prints of type and illustrations, the designer and typographer of Little, Brown and Company came down here and spent ten days, and we designed the book so that the text would be right with the picture.

BENNETT: Your books themselves are works of art.

LEA: It's almost like having a painting to frame, you see. It has nothing to do with the quality of the book, but it has something definitely to do with making the book a happy experience.

BENNETT: So you've been working on this book three or four years now?

LEA: Longer than that.

BENNETT: Have you stopped painting during that time?

LEA: Last year I worked from the end of January until the end of May on the book, and then I quit and did some painting. We've got to make a living. You don't make a living writing the way I write. *The Wonderful Country* and *The Brave Bulls* supported my wife and me for several years so we could go on and do other things. *The King Ranch* did also. But when you have a way of earning a living, and your writing is not a way of earning a living, when you're trying to go forward and keep it an adventure . . . . I had the opportunity to write a lot of books about the history of a lot of families. Or to go out to Hollywood to write scripts. This is not what I was born to do. I was born to listen to my own impulse about how to paint and write.

BENNETT: There is a three-to-five-year interval between your books.

LEA: This is painting all between them. Except that *King Ranch* thing. That book actually took me five years. It was hard to get it all together. I had the greatest encouragement from the whole Kleberg family, but just the great variety of material made it difficult.

BENNETT: You wrote a book in '68, but since then what?

LEA: I did a book purely for my friend, a book called *In the Crucible of the Sun*, which is about the Australian operation of the King Ranch people. I've been painting mostly for the last ten years. Sarah and I went out with Bob Kleberg. He said, "You've got to see this because you'll want to do something about it, but mainly I just want you to go out there and look." We went to Australia for a couple of months and just had a wonderful time, over the whole continent. They have eleven ranches out there, all in different kinds of climates—extreme variety of place. I told Bob, "I want to do paintings of each one of these places, and then some supporting text for the paintings, and have the one dependent on the other." I did. It was given away to friends of the ranch on three or four continents.

BENNETT: Did you go directly to the Art Institute out of high school?

LEA: Yes, the Chicago Art Institute. I was just barely seventeen.

BENNETT: Did you graduate?

LEA: You know, that part of an art school was inconceivable in those days. You went to an art school to learn how to paint and how to draw from life. You didn't go to get a diploma so you could teach in some school art department. The whole world has changed. People were really serious about becoming painters when I went to art school. There was only painting; now you can make pots or anything you want, and you're an artist.

BENNETT: And you left the institute when you went to work for John Norton.

LEA: No, I quit school to paint my first mural commission. I had worked two years at the Art Insitute to try to get into John Norton's class. At the beginning of my third year I finally made it—he was only for advanced students. I was in his class for a couple of months before I quit because I had a chance to do the mural. I've always wanted to be a mural painter. I was back at the Art Institute two or three months later—I was courting a girl there—and in the hall I saw John Norton. He said, "What the hell happened to you? Why don't you come back to the class?" I said, "Oh, I quit to do my own work, to make my own living." He said, "What are you doing?" I said, "I painted a mural out at River Forest." And he said, "Well, can I see it?" So I took him out there and showed it to him, and he said: "Well, I'd like to hire you. In my studio I've got a couple of commissions now, and I need somebody that knows what I'm doing to work on it." He had all these kids in his class and grown men of fifty and sixty years old who had studied in there for years, and he asked me. I was pretty happy.

I was with him for three years. In the depth of the Depression, why I was making enough money even to go to Italy to see the murals. Because John Norton hired me, paid me.

BENNETT: Wasn't an appreciation of John Norton the first thing you wrote?

LEA: Yes, his death was why I left Chicago. He had cancer of the stomach. They operated. I finished a couple of his commissions, one down in Birmingham, Alabama, and one in Saint Paul, Minnesota. He gave me this money and said: "Now's the time, while you've got it; you get back out to the country you know about, and do what you want to do. No future for you around here. You've got to cut it off anyway from me." This was very moving, for he was a very great man. So I did.

BENNETT: You still have his easel in your studio.

LEA: That book I wrote in—it was a little memorial volume that his friends got up a fund for, and the Lakeside Press in Chicago printed it. They asked me to do a discussion of his work. Another one of his friends, an architect, an older man, did the biographical part. Mine wasn't a particularly good thing, but it was a sincere tribute to a hell of a man.

BENNETT: That's when you came back to Santa Fe?

LEA: We came back out the week FDR made the bank holiday, and things were really broke. I had the money sewed in my undershirt. Banks were awful. I put some money down on it, and hired a Mexican, and we built a little one-room adobe house. That's where we lived.

BENNETT: That was with your first wife, Nancy. Was she also a painter?

LEA: Yes, and a writer too. She was writing very well when she died. She was never published. She left several things. The first thing Carl Hertzog and I ever did, I hired Carl to do a volume out of her notebook. That's all that has ever been published of Nancy's work.

BENNETT: Do you think of yourself as a painter who writes or as a writer who paints?

LEA: I like to think of myself as both, without qualifications. Writing is just as demanding as painting. I feel that I have a greater background, technically, in painting than I do in writing. But perhaps if I said I'm only a painter trying to write, I'd feel too amateurish to be as serious as I am about it.

BENNETT: Is your work in progress fiction?

LEA: Yes, but all my fiction is grounded on something that is absolutely real and historical. Rex Smith was a dear friend of mine in the war. When I knew him he was vice-president of American Airlines, but he was a writer, had been bureau head for a news service in Europe right after World War I. He became one of the great aficionados of the bulls in the world. Before he died, he wrote *Biography of the Bulls*, which the best anthology of a long bullfight literature. He asked me what I was doing one time, and I said I was writing a book. He said, "Good, what about?" "Well, something you know a little bit about but I do too—it's about the bulls in Mexico." He said, "Oh, my God, you'll never do it; I'm scared to do it." He said, "How can a gringo write about something he doesn't know anything about?" I said, "I'm going to write it just the way I want to." And I have never had any question from the whole profession of bullfighting; there is not one error in it. One time a bull critic in Spain wrote me: "I thought I had you. You said there was a certain kind of blood in the bloodline of this Mexican strain, and I had never heard of it, but now I learn there is some of that blood in the bulls of Mexico. I beg your pardon."

BENNETT: It has been published in Spain?

LEA: It has been published in Mexico and Spain both, with two different translations. It has been published in nine languages, including Hebrew.

BENNETT: You didn't do that one yourself, I take it. Have you ever tried to write anything in Spanish? Where did you learn Spanish?

LEA: I don't know it yet. I understand it better than I speak it. I speak crummy Spanish. I read it fluently. I guess I learned it when I learned English. You know, in those days we always had a bunch of servants in the house who spoke Spanish, and they taught me Spanish. I think I learned to count to a hundred in Spanish long before I did in English. It gives you the accent, but unless you speak it continuously, your grammar and all the things you learn when you become cultivated go to hell. When I am in a parlor in Mexico, I am very embarrassed and ashamed of my Spanish. I understand what's going on there, but I don't make a very elegant contribution to the conversation.

BENNETT: You don't try to translate your own things then?

LEA: I don't think I've ever translated anything that was published, except I did one little piece about Pancho Villa out of a book written by an old guy who knew him. *Southwest Review* printed it. It was Englished rather than translated. I would not trust myself with the nuance of translating.

BENNETT: You've said that when you wrote *The Brave Bulls* you just sat down and taught yourself to write.

LEA: I stood up and taught myself to write.

BENNETT: How did you do a thing like that?

LEA: I hadn't written very much. I wrote that Pacific-landing thing, that account of a thing that happened during the war. It was short, but it was strictly what I saw and what happened. I was passionate about not putting anything in there that I didn't actually see or feel. That's as much as I went to school with myself on my aim and purpose. But I had not wasted my life reading comic strips. I had read pretty good stuff, although I had never gone to the university and taken courses about perception of literature. I knew something about writing, how it affected me. When I went to write, I wasn't trying to write Hemingway or write Dos Passos or write anybody. I had known guys like Johnny Hersey; he and I were on the *Hornet* together for about a month before he got off—and I stayed on—during the

Guadalcanal campaign. The day the *Wasp* was sunk, I was too nervous, with all the torpedoes and everything, so I just did a little sketch that was a historical record, and I later made a painting of the death of the *Wasp*. I watched John that night—we were in the same bunkhouse together on the carrier—and he sat down to this little Hermes typewriter and typed this thing out on the death of the *Wasp* and how we had picked up survivors. He handed it to Oscar Dodson, who was the communications officer and censor, and Dodson said as far as he was concerned it was okay. We were going to oil—that's how we used to get the mail off, when the oiler came. John got his censored piece off by mail on the oiler, and it went all the way then back to the States. When I got back and went to the offices of the Time-Life Building, they had printed it without a single change of any kind, it was so perfect and so moving. I think of it often, how John Hersey could write so beautifully and just pull it out of the typewriter. The way I struggle! This is the difference between a guy who dreams in writing and a guy who dreams in painting. I just mention that because of the feeling of admiration I have for a guy who can think it and write it in one piece so easily.

BENNETT: All journalists write that way. But very few write like John Hersey. For more serious things, most people revise. Hemingway revised.

LEA: I'm sure. He could not have done that conversation he writes, particularly in his short stories, without the most infinite number of rewrites. I don't see how he could do it any other way.

BENNETT: The germ of many of his stories is in those newspaper stories he sent back from Europe.

LEA: It's bound to have been. All things that are good come out of a man's experience, and Hemingway's journalist stuff is his experience. He saw things happen.

BENNETT: I understand we don't have his less mature stories because his wife lost a trunk in a railway station.

LEA: I've always wondered how these fellows go around losing manuscripts. Including T. E. Lawrence. You read about how they lost manuscripts in railway stations and other places. I have the feeling that's a pretty good out.

BENNETT: So you learned to write by writing.

LEA: That's it. That's it.

BENNETT: First novels are often weak, but *The Brave Bulls* is a strong performance.

LEA: The reason I think it has some merit to it is that it's not autobiographical. It's a projection into another world. First novels are usually somebody's recounting of his former self.

BENNETT: Hemingway's first two are.

LEA: Yes, but I don't think there's any novel in the twentieth century that can approach *The Sun Also Rises*. That's a poem. This is what I mean by listening to the inner ear's poetry. That's a great piece of prose. He never touched it again.

BENNETT: Nothing you've written except *A Picture Gallery* is autobiographical.

LEA: That's right. It's a projection into another world, or I don't write it. The one that nobody liked, except me and a few other crazy people, *The Primal Yoke*, is about a guy I knew very well. I gave him part of the experience of the war that I knew. He didn't have it; he's younger than that. I turned it all around. In my book the son dies and the old man is the survivor; in real life the old man shot his wife, the boy's mother, and then himself. So I made a world which I didn't see, or particularly care to render faithfully, but the impulses were there.

BENNETT: I wonder why *The Primal Yoke* drew so much fire?

LEA: I think they were mainly insulted because it wasn't from the Southwest. It's an excellent book, and if people will only stop to look at it, they will see that I was trying to write a classical tragedy in which the gods were at work, and the guy never really had a chance. The mountain was like the mountain in Confucius. I used a quotation out of the *Analects* in the beginning. But, no, it didn't have cowboys or bullfighters or any Mexicans. I don't recall anything except that they said it was no good.

BENNETT: That's hardly just.

LEA: I don't care what any critic says, whether he's fair. On *The Wonderful Country*, *Time* said "He came a cropper, it's no good." And five years later they said it was in the class with *The Ox Bow Incident*, and it and one or two others were the only westerns ever written, and all that sort of shit. It doesn't matter. You get it put down, and if you know it's true to your own inner experience of the world, nobody else's opinion matters. You love it when other people like it, and of course you like it when it's popular enough to bring you some money that will endow you for future effort.

BENNETT: Once you know a thing's right——

LEA: No, once I had done the best I could. I look back on some of my paintings, and I think, Gee, I wish I had painted that arm different.

I know I could do it and see it better now, but I can't go back and do that.

BENNETT: Did you get any advice from friends when you began trying to write?

LEA: I didn't ask for any.

BENNETT: What books did you read before you began writing?

LEA: Some books made tremendous impressions on me. One of them that really formed some of my thought was Charles M. Doughty's *Travels in Arabia Deserta*. I read it by sheer accident. A friend of mine in Chicago—I didn't know him until I did a bookplate for him—had bought this book because it had an introduction by T. E. Lawrence. He said, "I find the damned thing unreadable; would you like to have it?" I was interested, you know, Lawrence of Arabia, *Seven Pillars of Wisdom* stuff, and I said, "Sure." I took it. And it *was* the desert; it was something I had been wanting to know about the world I lived in. I think all the books that you read that mean something to you are those that tell you something about the world you've already experienced. When I went to Morocco, and across what was then called Persia, during the war, I didn't understand too much what had been my great enthusiasm. But it was English literature that made it so wonderful. Doughty makes it great. Another book that still affects me, makes me happy that I know how a great man can give you a true and solid picture of the comedy and tragedy of being alive—that's *Candide*. Voltaire's *Candide* is one of my foundation books. I reread it every two or three years now. My whole life, books have been something to me very strong. I don't read current things any more at all. I go back into what I've already read, and my nourishment is still coming from that.

BENNETT: What painters have influenced you?

LEA: That's easier. When I was a kid, and hadn't seen anything except things in Santa Fe, I was dependent on reading in the El Paso Public Library. The librarian was a very great woman, and I was fortunate in knowing someone like that. If the book wasn't there, she would order it so I could read it. Maud Durlin Sullivan. Last year they had Peter Hurd and Carl Hertzog and Josie Cisneros and myself at the library associations of Texas and New Mexico, and Lawrence Clark Powell told how Maud Durlin Sullivan had handed books to me and Carl Hertzog and Josie Cisneros. I read Whistler's involved life with great interest. Then when I got to the Art Institute, there at last was not only a great gallery but the Ryerson Library, which is one of the great art libraries. So the whole treasures of the earth were open to me. The first person I really studied and admired as a painter was Eugène Delacroix, and the other one was Paul Gauguin. That enthusiasm carried through when I happened to be in Paris at one of the great commemorative exhibitions of the work of the Romantic painters at the Louvre. I got to see a great assembled collection of all of Delacroix's things. That's an enthusiasm that has lasted all my life. Of course, the murals he did at Saint Supplice are superb things and remain in your mind always. The murals that I truly worshiped, and the reason why I went to Italy—two weeks of Paris was enough for me in 1930; this was when Hemingway and all the other expatriates were holding forth, and this was pure poison to me, except the Louvre—so when I went to Italy, the two that formed my whole thought about painting were Piero della Francesca and Luca Signorelli. Piero at Arezzo. I spent some time at the little town of Arezzo. Going back twenty or thirty years later with Sarah, I found, gee, that Arezzo is now an industrial town, and the experts have retouched those Francesca murals. Signorelli did the great murals which were an influence on the young Michelangelo. He did a *Last Judgment* that's got them all topped.

BENNETT: Did you meet Hemingway?

LEA: Oh, hell, no! Rex Smith—they were both newspapermen, so he knew him quite well, and Rex was the one that put Hemingway in touch with bullfighting—said, "I would not undertake to have you meet him; you won't like him, and he won't like you." I said, "Okay, Rex."

BENNETT: Hemingway had a mean streak in him.

LEA: If you only have to do with his books, they're all right.

BENNETT: Have you written any shorter pieces?

LEA: Very few. I did a short story for the *Atlantic* once, and I did a bullfighting piece for the *Saturday Review* one time. For a while people would ask me to do a book or a piece on a holiday in Mexico, or the west coast of Mexico, or on West Texas for the *National Geographic* or something. But, you see, my incidental work is all painting. The only time I think of myself really as a writer is when I have a rounded thing, like a mural, only this is in words, and it's a whole book. The one time that I tried to do a thing that was documented, and had to have footnotes, was the bitterest, most prisonlike feeling I've ever had in my life, bound by facts, when I had to do the King Ranch history. I had to go back and try to decide whether Stephen Powers was a liar, or whether somebody else was throwing a curve in what he wrote about who wrote something to Charles A. Stillwell on a night in December, 1859, because it was my purpose in undertaking it to tell the story as near as it could be told without lies or prejudice and folderol pretty stuff about a very interesting phenomenon that happened in the grass part of the world.

BENNETT: It's a chore, going through documents.

LEA: It's hard to write about, this flicker stuff seen through barely translucent material. You know it's not reality. It only becomes something that you can write about when you've made up your mind about what's real and what isn't, and you know damned well in your heart you don't know.

BENNETT: "The sorry pablum of which history is made."

LEA: Yet some of it is a shaft of light which will pierce your heart every once in a while. So it's more than pablum at times.

BENNETT: Sometimes your books seem to be as interested in animals, in horses and bulls, as in human beings.

LEA: Horses and cattle were something I knew. Of course, my people were townfolk: my father was a lawyer and my mother a housewife. But we had lots of kinfolk who were ranchers, and all my summers as a boy—well, when I was an infant, we'd go to these various places out of town, where you're on a ranch and animals are your life. One of the reasons I admire Bob Kleberg and his young nephew Dick Kleberg so much—old Dick I was never so intimate with—was the fact these people loved animals and were dedicated to the welfare and improvement of animals. I'm sometimes disappointed over how humans can't be that way about one another. But I don't think my books are actually about that. None of my books start because of an animal.

BENNETT: Some writers do have a particular thing that moves them.

LEA: One of the things I've noticed about my books is there's always an old man, and he's usually admirable; he knows a lot. I've had three guys, four really, in my life from whom I've learned a great deal. I consider Bob Kleberg—he was maybe fifteen years older—as my same generation and not an influence. First, my father; we got along wonderfully, and he was my exemplar. Then John Norton was an exemplar. And then Frank Dobie. And then a man named John Lovell, who was an uncle of my contemporary. You know, old Balbuena in *The Brave Bulls* knew it all.

BENNETT: In *The Primal Yoke* there's old Claunch. There's also an animal, the horse Hemlock.

LEA: That was actually my horse I rode in the mountains in Wyoming. His name was Tamarack, and I just renamed him Hemlock.

BENNETT: But that book is really more about the relationship of person to country.

LEA: All of my books, if you'll look at them, are about that. Landscape is important. You see, I'm a landscape painter too. It's the roots a man feels, not his forebears but the soil that nourishes him. I got that very strongly from my dad, who left Missouri to come down here and became a Texan. He felt by the time he died that he had totally lost his Missouri roots. He came down on horseback from Chihuahua. He spoke Spanish so that he could deliver a final argument in Spanish before the court, and he didn't know a word of it until the age of twenty-two.

BENNETT: In *The Hands of Cantu*, were you attempting to substitute the drawn portraits for language description?

LEA: I am trying to deepen the delineation of the characters by using another medium. This is very conscious on my part.

BENNETT: Were you trying to eliminate description that way?

LEA: Yes. In the book that I'm writing now I'm doing a great deal of that.

BENNETT: You've actually been moving toward dialogue supplemented by your pictures?

LEA: This is right. But even in *The Brave Bulls* the book is mostly conversation. Dobie was always saying—I think he wrote it in one of the books he sent me—"What good is a book without pictures and conversation?" It's in *Alice in Wonderland*. So if you eliminate it all down to pictures and conversation, you might have a pretty good book.

BENNETT: They don't illustrate novels anymore. They printed those wonderfully illustrated novels in the nineties. It is a great pleasure to pick up one of your novels.

LEA: In *The Brave Bulls* and *The Wonderful Country* the illustrations are more ornaments. I carried the ornamental thing to its extreme in *The Primal Yoke*, and I think those are the best drawings that are in any of my books. By the time I got to *The Hands of Cantu*, I also had my publishers to the point where they were willing to let the Meriden Company reproduce these things in a novel, which is way too expensive for any publisher to attempt in a work of fiction. A kid couldn't get an old-line publisher to accept both his manuscript and his illustrations: "No, I'm sorry, we'll take one or the other, but we can't take both." Those reproductions in *The Hands of Cantu* were done by the best people in North America. They're quite expensive, and so you have to have a little favorable acceptance by a publisher who has known you for a long time. There aren't any other novels published like that. Name one. So one of my obligations is to use illustrations so they are a deepening element, a pungent part of what I'm trying to say.

BENNETT: A common element discussed by Texas writers is religion. But I can't think of any in your work, unless you count the Roman Catholic tang in the conversation of *The Hands of Cantu*.

LEA: I was brought up very strictly. My mother was a very devout Baptist. My brother and I—my brother is three and a half years younger—we were brought up from the cradle roll on to go to church for Sunday school, and then to stay and hear the sermon, and then go to Wednesday-night prayer meeting. The day I left El Paso to go to Chicago, Illinois, at the age of seventeen, I left church. Of course, I went to funerals and baccalaureate sermons and that sort of thing. After the war Sarah and I attended the Episcopal church some, and the Presbyterian. When my mother died, I painted a mural over the baptistry, and my father and I gave it to her church here. But I must say that I don't have much connection with the formal church anymore, and I have not dealt with that part of religion. I am a very devout man, but that's my own damned business.

BENNETT: You sound like Elmer Kelton.

LEA: I really liked him the time we met.

BENNETT: His *The Good Old Boys* is a good novel, and——

LEA: Listen, it's an excellent novel. It's a first-rate novel.

BENNETT: That old cowboy of his, Hewey Calloway, I've known him.

LEA: You bet, we all have. Fred Gipson had that same attitude toward the cowboy that Kelton has. He did one called *Cowhand* that's excellent. Gipson was kind of a tragic figure. He was a hell of a nice guy.

BENNETT: All your novels have a good deal about courage in them.

LEA: I think that's a great theme. I suppose it all stems from . . . . You see, all this writing has been done since World War II, and I saw all kinds of people in that war, under highly emotional circumstances.

BENNETT: The only novel you've written with an artist is *The Primal Yoke*?

LEA: I had fun with him.
BENNETT: Actually you had two artists.
LEA: Quite a few for one book, eh?
BENNETT: Do you feel there is any conflict between manliness and the aesthetic temperament?
LEA: I think an aesthetic temperament is a sure mistake for anybody to have. You know the old Navaho thing of "walking in beauty." I've often wondered what that means. I suppose it means the aesthetic temperament, but the Navahos don't think that; they think that beauty is simply belonging, and I think that's what aesthetics might be: a sense of belonging. To be a person involved with a creative art is a little different from being a person involved with either a performing art or a craft kind of art. I don't care how great a pianist you are, or violinist, if you didn't write the piece, you aren't near the guy the creator of that sonata is. In painting now there is a confusion between what is decorative and what is aesthetically pleasing. The only response I can get out of things like Jackson Pollock's dripping is that it's decorative, but to rank it as high creative art seems to me to be putting the emphasis in the wrong place. Of course, they can be pleasing, and I'm sure this fellow Pollock felt he was doing something creative. All the critics and double-domes say he was.
BENNETT: Which of your books do you like best?
LEA: That's one I won't answer, because they are all different.
BENNETT: That's quite true.
LEA: When I start writing one like the next, I have no business writing. Even such a dear friend as Rex Smith said, "You've got to write a sequel to *The Wonderful Country*." I said, "Rex, get the hell out." And the *Bulls*, I've had opportunities from a hell of a number of publishers to do something about that. I said what I wanted to say about the bulls. I wasn't talking about the bulls; I was talking about people, and in that particular thing that's what I wanted to say.
BENNETT: You consider them complete in themselves?
LEA: No, they're not complete, but they're as complete as I thought I could make them within the range that I set for myself. I wish they were all of them better, and I wish they were all of them *War and Peace*.
BENNETT: Have you ever attempted to write a book on the Pancho Villa times?
LEA: That's what I'm doing now. Pancho Villa is out here somewhere, and I made the big mistake of bringing .... This is one of

the troubles in this book. I suddenly realized that I don't want a historical figure telling me what to write; I want to create him entirely. So, I'm creating a figure who is connected with Villa, but who is entirely a creature of my own imagination. I can make him do and say what I think he should under the circumstances. You know, there are a lot of people who are still violently emotional at just the thought of Villa, or the thought of Carranza, or Zapata. They are fanatical, crazy. They make noise. They stir it up to here.

BENNETT: Have you ever considered a novel about World War II?

LEA: No, I haven't. I feel so lucky that I got home. It's still an emotional thing with me. There are a few of my friends with whom I went through some of that stuff that I see occasionally, but I don't have any desire to write a book about it. If I did, it would be placing myself back there, and the nearest I ever came to that was when I put it in another man's thought, in another man's language, when Hank Spurling tells about what it was to be a Marine. There's a whole chapter of first-person-singular narrative that shows what it was like to actually try to describe to a man that you revere what it's like to be where people that you don't know are trying to kill you. Now all of us are old. My old friends know it's there; I know it's there. But we don't want to write any damned book about it.

BENNETT: The best book about the Civil War was by a fellow who wasn't there.

LEA: Yeah, and had never been in combat.

BENNETT: Have you ever thought of writing anything about the Depression?

LEA: No, I'm not sociologically minded. We all went through that, and I lived on potato soup up there in Santa Fe for a long stretch. I know something about not having anything to eat, and having a sick wife, and living out in the country. I know all about the Depression, but I don't think I'd ever write anything about it because then I'd be supposed to be hating Wall Street or something.

BENNETT: There is quite a herd of novels like that.

LEA: Even Steinbeck is a didactic guy. I think *The Grapes of Wrath* is okay, but it's the kind of book that is almost better as a movie than it is as a novel. Like *From Here to Eternity*, which was a pretty doggone good book because they had a good movie writer that made a good movie out of *From Here to Eternity*. James Jones is my idea of a guy who wrote about something that maybe he knew something about but wasn't able to be unself-conscious about it.

BENNETT: I wonder if you have any particular favorites among Texas writers.

LEA: Well, he's not really Texas much anymore, but one of my good friends and a man I admire a great deal is William Weber Johnson. He lives in California now, and he's from near where Sarah lived in Illinois, but at one time he was around Texas. He wrote *Heroic Mexico*; it's the greatest book that's ever been written about the Mexican Revolution in Spanish or English or any other language. Bill and I are close. And Dobie was a good friend of mine and also .... It would be impossible to say. Have you read Lon Tinkle's book on Dobie? Lon tells it in there; I won't go into it. Dobie and I fell apart toward the end of his life, after a smart review he wrote on *The King Ranch*. He and I were never quite so close again, although we patched it up, and I was a pallbearer at his funeral. I liked old Webb. I still read Webb with great pleasure, and I think *Great Plains* is one of the great books. It's so like Walter, so dry, and so clean, just scrubbed well. No horse shit on his heel at all. Someone I've always liked—and he's a friend, and we get together at every opportunity we have—is Paul Horgan. But he's not really a Texas writer. He writes very differently from anything I do, and I guess we both of us know that. Except for Bill Johnson, Paul Horgan is as good a friend as I have. Lon Tinkle is, of course, dear to me. And Holland McCombs—he's a journalist. He helped me so much in getting the stuff together on the King Ranch book, practically wrecked himself doing that.

BENNETT: What about John Graves?

LEA: I admire his work. I don't know him well. He's a very, very straightforward gentleman, and I mean gentleman!

BENNETT: He's a terrific writer.

LEA: You bet.

BENNETT: Have you read Frank Vandiver?

LEA: I've just known him briefly, on the phone or something. No, one meeting at the Texas Institute of Letters, I think I met him there. I am a great admirer of his biography of Pershing. It's an excellent biography. Pershing was a good friend of my father's, and I even have a letter that Pershing wrote me from France when he was over there. To "Master Tom Lea." He was quite a guy in our family, and I think Vandiver has done a beautiful job.

BENNETT: Do you have an opinion on some other Texas writers?

LEA: No. You see I live a long way from most of these people. And I do it for a reason.

BENNETT: Do you have an opinion on what makes beauty in both painting and writing?

LEA: Well, everybody has thought about it. But I suppose I gave up pretty early trying to define the principle involved. I think beauty is something you recognize easily and analyze damned poorly. And I don't think Bernhard Berenson knew a doggone thing more about aesthetics than I do.

April, 1979

Works of the Writers

MAX APPLE
The Oranging of America and Other Stories. New York: Grossman, 1976.
Zip: A Novel of the Left and the Right. New York: Viking, 1978.

WILLIAM GOYEN
Aimee! [play]. First produced in Providence, R.I., Trinity Square Repertory Theater, 1973.
Arthur Bond: A Story. Winston-Salem, N.C.: Palaemon, 1979.
A Book of Jesus. Garden City, N.Y.: Doubleday, 1973.
Christy [play]. First produced in New York, American Place Theater, 1964.
The Collected Stories of William Goyen. Garden City, N.Y.: Doubleday, 1975.
Come, the Restorer: A Novel. Garden City, N.Y.: Doubleday, 1974.
The Diamond Rattler [play]. First produced in Boston, Charles Playhouse, 1960.
The Faces of Blood Kindred: A Novella and Ten Stories. New York: Random House, 1960.
The Fair Sister: A Novel. Garden City, N.Y.: Doubleday, 1963.
Ghost and Flesh [stories and tales]. New York: Random House, 1952.
The House of Breath [novel]. New York: Random House, 1950. 25th anniversary ed. New York: Random House-Bookworks, 1975.
The House of Breath [play]. First produced in New York, Circle-in-the-Square Theater, 1955.
The House of Breath, Black/White [play]. First produced in Providence, R.I., Trinity Square Playhouse, 1969.
In a Farther Country: A Romance. New York: Random House, 1955.
The Lazy Ones (Les Faneants), by Albert Cossery. Translated by William Goyen. New York: New Directions, 1949.
My Antonia: A Critical Commentary. New York: American R.D.M. Corp., 1966.
Nine Poems. New York: Albondocani, 1976.
A Possibility of Oil [play]. First produced in Hollywood, CBS Television, 1958.
Ralph Ellison's Invisible Man: A Critical Commentary. New York: American R.D.M. Corp., 1966.
Selected Writings of William Goyen. New York: Random House, 1974.
Wonderful Plant: A Novella. Winston-Salem, N.C.: Palaemon, 1980.

John Graves

Blue and Some Other Dogs. Austin: Encino, forthcoming.
From a Limestone Ledge. New York: Knopf, forthcoming.
Goodbye to a River. New York: Knopf, 1960.
Hard Scrabble; Observations on a Patch of Land. New York: Knopf, 1974.
Home Place: A Background Sketch in Support of a Proposed Restoration of Pioneer Buildings in Fort Worth, Texas. Fort Worth, 1958.
The Last Running; A Story. Austin: Encino, 1974.
The Nation's River. Washington, D.C.: Government Printing Office, 1968.
Texas Heartland: A Hill Country Year. With Jim Bones. College Station: Texas A&M University Press, 1975.
The Water Hustlers. With Robert H. Boyle and T. H. Watkins. San Francisco: Sierra Club, 1971.

A. C. Greene

A Christmas Tree. Austin: Encino, 1973.
Dallas: The Deciding Years—A Historical Portrait. Austin: Encino, 1973.
Elephants in Your Mailbox. By Roger Horchow with A. C. Greene. New York: Times Books, 1980.
The Last Captive. Austin: Encino, 1972.
Living Texas: A Gathering of Experiences. Compiled and edited by A. C. Greene. Austin: Hendrick-Long and Encino, 1970.
A Personal Country. New York: Knopf, 1969. (Rev. edition. Introduction by Larry L. King. College Station: Texas A&M University Press, 1979.)
A Place Called Dallas: The Pioneering Years of a Continuing Metropolis. Dallas: Dallas County Heritage Society, 1975.
The Santa Claus Bank Robbery. New York: Knopf, 1972.
Views in Texas, 1895-96: A Photographic Tour of Texas Made in the Winter of 1895-96 by Henry Stark. Additional commentary by A. C. Greene. Austin: Encino, 1974.

Leon Hale

Addison. Garden City, N.Y.: Doubleday, 1979.
Bonney's Place. Garden City, N.Y.: Doubleday, 1972.
Buck Schiwetz' Memories, by E. M. Schiwetz. Introduction by Leon Hale. College Station: Texas A&M University Press, 1979.
The Texas Gulf Coast: Interpretations by Nine Artists. Introduction by Leon Hale. College Station: Texas A&M University Press, 1979.
Texas Out Back. Austin: Madrona, 1973.
Turn South at the Second Bridge. Garden City, N.Y.: Doubleday, 1965. (Reprint. College Station: Texas A&M University Press, 1980.)

Shelby Hearon

Armadillo in the Grass. New York: Knopf, 1968.
Barbara Jordan: A Self Portrait. By Barbara Jordan and Shelby Hearon. Garden City, N.Y.: Doubleday, 1979.
Hannah's House. Garden City, N.Y.: Doubleday, 1975.
Now and Another Time. Garden City, N.Y.: Doubleday, 1976.

A Prince of a Fellow. Garden City, N.Y.: Doubleday, 1978.
The Second Dune. New York: Knopf, 1973.

PRESTON JONES

Juneteenth: A Comedy in One Act [play]. First produced in Louisville, Ky., Actor's Theater, 1979. Published in *Vision* magazine, Dallas, June, 1979.
The Last Meeting of the Knights of the White Magnolia: A Play in Two Acts. First produced in Dallas, Dallas Theater Center, 1973. New York: Dramatists Play Service 1976.
Lu Ann Hampton Laverty Oberlander: A Play in Three Acts. First produced in Dallas, Dallas Theater Center, 1974. New York: Dramatists Play Service, 1976.
The Oldest Living Graduate: A Play in Two Acts. First produced in Dallas, Dallas Theater Center, 1974. New York: Dramatists Play Service, 1976.
A Place on the Magdalena Flats. First produced in Dallas, Dallas Theater Center, 1976.
Remember. First produced in Dallas, Dallas Theater Center, 1979.
Santa Fe Sunshine: A Comedy in Two Acts. First produced in Dallas, Dallas Theater Center, 1977. New York: Dramatists Play Service, n.d.
A Texas Trilogy. New York: Hill and Wang, 1976. (Includes *The Last Meeting of the Knights of the White Magnolia, Lu Ann Hampton Laverty Oberlander,* and *The Oldest Living Graduate.*)

ELMER KELTON

After the Bugles. New York: Ballantine, 1967.
Barbed Wire. New York: Ballantine, 1957.
Bitter Trail. New York: Ballantine, 1962.
Bowie's Mine. New York: Ballantine, 1971.
Buffalo Wagons. New York: Ballantine, 1956.
Captain's Rangers. New York: Ballantine, 1968.
The Day the Cowboys Quit. Garden City, N.Y.: Doubleday, 1971.
Donovan. New York: Ballantine, 1961.
The Good Old Boys. Garden City, N.Y.: Doubleday, 1978.
Hanging Judge. New York: Ballantine, 1969.
Horsehead Crossing. New York: Ballantine, 1963.
Hot Iron. New York: Ballantine, 1956.
Joe Pepper. By Lee McElroy, pseud. Garden City, N.Y.: Doubleday, 1975.
Llano River. New York: Ballantine, 1966.
Long Way to Texas. By Lee McElroy, pseud. Garden City, N.Y.: Doubleday, 1976.
Looking Back West: Selections from the Pioneer News-Observer. San Angelo, Tex.: Talley, 1972.
Manhunters. New York: Ballantine, 1974.
Massacre at Goliad. New York: Ballantine, 1965.
Shadow of a Star. New York: Ballantine, 1959.
Shotgun Settlement. By Alex Hawk, pseud. New York: Paperback Library, 1969.
The Texas Rifles. New York: Ballantine, 1960.

The Time It Never Rained. Garden City, N.Y.: Doubleday, 1973.
Wagontongue. New York: Ballantine, 1972.
The Wolf and the Buffalo. Garden City, N.Y.: Doubleday, 1980.
Yesterday in Ozona and Crockett County. by V. I. Pierce. Edited by Elmer Kelton. Ozona, Tex.: Crockett County Historical Society, 1980.

LARRY L. KING

... And Other Dirty Stories. New York: NAL-World, 1968.
The Best Little Whorehouse in Texas. With Peter Masterson, songs by Carol Hall. First produced in New York, Actor's Studio, 1977. (In *The Best Plays of 1977-78.* New York: Dodd, Mead, 1978.)
Confessions of a White Racist. New York: Viking, 1971.
Kingfish. With Ben Z. Grant. First produced (by Barbara S. Blaine) in Washington, D.C., New Playwrights' Theater, 1979.
Of Outlaws, Con Men, Whores, Politicians, and Other Artists. New York: Viking, 1980.
The Old Man and Lesser Mortals. New York: Viking, 1974.
Oliphant! a Cartoon Collection, by Pat Oliphant. Introduction by Larry L. King. New York: Andrews and McMeel, 1980.
The One-eyed Man. New York: New American Library, 1966.
Places People Live: An Urban and Social Geography. With Gary H. Searl and Ryan V. Anderson. Dubuque, Iowa: Kendall-Hunt, 1971.
Wheeling and Dealing: Confessions of a Capitol Hill Operator, by Bobby Baker with Larry L. King. New York: Norton, 1978.

TOM LEA

The Brave Bulls: A Novel. Boston: Little, Brown, 1949.
Bullfight Manual for Spectators. El Paso: Hertzog, 1949.
Fort Bliss: One Hundredth Anniversary, El Paso, Texas. El Paso: Guynes, 1948.
A Grizzly from the Coral Sea: Conversation and Pictures. El Paso: Hertzog, 1944.
The Hands of Cantu. Boston: Little, Brown, 1964.
In the Crucible of the Sun. Kingsville, Tex.: King Ranch, 1974.
The King Ranch. Boston: Little, Brown, 1957.
Peleliu Landing. El Paso: Hertzog, 1945.
A Picture Gallery. Boston: Little, Brown, 1968.
The Primal Yoke: A Novel. Boston: Little, Brown, 1960.
Randado. El Paso: Hertzog, 1941.
The Wonderful Country. Boston: Little, Brown, 1952.

LARRY MCMURTRY

All My Friends Are Going to Be Strangers. New York: Simon and Schuster, 1972.
Daughter of the Tejas, by Ophelia Ray [with Larry McMurtry]. Greenwich, Conn.: New York Graphic Society, 1965.
Film Flam. Austin: Encino, forthcoming.
Horseman Pass By. New York: Harper, 1961.

In a Narrow Grave: Essays on Texas. Austin: Encino, 1968.
It's Always We Rambled: An Essay on Rodeo. New York: Frank Hallman, 1974.
The Last Picture Show [novel]. New York: Dial Press, 1966.
The Last Picture Show [screenplay]. With Peter Bogdanovich. Hollywood: Columbia Pictures, 1972.
Leaving Cheyenne. New York: Harper and Row, 1963.
Moving On. New York: Simon and Schuster, 1970.
Somebody's Darling. New York: Simon and Schuster, 1978.
Terms of Endearment. New York: Simon and Schuster, 1975.

FRANCES MOSSIKER

The Affair of the Poisons: Louis XIV, Madame de Montespan, and One of History's Great Unsolved Mysteries. New York: Knopf, 1969.
More Than a Queen: The Story of Josephine Bonaparte. New York: Knopf, 1971.
Napoleon and Josephine: The Biography of a Marriage. New York: Simon and Schuster, 1964.
Pocahontas: The Life and the Legend. New York: Knopf, 1976.
The Queen's Necklace. New York: Simon and Schuster, 1961.

Index

Abilene Christian University, 37, 47, 52
Abilene Reporter-News, 7, 37, 43-44, 46-48, 52, 54, 56, 60
Abilene Southern Railroad, 48
"Abilene Streetcar System" (Greene): 48
Accent, 241
Ace Books, 182
Addison (Hale): 87, 137, 140-143, 145, 149, 151-153
Adventures of Hap Hazard, The (King): 250
Adventures of Huckleberry Finn, The (Twain): 253
Adventures of Tom Sawyer, The (Twain): 250, 253
Affair of the Poisons, The (Mossiker): 42, 219-221
After the Bugles (Kelton): 183, 191, 202
Aimee! (Goyen): 246
Akers, Norman (fictional character): 147
Alamo, The (film): 140
Alexander, L. D. (fictional character): 171-173, 176
Alexandria Quartet, The (Durrell): 81
Alice in Wonderland (Carroll): 285
Allen, John Houghton, 42
Allen, Louise, 138
Allen, Woody, 175
All My Friends Are Going to Be Strangers (McMurtry): 27, 31-35
Almanach de Gotha, 206
Altman, Robert, 51, 153
American Film, 19
American Historical Association, 59
American Literary Translators Association, 207, 216
American Review, The, 92
American University, 18
Analects (Confucius): 281
Anatomy of Melancholy, The (Burton): 92
Anders, John, 168
Anderson, Edward, 7, 152-153
... And Other Dirty Stories (King): 249
Angoulême, Duchesse d', 225
Apache Gold and Yaqui Silver (Dobie): 214
Apple, Debra, 4
Apple, Jessica, 107
Apple, Max: background of, 4, 6; short stories of, 10, 20; others' opinions of, 40, 87-88, 236, 264; interview with, 89-109; writing habits of, 93, 98, 100-101
Apple, Sam, 107
Angie (television series): 7, 232
Arcadio (fictional character): 232, 240, 242, 244
Arcadio (Goyen): 231
Archer, William, 169
archy and mehitabel (Marquis): 156
Armadillo in the Grass (Hearon): 39, 111, 119-120, 127-128, 131
Armstrong, Louis, 257
Army, U.S., 249, 254, 260, 267, 279
Army Air Corps, 139, 149-150
Art Institute of Chicago, 269, 273, 276-277, 282
Ashton-Warner, Sylvia, 133
As I Lay Dying (Faulkner): 33
Associated Press prizes, 49
Atheneum Publishers, 255
Atlantic, The, 48-49, 283
Auden, W. H., 234
Austin Community College, 130
Austin Writers Roundup, 143
Autry, Gene, 179
Babel, Isaac, 96, 104
Bachellor, Claude, 262
Bailey, Pearl, 243
Baker, Eugene, 40
Baker, Paul, 157, 160, 165, 236, 246
Balbuena, Tiburcio (fictional character): 284
Ballantine Books, 182-183, 196
Balzac, Honoré de, 17, 235
Bantam Books, 108
Baptists, 11, 53, 286
Barca, Calderón de la, 174
Barker Collection, University of Texas, 203
Barnard College, 205-206
Barnstone, Ann, 68
Barr, Amelia, 6, 42
Barrow, Clyde, 51
Barth, John, 107
Barthelme, Donald, 10, 42, 107, 236-237
Baylor University, 159-160
Beagle, Peter, 21
Beck, Tony, 59
Bedichek, Roy, 4, 17, 119, 190, 237
Bello, Luis (fictional character): 274
Bellow, Saul, 97, 108
Benjamin, Walter, 19

298 Index

Bennet, Arnold, 27-28, 75, 171, 230, 274
Bennett, David, 75
Bennett, Shay, 8, 11
Bentley, Max, 51
Berenson, Bernard, 290
Best Little Whorehouse in Texas, The (King): 9, 176, 252, 263-264, 266
Bettmann Archives, 215
Beugnot, Comte, 217
Bible, The, 86, 87, 139
Bibliotheque Nationale, 215
Big Little Books, 253
Billboard, 49
Biography of the Bulls (Smith): 278
Bishop, Dr. Selma, 46
Black, Chili, 177
Black Sparrow Press, 246
Blaine, Barbara, 249
Blanton, Cullie (fictional character): 263
Blessed McGill (Shrake): 41, 264
Blood Will Tell (Cartwright): 41
Blue and Some Other Dogs (Graves): 72
Boatright, Mody, 190
Bobbsey Twins (fictional characters): 96
Bode, Elroy, 88
Boheme, La, 179
Boleyn, Anne, 116
Bond, W. D., 52
Bonney's Place (Hale): 39, 87, 135, 140, 146-148, 151-153
Book Beat (television series): 150
Book of Daniel, The (Doctorow): 97
Book of Lists, The (Wallechinsky, Wallace, and Wallace): 146
Borges, Jorge, 107, 116
Boston Law School, 128
Bottlescars (Hale newspaper column): 138
Bourbons, the, 208
Bourland, Harvey, 61
Bowen, Eliabeth, 227, 235
Bower, Bertha M., 193
Boys of Summer (Kahn): 96
Bradbury, Ray, 154-155
Brady, Martin (fictional character): 274
Brahms, Johannes, 241
Brammer, Billy Lee, 42-43, 259-260, 264
Brann, W. C., 254, 264
Brave Bulls, The (Lea): 6, 214, 269, 272, 274, 276, 279, 280-281, 284, 285, 287
Brett, Bill, 154
Brett, Dorothy, 227, 238
Bright and Early Barn (Nunn painting): 60

British Broadcasting Corporation (BBC): 224
Brown, James, 20
Browning, Robert, 52
Broyles, William, 86
Buckwitz, Harry, 167
Burford, William, 10
Burgess, Anthony, 86
Burton, Robert, 97-98
But Not for Love (Shrake): 41
"Ça Ira" (song): 215
Caldwell, Taylor, 208
Calloway, Hewey (fictional character): 8, 184, 187, 191, 194, 198-199, 286
Cameron, Angus, 39, 50, 59
Campbellites, 41
Candide (Voltaire): 282
Cannery Row (Steinbeck): 81
Capps, Benjamin, 40, 189
Carlisle, Brad, 251
Carlyle, Thomas, 7, 212, 216, 218
Carranza, Venustiano, 288
Carson, Johnny, 197
Carter, Jimmy, 68, 102
Carter, Robert Goldthwaite, 203
Cartwright, Gary, 8, 40-41, 225
Cash, Johnny, 73
Catch-22 (Heller): 138
Cather, Willa, 5, 133, 239
Cellini, Benvenuto, 128
Centennial (Michener): 141
Cerf, Bennett, 50
Chambers family (fictional characters): 121, 124, 125
Chandler, Raymond, 97
Chekov, Anton, 96, 104
Cheyenne Indians, 33
Chip of the Flying U (Bower): 193
Choate, Gwen, 50-51
Chopin, Fréderic, 241
Christie, Agatha, 125
Christmas Tree, A (Greene): 10, 53-54
Cinderella, 127
Cisneros, José ("Josie"): 282
City of Night, 10
Claunch, Merlin (fictional character): 285
Clayhanger Family, The (Bennet): 27
Coburn, D. L., 10, 40, 168-169
Coindreau, Maurice Edgar, 237
Cole, Art, 267
Coleman, James, 172
College of Santa Fe, 161
Colliers, 139
Columbia University, 63, 66
Comanche Indians, 57, 184-185, 191
Comancheros, 191

Come, the Restorer (Goyen):
231-232, 244
Confessions of a White Racist (King):
260-261
Congress, U.S., 249-250, 254, 258-260
Connolly, Cyril, 227
Conrad, Joseph, 20, 274
Cooper, Gary, 179, 197
Coover, John, 97, 107
Cortez, Gregorio, 191
Count of Monte Cristo, The
(Dumas): 178
Cousins, Maggie, 218
Cowhand (Gipson): 286
Cowley, Malcolm, 21
Crane, Stephen, 46
Crawford, Max, 36, 264
Crawford, Milo (fictional character): 172
Creasy, John, 193
Crosby, Bing 179
Cullen, Maifred Hale, 156
Cunningham, Dr. A. B., 138
Curious in L.A. (Smith): 169
Curran (fictional character): 245
Dalhart, Vernon, 198
Dallas: The Deciding Years (Greene):
44, 58
Dallas Morning News, 209, 149
Dallas Rediscovered (McDonald): 58
Dallas Theater Center, 40, 157, 162, 173
Dallas Times Herald, 7, 37, 41, 43-44, 49
Dance to the Music of Time, A
(Powell): 81, 97, 125
Davis, Sammy, Jr., 243
Day the Cowboys Quit, The (Kelton):
195-196, 201-202
Death Comes to the Archbishop
(Cather): 133
Deck, Danny, 33
DeGolyer, Everett Lee, 216
Delacroix, Eugene, 283
De Persia (fictional character): 232, 243-244
Devil's General, The (Zuckmayer): 157
Dewlen, Al, 8
Diamond Rattler, The (Goyen): 246
Diary of a Madman (Coggio, Luneau, and Rudd): 169
Dickens, Charles, 17, 263
Different Drummer, A (McKinney): 169
Dobie, J. Frank: 12, 53, 256; influence of 5, 39; and Tom Lea, 9, 84; McMurtry on, 17; Greene on, 39, 57; Graves on, 84, 87; Kelton on, 181, 189-190; Mossiker on, 214, 218; Goyen on, 236-237; King on, 255,
264; Lea on, 274, 284, 285, 289
Dr. Faustus, 105
Doctorow, E. L., 97, 99, 108
Dodd, Sheriff Ed Earl (fictional character): 266
Dodge, Mabel, 227, 238
Dodson, Oscar, 280
Dogs of War, The (Forsyth): 255
Donahue, Jack, 152
Dos Passos, John, 279
Dostoevski, Fëdor, 96
Doubleday and Co., 51, 149, 153, 183, 185, 196, 208, 218, 243
Doughty, Charles M., 282
Drabble, Margaret, 133
Duane (fictional character): 32
Duff, Kathryn, 7
Dugger, Ronnie, 88, 254
Duke University, 256
Dumas, Alexandre père, 216
Durrell, Lawrence, 81
Earnest, Joe, 177
"East of the Sun, West of the Moon," 126
Editions René Julliard, 212
Edwards, Ben, 160
Edward VII (St. Aubyn), 218
Eleanor (fictional character): 125
Eliot, George, 17, 105
Eliot, T. S., 43, 234-235
Ellison, Ralph, 239
Eminent Victorians (Strachey): 215
Emmerich Descending (King): 263
Encino Press, 19, 54, 56, 67, 72-73
Engel, Benno, 60
English, Jacky, 249
Enid Morning News, 46
Episcopalians, 11, 45, 86, 125, 286
Esquire, 254
Estes, Winston, 40, 168
Evangelicals, 125
Eye of the Beholder, The (Jones): 161
Eye of the Needle (Follett), 255
Fair Sister, The (Goyen): 7, 243
Falstaff (fictional character): 91
Faulkner, William, 17, 41, 76-77, 192, 253
Fear of Flying (Jong): 121
Fenstemaker, Arthur (fictional character): 259-260
Fenstemaker, Hoot Gibson (fictional character): 260
Ferber, Edna, 6
Film Flam (McMurtry): 19
Finberg, Francis, 51
Fisher, John, 45
Flagg, Charlie (fictional character): 183-184, 189-190, 198, 200

Flagg, Mary (fictional character): 201
Flaubert, Gustave, 26, 235, 273-274
Fleischer, Von Humboldt (fictional character): 108
Flynn, Robert, 168
Foley, Martha, 80
Folger Theater Group, 249
Follett, Ken, 255
Fonda, Henry, 34
Ford, Gerald, 103
Foreman, Paul, 156
Forster, E. M., 270
Forsyth, Frederick, 255
Forsythe, Elizabeth, 42
Forsythe, Henderson, 176, 266-267
Fort Chadbourne, 184
Fort Concho, 184
Fort Griffin, 184
"Fortune Hunters, The" (Greene): 53
Four Quartets (Eliot): 235
Francesca, Piero della, 283
Frank, Stanley, 185
Frazer, Sir James, 245
French language, 75, 206, 219, 233, 274
Freud, Sigmund, 12, 129-130, 224
From Here to Eternity (Mailer): 178, 288
Fuels, Minerals and Human Resources (Reed): 129
Fustian Days (Brammer): 260
Ganchion family (fictional characters): 241, 243, 246
"Gas Stations" (Apple): 102
Gauguin, Paul, 100, 283
Gay Place, The (Brammer): 259-260
Geisenberger family, 206
Georgel, l'Abbe, 217
George Mason University, 18
Georgia Review, 103
Gerhart, Willis, 45
German language, 201, 216, 219, 233
Giant (Ferber): 6
Gibson, Jewell, 153
Gillett, Jim, 57, 275
Gillis, Everett, 10
Gin Game, The (Coburn): 10, 40, 169
Ginsberg, Allen, 17
Gipson, Fred, 85, 286
God, 44, 120, 125, 198, 239
"God in West Texas" (Greene): 50, 58
Goetzmann, William, 42
Golden Bough, The (Frazer): 245
Golden Notebook, The (Lessing): 133
Goodbye to a River (Graves): 3, 7, 67, 69, 75, 76, 78, 79, 80, 83, 84, 154, 264
Good Old Boys, The (Kelton): 8, 183, 184, 189, 191, 192, 194, 195, 198, 201, 286
"Good Old Girl" (Hall): 267
Goodwyn, Frank, 189
Gorky, Maxim, 91
Gottlieb, Robert, 209, 218
Goulden, Joe, 42
Goyen, William: background of, 6-7, 10, 13; others on, 17, 65; interview with, 227-247; writing habits of, 228-229, 230, 232-233
Grace Note in a Hard World (Lea): 275
Grand Old Opry, 199
Grant, Ben Z., 264
Grapes of Wrath, The (Steinbeck): 288
Graves, Helen, 84
Graves, Jane, 84
Graves, John: background of, 3-4, 7, 12, 13; McMurtry on, 21, 36; Greene on, 39; interview with, 63-88; writing habits of, 73-74; Hearon on, 118-119; Hale on, 144-145, 154; Jones on, 168; Mossiker on, 211, 214; Goyen on, 234, 236; King on, 264; Lea on, 289
Great Frontier, The (Webb): 80
Great Plains, The (Webb): 289
Green, Ben, 154
Greene, A. C.: background of, 7-8, 10, 12; interview with, 37-62; writing habits of, 43-44; Graves on, 87; Hale on, 152; Jones on, 168; Kelton on, 189; Mossiker on, 214; King on, 264
Greene, Betty, 52, 59-60
Greene, Eliot, 56
Green Grow the Lilacs (Riggs): 161
Greenway, Aurora (fictional character): 31
Grey, Zane, 5, 181, 193
Grimm, Clyde, 237
Guggenheim Fellowship, 67
Gunther, John, 208
Gutwillig, Bob, 262
Hale, Leon: background of, 8, 12; others on, 39, 87, 108, 211; interview with, 135-156; writing habits of, 141-142, 154-155
Hale, Marshall, 272
Haley, J. Evetts, 84
Haley, Oliver, 168
Half a Look of Cain (Goyen): 244
Hall, Adrian, 246
Hall, Carol, 266
Hall, Monte, 92
Hamlet, 105
Hammersley, Violet, 214
Hammonds, Mike, 176
Hampton, Skip (fictional character): 174

Hands of Cantu (Lea): 39, 271, 285-286
Hannah's House (Hearon): 8, 39, 114, 120-121, 123, 126-127, 130-131
Hardeman, Dorsey, 55
Hardin-Simmons University, 19, 37, 48, 52
Hard Scrabble (Graves): 7, 67, 70, 74, 78-80, 83, 145, 264
Hardy, Thomas, 17, 100
Harper's, 45, 257
Harris, Leon, 41
Hartley, Margaret, 7, 53, 237
Harvard University, 127-128, 260
Havens, Sam, 168
Hawthorne, Nathaniel, 235
Haycox, Ernest, 189
Hearon, Anne Shelby, 116, 130
Hearon, Bob, 130
Hearon, Reed, 130
Hearon, Shelby, background of, 8; others on, 39, 87, 108, 236; interview with, 111-134; writing habits of, 115-117
Hebrew language, 279
Heitchew, Houston, 51
Heller, Joseph, 108, 138
Hemingway, Ernest, 135, 170, 188, 279, 280-281, 283
Henderson, Jimmy and Jo (fictional characters): 121-125
Heroic Mexico (Johnson): 289
Herrera, "Maximo," 269
Hershey, John, 279
Hertzog, Carl, 83, 272, 275, 278, 282
High Pockets (Tunis), 96
Hill, Gladys, 55-56
Hill, Robert, 54
Hitchcock, Hugh, 199
Hockaday, Miss Ela, 206
Hoffmann, E. T. A., 221
Hold Autumn in Your Hand (Perry): 17, 81
Holiday, 19, 66, 70
Home Away From (Smith): 169
Hoover, J. Edgar, 101
Hopalong to Hud (Sonnichsen): 82
Hopwood Contest, 92
Horgan, Paul, 5, 140, 287
Hornet (aircraft carrier): 279
Horsehead Crossing (Kelton): 202
Horseman Pass By (McMurtry): 9, 15, 18, 20, 25, 27, 31-32, 86, 189, 214
Horse Trading (Green): 154
Horton, Flap (fictional character): 33
Hot Iron (Kelton): 182-183
House of Breath (Goyen): 7, 227, 235, 238, 241, 245-246
Houston, Sam, 51-52

Houston Post, 8, 135, 142
How Not to Write a Play (Kerr): 170
Hud. See *Horseman, Pass By*
Hughes, Howard, 100
Humble Oil, 139
Humbolt's Gift (Bellow): 108
Humphrey, William, 17, 40-41, 86
Hundred Yard War, The (Cartwright): 41
Hungry Men (Anderson): 51
Hurd, Peter, 282
Igo, John, 7
I'll Die Before I Run (Sonnichsen): 56
I'm Okay, You're Okay (Harris): 122
In a Farther Country (Goyen): 242-243
In a Narrow Grave (McMurtry): 5, 17, 19, 35
Indianology (Lehmann): 56-58
"Inside Norman Mailer" (Apple): 102
Interiors (film): 175
In the Crucible of the Sun (Lea): 84, 276
Irving, Henry, 176
Irwin, John, 103
Is There Life After High School? (Keyes): 172
Italian language, 233
James, Henry, 213-214
James, Will, 181
James, William, 11
Jenkins, Dan, 41, 264
Jenkins, Nick (fictional character): 97-98
Jesus, 240, 244
Jews, 4, 11, 89, 207
Jiménez, Juan Ramón, 71
Job, Book of, 200
Johna (fictional character): 230
Johnson, Howard, 98, 100-101
Johnson, Lyndon, 259-260, 263
Johnson, Sam Houston, 260
Johnson, Samuel, 5
Johnson, William Weber, 289
Jones, James, 288
Jones, Margo, 238
Jones, Mary Sue, 157, 173
Jones, Preston: background of, 6, 8, 10-11; Greene on, 40, 53; Graves on, 87; interview with, 157-178; writing habits of, 162-165; Goyen on, 236; King on, 264-265
Jordan, Barbara, 39, 117, 127, 133-134
Josephine, Empress, 206, 219, 224
Joshua Bean and God (Gibson): 153
Joyce, James, 105-106
Julio (fictional character): 191
Jung, Carl, 129, 134
Kafka, Franz, 107

302 Index

Kefirovsky, Vasirin (fictional character): 103
Kelton, Ann, 9, 179, 182, 201
Kelton, Elmer: background of, 8-9; others on, 87, 124, 153, 286; interview with, 179-203; writing habits of, 185, 186, 187, 188
Kelton, Steve, 193
Kennedy, John F., 250
Kerouac, Jack, 17, 26
Kesey, Ken, 21
Keyes, Ralph, 172
Kid from Tompkinsville, The (Tunis): 96
King, Bradley Clayton, 251
King, Larry L.: background of, 6, 9-10, 12; others on, 40, 154; interview with, 249-267; writing habits of, 252, 263
King, Lindsey Allison, 249
King, Richard, 84
Kingfish (King and Grant): 264, 266
King Ranch, The (Lea): 10, 84, 276, 283
Kingston, Maxine Hong, 108
Kiwanis, 49
Kleberg, Bob, 276, 284
Kleberg, Dick, 284
Kleberg family, 84, 276
Knopf, 50, 83, 207-209, 218
Kojak (television series): 109
Krause, Avery (fictional character): 112-113, 115, 118, 120, 132
Kristin Lavransdatter (Undset): 133
Ladd, Diane, 174
Laguna Gloria, 60
Laing, R. D., 112-113
Lakeside Press, 227
Landrum, Beverly Foster ("Bananas") (fictional character): 114-115, 121, 126, 132
Lasswell, Mary, 40
Last Captive, The (Greene): 45, 56-57
Last Judgment, The (Signorelli painting): 283
Last Meeting of the Knights of the White Magnolia (Jones): 162, 166-168, 171, 173
Last Picture Show, The (McMurtry): 15, 27-29, 34-35, 108, 189, 264
Last Running, The (Graves): 67, 71
Laughton, Charles, 162
Lawrence, D. H., 227, 238
Lawrence, Frieda, 227, 237-238
Lawrence, T. E., 280, 282
Lea, Nancy, 278
Lea, Sarah, 9, 286
Lea, Tom: 66; background of, 6, 9, 10-11; Greene on, 39; Graves on, 83-84; Apple on, 99; Kelton on, 189; Mossiker on, 214; Goyen on, 236; interview with, 269-290; writing habits of, 269-272, 274
Lea, Tom, Sr., 269
Lea Ranch, 193
"Least Jot and Tittle, The" (Greene): 53
Leaving Cheyenne (McMurtry): 18, 27, 33, 189
Le Carre, John, 255
Lee, Dr. Roy, 144
Lehmann, Herbert, 45, 56-57
Lehrer, Jim, 49
Lem the Lion (fictional character): 32
Lessing, Doris, 133
Liberty, 139
Life, 66, 269, 271-272
Life and Literature of the Southwest (course): 5, 53
Life is a Dream (Calderón de la Barca): 174
Life on the Mississippi (Twain): 253
Linden, Bill, 20
Liszt, Franz, 241
Literary Guild, 262
Little, Brown and Co., 39, 275
Lloyd-Jons, Godwin, 33
Lone Star Preacher (Thomason): 87
Long, Earl, 263
Long, Huey, 263-264
Long Day's Journey Into Night (O'Neill): 160, 178
Long Day's Journey Into West Texas (Jones): 170-171
Loose Herd of Texans, A (Porterfield): 88
Louis XIV, 220
Love, Larry (fictional character): 93-95
Lovell, John, 284
Love Song of J. Alfred Prufrock, The (Eliot): 235
Low Man on a Totem Pole (Smith): 253
Lowry, Beverly, 39, 119, 152
Lu Ann Hampton Laverty Oberlander (Jones): 165, 167-168, 170, 173-174
Lusty Texans, The (Rogers): 62
Lutherans, 125
Macaulay, Rose, 227
McCall, Monica, 218
McCalls, 53
McCamey, Bonham J. (fictional character): 151
McCombs, Holland, 289
McCormick, Ken, 218
McCracken, James, 55
McCullars, Carson, 133
McDonald, William, 58, 62

McElroy, Lee (Kelton pseudonym): 183, 193
McGee-Chavez, Marietta (fictional character): 243-244
McGinty, Kate (fictional character): 199
McGraw-Hill Book Co., 238-240
McKinney, Gene, 169
Maclovio (fictional character): 274
McMurry College, 3, 54
McMurtry, James, 11, 15, 85
McMurtry, Larry: 123, 198; background of, 5-6, 9, 10, 11; interview with, 15-36; writing habits of, 22, 24; Greene on, 39, 40; Graves on, 65, 70, 85-86; Apple on, 108; Jones on, 168; Kelton on, 189, 192; Mossiker on, 214; Goyen on, 234, 236; King on, 264
McPherson, Aimee Semple, 246
Madero, Francisco, 269
Mahmud III, 225
Mailer, Norman, 104
Making of a Broadway Hit, The (King): 253
Manhunters (Kelton): 191, 198, 200, 202
Mann, Thomas, 105, 128
Marcus, Stanley, 50, 54
Marie Antoinette, 205, 217, 225
Marines, U.S., 37, 63, 65, 87, 288
Marquis, Don, 8
"Marseillaise, The" (song): 215
Massacre at Goliad (Kelton): 183, 202
Matthiessen, Peter, 68-70
Maugham, W. Somerset, 100, 214
Maxwell, Allen, 237
Mencken, H. L., 253
Methodists, 11, 87, 125-126, 139, 198, 239
Michelet, Jules, 217
Michener, James, 141
Milestones (Bennett): 171
Miller, Arthur, 169
Miller, J. P., 65
Miller, Marvin, 51
Miller, Vassar, 10
Miller, Warren, 262
Milton, John, 86
Miracle of Thirty-fourth Street (musical play): 56
Misérables, Les (Hugo): 96
Mr. Roberts (Heggen): 178
Mitchell, Bill, 82
Mitchell, Cooney, 82
Mitchell, John, 71
Modernism, 104
Montespan, Madame de, 206
Moore, Randy, 172

More Than a Queen (Mossiker): 219, 225
Morris, Willie, 42, 45, 254, 257, 261, 265
Morrow, Maude, 52
Mossiker, Frances: background of, 10, 14; others on, 41-42, 59; interview with 205-225; writing habits of, 211
Mossiker, Jake, 59
Mother Earth News, 80
Motte de la Valois, Madame de la, 216-217
Moving On (McMurtry): 22, 27, 31-32, 35
Mozart, W. A., 9
Murder in Space City, 35
Nabokov, Vladimir, 86, 118
Napoleon, 42, 205, 207, 218-219, 224
Napoleon and Josephine (Mossiker): 42, 218-219, 224
Nashville Banner, 251
National Barn Dance (radio program): 199
National Book Awards, 50
National Endowment for the Arts, 95
National Geographic, 283
Navy, U. S., 37, 46, 227
Nelson, Willie, 73
New American Library, 262, 265
Newsweek, 126
New Yorker, 10, 67
New York Times, 20, 261, 265
New York Times Book Review, 148
Nichols, Mike, 264
Night of the Hunter, The (film): 162
Nine Years Among the Indians (Lehmann): 56-58
Nobel Prize, 71, 77, 133, 165-166
"Noon" (Apple): 92, 102
Nooncaster, Aubra, 251
Norris, J. Frank, 53
North Texas State University, 15, 18-19
North to Yesterday (Flynn): 168
Norton, John, 269, 277, 284
Now and Another Time (Hearon): 112-115, 120-122, 124-128, 131-132
Nunn, Ancel, 59, 60
Nunn, Renata, 60
Oarson, Owen (fictional character): 30
O'Connor, Flannery, 20
O'Connor, Frank, 21
Odessa American, 251
Of Con Men, Outlaws, Whores, Politicians and Other Artists (King): 260
Ohio State University, 166
Oil King (fictional character): 244, 246

Index

Oldest Living Graduate, The (Jones): 165, 167-168, 171, 174, 177
Old Fart (fictional character): 79, 83
Old Wives' Tale, The (Bennett): 230
Oliphant, Pat, 254
One-eyed Man, The (King): 9, 262
O'Neill, Eugene, 124
On the Border With Mackenzie (Carter): 203
On the Road (Kerouac): 17
Oppenheimer, Evelyn, 149
"Oranging of America" (Apple): 92, 98, 101-102
Oranging of America, The (Apple): 102, 264
Ordways, The (Humphrey): 41
Orozco, Pascual, 269
Our Town (Wilder): 169
Ox Bow Incident, The (Clark): 281
Paige, Janis, 56
Painted Dresses (Hearon): 115, 123, 125, 128
Paisano Fellowship, 59-60
Paisano Ranch, 60
Pappas, Bill, 161
Paradise Lost (Milton): 86
Paris Review, 68, 107
Parker, Bonnie, 51
Patsy Carpenter (McMurtry): 22
"Patty Cake, Patty Cake" (Apple): 102
Peel, Jill (fictional character): 29-30
Pendergrast, Sam, 153
Penn, William, 52
Pennsylvania State University, 166
Percy, Joe (fictional character): 30-31, 33
Percy, Walker, 261
Perelman, S. J., 10, 17, 138
Perini, Vince, 55
Perry, George Sessions, 17, 42, 81
Pershing, John J., 289
Personal Country, A (Greene): 44-45, 50-51, 53-54, 58-59, 62, 87, 214, 264
Philadelphia Inquirer, 46
Phillips, Robert, 237
Phillips University, 52
Picasso, Pablo, 270
Pirandello, Luigi, 212
Place Called Dallas, A (Greene): 58
Place Called West Texas, A (Greene): 50
Place on the Magdalena Flats, A (Jones): 161, 170, 175, 178
Playboy, 266
Pocahontas (Mossiker): 207-208, 213, 221-222, 224
Polk, Duvan, 7
Pollock, Jackson, 287

Porter, Katherine Anne, 5-6, 39, 85, 238
Porterfield, Bill, 88
Portnoy's Complaint (Roth): 148
Possibility of Oil, A (Goyen): 246
Post-modernism, 104
Pound, Ezra, 234-235
Powell, Anthony, 81, 97, 99, 125
Powell, Lawrence Clark, 282
Powers, Stephen, 283
Presbyterians, 11, 81, 126, 286
Price, The (Miller): 169
Primal Yoke, The (Lea): 275, 281, 285-287
Prince and the Pauper, The (Twain): 253
Prince of a Fellow, A (Hearon): 8, 112-115, 118, 120-121, 123-127, 131
Proud Flesh (Humphrey): 41
Proust, Marcel, 128, 213-214
Publisher's Weekly, 48, 116
Puccini, Giacomo, 9
Pulitzer Prize, 10, 42
Queen's Necklace, The (Mossiker): 42, 205, 209-213, 216, 219
Raabe, Minna (fictional character): 112-114, 118, 120
Ragtime (Doctorow): 97
Railroad Magazine: 48
Raintree County (Lockridge): 178
Raleigh, Sir Walter, 274
Rambouillet, Madame de, 205
Ranch Romances, 182
Random House, 50
Rasmussen, Boy (fictional character): 193, 199
Readers Digest, 184
"Real Estate" (Apple): 102
Rechy, John, 10, 88
Redbook, 116, 131
Remember (Jones): 8, 40, 157, 163-165, 169
Repusseau, Patrice, 237
"Rhody's Path" (Goyen): 246
Rice University, 13, 15, 18, 21, 63, 65, 89, 93, 100, 103, 108, 227, 233, 236, 239
Richardson, Rupert, 10, 40, 54
Riggs, Lynn, 5
Riley, Drexel, 161
Rister, Carl Coke, 54
Robbins, Harold, 100
Roberts, Doris (Mrs. William Goyen): 7, 227, 233
Rockefeller, Nelson, 257-258
Rogers, Jimmie, 198
Rogers, John William, 62
Rohan, Cardinal de, 217

Rolling Stone, 107
Rollins, Hyder Edward, 52
Roman Catholics, 11, 174, 286
Roosevelt, Franklin D., 278
Rose-Mama (fictional character): 147
Ross, Diana, 243
Roth, Phillip, 97, 148
Running Iron (Kelton): 183
Runyon, Damon, 137, 146
Rushing, Jane Gilmore, 7
Ryerson Library, 282
"Saint Julien" (Flaubert): 235
Sam the Lion (fictional character): 32
San Angelo Standard Times, 179, 183, 186, 194, 198
Santa Claus Bank Robbery (Greene): 45, 53-56, 87, 264
Santa Fe Sunshine (Jones): 175
Sarah Lawrence College, 115, 130
Saturday Evening Post, 17, 87, 139
Saturday Review, 209, 283
Savata (fictional character): 243
Sayles, Hal, 47-48
Scarborough, Dorothy, 81, 82
Second Dune, The (Hearon): 8, 112-114, 120, 123, 126-127, 131
Seib, Harry, 47
"Selling Out" (Apple): 102
Semi-Tough (Jenkins): 41, 264
"Seven Brides for Seven Brothers" (tale): 126
Seven Pillars of Wisdom (Lawrence): 282
Sévigné, Madame de, 206-208, 210-213, 220, 224-225
Shakespeare, William, 12, 77, 105, 127, 210, 222, 234
Shattuck, Roger, 214
Shaw, Bernard, 80, 145, 176
Shedd, Dick, 168
Shoal Creek Publishers, 152
Short, Luke, 189
Shrake, Edwin ("Bud"), 40-41, 264
Shulman, Max, 137
Sierra Club, 67, 71
Signorelli, Luca, 283
Simenon, Georges, 115, 187
Simon, Neil, 175
Simon and Schuster, 209, 218
Sitwell, Edith, 227
Six Women (Goyen): 238
Six Years with the Texas Rangers (Gillett): 275
Smith, C. W., 108
Smith, Captain John, 222, 224
Smith, Glenn, 169
Smith, H. Allen, 253, 255

Index 305

Smith, Rex, 278, 283, 287
Smith College, 206
Snapp, Eddie, 160-161
Snapp, Pauline (Mrs. Eddie): 161
Somebody's Darling (McMurtry): 27, 29-31, 33
Sonnichsen, C. L., 10, 56, 82
Sonny (fictional character): 32
Sophie's Choice (Styron): 234
Sorbonne, 205-206
Southern Baker (magazine): 48
Southern Methodist University, 42, 59, 222
"Southwest Literature?" (McMurtry): 5, 17
Southwest Review, The, 7, 19, 53, 237, 279
Spanish language, 75, 201, 219, 233, 271, 273, 279, 285
Spawning Run, The (Humphrey): 41
Specht, Joe, 8, 19
Speck, Dr. Frank, 222
Spender, Stephen, 227
Sports Illustrated, 70
Spurlig, Hank (fictional character): 288
Staked Plain, The (Tolbert): 190
Stamey, Joe, 55
Stanford University, 15, 18, 20
Stanley Walker Award, 154
Stegnor Fellowship, 18, 21
Stein, Gertrude, 116, 119
Steinbeck, John, 81, 165-166, 288
Stendhal, 17
Stewart, James, 34
Stillwell, Charles A., 284
Stowers, Carlton, 7
Strachey, Lytton, 215
Strauss, Harold, 77
Streetcar Named Desire, A (Williams): 267
Street Full of People (Estes): 168
Streets of Laredo (McMurtry): 34
Strout, Dr. Alan, 121, 138, 197
Styron, William, 234
Such Sweet Sorrow (Snapp): 161
Sullivan, Maud Durlin, 282
Summer Before the Dark, The (Lessing): 133
Sun Also Rises, The (Hemingway): 281
Swan, Praxiteles (fictional character): 87
Swedish language, 219
Synge, J. M., 234
Tallyrand, 213
Terms of Endearment (McMurtry): 31-32
Ternay, Comte de, 210
Terry, Ellen, 176

306 Index

Texas A&M University, 142
Texas A&M University Press, 59, 88
Texas Christian University, 18, 21, 63, 66, 166
Texas Institute of Letters, 11, 51, 88, 152, 154, 214, 289
Texas Monthly, 39, 67-69, 72, 75, 116
Texas Observer, 20, 254
Texas Quarterly, 19
Texas Rangers, 57, 200
Texas Tech University, 135, 137, 139, 142, 204, 249, 251-252
Texas Trilogy, A (Jones): 8, 157, 160, 167, 170-173, 176-177
Texas Water Plan, 67
That Championship Season (Miller): 266
"They Call Me Whitey" (King): 261
Thieves Like Us (Anderson): 51, 152-153
Thomason, John W., 87, 152
Thoreau, Henry, 69
Thorp Springs Press, 156
"Three American Portraits as Elegy" (Goyen): 241
Thurber, James, 17
Time It Never Rained, The (Kelton): 8, 153, 185, 189, 194, 198, 200-201
Tinkle, Lon, 50, 255, 274, 289
Toby and Company (King and Oliphant): 254, 264
Todasco, Ruth, 205
Tolbert, Frank X., 189-190
Tolstoy, Leo, 17, 96, 105
Toreador (newspaper): 138
Travels in Arabia Deserta (Doughty): 282
Trinity, Texas, 6, 242
Trinity University, 157, 160
Trollope, Anthony, 93-94
Troupe, Tom, 169
Truitt, Rev. James, 82
Truitt family, 82
Truitt-Mitchell feud, 82
Truman, Harry, 261
Tularosa (Sonnichsen): 10
Tunis, John R., 96
Turner, Martha Ann, 152
Turn South at the Second Bridge (Hale): 143-146
Twain, Mark, 17, 250, 253
Udall, Stewart, 66, 68
"Understanding Alvarado" (Apple): 102-103
Undset, Sigrid, 133
Unitas, Johnny, 257-258
University of Aix, 206
University of Chicago, 130, 235
University of Illinois, 241
University of Kentucky, 129

University of Michigan, 89, 91
University of New Mexico, 157, 160-161, 173
University of Texas, 5, 37, 42-43, 53, 63, 66, 111, 130-132, 179
University of Texas Archives, 56
University of Texas Press, 81
University of Virginia, 126, 129
Updike, John, 106
Upstairs, Downstairs (television series): 109
Ursuline Academy, 167
Valley of the Dolls (Susanne): 109
Vanderbilt University, 129
Vandiver, Frank, 10, 289
"Vegetable Love" (Apple): 102, 104
Vestal, Stanley, 5
Vigee-Lebrun, Madame, 225
Viking Press, 265
Villa, Francisco ("Pancho"): 5, 274, 279, 287-288
Vision of St. Eustice, A (Goyen): 245
Visit, The (Durrenmatt): 161
Viva Max (Lehrer): 49
Vliet, R. G., 42
Voltaire, 282
Wagner, Richard, 241
Wagontongue (Kelton): 192
Walls Rise Up (Perry): 17, 81
Waltz Across Texas (Crawford): 264
War and Peace (Tolstoy): 287
War Between the Tates, The (Lurie): 121
Waterfall, The (Drabble): 133
Watergate, 212, 217
Waterhouse, Russell, 83
Water Hustlers, The (Graves): 71
Watty, 79
Wayne, John, 34, 140
Webb, Damon, 61
Webb, Walter Prescott, 4, 17, 80, 119, 190, 214, 237, 289
Weeth, Chuck, 55
Well, The (Goyen): 245
Welty, Eudora, 98-99, 133
Western Writers of America, 193, 196
West Texas Historical Association Yearbook, 54
West Texas Livestock Weekly, 179, 185
Whistler, James McNeill, 282
White, E. B., 17
White, Fred, 58
Whorehouse Papers, The (King): 253
Wilder, Thornton, 169
William and Mary College, 222
Williams, George, 13, 65, 234
Williams, Jeanne, 193
Williams, Tennessee, 227

Wilson, Edmund, 99
Wind, The (Scarborough): 81
Wittliff, Bill, 56-57, 60-61, 67, 73, 86
Wittliff, Sally, 60
Wolfe, Thomas, 162
Women's Movement, 28, 132-133
Wonderful Country, The (Lea): 39, 84, 189, 275-276, 281, 285, 287
Woodard, Nell (fictional character): 115
Woods, Audrey, 236
Wooten, Don, 58
World War I, 278
World War II, 11, 179, 269, 272, 286, 288
Wright, Frank Lloyd, 157
Writer, The, 116
XELO radio station, 199
XEPN radio station, 199
XIT Ranch, 201
Yale Divinity School, 126
Yale Series of Younger Poets, 42
Yeats, W. B., 43, 234
"Yogurt of Vasirin Kefirovsky, The" (Apple): 102
Zapata, Emiliano, 288
Zen, 118
Zip (Apple): 105-106